The Cambridge Introduction to
Queer and Trans Studies

The book provides a detailed analysis of important work in queer and trans studies over the past thirty years. Stretching from early figures (such as Eve Kosofsky Sedgwick, Judith Butler, Cathy Cohen, José Muñoz, and Sandy Stone) to the most recent scholarship, it offers a rich account of these fields' major ideas and contributions while indicating how they have evolved. Centering race and empire, the book offers extended discussion of work in Black, Indigenous, Latinx, and Asian American studies as well as engaging the Global South. The *Introduction* further addresses historical considerations of sexuality and gender identity, and queer and trans temporalities, while also providing a robust account of social and political movements that preceded the emergence of queer and trans studies as scholarly fields. Accessible for those unfamiliar with these areas of study, it is also a great resource for those already working in them.

Mark Rifkin is Professor of Global Gender and Sexuality Studies and Indigenous Studies at the University at Buffalo. He is the author of eight other books, including *The Politics of Kinship: Race, Family, Governance* (2024), *Beyond Settler Time: Temporal Sovereignty and Indigenous Self-Determination* (2017), and *When Did Indians Become Straight?: Kinship, the History of Sexuality, and Native Sovereignty* (2011). His work has won a number of national awards, including the John Hope Franklin Prize for best book in American Studies, the Subsequent Book Prize from the Native American and Indigenous Studies Association, and the Best Special Issue award from the Council of Editors of Learned Journals. He also has served as president of the Native American and Indigenous Studies Association.

The Cambridge Introduction to Queer and Trans Studies

MARK RIFKIN
University at Buffalo

CAMBRIDGE
UNIVERSITY PRESS

Shaftesbury Road, Cambridge CB2 8EA, United Kingdom

One Liberty Plaza, 20th Floor, New York, NY 10006, USA

477 Williamstown Road, Port Melbourne, VIC 3207, Australia

314–321, 3rd Floor, Plot 3, Splendor Forum, Jasola District Centre, New Delhi – 110025, India

103 Penang Road, #05–06/07, Visioncrest Commercial, Singapore 238467

Cambridge University Press is part of Cambridge University Press & Assessment, a department of the University of Cambridge.

We share the University's mission to contribute to society through the pursuit of education, learning and research at the highest international levels of excellence.

www.cambridge.org
Information on this title: www.cambridge.org/9781009435666

DOI: 10.1017/9781009435635

© Cambridge University Press & Assessment 2026

This publication is in copyright. Subject to statutory exception and to the provisions of relevant collective licensing agreements, no reproduction of any part may take place without the written permission of Cambridge University Press & Assessment.

When citing this work, please include a reference to the DOI 10.1017/9781009435635

First published 2026

A catalogue record for this publication is available from the British Library

A Cataloging-in-Publication data record for this book is available from the Library of Congress

ISBN 978-1-009-43566-6 Hardback
ISBN 978-1-009-43561-1 Paperback

Cambridge University Press & Assessment has no responsibility for the persistence or accuracy of URLs for external or third-party internet websites referred to in this publication and does not guarantee that any content on such websites is, or will remain, accurate or appropriate.

For EU product safety concerns, contact us at Calle de José Abascal, 56, 1°, 28003 Madrid, Spain, or email eugpsr@cambridge.org

For Beth

Contents

Acknowledgments	*page* viii
Introduction	1
1 Reading and Revising the 1990s	19
2 Genealogies of Queer and Trans Studies	54
3 Histories of Sexuality and Gender Identity	99
4 Queer/Trans of Color and Indigenous Critique	136
5 Global Dynamics, Refusals, and Reorientations	171
Notes	207
Bibliography	245
Index	282

Acknowledgments

Thanks so much to Ray Ryan and the entire team at Cambridge University Press. Working on this project during the pandemic and its aftermath at times has been quite challenging, and I'm deeply appreciative of Ray's patience during this process.

While working on this book, I switched institutions and so would like to thank everyone in English and Women's, Gender, and Sexuality Studies at UNC Greensboro (where I spent a wonderful sixteen years) and my incredible new colleagues in Global Gender and Sexuality Studies and Indigenous Studies at the University at Buffalo, where I've found a new home. During most of the time while I was writing this book, I benefited greatly from being the Linda Arnold Carlisle Professor of Women's, Gender, and Sexuality Studies (WGSS) at UNC Greensboro, and I am deeply grateful to Linda Carlisle for all that she's done to support the work of the WGSS Program over the decades.

Thanks to everyone who has worked assiduously and often in difficult and precarious conditions to build the fields of queer and trans studies over the past thirty plus years. I stand on your shoulders and hope to do justice to the incredible insights and power of the work you've done.

I also would like to thank my friends and family for their continuing love and support (particularly Erika Lin, Gail Dichter, and Sharon and Neal Rifkin). To my husband Rich – I don't have the words, but you can see it in my eyes.

This book would not exist if not for Beth Freeman. She recommended me to Ray, served as an important mentor, and offered her friendship and support over many years. I have worked hard to try to live up to her belief in me. This book is dedicated to her memory.

Introduction

I can't remember the first time I heard the word queer – or trans/transgender, for that matter. With queer, it probably was hurled at me as a slur on some playground or in some school hallway (although *fag* was the preferred term of denigration). While I'm also not sure when I first encountered the reclaimed, defiant sense of queer, I do recall shouting, "We're here, we're queer, we're fabulous, don't fuck with us" at any number of demonstrations across the 1990s. I think it's safe to say that I'm part of the first queer studies generation. I started college only two years after the publication of the field-making double feature of Eve Kosofsky Sedgwick's *Epistemology of the Closet* (1990) and Judith Butler's *Gender Trouble* (1990), only a year after Teresa de Lauretis coined the phrase *queer theory* in print (1991).[1] During those same years, I read Kate Bornstein's *Gender Outlaw* (1995) and was transformed by Leslie Feinberg's fictionalized autobiographical novel *Stone Butch Blues* (1993). This period is my intellectual coming-of-age, when I came to the world- and self-remaking realization that sexuality, gender, all of it, is socially constructed, that my ingrained sense of the natural was learned and historically built, and that, as a result, maybe any number of things around me – and possibly in me – might be changeable (or at least less invariably embedded and intractable as they seemed). This heady, 1990s sense of possibility, and of the ways intellectual work can reshape consciousness, has for the last several decades continued to orient my relation to queer and trans studies as scholarly fields, which is the subject of this book.

What do queer and trans studies do? What conclusions do they offer? What do *queer* or *trans* mean, and how do we know them when we see them (or are them)? Queer at its broadest refers not solely to homosexuality, homoeroticism, or whatever lies outside dominant straightness, but also to the critique of ideological and institutional structures that present "opposite sex" desire, monogamous couplehood and marriage, and the nuclear family household as inherently natural, healthful, and necessary for human development and thriving. Such structures can be called *heteronormativity*. In a similar vein, trans can be said not only to refer to persons whose self-perceived and lived gender is different than the gender conventionally assumed for the sex that person was assigned at birth (usually based on an assessment of the infant's, or fetus's, genitalia), but also to the critique of ideological and institutional structures that presume a necessary, natural congruence between body shape/physiology, gendered self-expression, and social role. Those structures can be called *cisnormativity* (*cis* in Lain means on this side, as opposed to *trans* as a movement across).² We also might describe queer and trans analysis and critique as allied, although not identical in their foci, aims, and methods. Having offered these initial definitions, my goal in the rest of the book is to expand, complicate, reframe, and challenge them. Much of the work of queer and trans studies lies not so much in trying to provide clear terms and definitive answers as, instead, finding ways of seeking to understand, sit with, work through, and live in the general conceptual and political messiness of the world. That messiness includes the complexities, unruliness, contradictions, and multilayered possibilities of identity, power, privilege, desire, and embodiment as well as the difficulties, debates, and disagreements involved in envisioning and pursuing more equitable and just relations.

That being said, we might start out with the idea of treating queer and trans less as *identities* than as *analytics*. To understand them as identities suggests that these terms refer to kinds of persons whose belonging to that group is based on particular criteria, such as sexual object-choice (the sex of the persons whom you desire) or gender expression (the ways you enact your gender, especially if it's not consistent with the gender attributed to your body at birth). While we might talk about how ideas about who belongs to those categories change over time, or about how those categories (as well as related ones) emerge historically, intellectual work that is identity-based would treat these categories (or similar ones) as the primary starting point and organizing framework. Thinking about queer and trans as analytics, though, means that these areas of study pose particular kinds of questions and provide tools for thinking about a range of topics: they are *modes of analysis* rather than (solely) *kinds of identity* that attach to a specific group of persons or that provide the basis for those persons to see themselves as belonging to a coherent group.

What, then, defines queer and trans modes of analysis or determines whether something belongs in queer and trans studies? In addressing this question, we can turn to two early-ish writings in these fields that foreground and elaborate the distinction between identity and analytic in ways that center questions of inclusion/exclusion and their implications – Cathy Cohen's "Punks, Bulldaggers, and Welfare Queens" (1997) and Emi Koyama's "Whose Feminism Is It Anyway?" (2006). In her ground-clearing essay,

Cohen takes "queer" intellectual and activist work to task not only for their implicit whiteness but for the ways they largely envision queer as naming an identity formation rather than offering a broad-based critique of processes of normalization. While at its best queer foregrounds "the socially constructed nature of sexuality and sexual categories, but also the varying degrees and multiple sites of power distributed within all categories of sexuality," "queer politics has often been built around a simple dichotomy between those deemed queer and those deemed heterosexual." In presuming a unified identity, that binary ignores the distinctions in power and privilege among those who might be understood as queer, including class and racial differences, as well as attendant forms of racism and classism among queers and in queer spaces. Moreover, that simple dichotomy – straight versus queer – rests on an "unchallenged assumption of a uniform heteronormativity from which all heterosexuals benefit."[3] Queer, then, refers to those who are not heterosexual, leaving aside the ways the "'nonnormative' procreation patterns and family structures of people who are labeled heterosexual have also been used to regulate and exclude them." Attending to the legacies of enslavement, including the racialized figure of *the welfare queen*, Cohen illustrates that, while many people of color may be classified as straight, conceptions of sexual deviance have been attached to people of color regardless of their sexual object choice. In this way, we can see the "roots of heteronormativity in white supremacist ideologies," and although Cohen is dubious about the capacity of *queer* thinking and activism to address these issues, her argument demonstrates how queer analysis can move beyond identity in important and productive ways.[4] In a resonant vein, Koyama's essay shows how engaging transness opens toward a searching analysis of the politics of the category of *woman*. Addressing the Michigan Womyn's Music Festival's policy that only allowed entry to "womyn-born-womyn," directly excluding trans people, Koyama argues, "most if not all rationales for excluding transsexual women are not only transphobic, but also racist. To argue that transsexual women should not enter the Land [where the festival was staged] because their experiences are different would have to assume that all other women's experiences are the same, and this is a racist assumption." She adds, "white skin is just as much a reminder of violence as a penis."[5] The exclusion of trans women not only de facto defines *women* in biological ways (itself questionable as a feminist position), it posits a unity of experience based on shared *womanness* that effaces differences within that category, forms of privilege and oppression among "women" around those differences, and the significance of relations with others who share those identities that exceed the category of woman. Starting from the exclusion of trans people, Koyama's analysis turns toward highlighting the politics of naturalized gender identity and its alignment with whiteness.

As opposed to foregrounding identities, then, the *Introduction* approaches queer and trans as kinds of intellectual frameworks that raise questions about *sexuality* and *gender* as concepts and categories, illustrating what comes into view when one ceases to treat them as obvious or commonsensical. As they have emerged, accrued, and changed over the past three decades or so, queer and trans studies seek to trouble the presumed clarity of what "sexuality" and "gender" mean and do. In contrast to an ethos of ethical and political transparency that often seems to dominate popular and activist discourses, the implicit sense that there is a correct kind of analysis or framework that if adopted in and of itself can resolve all disagreements and provide an unimpeachable way forward toward justice, this volume is invested in exploring the intractable messiness of social life and the difficulties involved in trying to say something meaningful about it. Here I mean that questions of how power works, how institutionalized forces shape forms of individual and collective experience, how intimate life and felt embodiment articulate to public languages and systems, how multiple kinds of struggle might connect, and how varied projects of critique and seeking to live life otherwise rub and run up against each other and evade simple, unitary formulations. This book, then, aims to highlight the ways queer and trans studies have sought to speak to urgent issues in the world while also holding onto a sense of its irresolvable, multidimensional complexity. It shows how these fields in troubling ideas about the givenness of sexuality and gender also upend a wide range of other conventional givens about personhood, peoplehood, what a fairer world would entail, how we understand our places within that world and this one, and how to get there. I spend a good deal of time tracing specific lines of argument to illustrate queer and trans thought in its thinking, the *how* through which these fields navigate and unsettle the social landscapes we inhabit while also being reflexive about the limits of their own conceptual tools. That searching sense of undoing the taken-for-granted and seeking to attend to the crises people have been and are living in while not knowing beforehand exactly what will come to matter or where intellectual work will take you seems a hallmark of queer and trans scholarship. More than any specific content, that sense is the takeaway for readers.

As one might expect, there are any number of ways to tell the story of what these fields have been and keep becoming. The story I aim to tell is centered on how, moving beyond the hetero/homo and cis/trans binaries, scholarship in these fields addresses how what we think we know about sexuality and gender is inevitably crossed by and constitutively intertwined with race, class, ability, nationality, religion, ambient ecologies, and extant political and economic systems. The discussion offered here is rooted in a refusal to understand sexuality and gender, or *queer* and *trans*, as indicative of a single-issue politics that seeks to isolate a category of discrimination/oppression and to consolidate those subjected to it as a unified group so as to advocate on their behalf. Queer and trans as modes of analysis provide frameworks for understanding how sexual and gender identities themselves are shaped by and experienced through other kinds of identity. Perhaps more importantly, though, work in queer and trans studies has provided tools for tracing how dynamics of sexuality and gender are crucial to the making and sustaining of racial, capitalist, and imperial formations. This book aims to address queer and trans work in the humanities and qualitative social sciences over the last thirty years (particularly coming out of the United States) while resonating with where these fields' current energies are, in many ways reading backward from the present to generate a usable past for these adjacent, often aligned, but not interchangeable areas of study.

An Introduction to Introductions

I've been suggesting that queer and trans studies – and this introduction to them – are less invested in providing a window onto queer and trans persons (however defined) than raising questions about the assumptions, organizing principles, and erasures at play in existing (dominant?) ways of thinking about gender and sexuality. In this vein, in offering a survey of some of the major intellectual strategies in these fields that can help orient readers, I'd like to turn to other introductions that illustrate how these ideas have been developed, reshaped, and contested over the years. Whether to collections of essays or as freestanding monographs (like this one), such introductions themselves reflect on the state of these fields and articulate major trends within them. In this way, a survey of a collection of important introductions can provide a sense of how queer and trans analytics have been understood and of significant ways these areas have been theorized as fields of study.

The question of the capaciousness of queer and trans studies, the extent to which they can develop multidimensional models of subjectivity and oppression, has been a concern of these fields from the beginning. While often presented as a later turn, some of the earliest introductions foreground issues of what we might term intersectionality – the mutually defining copresence of varied kinds of identity and domination – as central to queer and trans analysis.[6] In her initial discussion of "queer theory," a phrase she invented,

Teresa de Lauretis presents this incipient area of study as seeking to "problematize some of the discursive constructions and constructed silences in the emergent field of 'gay and lesbian studies,'" and one of the principal silences is with regard to race: "The difference made by race in self-representation and identity argue for the necessity to examine, question, or contest the usefulness and/or the limitations of current discourses on lesbian and gay sexualities."[7] In this early articulation of *queer* as a scholarly concept, it appears as a way of opening up what constitutes the study of "sexualities" by raising questions about the scope and character of *gay and lesbian* as an organizing frame, particularly drawing attention to the *silences* within existing intellectual and political formulations. More than seeking simply to add additional constituencies to these existing categories, queer gestures toward the need to think in different ways about *identity* and *representation*, suggesting that attending to race, for example, alters how we conceptualize sexuality. This kind of intellectual work

> not only illuminates how various dimensions of social experience – race, sexuality, ethnicity, diaspora, gender – can cut across or transect one another resulting in their potential mutual transformation; it also "queers" the status of sexual orientation as itself the authentic and centrally governing category of queer practice, thus freeing up queer theory as a way of reconceiving not just the sexual, but the social in general.[8]

The editors of the special issue "Queer Transexions of Race, Nation, and Gender" (1997) present queer analysis as part of a process of decentering "sexual orientation" as a stand-alone issue/identity in favor of addressing how various kinds of identity and forms of social positioning *transect* and coconstitute each other.

From this perspective, queer studies entails less the analysis of sexuality per se (sexual identity or specifically gay and lesbian persons) than the consideration of how sexuality as a category or concept necessarily operates within a wider set of social relations, also reciprocally understanding the form and content of sexuality (whatever it might mean) as shaped by that complex network of relations. If queer studies addresses transections among identities and struggles against domination and the silences produced by conventional models and discourses of sexual identity, that set of concerns leads toward an analysis of how Euro-American notions of sexuality have also been an important part of projects of empire. As the editors of the collection "What's Queer about Queer Studies Now?" (2005) observe, work in the field "has examined the numerous ways in which racialized heteropatriarchy has been universalized as a Western discourse of (sexual) development, as a project of modernity and modernization, as a colonial and civilizing mission, as an index of political and social advancement, and as a story of human liberty and freedom."[9] Western formulations of proper sexuality (which themselves are shaped around racial ideals and imperial histories) bolster the West's narrative of its own superiority, as contrasted with nonwestern deviance and backwardness, and such ideals also help shape forms of Western intervention, seeking to reorganize dynamics of eroticism, intimacy, household-formation, and kinship in other places. Some of the introductions take other scholarship in the field to task for failing to engage these issues and for de facto centering whiteness and promoting Eurocentrism, but the engagement with race and empire in these introductions indicates that part of "the political promise of the term [queer has] resided specifically in its broad critique of multiple social antagonisms, including race, gender, class, nationality, and religion in addition to sexuality."[10]

Similar concerns have shaped the direction of trans studies. As Susan Stryker and Aren Z. Aizura (2013) indicate, "Gender is not merely the representation in language and culture of a biological sex; it is also an administrative or bureaucratic structure for the management of sexual difference and reproductive capacity," and in this way, "*transgender* is intimately bound up with questions of nation, territory, and citizenship, with categories of belonging and exclusion, of excess and incorporation, and with all the processes through which individual corporealities become aggregated as bodies politic."[11] *Transgender* here does not simply provide a collective way of naming a variety of kinds of gender identity and expression (particularly those deemed nonnormative because they do not accord with what is taken to be a person's *biological sex*). Rather, the term speaks to the broader processes through which gender is defined, through which it is attached to notions of supposedly innate sexual difference, through which such definition and difference affect the management of social and biological reproduction, and the implications of all of those dynamics for how persons are grouped together and regulated within administrative and legal structures. More than highlighting particular embodiments and experiences of gendered selfhood, trans studies considers how ideologies of gendered embodiment intertwine with the numerous other ways bodies are given meaning within (and are managed by) social and political systems. Even as trans studies opens possibilities for addressing a wide range of processes of gendering and conceptions of embodiment, both intimately felt and imposed, scholars also stress the problems of treating *transgender*, or any other category of gender variance, as if it were universally applicable. As Susan Stryker notes in the introduction to the first *Transgender Studies Reader* (2006),

> The conflation of many types of gender variance into the single shorthand term "transgender," particularly when this collapse into a single genre of personhood crosses the boundaries that divide the West from the rest of the world, holds both peril and promise. It is far too easy to assimilate non-Western configurations of personhood into Western constructs of sexuality and gender, in a manner that recapitulates the power structures of colonialism.[12]

In the second edition, Stryker and Aizura ask, "What kinds of questions and practices, then, can transgender studies offer that advance an anti-colonialist agenda, and that resist the subsumption of non-western configurations of personhood into western-dominant frameworks that privilege either 'homo' or 'trans,' or assume the ontological given-ness of the concepts man and woman? What might an anti-colonial or decolonizing transgender studies look like?"[13] In addition to tracking how gender and the distinction between sexed bodies is constructed in ways that affect and are affected by other kinds of identification, work in trans studies further traces the silences created by treating Euro-American terms and concepts as common sense, instead seeking to envision possibilities beyond such colonial interpellation and erasure.

As suggested by the discussion thus far, these fields both aim to challenge assumptions about the givenness of sexual and gender identities. The term *transsexual* was popularized in the 1950s by Harry Benjamin as a way of talking about persons who sought to change their sex through surgical intervention (what previously was called a *sex change*), as opposed to *transvestites* who sought pleasure through cross-dressing but did not seek to live as or become the *other sex*. In the 1990s, *transgender* came to represent "a political alliance between all individuals who were marginalized or oppressed due to their difference from social norms of gendered embodiment," potentially including those who were described (and described themselves) as transsexuals.[14] Inclusion in the category of transgender, though, did not and does not assume a desire for gender-affirmative surgery and can include persons who do not see themselves as *men* or *women* (often using the term *non-binary*). In opening up possibilities for thinking about a range of kinds of gendered embodiment and possibilities for transition, as Stryker observes, "Transgender phenomena call into question both the stability of the material referent 'sex' and the relationship of that unstable category to the linguistic, social, and psychical category of 'gender.'"[15] Those questions, she suggests, are central to formulating the work of trans studies as a field, which

> broadly conceived, ... is concerned with anything that disrupts, denaturalizes, rearticulates, and makes visible the normative linkages we generally assume to exist between the biological specificity of the

sexually differentiated human body, the social roles and statuses that a particular form of body is expected to occupy, and subjectively experienced relationship between a gendered sense of self and social expectations of gender-role performance, and the cultural mechanisms that work to sustain or thwart specific configurations of gendered personhood.[16]

Thus, rather than solely attending to persons who might be characterized as transsexual or transgender, this area of study aims to contest the supposed obviousness of biological sex, gendered social roles, and gendered self-understanding and the presumed relations among them while also highlighting the networks of principles, practices, and policies through which such notions of gendered personhood are made to appear self-evident. This project of disrupting and denaturalizing sex/gender offers a "political imaginary that moves beyond a rights-and-representation based framework," one where the goal would be to advocate for a clearly delimited marginalized group to be recognized by the state as the subject of rights and of anti-discrimination protection.[17] In contrast to that conception of transgender, trans studies considers the shifting and layered ways sex and gender are (re)made as social categories and the implications of those processes for various experiences of embodiment and gendered selfhood.

Queer studies also shifts away from a focus on "identifiable subjects laying claim to liberal rights, recognition, normalization, and inclusion."[18] It engages systems of power that produce and naturalize ideologies of identity, eroticism, health, and homemaking. Annamarie Jagose (1996) notes, "It is difficult to think of 'homosexuality' not as a self-evidently descriptive term for certain identifications or inclinations but as a historically and culturally contingent category," adding, "It is particularly hard to denaturalise something like sexuality, whose very claim to naturalisation is intimately connected with an individual sense of self, with the way in which each of us imagines our own sexuality to be primary, elemental and private."[19] Considering the contingency of the identities through which we characterize ourselves and others not only opens the potential for challenging their apparent obviousness but directs attention toward the institutional and ideological dynamics that create and sustain that sense of obviousness. In this vein, Nikki Sullivan (2003) suggests that "a deconstructive analysis would highlight the inherent instability of the terms, as well as enabling an analysis of the culturally and historically specific ways in which the terms and the relation between them have developed, and the effects they have produced."[20] In this sense, a queer approach not only contests the naturalness of heterosexuality (as opposed to, say, simply challenging the supposed deviance of homosexuality) but addresses the ways the differential distinction between the two – the hetero/homo binary itself – means that the one depends on and is defined through the existence of the other ("the homo in relation to the hetero ... operates as an indispensable interior exclusion – an outside which is inside ... making the articulation of the latter possible").[21] Moreover, their existence as a linked pair is dependent on historically shifting social processes. As Michel Foucault (1976) has famously argued, in Europe acts of sodomy had been condemned and prosecuted as a "temporary aberration," a prohibited kind of behavior, but with the invention of the category in the nineteenth century, "the homosexual was now a species": the "homosexual became a personage, a past, a case history, and a childhood" – a type of person defined by a notion of sexual identity that newly was used as a way of cataloguing people.[22] Queer as a critical concept, then, does not refer to a collection of kinds of persons who are part of a "community" that in some sense has "a common identity" or that "by nature" share certain "things in common"; "it does not offer itself as some new and improved version of lesbian and gay but rather as something that questions the assumption that those descriptors are self-evident."[23] Further, queer draws attention to the complex ways such a sense of self-evidence is generated and maintained – with respect to notions about normality and deviance, distinctions among sexual identities, and even the idea of *sexuality* itself.

Queer and trans studies further foreground the multiplicity and potential mutability of identity, both in the sense that any identity is crosscut and coconstituted by other identities (discussed above) and that experiences of subjectivity and selfhood are themselves complex and not simply derivable from external criteria. In this vein, we might think about the influence of poststructuralism and psychoanalysis on these fields. The former addresses critiques of the notion of a stable truth and of the idea that there is a grounding real/nature outside of historically shifting cultural frames. As Jagose suggests, "within poststructuralism, the very notion of identity as a coherent and abiding sense of self is perceived as a cultural fantasy rather than a demonstrable fact."[24] With respect to psychoanalysis, "the theory of the unconscious has radical implications for the common-sense assumption that the subject is both whole and self-knowing," and considering the role of unconscious feelings and desires within everyday experience emphasizes how identity "is an effect of identification with and against others: being ongoing, and always incomplete, it is a process rather than a property."[25] Moreover, particularly within trans studies, "the embodied experience of the speaking subject" is "a proper – indeed essential – component of the analysis of transgender phenomena; experiential knowledge is as legitimate as other, supposedly more 'objective' forms of knowledge."[26] As against claims about a person's supposed *real* sex, trans analysis values subjectively experienced sex/gender while also recognizing how that sense is itself historically and socially situated and possibly variable over the course of a person's lifetime.

One of the principal ways that scholars have sought to address social dynamics with regard to sexuality and gender without starting from the presumption of determinate identities is by presenting queer and trans analyses as critiques of various kinds of *normativity*. In what is often cited as the first use of the term heteronormativity, Michael Warner (1993) notes the prevalence of "a heteronormative understanding of society," adding that "political struggles over sexuality ramify in an unimaginabl[y] large number of directions. In the everyday political terrain, contests over sexuality and its regulation are generally linked to views of social institutions and norms of the most basic sort." From this perspective, "'queer' gets a critical edge by defining itself against the normal rather than the heterosexual" and by "pointing out a wide field of normalization."[27] More than simply pointing to those who are heterosexual as privileged, queer analysis engages the wide range of ways extant social institutions generate and manage the terms of "sexuality," presenting those ideas and structures as simply given (as the basis for social organization, reproduction, health, etc.) rather than as actively (re)made through the work of discourses, institutions, and regularized practices. Warner and Lauren Berlant further develop this framing in their essay "Sex in Public" (1998), observing, "Intimate life is the endlessly cited *elsewhere* of political public discourse, a promised haven that distracts citizens from the unequal conditions of their political and economic lives, consoles them for the damaged humanity of mass society, and shames them for any divergence between their lives and the intimate sphere that is alleged to be simple personhood."[28] This normalization of the bourgeois private sphere of home and family (the supposed space of intimacy as differentiated from the public sphere and the world of politics) not only makes it appear as natural, as the necessary condition for personhood itself, it also normalizes/naturalizes the capitalist and state structures that make possible the existence of the private sphere and the systems of inequality those structures engender. As a way of marking this broader systemic mode of analysis, some scholars draw on what has been called *subjectless critique*, which insists that "queer has no fixed political referent" in the sense that it offers "a continuous deconstruction" of a single-issue kind of advocacy that holds steady the existing political and economic structures and "lay[s] claim to liberal rights, recognition, normalization, and inclusion."[29] The presentation of the field(s) as *subjectless* highlights the absence of queer or trans identity as a grounding feature, instead emphasizing the turn toward interlocking ideologies, policies, and practices that (re)produce and seek to materialize notions of the normal. (Although other scholars have suggested that such supposed subjectlessness can lose track of the importance of subject position in understanding the dynamics and politics of lived desire and embodiment.)[30]

The concept of heteronormativity, then, points toward the ideologies and social arrangements through which linked ideas about desire, eroticism, intimacy, gender, home, and family take shape and come to seem obvious and simply given, including the idea that sexual identity is a necessary and ingrained feature of human experience. The use of queer as a verb – *queering* – draws on this sense of queer as a challenge to the normal. As Sullivan suggests of her introduction to the field, "the aim of this book is to queer – to make strange, to frustrate, to counteract, to delegitimise, to camp up – heteronormative knowledges and institutions," and Siobhan Somerville (2020) observes how, in contrast to the idea of queer "as an umbrella term for a range of sexual and gender identities," queer-as-verb "signal[s] a critical stance ... that is skeptical of existing identity categories and more interested in understanding the production of normativity."[31] Reciprocally, the concept of *cisnormativity* "mark[s] the ongoing assumptions about the psychic and social congruence between birth assignment and sex/gender identifications," and it indicates a "political awareness of the ways that social institutions and built environments train all people to pass as a single, consistent, legible, and acceptable gender," while attending to how "binary gender norms and gender hierarchies are established and maintained through violence against those who visibly deviate from them."[32]

This critique of normativity, though, also extends to queer and trans people. *Homonormativity*, coined by Lisa Duggan (2002), refers to the effort by members of sexual minorities to fit into a heteronormative model: "While in prior decades gays and lesbians sustained a radical critique of family and marriage, today many members of these groups have largely abandoned such critical positions, demanding access to the nuclear family and its associated rights, recognitions, and privileges from the state."[33] This "incorpor[ation] into (neo)liberal regimes of ... marriage and kinship, of markets and property, and as reproductive actors and agents of the state (in military service, for example)" illustrates "LGBTQ alignments with nationalist and racist ideologies" that are "constitutive of a normative queer liberal rights project."[34] This dovetailing of queer people seeking forms of state recognition with acceptance of forms of racializing and imperial domination – including when supposed support for queer rights serves as an alibi for a country's claims to be enlightened and democratic despite violence against people of color (at home and abroad) – has been called *homonationalism*.³⁵ *Transnormativity* has been described as a "universalized trajectory of coming out/transition, visibility, recognition, protection, and self-actualization" that "largely remains uninterrogated in its complicities and convergences with biomedical, neoliberal, racist, and imperial projects."³⁶

Some, though, have questioned organizing the field(s) around the critique of normativity(/ies). If "queer opts for denaturalisation as its primary strategy," "can queer theorizing proceed without a primary commitment to antinormativity?"³⁷ Robyn Wiegman and Elizabeth Wilson (2015) have suggested that this commitment to challenging norms illustrates how "the allure of moving *against* appears to have had greater critical currency than the more intimate and complicit gesture of moving *athwart*," adding that there seems to be a shared scholarly "conviction that norms are conceptually and politically limiting" and that they operate "univocally on the side of privilege and conventionality."³⁸ To be *against* endows a sense of being outside of relations of power, potentially enacting a "romanticization of the outside as a privileged site of radicality."³⁹ To be *athwart*, though, implies being in the middle or at an odd angle, perhaps carrying the image of being caught in currents. This perspective suggests that norms may not coalesce as a singular source of authority/oppression – *the* normative, for which queer and trans provide an unimplicated position of fluidity, freedom, liberation, justice, etc. Instead, queer and trans might address the complex currents that bring a person, group, scene, or situation into and out of conjunction with multidimensional forms of institutionalized power, and they might generate modes of analysis whose aim is less tracking and condemning complicity with dominant ideologies and systems than attending to the range of ways ideas and practices of desire, embodiment, and intimacy circulate, what they do, and how they facilitate or foreclose various possibilities for individual and collective worldmaking. In this way, *transing* may differ in important ways from queering. More than tracking and contesting forms of cisnormativity, or even transnormativity, transing might be thought of as multiplying possibilities for gendered perception and experience and for conceptualizing them: "proliferating ecologies of embodied difference" and "begin[ning] to articulate what might be called a general 'somatechnics,' or analytics of embodied difference."⁴⁰ If queering tends to draw attention to the limits of ostensibly shared identity as a means of political analysis and organizing, shifting focus to engagement with more encompassing and multipronged systems of normalization (to which sexual minority subjects may in various ways contribute as privileged beneficiaries), transing, perhaps, emphasizes less the violence of normalization than the range, complexity, layeredness, and mutability of processes of gendered meaning, expression, relation, and sensation.

Organization

The structure of the book aims to introduce readers to a range of concepts, questions, and intellectual strategies in these scholarly fields in a way that allows for ideas about sexuality and gender to be further and differently problematized with each chapter. To this end, it begins with discussion of some of the scholars whose work often is positioned as the beginning moment of queer studies in the 1990s, presenting them less as an origin than an ongoing touchstone for discussions and debates. From here, the book offers two different kinds of histories – one on movements frequently discussed as leading to queer and trans studies and the other on queer and trans histories, historiographies, and temporalities. These two chapters less offer a history than highlight the intellectual issues raised by how these fields turn to the past and articulate its relation to the present and future. The final two chapters might be described as shifting from time to space, at different scales. One chapter addresses dynamics of race, diaspora, and empire in relation to the United States (both because it's where I am situated and it's the site from and about which a significant amount of queer and trans work has been generated), and the final chapter turns outward, engaging scholarship on nonwestern and Global South peoples and places, since such work historically has not been centered in these fields. As this description suggests, the arrangement of the project is not based on something like progressive waves (such as in how histories of feminism are often described) or the description of foundational ideas/approaches into which additional persons, places, or topics simply can be included. Transness, class, race, religion, and the Global South, for example, are not contents to be slotted into established frameworks but themselves shape and reshape what queer and trans studies do and the *how* of their doing. For this reason, much of the scholarship discussed in any particular chapter could also readily be addressed in another chapter, and the placement is less about the topic to which something properly belongs than what struck me as most narratively effective in laying out the points for a given section or chapter.

Although the intellectual and political currents that might be understood as shaping what became queer and trans studies certainly precede the 1990s, this decade is when these areas of study begin to take shape as distinct fields in the humanities. In order to explore that process, as well as the ways the fields have grown through returning to and challenging those emergent analyses, Chapter 1 focuses on the work of Judith Butler and Eve Kosofsky Sedgwick. It will offer an account of the major strands of their thinking, how their work evolved over the course of the 1990s and early 2000s, and the ways some important (re)formulations can be traced directly or indirectly back to these writers. Sedgwick engages with the entangled relations between sexuality, knowledge, and feeling and Butler with the coconstitutive connections among gender, sexuality, and notions of embodiment. Both are avowed feminists and antihomophobic thinkers, both understood their academic work as arising out of and embroiled in activism and contemporary political struggles, and both foreground how the taken-for-grantedness of certain ideas about personhood and social difference significantly limit our ability to see the world and access non-dominant possibilities for being in it. Butler's and Sedgwick's critiques of what were commonsensical ideas about gender and sexuality still raise powerful questions about bodies, identity, and collective movements, even as later scholarship puts pressure on the implicit frameworks that shape how those questions are posed and addressed in their work.

Queer and trans studies often have been presented as emerging out of previous social and intellectual movements from the 1960s onwards. Over the past couple of decades, queer and trans scholarship has created, circulated, and revised stories about these movements, and Chapter 2 will consider some that often have been cited as laying the groundwork for the development of queer and trans studies as scholarly fields. These earlier movements in the context of the United States, themselves overlapping in complex ways, include gay liberation, lesbian feminism, women of color feminism, AIDS (acquired immunodeficiency syndrome) writing and activism, and early transgender writing and activism. However, we might approach them not so much through a conventional intellectual history – these ideas directly caused or led to those – than as sites of inspiration and provocation to which later scholars return. These recursive and revisionary journeys through the past speak to a process of creating genealogies that help anchor the present while also understanding the past as less an origin than a continuingly generative resource for reframing how we think.

If we do not understand terms like *queer* and *trans* as indicating historically unchanging kinds of identities and bodily experiences, then attending to the histories of contemporary terms, categories, and conceptual frameworks is vital in seeing that they have been constructed, how they have been so, and the institutional and ideological dynamics at play in those processes. How do you both draw on contemporary concepts, categories, and identities to make sense of the past in ways that are meaningful for the present *and* challenge their apparent obviousness? How do you both trace the structural continuities of forms of power and privilege across time *and* draw attention to other ways of being that have been effaced or supplanted by newer configurations of sexual and gender identity? Chapter 3 engages these historiographic issues, and the significance of history for queer and trans studies, from several different angles, including the stakes of centering race and empire, the ways scholars have conceptualized eroticism and embodiment in periods before the advent of the concepts of homosexuality and transsexuality, the question of whether particular historical persons and social dynamics should be understood as *queer* or *trans*, and the emergence from the late nineteenth century through the mid twentieth century of the dominant categories of sexual and gender identity we've inherited from that period. The chapter will close with scholarly articulations of queer and trans temporalities – the effort to rethink how we understand the experience of being-in-time.

More than simply attending to the experiences of nonwhite subjects deemed deviant due to their object-choice and/or gender expression, queer and trans of color critique engages the ways sexuality and gender themselves gain meaning in the context of systems of racial differentiation and, reciprocally, how struggles for justice, abolition, freedom, and decolonization must attend to sexuality and gender as both vectors of domination and sites of liberatory imagination and expression. Chapter 4 considers in greater detail how ingrained inclinations toward savagery, criminality, and inassimilable alienness are attributed to racialized populations in the United States through invoking their supposed failures to enact proper gender and sexuality – to live in heteronormative and cisnormative ways. Additionally, I will consider how queer and trans of color critique addresses the specificities in how particular racialized groups are defined through systems of sexual and gender normativity and how they have engaged those systems in multidimensional ways. This chapter will consider these issues by attending to queer and trans work in Black studies, Latinx studies, Asian American studies, and Indigenous studies, tracing differences and disagreements within those fields and tracking dialogues among/across them.

When thinking about the world outside of "the West" (the United States, northern and western Europe, and predominantly white settler-states like Canada and Australia), scholarship can fall into generalizing frameworks in which comparison with the West predominates or in which the world is divided up into "areas" that are treated as self-identical blocks, also de facto portrayed as more or less sealed off from each other. As Chapter 5 discusses, the presence of such patterns raises a series of intellectual and methodological questions: how can we reckon with the effects and ongoing histories of imperialism and occupation, uneven transnational dynamics of exploitation and extraction, and racial capitalism while not understanding those subjected to oppression and domination as merely passive in the face of those processes? How do we engage with forms of difference while understanding them as multidimensional, permeable, and changing, rather than freezing them in ahistorical and essentialized accounts of local/national/regional culture? How do we attend to forms of place-based specificity (at whatever scale) while engaging the heterogeneity and diversity of the area, country, and/or population under discussion and while also addressing dynamic relations with other peoples and places – both chosen and coerced? Moreover, how do we decenter "the West" without recentering it in that very process (as the thing whose negation ends up defining the shape and character of our studies)? In considering how queer and trans studies have taken up these challenges, this chapter is organized into three sections. The first considers critiques of imperialist and capitalist influence as well as critiques of those critiques, due to what other scholars have suggested can be their homogenizing tendencies. The second section focuses on articulations of national/local difference and how to understand it in relation to layered histories and contemporary transnational formations. The final section will address circulations and exchanges, particularly as they generate forms of regional interrelation – connections that themselves do not simply follow from Western/Global North formulations and frameworks, despite the latter's presumed dominance.

Note on Audience and Use

The audience for this book includes undergraduates, graduate students, faculty, and members of the general public. The volume provides useful background on important figures, arguments, and texts in these fields. While designed to be read from beginning to end, each chapter also works as a freestanding discussion of its organizing topic, and in many ways, each section in the chapters potentially could be read as a freestanding unit. This modular-ish structure is meant to allow ease of engagement, for reading and teaching. In this vein, although the book is meant to sustain itself as a stand-alone volume, I've also tried to bear in mind its potential pedagogical uses, which has included trying to provide a range of sources for all of the topics discussed so that someone could easily either assemble a reading list for further exploration on their own or develop a syllabus around the topic(s). It's been important to me that this volume be accessible enough for someone first starting out with these fields and that it also retain the complexity and specificity that would make it helpful for those experienced in scholarly work who want to learn more about queer and trans studies *as well as* scholars already working in (or closely adjacent to) queer and trans studies who want to learn more about other aspects of these fields. I very much hope this book can serve those various purposes and constituencies while conveying the richness of these areas of study, which have meant and continue to mean so much to me (in my ever-evolving "I'm a queer '90s baby" way).

Chapter 1
Reading and Revising the 1990s

Beginnings are difficult. Beginnings are difficult, because the beginning often is not just a starting place, a convenient entry point, but often is taken to be the origin. Presenting something as the original not only blots out what came before but presents everything that follows as somehow contained within or derived from that initial point (think the Big Bang). "Queer and trans studies began in the 1990s." That statement in many ways rings true, since many of the texts still cited as starting points for these fields were published then and much that gave rise to these areas of study did coalesce over that decade. In this sense, the work of Eve Kosofsky Sedgwick and Judith Butler is at the beginning of that beginning, giving shape to and propelling the intellectual conversations that would take shape as queer and trans studies. Historical beginnings, though, are also retrospective, decided on after a movement of one kind or another has become established and it looks back to give itself a history – including a starting point. In this sense, Sedgwick and Butler are celebrated figures who've come to be presented as foundational after-the-fact. Exploring their scholarship during the 1990s and early 2000s, and its resonance for what came afterward, though, does offer some important intellectual entry points for engaging these fields.

This chapter turns to Sedgwick's and Butler's work as a way of detailing some ideas, questions, formulations, and conceptual difficulties that have become important to queer and trans studies over the last three decades. Sedgwick engages with the entangled relations between sexuality, knowledge, and feeling and Butler with the coconstitutive connections among gender, sexuality, and notions of embodiment. Both are avowed feminists and anti-homophobic thinkers, both understood their academic work as arising out of and embroiled in activism and contemporary political struggles, and both foreground how the taken-for-grantedness of certain ideas about personhood and social difference significantly limit our ability to see the world and access non-dominant possibilities for being in it. These thinkers also insist on the non-universality of dominant notions of gender and sexuality – that ideas about the naturalness of particular configurations of identity and desire simply are not true in all times and places. However, they also often de facto center whiteness and normalize imperial dynamics even as these scholars also indicate commitments to antiracist and anticolonial intellectual and political work. Butler's and Sedgwick's critiques of what were commonsensical ideas about gender and sexuality still raise powerful questions about bodies, identity, and collective movements, even as later scholarship puts pressure on the implicit frameworks that shape how those questions are posed and addressed in their work.

It Was Gender All Along

In *Gender Trouble*, Butler begins by investigating the idea that there is a meaningful unified category of "women" for which feminism as a political movement can speak. They engage the assumption that "there must be a universal basis for feminism, one which must be found in an identity assumed to exist cross-culturally." That presumption also quite often is accompanied by "the notion that the oppression of women has some singular form discernible in the universal or hegemonic structure of patriarchy or masculine domination." However, the claim that patriarchy operates more or less the same way everywhere – and that women, as the objects of that oppression, share an inherent set of experiences and interests – is itself imperialistic. It "support[s] highly Western notions of oppression" while also "construct[ing] a 'Third World' or even an 'Orient' in which gender oppression is subtly explained as symptomatic of an essential non-Western barbarism."[1] If there's a shared womanness resulting from the ways patriarchy operates all around the world, why is it, Butler asks, that Euro-American feminist accounts of that oppression so often cast non-European places and people of color as so much more patriarchal? Or, put another way, how do notions of a shared patriarchy, and shared womanness, reinforce racializing and colonial assumptions about non-European and nonwhite backwardness and savagery? Challenging the existence of such a global, transcultural patriarchy, though, leaves one with the question, what exactly unites the people categorized as *women*?

One way of approaching this issue is to say that while their social circumstances may differ, women are united in a shared femaleness, having a particular kind of sexed body (one of two models in which human bodies come). Having a female body – sex – is distinguished from how that body gains social meaning in cultural practices – gender. Butler observes that this distinction between sex and gender was "intended to dispute the biology-as-destiny formulation," the assumption that certain particular kinds of social practices (like femininity and ways of being a mother) simply follow naturally from having a female body.[2] As Butler argues, though, "If gender is the cultural meaning that the sexed body assumes, then a gender cannot be said to follow from a sex in any one way. Taken to its logical limit, the sex/gender distinction suggests a radical discontinuity between sexed bodies and culturally constructed genders." This logical disjunction raises the question, "what is 'sex' anyway"? Differentiating *sex* and *gender* leaves the former with no way of shaping the latter, thereby leaving unclear what sex is supposed to mean with regard to gender. Butler observes, "sex proves to have been gender from the start."[3] In making this statement, they're indicating that ideas about the body as having a natural, presocial form are themselves an expression of cultural narratives and, thus, a function of gender. In this way, *gender* provides a way of naming not so much culturally differing assumptions about the meanings and social roles of sexed bodies as the entire system of culturally and historically produced meanings through which bodies are divided into two types called *sex*. Butler indicates, "gender must also designate the very apparatus of production whereby the sexes themselves are established. As a result gender is not to culture as sex is to nature: gender is also the discursive/cultural means by which 'sexed nature' or 'a natural sex' is produced and established as 'prediscursive,' prior to culture."[4] Gender as a process of socially categorizing and differentiating bodies in ways that make them socially meaningful creates the categories of sex, which then are treated as if they referred to something that simply was given outside of all language, culture, or history.

Rather than understanding man and woman as commonsensical categories that correlate to necessary identities in human reproduction, Butler reverses that logic, viewing the naturalization of "the heterosexual matrix" as significant in shaping how gender is constructed. They argue, "The institution of a compulsory and naturalized heterosexuality requires and regulates gender as a binary relation in which the masculine term is differentiated from a feminine term, and this differentiation is accomplished through the practices of heterosexual desire."[5] *Heterosexual* here refers to more than desire for someone of "the opposite sex"; it's an institutionalized ideological system in which desire is supposed to take only one form that also correlates with family formation and household-making (the nuclear family) and in which the companionate, monogamous hetero-couple is understood as the fundamental building block of social life. This series of interdependent and cross-referencing assumptions depends on there being two binarized genders envisioned as tied to reproductive bodily types. From this perspective, other configurations of desire appear as perverse deviations, also defined in terms of binarized genders: "for heterosexuality to remain intact as a distinct social form, it *requires* an intelligible conception of homosexuality and also requires the prohibition of that conception in rendering it culturally unintelligible." Homosexuality, defined in terms of same-sex object-choice, then, is not so much outside the system of compulsory heterosexuality as produced as a category within that system – a category that also relies on notions of sexed bodies but that is demonized as aberrant and unnatural within that system. As Butler notes, "lesbian desire is no more and no less constructed than other modes of sexuality."[6]

In developing the notion of sex as an effect of gender, Butler challenges what they refer to as the "metaphysics of substance" – the idea of a kind of being or identity that we could reference that exists totally apart from existing social frameworks.[7] They characterize the metaphysics of substance as "humanist conceptions of the subject [that] tend to assume a substantive person who is the bearer of various essential and nonessential attributes."[8] Such conceptions posit the existence of an experience of embodiment or personhood that is prior to or outside of historically and culturally situated social meanings. For example, with regard to Simone de Beauvoir's argument that "one is not born a woman," suggesting a kind of personhood that precedes social gendering, Butler asks, "Are there humans who are not, as it were, always already gendered? The mark of gender [including the gendered construction of bodies as sexed] appears to 'qualify' bodies as human bodies." Butler indicates that in other feminist critiques of gender oppression and compulsory heterosexuality, "there appears to be a truer reality, an ontological field of unity against which these social fictions are measured."[9] Dominant ideologies of gender and sexuality are seen as layered over or obfuscating a realm of experience that defies such cultural inscriptions. However, as with the discussion of the problems of defining *sex* as distinct from *gender*, Butler argues that the sense of such a before or beneath is the result of existing social systems of meaning: that such systems actively produce that sense of the natural, the given, the presocial. In *Bodies That Matter*, Butler seeks to respond to criticisms that their theorization of gender does not account for the materiality of the body by addressing the ways that the idea of accessing a sense of the body beyond language and culture is itself a function of how embodiment is materialized *through* language and culture. Butler observes, "The body posited as prior to the sign [by which it is referenced or figured] is always *posited* or *signified* as *prior*."[10] Asserting, in language, the existence of a body and form of bodily experience that precedes and exceeds all acts of cultural naming creates, in language, a sign of that supposed otherness/alterity – generating an image or impression of such *beforeness* or *outsideness* rather than simply designating a thing that exists in an asocial way. In this vein, Butler insists, "it is no longer possible to take anatomy as a stable referent that is somehow valorized or signified through being subjected to an imaginary schema," like cultural forms and psychological investments/ identifications; "[o]n the contrary, the very accessibility of anatomy is in some sense dependent on this schema and coincident with it." In this way, the *materiality* of embodiment cannot be understood outside the ways extant cultural norms and modes of power produce the lived effects of how we see, feel, and envision our bodies and those of others, which we treat as if they were empirical and obvious – the "material effects" of such social dynamics "are taken as material data or primary givens."[11]

If there is no inherent, natural body or set of bodily relations that provide the basis for social relations, then dominant ideas about the body, gender, and desire, Butler argues, come to seem natural through routine repetition – being continually performed. That ongoing performance, or *performativity*, is what constructs and maintains identities, bodies, social relations, and personal experience in ways that enact the heterosexual matrix and its genderings. In current popular usage, performative tends to mean false or surface, a kind of act for others, as in the idea of performative activism. Butler, though, uses the term to conceptualize identities of all kinds as produced and reproduced through the ways they are enacted in everyday circumstances. Butler observes, "In this sense, gender is always a doing, though not a doing by a subject who might be said to preexist the deed": "identity is performatively constituted by the very 'expressions' that are said to be its results." They later add, "gender is itself a kind of becoming or activity . . . not to be conceived [of] as a noun . . . but rather as an incessant and repeated action of some sort."[12] If there is no individual sense of a body or a kind of individual personhood that precedes the enactment of gender, then there is no subject who chooses or decides to live out a particular gender. What seems like the *expression* of an inner or innate sense of self, or of the supposed natural tendencies that follow from having a particular kind of sexed body, is actually, Butler indicates, the built-up effects of *performing* socially constructed forms of gender. In *Bodies That Matter*, Butler supplements their notion of performativity with the idea of citationality. They suggest that "agency" is "a reiterative or rearticulatory practice, immanent to power, and not a relation of external opposition to power."[13] The example of a judge's ruling often serves as a go-to for Butler to explain how this process works. The justice "speaks in the name of the law," although not creating it, and in doing so, the judge "'cites' the law." The judge's judgment takes part in a "signifying chain" predicated on "the authority of the law" even as legal meanings and implications may be altered in the repetition or citation – "reworking a set of already operative conventions." That "citational legacy" provides the framework in which both conformity and resistance take place, shaping what will appear as an intelligible claim or experience.[14] In this way, people can be said to live their gender and sexuality in ways that cite existing norms, even while that very reiteration also can provide the occasion for reworking and shifting them: "The 'I' who would oppose its construction is always in some sense drawing from that construction to articulate its opposition."[15]

While socially intelligible personhood depends on such a continuing performance/citation, that dynamic does not mean that gender is always enacted in ways that reinforce the obviousness and naturalness of those norms. The central role of repetition in realizing those norms means that they are subject to shifts and slippages that bring their givenness into question. Through the everyday performance of gender, "'the normal,' 'the original' is revealed to be a copy," a copy – a reiterated reproduction – that has no original – no ground in some identity, set of sensations, or biological mandate that lies outside of the historically and culturally specific "matrix of power" in which all of these gendered experiences take place.[16] In perhaps one of the most famous and most misunderstood moves in *Gender Trouble*, Butler turns to drag to illustrate these points. In their argument, drag "become[s] the site of parodic contest and display that robs compulsory heterosexuality of its claims to naturalness and originality": "*In imitating gender, drag implicitly reveals the imitative structure of gender itself – as well as its contingency.*"[17] Drag provides a concrete example of the ways one might conceptualize gender less as emanating from an internal core of selfhood or from the supposed predispositions of one's "sex" than as a collection of social meanings produced and reproduced through their enactment. In turning to drag as a metaphor for visualizing the idea of gender performativity, though, Butler can make processes of gendering seem like a form of theater, a volitional act on the part of a subject who actively chooses to put on the signs of a gender and who equally can choose to take them off – whose subjectivity and experience of personhood is not integrally tied up in the gender they perform. Instead, for Butler, gendered selfhood and embodiment emerge through ongoing participation in a matrix of sustained and interdependent cultural forms, but those forms themselves are malleable and change over time, as revealed by the ways they need to be performed in order to be realized.

As noted earlier, Butler challenges the feminist claim to the idea of a universal patriarchy and a unified sense of womanhood, but when addressing compulsory heterosexuality and processes of gendering, Butler often speaks as if there were only one set of norms governing such cultural processes, usually figured as "the law" (drawn from the psychoanalytic and structuralist thinkers with whom Butler engages). However, even as Butler often uses *the law*, singular, to conceptualize how identity is generated and experienced, they also make an effort to address the multiplicity of modes of domination. Butler asserts, "it seems crucial to rethink the scenes of reproduction and, hence, of sexing practices not only as ones though which a heterosexual imperative is inculcated, but as ones through which boundaries of racial distinction are secured as well as contested."[18] Race, gender, and sexuality are intertwined, such that "to claim that sexual difference is more fundamental than racial difference is effectively to assume that sexual difference is white sexual difference, and that whiteness is not a form of racial difference."[19]

In considering how persons negotiate the system of norms in which they find themselves and by which they come to know and experience themselves, Butler at times introduces an implicit queer/trans split in their thinking about opposition to that system. They tend to privilege kinds of performativity that readily can be seen as crossing or contesting dominant terms, rather than as identifying with them. In this vein, *queer* becomes a way of marking forms of personal identity and political organizing that aim to disrupt dominant understandings of gender and sexual normality, and that aim also involves seeking to mark the limits of queer – what it effaces, occludes, and renders unspeakable. Simply "legitim[izing] homosexuality" does not transform existing systems of sex/gender, instead reinvesting in "the force of normalization" and requiring "a queer resignification" that can "expand and alter" existing modes of "normativity." Butler suggests that drawing attention to processes of normalization, and how they shape possibilities for identification and action, is a necessary element of political work and should be part of the self-reflexive intellectual aims of queer analysis. They note that "the genealogical critique of the queer subject will be central to queer politics to the extent that it constitutes a self-critical dimension within activism, a persistent reminder to take the time to consider the exclusionary force" of the terms and de facto norms that very activism mobilizes.[20] However, the text implicitly contrasts such a self-reflexive political consciousness with a desire to embody social norms – a tendency Butler repeatedly attributes to trans women of color. In discussing the film *Paris Is Burning* and its focus on house-ballroom culture in New York, Butler highlights the representation of Venus Xtravaganza, a trans Latina who is part of that scene and who viewers learn was murdered by a man with whom she had sex. In the film, Venus expresses her desire for gender-affirming surgery, which she describes as allowing her to live a life of suburban couplehood, and Butler reads this desire, including the pursuit of surgery, as an "uncritical miming of the hegemonic."[21] Moreover, they argue that Venus's vision for herself is of a piece with the notion of *realness* that is part of the categories and ways of judging performance in the balls themselves: "The citing of dominant norms does not, in this instance, displace the norm; rather it becomes the means by which that dominant norm is most painfully reiterated as the very desire and the performance of those it subjects."[22] If queer subjects challenge norms by emphasizing their constructedness and the force of their imposition, trans subjectivity appears here as merely identifying with and confirming the naturalness of those norms. Trans women of color in Butler's account seem too invested in white, bourgeois, heterosexual ideals to perform identity in ways that would challenge or displace them.

In *Undoing Gender*, though, Butler revisits and revises this problematic way of framing transgression and subversion. They highlight the immense difficulties of creating a "livable life" when a person or group is treated as impossible within dominant social frameworks, particularly focusing on gender nonnormativity and trans identities. At the outset, they pose the question of the relation between having a recognized kind of gender and having one's personhood acknowledged: "If I am a certain gender, will I still be regarded as part of the human? Will the 'human' expand to include me in its reach"?[23] Some genders will remain unintelligible – cast as unreal, fake, impossible – in a system in which gender continues to be understood as deriving from one's supposed biological sex (which one nonconsensually is assigned at birth). Persons who live such genders will not be seen as fully persons, but, instead, as a kind of monstrous deformation of the human. With regard to that process of enforced ascription (your *real* gender follows from your *real* sex which usually follows from others' assessment of your genitals), Butler notes, "I would hope that we would all remain committed to the idea that no one should be forcibly compelled to occupy a gender norm that is undergone, experientially, as an unlivable violation."[24] Butler affirms "experiential" gender separate from whether that experience supposedly idealizes existing gender norms. Moreover, while continuing to point toward the importance of "expos[ing dominant cultural forms and ideals] as nonnatural and nonnecessary" in order to "def[y] normative expectation[s]," *Undoing Gender* offers new intellectual support for the significance of being recognized. To want to be seen as real by others and fully valued as a person, including in terms of one's gender, cannot be dismissed as merely a desire for assimilation: "it seems crucial to realize that a livable life does require various degrees of stability"; "What is most important is to cease legislating for all lives what is livable only for some." The "desire for norms that might let one live," then, is not equivalent to an uncritical identification with normative ideals (which also engages some of the questions about the limits of the critique of normativity raised in my introduction).[25] The argument for greater access to gender-affirming medicine, which Butler makes, need not be seen as at odds with critiques of various kinds of gender normalization (including those enacted in the process of being diagnosed as having gender dysphoria, which for many is the precondition for getting funded access to gender-affirming hormones, surgical interventions, and technologies). Butler indicates, "I want to maintain that legitimation is double-edged: it is crucial that, politically, we lay claim to intelligibility and recognizability; and it is crucial, politically, that we maintain a critical and transformative relation to the norms that govern" what will be understood as recognizable.[26]

Trans Experience and Gendered Power

If gender is performative, as Butler argues, what does that mean for understanding trans experiences of embodiment, particularly with respect to the process of transition itself? Some trans scholars have questioned how Butler's work addresses the physicality of the body and the complex ways that trans people negotiate that sexed materiality as part of affirming their gender, and they have pointed to the ways that trans subjectivity and embodiment can function as a figure within queer visions of anti-normativity in ways that efface the experiences of trans people. Others have suggested that the felt sense of being in a sexed body that does not reflect one's gender itself points to the ways the social meaning of bodies is not reducible to a self-evident, presocial materiality that the body simply has. Such work also addresses the kinds of historically and culturally situated frameworks at play in representing trans identities. Further, scholars have challenged the racial and imperial assumptions that can be part of efforts to describe and theorize *trans experience*, as if it were a unified category or as if all those who would be understood as gender-nonconforming in Euro-American terms will necessarily understand themselves as *trans*.

Queer discussions of embodiment can remake what otherwise would be seen as accounts of trans experience into examples of gender indeterminacy in ways that advance critiques of heteronormativity but leave aside the lived experiences of many trans people. As Viviane Namaste suggests, "what merits attention is the fact that some individuals have transgressed a sex/gender binary," and the focus on such supposed transgression creates "neglect of everyday life for transgendered people."[27] Rather than suggesting that trans people somehow illustrate the limits of the dominant sex/gender system, scholarship should start from "the mundane assumption that [transsexual/transgendered] people exist" and "examine the workings of discourse [and institutional] practices that inscribe, efface, and order transgendered lives, bodies, and experiences."[28] In perhaps the most famous trans critique of Butler's account of performativity, Jay Prosser argues that "transition has become the lever for the queer movement to loosen the fixity of gender identities," making what are seen as "gender crossings" into "a key queer trope" of the absence of a natural basis for the heterosexual matrix and the possibility of a wide range of kinds of nonheteronormative genders and sexualities. What is lost in the process, though, is "the referential transsexual subject," the person whose desire for transition is not about challenging gender norms but about addressing the nonalignment of their experienced gender with their physical sex.[29] The effort, from a trans perspective, to align gender and bodily characteristics can be mischaracterized from a queer perspective as merely confirming conventional gender ideals (as in Butler's reading of *Paris Is Burning*). In his study of transsexual men, Henry Rubin notes, "Ordinary lives, unmarked by suspicion and hostilities, should not be confused with gender conformity."[30] In this vein, Julia Serano observes that many transsexuals "feel that the transgender movement tends to privilege those identities, actions, and appearances that most visibly 'transgress' gender norms," which has "led to the creation of another oppositional binary of sorts, pitting those transgender people who identify outside the gender binary (and who are therefore presumed to challenge gender norms) against transsexuals (who are accused of supporting the gender status quo by transitioning to their identified sex)."[31]

From this perspective, *transgender* can be seen as aligned with conceptions of gender performativity that fail to recognize the transsexual aim of transition, to simply *be* and be recognized as the women or men that they are – "feeling at home in my own sexed body."[32] In "An Affinity of Hammers," Sara Ahmed suggests, "An existence can be nullified by the requirement that an existence be evidenced. The very requirement to testify to your existence can end up being the very point of your existence."[33] Trans critiques of Butlerian notions of performativity draw attention to the physicality of transition, the importance of differentiating the sexed body from a person's felt gender (in order to understand the potential dissonance between them and the need to bring them into alignment – affirming felt gender), and the realness of that sense of felt gender (a trans woman *is* a woman, a trans man *is* a man). Prosser argues that Butler's emphasis on modes of psychological identification and projection "refigures sex from material corporeality into phantasized surface." If sex is just an embodied projection of ideologies of gender, how can such a theory capture the difference between physical sex and felt gender that is crucial to trans experience? Prosser asks, "If there is no sex left over, no immanent sexed part to the self that is not already gender, what substance is there for the transsexual to change"?[34] Attending to this difference between physical body and internal understanding is also necessary for engaging what Serano terms "cissexual privilege." Referring to "people who have only ever experienced their subconscious sex and physical sex as being aligned," *cissexual* – or *cisnormativity* – provides a way of talking about the effects of the "double standard that promotes the idea that transsexual genders are distinct from, and less legitimate than, cissexual genders." In order to understand how that delegitimization works, there needs to be a recognition of the ways that sexed embodiment may differ from felt gender. Serano suggests that absent such recognition, queer conceptions of performativity can enact an "ungendering" of trans people by not recognizing the sex affirmed through the process of transition.[35]

However, even while critiquing what they suggest is a tendency in queer studies to foreground the critique of the gender binary at the expense of attending to trans experiences (which may "produce the feeling that one is being made into an impossibility"), some trans studies scholars remain concerned about the ways accounts of gendered realness also can end up "naturalizing sexist gender differences."[36] Instead, such accounts emphasize the need for intellectual frameworks that can "illuminate the experiences of transgender people and give an account of our claims to sex and gender," including attending to the meanings of gender categories – like *woman* – as used and felt within different contexts, while also refusing the kinds of "reality enforcement" with respect to essentialized ideas of sex/gender that are used to deny trans people's narration of their own bodies and identities.[37] Riki Anne Wilchins presents her own transition in terms of the imposition of gendered meanings on her body. She notes, "Trans-identity is not a natural fact. Rather, it is a political category we are forced to occupy when we do certain things with our bodies." Drawing on Butler's work, she further argues, "There is an entire social apparatus whose sole purpose is to determine, track, and maintain my sex. Perhaps sex is not a noun at all. Perhaps it is really a verb, a cultural imperative . . . in the face of which none of us have a choice."[38] Wilchins does not characterize her own transition as coming to occupy a material sex in which she is at home, but instead, she presents it as a way of navigating processes of *sexing* – the making of "sex" within the "social apparatus" through which gendered meanings are circulated and institutionalized.

Taking trans experiences as the model for gendered embodiment, rather than treating them as an exception or aberration, becomes a way of challenging cisnormative notions of *realness* by expanding and texturing Butler's analysis of how cultural construction works. Gayle Salamon observes, "the body one feels oneself to have is not necessarily the same body that is delimited by its exterior contours, and that is the case even for any normatively gendered subject." There is no given embodiment that is outside a person's experience of their body as lived within particular social circumstances. Salamon notes, "we only have recourse to our bodies through a body image, a psychic representation of the body that is constructed over time," adding, "The body image is always contextually situated, in relation to other bodies and to the world, and its construction is a social phenomenon." In this way, "What social construction offers is a way to understand how that felt sense arises, in all its historical and cultural variations, with all its urgency and immediacy."[39] The most intimate feelings of embodiment are, at all levels, social, and they emerge out of our experiences of living in the world and the ways our bodies gain meaning (including to ourselves) through such living, which is always in a historically and culturally situated context. For this reason, a person's phenomenological – felt/lived – experience of sex/gender cannot be judged against some supposed asocial truth of the body: "what constitutes something as real is not its [supposedly presocial] materiality but a horizon of possibility, an openness to all the different experiences that it represents to any given person" within specific, located circumstances.[40] The effort to attend to the trans everyday, to possibilities for living an ordinary life in ways that are not organized around contesting normativity per se, also can draw on Butler's notions of performativity in order to consider the possibilities of the law and citizenship for trans people. Isaac West suggests the importance of "avoid[ing] equating the demand to be recognized as a citizen with an uncritical adoption of norms." He argues, "The charge of assimilation holds only if discourse and legal subjectivity are figured as fixed processes divorced from particular contexts and located within cultural logics with inalterable scripts whereby culture is reproduced without a difference," rather than considering "the radical potential of performative contradictions" in the enactment of legal norms and claims to citizenship rights and belonging. In this way, West argues, trans assertions of citizenship can play on, across, and between legal norms in order to try to secure conditions of ordinary livability.[41]

Gender identity, though, takes shape in relation to a range of social dynamics, such as race, nationality, imperialism, and global capitalism. Such interdependence can be seen in typical ways of representing trans identity and the process of transition, as well as in the connections between gendered ideals and whiteness. For example, the figure of a desire for and journey toward home through transition appears prominently in accounts of trans experience, particularly those that seek to challenge or refuse notions of gender performativity. However, what do such narratives assume about mobility and belonging, how they operate, and who has access to them? Nael Bhanji observes, "The journey home of the transsexual may come at the expense of a recognition that others are permanently dislocated from home – that they occupy the inhospitable territories in between," particularly those who are migrants and refugees.[42] Immigration and diaspora are often caused by war, poverty, and oppression and often lead to racism, xenophobia, and criminalization in the places to which migrants have moved. Describing transition as a process of movement, a crossing in order to come home, then, can erase the experiences of unhomeliness and nonbelonging faced particularly by trans migrants of color coming to Europe and the United States, suggesting the need for greater attention to the work performed by "the spatial and geographical figures that animate understandings of transition and gender reassignment." Addressing the ways trans people use international travel to bypass particular state-mandated programs of diagnosis and surveillance that can regulate access to gender-affirming medical treatment, Aren Aizura observes, "Mobility here does not simply mean having the economic resources to travel overseas .... It implies the capacity to produce a fantasy of oneself as a consumer of medical procedures and the good life rather than a patient defined by the limitations of publicly available health care."[43] In addition, the pharmaceuticals often used in processes of transition and gender affirmation are themselves embedded within uneven global capitalist formations. As Michelle O'Brien notes, "When I give myself an injection of Delestrogen, I am locating myself and am located within global flows of power. I am connected to the complex political, economic, and social histories of how these drugs were manufactured and by whom .... I am participating within the system of transnational capital." She adds, "The politics of our bodies – as trans people, as drug users, as people living with HIV – require a sophisticated grasp of multiple contradictions. We are dependent on the very systems that oppress us," a realization that she suggests leads toward kinds of analysis that are not about "purity" but about understanding the complexities of "relationships of participation, resistance, complicity, and challenge."[44]

Somewhat exoticizing representations of nonwestern and Indigenous peoples also can play a significant role in forms of (white) trans self-articulation. For example, trans writers have drawn on the idea of the *third gender* as a way of challenging dominant ideologies. This concept was developed by anthropologists to refer to kinds of identity in non-Euro-American societies that do not fit dimorphic notions of sex/gender. As Evan

B. Towle and Lynn Marie Morgan note, this invocation by Euro-Americans of third genders or of specific nonwestern categories of identity, such as the *hijra* in India or the Lakota *winkte*, "seek[s] legitimacy in narrow or sanctified appropriations of [other] cultural histories [and] practices" in ways that "reify [and] romanticize presumed gender variability in non-Western societies."[45] Not only do such appropriations offer a thin and decontextualized sense of how such gender dynamics and systems work, as Towle and Morgan argue, they position such societies as backward or bygone predecessors to the modern Euro-American present while also failing to investigate more fully the historically situated processes of cultural construction that give rise to gendered meanings in the society they seek to critique – the one they themselves inhabit. Towle and Morgan suggest that such projections also tend to leave aside the operation of imperial dynamics in the present and the struggles for self-determination by the peoples who serve as the material for this mode of trans comparison.

In this way, work in trans studies can be seen as further building on Butler's feminist critique of the supposed universality of *women*'s experience and of an undifferentiated patriarchy. Trans movements can assert their own forms of universality that displace differences in how institutionalized systems of power impose and regulate sex/gender, particularly with regard to race and racialization. As C. Riley Snorton and Jin Haritoworn have argued, trans people of color generate greater value in death than they do care and consideration in life. Annual Transgender Day of Remembrance celebrations circulate tabulations and images of those killed in ways that imply a shared trans vulnerability to violence that is meant to rally support for greater legal protections for trans people. However, "[i]mmobilized in life, and barred from spaces designated as white (the good life, the Global North, the gentrifying inner city, the university, the trans community), it is in their death that poor and sex working trans people of color are invited back in; it is in death that they suddenly come to matter."[46] The representation of trans people of color who have been murdered, largely trans women, becomes a vehicle for advancing an ostensibly encompassing *transgender* political agenda that largely does not address the circumstances in which those so featured live and in which they seek means to survive. Trans of color deaths are construed as a function of a generic transness, having little to do with structural racisms, impoverishment, and criminalization. Further, people of color are viewed as failing to perform normative sex/gender in ways that mean that their experiences of gendered embodiment – and the ways gender regulation and discipline operate as part of racist oppression – do not necessarily fit within a transgender political or intellectual framework primarily organized around gaining recognition and resources for gender-crossing or transition.[47] In *decolonizing trans/gender 101*, b. binaohan observes that, as a Filipino *bakla*, "It had never really occurred to me ... that the trans community was under the impression that it was including people like me": "when we look globally, we can locate a bunch of people and identities who, when reading reports/studies/research, are often labeled as 'trans women,' but, of course, this is an ill-fitting and, more importantly, imperialist translation of a great variety of genders."[48] In this vein, Jian Neo Chen suggests that "[t]rans of color expressions and practices use the *surplus* that constitutes racial gender embodiment as the material for social struggle, reconstruction, and transformation."[49] The presumed excessiveness and deviance of people of color's modes of gender identity/expression – the "surplus" that is outside of ideals oriented around white bodies and social forms – becomes the basis for trans of color self-identifications and worldmaking, which cannot simply be incorporated into a de facto white-centered vision of transgender identity or rights. Moreover, uses of transgender can separate gender and sexuality as categories in ways that misrepresent the self-understandings of people of color. Tracking the ways the term transgender gained prominence by being circulated within social service and activist organizations in the late 1990s, David Valentine illustrates how that process aimed to coalesce the kind of "political and social entity that is needed in contemporary U.S. discourses of civil rights and identity politics."[50] He demonstrates how many people of color who understood their own gender and embodiment through the category of *gay* were classified by others as *transgender*, thereby seeking to include people into a struggle for rights and institutional recognition conducted on others' terms.

A good deal of scholarship in trans studies has sought to shift from chronicling the choices and experiences of trans people (who may or may not understand themselves in such terms) to developing a transfeminist analysis of overlapping and interdependent systems of power in which sex/gender is made, monitored, and regulated.[51] Dean Spade illustrates how centering the experiences of the most marginalized gender-nonconforming people (including the undocumented and incarcerated) leads to a shift from a focus on a delimited set of persons who can be categorized as transgender to consideration of the kinds of disciplinary and population-making power exercised by the state and service institutions in generating, regulating, and policing modes of gender and gendered realness. Such administrative systems do not so much neutrally catalog the qualities of the people in them as "actually invent and produce meaning for the categories they administer," like gender and race, and "those categories manage both the population and the distribution of security and vulnerability."[52] As Andrea Ritchie suggests with regard to policing, "What is determined disorderly or lewd is often in the eye of the beholder, an eye that is informed by deeply racialized and gendered perceptions," and she later adds, "failure to meet individual police officers' subjective expectations of gender appropriate behavior is read as embodying 'disorder,' giving rise to a minimum of intensified scrutiny that often escalates to verbal and sexual harassment, detention, and citation or arrest," expectations "rooted in white supremacist heteropatriarchy."[53] As with Butler's analysis, the kind of "critical trans politics" Spade articulates addresses processes of "subjection," "how we know ourselves as subjects through these systems of meaning and control – the ways we understand our bodies, the things we believe about ourselves and our relationships."[54] Unlike Butler, though, the discussion of how those institutional frameworks construct forms of identity is less focused on individuals' experience of themselves as subjects than the collective effects of political, economic, judicial, and social service systems that produce increased vulnerability for particular persons and groups as a result of how those identities work in interdependent ways. Such an attention to institutional frameworks and how they provide the terms of intelligibility for everyone's gender retains a sense of identity as performed within dominant systems of meaning while deemphasizing individual acts as sites for opposing such systems.

Mapping the Closet and Feeling Queer

In *Epistemology of the Closet*, Sedgwick begins with the chapter "Axiomatic," arguably the most important piece in the formation of queer studies as a scholarly field, laying out a series of foundational principles that will guide her analysis. Rather than providing a firm basis for broad claims, though, these ideas are meant to be experimental: "A point of the book is *not to know* how far its insights and projects are generalizable." Sedgwick presents her argument as an exploration, suggesting that a key part of the kind of intellectual work she's doing is not to know beforehand exactly where these ideas will go – what they'll encompass and what kinds of relations will come to be important. This sense of what we might call conceptual indeterminacy, perhaps even promiscuity, is quite different than an approach where the social structures and dynamics to be discussed are already clearly delineated. In the same vein, the first of Sedgwick's axioms is, "*People are different from each other.*" She explains, "It is astonishing how few respectable conceptual tools we have for dealing with this self-evident fact. A tiny number of inconceivably coarse axes of categorization have been painstakingly inscribed in current critical and political thought: gender, race, class, nationality, and sexual orientation are pretty much the available distinctions." These categories may provide important information about social positioning and point toward ways of mapping how power works, but, Sedgwick suggests, not only can they not capture the full variety of personal feelings, desires, and self-understandings, they can efface the presence of less generalizable terms and concepts that people use to make sense of themselves, others, and their relations to them – what Sedgwick calls forms of "*nonce* taxonomy." For example, something like categories of sexual identity – homosexual and heterosexual – can erase the fact that "[e]ven genital acts mean very different things to different people," including what counts as a *sexual* act, the role of fantasy in forms of desire, the importance of having a longstanding intimate connection or not, and relative emotional attachment to particular kinds of acts or scenarios.[55] Sedgwick aims to open intellectual room for recognizing and engaging unexpected dynamics and for viewing as significant ways of being, individual and collective, that do not necessarily fit existing rubrics of scholarly and political analysis.

Many of the rest of the axioms she offers seek to create this kind of capaciousness for the study of *sexuality*, including with regard to what will be seen as belonging to that category or as relevant in understanding whatever may be classified as such. The effort to determine whether one's sexual identity and kinds of desire arise from some sort of biological programming or the social context of maturation – "*seemingly ritualized debates on nature versus nurture*" – occurs against the backdrop of "gay-genocidal nexuses of thought," the desire to eliminate gayness. Seeking to adjudicate how any given person becomes gay, Sedgwick argues, cannot be separated from the larger social aim of trying to specify an origin that can be treated/eradicated. Similarly, efforts rigidly to distinguish sexual identity today from the forms homoerotic desire took in the past are equally deadening and dead-ended: "*The historical search for a Great Paradigm Shift may obscure the present conditions of sexual identity.*"[56] Here she's referring to the idea, often attributed to Michel Foucault (as discussed in the Introduction), that in the late nineteenth century a conceptual shift occurred from there being persons who committed particular outlawed sexual acts with persons of the same sex (such as anal intercourse) to there being a *kind of person* who innately desired erotic connection with people of the same sex – the homosexual. Moreover, that supposed fundamental change in understanding the meaning and social implications of desire itself is largely split into two versions: the defining of the homosexual as a gender invert (desiring other men in the ways a woman would and taking on other feminine characteristics – such as in the image of the sissy); and the notion of homosexuality as purely a matter of object-choice (the sex of the person with whom you want to have sex) separate from anything having to do with gender per se.[57] These two models of homosexuality also can be presented as part of a historical development, the former gender-based model eventually giving way to the latter/later object-choice-based one. However, Sedgwick cautions that all these attempts to indicate a definite change in how sexual acts and sexual subjectivity are understood – the idea that "homosexuality as we conceive it today" is fundamentally distinct from some set of assumptions about acts, gendered orientations, or desires in a previous historical period – tend to impoverish our sense of the complexities of both the past and the present, creating the impression of "a coherent definitional field rather than a space of overlapping, contradictory, and conflictual forces." Further, such contradiction and conflict among models ("the unrationalized coexistence of different models") does a great deal in shaping how discourses of sexuality and the dynamics of power in which they participate actually operate in the past and present.[58]

Sedgwick emphasizes the incongruity among notions of (homo)sexuality and the importance of attending to such incongruity in understanding how heteronormativity operates. For example, she distinguishes between *minoritizing* and *universalizing* understandings of (homo)sexual identity, "between seeing homo/heterosexual definition ... as an issue of active importance primarily for a small, distinct, relatively fixed homosexual minority" and "seeing it ... as an issue of continuing, determinative importance in the lives of people across the spectrum of sexualities."[59] She suggests that the pervasive slipperiness between minoritizing and universalizing frameworks – particularly the ways they incoherently inhabit and animate each other – makes the issue of sexual desire and identity central to a series of other significant, and slippery, distinctions that figure prominently in dominant Euro-American ways of understanding personhood, embodiment, and social well-being. These binaries include natural/unnatural, healthy/diseased, public/private, secret/visible, authentic/artificial, and voluntary/addictive. The issue is how dynamics of knowledge and ignorance around sexual matters also attach to other, often seemingly unrelated matters of disease, perversity, degeneracy, and social danger. Do these ostensible challenges to social order and well-being have to do with a determinate group that can be isolated and contained (minoritizing)? Or do they threaten to engulf the entire population (universalizing)? Can those who endanger public welfare in this way be known, and if so, how? That structure of slipperiness, incoherence, and simultaneity *is* "the closet," in Sedgwick's terms. To attempt to specify who or what kind of hidden relation carries morally suspect meanings or intentions also potentially brings with it a feared proximity to those very forms of deviance, degeneration, and unnaturalness by which you can get tainted if you get too close. As Sedgwick observes, "to know and be known [as the problem] become the same process," later adding:

> We must know by now, in the wracking jointure of minoritizing and universalizing tropes . . ., better than to assume that there is *a homosexual man* waiting to be uncovered in each of the closets constituting and constituted by the modern regime of the closet; yet it is by *the homosexual question*, which has never so far been emptied of its homophobic impulsions, that the energy of their [the closets'] construction and exploitation continues to be marked.[60]

As a structure of knowledge and social relations, the closet does not so much contain an identity as create the volatile and changing circumstances by which deviancy and perversity can be seen as lodging in particular persons *and* always potentially threatening to infect the populace from its ostensibly hidden locations.

While personal feelings, relations, and desires may unfold within larger social dynamics, Sedgwick suggests that they often do not line up with dominant terms or notions of identity. In *Tendencies*, Sedgwick turns to *queer* as a means of conceptualizing those wayward forms of identification, sensation, and narration. As part of considering how "queer representation" gets "smuggled" into mainstream forms of representation, she reflects on her own emotional attachments as a child:

> for many of us . . . the ability to attach intently to a few cultural objects, objects of high or popular culture or both, objects whose meaning seemed mysterious, excessive, or oblique in relation to the codes most readily available to us, became a prime resource for survival. We needed for there to be sites where the meanings didn't line up tidily with each other.[61]

Valuing and drawing attention to how things *do not line up* is a central part of what Sedgwick sees as the power of queer analysis. It challenges dominant notions of normality – with regard to (homo)sexuality, gender, the family, etc. – by treating those ideals as fusing together collections of disparate parts that conceptually can be disaggregated and analyzed for the ways they need not line up with each other and quite often don't. To do *queer* work is to render "those culturally central, apparently monolithic constructions newly accessible to analysis and interrogation" by showing "the ways in which meanings and institutions can be at loose ends with each other." In this vein, Sedgwick observes, "what's striking is the number and *difference* of the dimensions that 'sexual identity' is supposed to organize into a seamless and univocal whole." Against this homogenizing assemblage, Sedgwick suggests that queer can reference "the open mesh of possibilities, gaps, overlaps, dissonances and resonances, lapses and excesses of meaning when the constituent elements of anyone's gender, or anyone's sexuality aren't made (or *can't* be made) to signify monolithically."[62]

For example, meaningful forms of desire allegedly are defined by sexual object-choice, are part of someone's core sense of themselves, and provide the basis for long-term relationships. However, in her discussion of the depiction of masturbation in Jane Austen's fiction, Sedgwick highlights how autoeroticism is an incredibly common form of erotic practice and fantasy that fits none of those assumptions. Attending to the portrayal of *this* kind of desire peels away erotic activity and imagination from the conglomeration of pieces that are supposed to adhere to each other as *sexual identity*; masturbation "today completely *fails* to constitute anything remotely like a minority identity." Perhaps even more notably, addressing the prominence of masturbation and the masturbator as part of "the Victorian multiplication of sexual species" helps highlight the ways conventional ideas of sexual subjectivity have "all but boiled down to a single, bare ... dichotomy" of homo versus hetero. Sedgwick's effort to "make available the sense of an alternative, passionate sexual ecology," then, works by separating the presence of forms of desire, pleasure, and fantasy from their presumptive embedding in or subordination to the homo/hetero binary or the question of sexual object-choice.[63]

Rather than simply affirming non-straight identity, Sedgwick repeatedly underlines the importance of contesting the ideological and institutionalized assumptions that create conceptual units like *the family*. The idea of "family" agglomerates together "a surname; a sexual dyad; a legal unit based on state-regulated marriage; a circuit of blood relationships; ... an economic unit of earning and taxation; ... a mechanism to produce, care for, and acculturate children; a mechanism for accumulating material goods over several generations; a daily routine; a unit in a community of worship; a site of patriotic formation." Instead of trying to reconfigure the ideal of family, "the most productive strategy (intellectually, emotionally) might be, whenever possible, to disarticulate [these parts from] one from another, to disengage them – the bonds of blood, of law, of habitation, of privacy, of companionship, and succor – from the lockstep of their unanimity in the system called 'family'": "Redeeming the family isn't, finally, an option but a compulsion; the question would be how to *stop* redeeming the family."[64] One way that Sedgwick does so, in "Tales of the Avunculate," is through tracing the ways the figures of "uncle" and "aunt" in gay subcultures refer both to kinds of sexual dynamics (penetrative versus receptive) and to relations of care. That discussion, though, opens up to broader consideration of how these figures contest assumptions about the insulated centrality of the nuclear family, expanding beyond the parent–child unit as the singular site of intergenerational affection and childcare. Speaking of the roles of aunts and uncles, she also notes that, since they "are adults whose intimate access to children needn't depend on their own pairing or procreation," "it's very common, of course, for some of them to have the office of representing nonconforming or nonreproductive sexualities to children."[65] Sedgwick's queer method emphasizes the critical potential of foregrounding not-easily-categorized deviations from standard models of identity and kinds of relations and attachments that do not *line up* with conventional assumptions about what "sexuality" means and how it works.

In *Touching Feeling*, Sedgwick further develops this impulse to dwell in forms of sensation and experience that move in ways that exceed what she characterizes as *dualistic* thinking – hidden versus revealed, dominance versus subversion, acceptance versus repudiation. While scholars embrace Michel Foucault's critique of what he terms "the repressive hypothesis," Sedgwick indicates that a great deal of work in queer studies continues to focus on versions of repression. The idea that certain kinds of acts, desire, subjectivity are *repressed*, Foucault suggests, positions the person who reveals such supposed repression as a heroic figure of liberation in ways that actually reinforce the forms of power that *produce* those acts, desires, and forms of subjectivity as meaningful – what seems like freedom from power (calling for an end to repression) just reinvests in the unquestioned givenness of those same terms and social categories.[66] Sedgwick suggests that scholars still emphasize "a negative relation" to power in which dominant forms work to inhibit or stifle alternatives and in which the aim of politically engaged scholarship is to reveal those patterns of force.[67] Instead of aiming to expose such oppressions and calling for movement *beyond* these repressive structures, Sedgwick offers *beside* as another option. She seeks to open more room for thinking about how people engage in a wide range of ways with existing social frameworks: "desiring, identifying, representing, repelling, paralleling, differentiating, rivaling, leaning, twisting, mimicking, withdrawing, attracting, aggressing, warping, and other relations."[68] As opposed to thinking about subjectivity and emotional experience in relation to "a single bar," what Butler often describes as "the law" and its repressive/prohibitive effects, Sedgwick emphasizes how the physiological sensations and psychological dynamics of *affect* both point toward the importance of social context in the emergence of individual feelings *and* how that context does not mechanically determine the character and texture of such feelings.[69] Even extremely negative and apparently destructive forms of affect, such as shame, might be thought of less as merely an effect of homophobic denigration ("'toxic' parts of a group or individual identity that can be excised") than as a part of how identity is shaped and experienced that might be subject to "reframing, refiguration, transfiguration," even eroticization.[70] Such feelings should not be dismissed as pathological or simply internalized self-hatred, but seen as potentially enabling kinds of relation and attachment – and as connecting to an unpredictable spectrum of other feelings – that do not necessarily line up with politically engaged intellectual models of proper identity or how to enact radical lifeways.

Sedgwick's turn to affect is about creating additional possibilities for tracing how people, including marginalized and minoritized subjects, live within existing categories and institutional systems, how they work with and on such forms – touch them – but in ways that neither simply reaffirm those forms' givenness nor necessarily outright refuse them. This approach attends to feelings phenomenologically – how they are experienced as part of being in the world – rather than diagnostically, as symptomatic of the operation of a kind of social structure whose dynamics are treated as more or less already analytically known beforehand.[71] In this way, Sedgwick suggests that queer analysis can revalue a range of everyday forms of feeling, understanding them as worthy of discussion less because they are inherently nonnormative than because attending to them challenges ideas about how feelings, experiences of embodiment, and identifications are supposed to line up in (hetero) normative ways.

Minoritarian Feeling and the Limits of Closet Thinking

For Sedgwick, the closet represents how minoritizing and universalizing framings of (homo)sexuality are run into each other in ways that generate flexible forms of heterosexual privilege and that amplify the sense of sexual deviance as a proliferating and dangerous contagion. Conversely, queerness and affect offer ways of displacing this dynamic by emphasizing how feelings and identities don't (need to) line up in predictable ways. Later scholars, though, have raised questions about how other kinds of minoritized identities fit into this understanding of the closet. Sedgwick's formulation of the homosexual question – and, thus, of the closet – tends not ask how race and ongoing histories of empire shape the dynamics of denigration, secrecy/visibility, and feared contagion she describes. In addition to exploring further the possibilities of affect for queer intellectual and political work, including negative feelings like depression and rage, scholars also have considered the ways that desire and sensation – including queer forms – do not necessarily challenge existing systems of power and privilege but, instead, can serve as the vehicle for materializing and normalizing such systems.

How do racially minoritized queer and trans people negotiate their minoritization and the ways that straightness and whiteness are made to *line up*? José Esteban Muñoz describes such self-making as achieved through *disidentification*, which he characterizes as "the survival strategies the minority subject practices in order to negotiate a majoritarian public sphere that continuously elides or punishes the existence of subjects who do not conform to the phantasm of normative citizenship" – such as through their nonwhiteness, non-Angloness, and non-straightness. Those strategies involve "working on and against" dominant ideals, images, and institutions by "scrambl[ing] and reconstruct[ing] the encoded message . . . in a fashion that both exposes the encoded message's universalizing and exclusionary machinations and recruits its workings to account for, include, and empower minority identities and identifications."[72] Disidentification collects and refashions various cultural materials and imaginings to create more livable kinds of subjectivity, individual and collective. Muñoz refers to that everyday labor as *worldmaking*, which "slic[es] into the façade of the real that is the majoritarian public sphere. Disidentificatory performances opt to do more than simply tear down the majoritarian public sphere. They disassemble that sphere . . . and use its parts to build an alternative reality."[73] In *Queer Phenomenology*, Sara Ahmed suggests that to be *oriented* is to repeat familiar ways of doing things that have become familiar through their repetition. She notes, "Within the concept of direction is a concept of 'straightness.' To follow a line might be a way of becoming straight, by not deviating at any point": "to be 'in line' is to direct one's desires toward marriage and reproduction; to direct one's desires toward the reproduction of the family line." In this way, the nuclear family enacts a "process of alignment" that brings intimacy, reproduction, and placemaking into conjunction.[74] Such ways of creating lines of straightness extends to racial identity. Ahmed argues, "race would follow the vertical line of the conventional family tree. Genealogy itself could be understood as a straightening device, which creates the illusion of descent as a line," and in doing so, whiteness comes to appear "*as if* it were a property of bodies."[75] The family line plays a vital role in lining up racial identity as a status or set of qualities simply passed through families, and together, these intertwined alignments (normative reproduction and racial identity) make the historical and everyday dynamics of Euro-American social organization seem like just the common-sense facts of human procreation.

While these analyses of disidentification and (re/dis)orientation might be described as significant elaborations of Sedgwick's discussion of the process of assembling and disassembling social norms, rereadings of her use of the figure of the closet have been more directly critical of the absences and gaps in Sedgwick's account. They draw attention to how her framing of the closet largely edits out the formative roles played by race and empire in Euro-American ideologies of sexuality. Based on the idea of a lurking sexual perversity that has yet to be revealed, and that therefore threatens to contaminate others, the closet presumes a baseline of normality imperiled by the potential eruption of deviancy and/or its surreptitious corruption of the otherwise innocent/healthful. Yet, not only have people of color been seen as sexually aberrant due to their nonwhiteness, that supposed abnormality in terms of desires, intimate relationships, and family formations has been cast as illustrative of backwardness – as a sign of nonwhite barbarity from which Euro-Americans have progressed. As Greg Thomas argues, "The West can and does regard itself as universal without averting its gaze at all, for the dark body of the non-West is coded as an eternal sign of the inferior evolutionary development of non-white humanity." Thus, in emphasizing the closet – and the dynamics of homo/heterosexual definition that swirl around its shifting dimensions – as central to understanding modern Western culture, Sedgwick indirectly reinvests in a West and the rest framework that, in Thomas's terms, "rhetorically purifies sexuality of race, ignoring the history of racialization, which is simultaneously a history of sexualization."[76]

Attending to such ongoing histories of racialization involves considering how the distinction between homosexuality and heterosexuality is itself immersed within whiteness, how people of color are positioned as premodern, and how the relation between minoritizing and universalizing discourses works differently once one takes colonialism and the color-line into account. Euro-American ideas of sexuality and sexual normality emerge within social formations already defined by racial difference, such that, as Marlon B. Ross argues, the "homosexual subject" appears as "racially retarded" since "the perceived racial difference of an African or Asian male could be used to explain any putatively observed sexual deviance." Beyond the figure of the closet, then, there is a need to attend to the "alternative sexual modernities" both generated by these processes of racialization and lived by people of color whose erotics, intimacies, and self-understandings do not simply follow the terms of dominant discourses of (white) sexual identity.[77] The figure of the closet also underemphasizes the extent to which articulations of (white) homosexuality rely on citations of and identifications with nonwhite persons and groups, who become a legitimizing metaphor for (white) sexual minorities – a similar dynamic as discussed earlier with regard to trans identities. As Hiram Pérez argues, "The privacy of the closet, of the epistemological and ontological spaces designated as *inside*, depends upon the publicity of the brown body," from which white bodies are civilizationally differentiated while the brown body simultaneously serves as a figure of a premodern sexual license or freedom with which white queers can identify. Pérez further observes, "The consolidation of white privacy (shame, humility, civilization) remains contingent upon colonial and white supremacist violence, while covering the lost (primitive, shameless, perverse) sexuality projected onto the savage(d) body."[78] Insofar as queer theory presents itself as resisting modes of heteronormalization, depictions of nonwhite others, Pérez suggests, are mobilized in ways that position them stereotypically as signs of unrestricted pleasure and the performance of an unconstrained shamelessness rather than as distinct, complex selves who are also engaged in processes of theorizing and who are subject to various forms of white oppression and aggression (including through what seems like celebratory identification). Conversely, as Jin Haritaworn illustrates, charges that people of color are homophobically and transphobically *hateful* collude in gentrification and criminalization by presenting them as impediments to (white) love and self-expression and, thus, needing to be monitored, policed, and displaced to make spaces *safe* for (white) queer and trans communities. Haritaworn argues that "in the panics over 'dangerous places' in queerly gentrifying cities such as London or Berlin, [white] queers from all over the global north become residents the minute they arrive, while those [communities of color] who have been there for generations are erased from dominant multicultural maps." Instead, they are treated as "a perpetrator population" that is "always already seen as hateful, where *hate* functions as a racialised psy[chological] discourse."[79]

In a related vein, white queers present themselves as inheritors of Indigenous sexual and gender diversity in ways that erase the contemporary existence of Indigenous peoples as well as nonnatives' participation in ongoing modes of settler colonial occupation. Scott Morgensen observes that nineteenth-century discourses "represent[ed] white subjects [categorized as sexually deviant] as degenerates who had regressed to earlier stages of racial evolution," adding that many contemporary white queers have reclaimed that portrayal, "mak[ing] primitivity a resource that settler subjects access when asserting their national belonging."[80] In casting themselves as bearers of a supposedly primitive kind of sexual deviancy, white queers can position themselves as modern heirs of Indigenous presence on the lands claimed by settler-states like the United States and Canada. Such gestures, including queer rural back-to-the-land movements and expressions of neo-paganism, assert "a relationship to Native land and culture that does not feel like the conquest that they know they inherit," also presenting "an Indigenous nature" as fundamentally "driving queer politics."[81]

Work over the past thirty years also has questioned the field's implicit investment in what Jack Halberstam has characterized as *metronormativity*. Halberstam observes, "While the story of coming out tends to function as a temporal trajectory within which a period of disclosure follows a long period of repression, the metronormative story of migration from 'country' to 'town' is a spatial narrative within which the subject moves to a place of tolerance after enduring life in a place of suspicion, persecution, and secrecy."[82] That spatial distinction, though, is also temporal and racial. The non-urban appears as a place of backward, regressive whiteness. As Scott Herring indicates, "Metronormativity often appears as a travel narrative that demands a predetermined flight to the city; a mythological plot that imagines urbanized queer identity as a one-way trip to sexual freedom, to communal visibility, and to a gay village," and this vision is partially powered by "the unfounded assumption that urbanized areas are more racially diverse and racially inclusive than ruralized ones."[83] Moreover, it envisions that escape from rural spaces can be nothing other than liberating for queer and trans people. However, while Eli Clare notes, "My loss of home is about being queer," he refers to his dislocation from that home space as "*exile*," indicating "a sense of allegiance and connection – however ambivalent – to the place left behind, an attitude of mourning rather than of good riddance." Clare also notes how the disdain for rural whites due to their supposed backwardness and investment in forms of racism and colonialism tells a deeply classist story in which they "are more complicit with environmental destruction [and other forms of violence] than the rest of us."[84] Highly publicized instances of homophobic and transphobic violence in non-urban places, such as the murders of Matthew Shepard and Brandon Teena, circulate as evidence of an atavistic and homicidal heterowhiteness that supposedly pervades what's cast as the hinterlands. This story of urban sophistication, acceptance, and diversity effaces the oppressions and dispossessions at play in the city (including forms of gentrification in which white queers actively participate).[85] In addition, it casts *the rural* as a particularly concentrated space of sexual and gender normativity, effacing the long history in the twentieth century of seeking to impose heteronormative and cisnormative ideals on such areas as well as positioning the non-urban "as America's perennial, tacitly taken-for-granted closet" (despite the fact that in such settings "sexual and gender nonconformity are widely known but treated as open secrets inappropriate for, or just too obvious to warrant, public conversation").[86] Such metronormative assumptions also whitewash spaces outside the city, thereby rendering invisible the lives of queers and trans people of color in rural *and suburban* spaces. Attending to the suburbs, Karen Tongson argues, challenges the tendency, including in Sedgwick's work, to associate the queer with the *subcultural* and the subcultural with the "politically radical."[87] Instead of continually foregrounding a minoritized, white, urban, male homo avant-garde, there's a need to acknowledge the presence of a wider range of queer and trans subjects in a wider range of places living in a wider range of ways that need not be understood as inherently politically transformative. As Tongson asks, "what happens when subjects opt in to one problematic context as they try to opt out of another?"[88]

If Sedgwick's later work seeks to think about kinds of feeling, living, and relating that go on *beside* dominant norms, rather than necessarily directly opposing them, later scholars have argued that such bad feelings (like humiliation, disgust, depression, and rage) can help in tracking the lived effects of ongoing histories of oppression and can provide insight into how minoritized persons and peoples work to create livable lives for themselves. Such analysis also helps reframe what counts as a political activity or response. Ann Cvetkovich asks, "What if depression, in the Americas at least, could be traced to histories of colonialism, genocide, slavery, legal exclusion, and everyday segregation and isolation that haunt all our lives"? She contrasts this perspective with a common pattern on the Left, including in queer and trans activisms, "of assuming that the expression of feeling has to become something else to make it count as political," "looking for a deeper meaning or a 'real' politics that lies elsewhere" than in "emotional expression."[89] In her earlier work, Cvetkovich suggests that trauma can be understood as giving rise to broader networks of queer relation that respond to the consequences of existing forms of heteropatriarchy and institutionalized homophobia. Among the "trauma cultures" Cvetkovich addresses are lesbian survivors of sexual abuse, AIDS activists, and caretakers of people with HIV/AIDS, and she suggests that they "maintain a place for shame and perversion within public discourses of sexuality rather than purging them of their messiness in order to make them acceptable."[90] Engaging the historical construction and everyday experience of blackness, Darieck Scott argues that the kinds of feelings that white supremacy produces can do valuable work as part of Black self-making. He argues that "to be black means to have-been-blackened, to have been rendered abject," a process he characterizes as "the queerness" of Black histories and which he contrasts with the idea of "an ostensibly liberated black wholeness" that imagines itself as utterly breaking free from "a history of sexual domination."[91] Rather than arguing for the importance of an unviolated sense of selfhood, Scott suggests that a "willing embrace of the defeat, abjection, and violation that blackness inescapably is" as a result of these formative histories allows one to access another kind of *power* not based on mastery of self or others – one that "provides an opportunity for different configurations of gender and sexuality" not predicated on Euro-American models of personhood.[92]

In a similar vein, we might question notions of *pride* that emphasize "the need to resist damage and affirm queer existence" and of *transition* that cast it as an "entrée into a kind of gender euphoria."[93] Efforts to cast queer and trans identity in a purely affirmative mode efface the accretive emotional effects of continuing denigration and discrimination while also creating a normative image of proper subjectivity that denies the range of ways of living queerness and transness. Heather Love insists that "the outrages and humiliations of gay and lesbian history" need to be addressed, particularly given the ways they continue to shape "the ongoing suffering of those not borne up by the rising tide of gay normalization." Such supposedly "[b]ackward feelings" of shame and humiliation "indicate continuities between the bad gay past and the present" while "show[ing] up the inadequacy of queer narratives of progress."[94] Hil Malatino tracks the ways that negative feelings are part of "a trans technology of survival."[95] For example, he suggests that "[r]age is a legitimate response to significant existential impediments, to roadblocks that minimize, circumscribe, and reduce one's possibilities." Such a response "seeks to transform, and destroy, such impediments," and, similarly, "burn-out" speaks to trans negotiations of authority in medical contexts in which trans subjects' "epistemic authority" is discounted and in which "need and debt" structures the experience.[96] More than highlighting how individual experiences can fail to line up with both dominant ideals and homonormative/transnormative ones, bad feelings also can become the basis for forms of collectivity. Addressing the work of the organization Gay Shame in San Francisco, Eric Stanley emphasizes how an "affective commons" can emerge around the effects "of the devastation of racial capitalism's modes of extraction," including the participation and investment of state-recognized LGBT institutions, like community centers, in programs of gentrification. As against such bids for inclusion that help normalize other forms of structural violence, Stanley suggests that Gay Shame generates a "commons of hate" – a "motley assembly of outsiders, freaks, and queers" that is sustained less by a program of advocacy than rage at LGBT efforts to accommodate dominant social and economic frameworks.[97] Bad feelings, then, point toward continuing inequities, the phenomenological experience of living amid them, the emotionally complex dynamics of disidentification from existing norms, and the lessons learned about possibilities for collective care and worldmaking amid such processes (even if those possibilities don't look like *proper* political organizing).

At the Edge of the Human

In different ways, both Butler and Sedgwick address the question of how embodied beings come to be understood as *human*. They trace the dynamics of intelligibility through which kinds of desires, feelings, sensations, and experiences of embodiment are seen as expressive of personhood or as indicative of perversion/monstrosity. Queer and trans work in disability studies and on the distinction between the human and nonhuman can be seen as building on Butler and Sedgwick's work, even indirectly, in considering how heteronormativity and cisnormativity shape the terms of intelligibility for personhood, how bodily traits and dispositions line up in ways that allow someone to be understood as fully human (and, conversely, how the boundaries of that category are policed with regard to gender and sexuality), and how other modes of being and becoming live on beside these institutionalized conceptions of personhood.

Disability studies starts from the premise that the concept of *disability* less refers to some particular set of supposed impairments than the fact that particular *bodyminds* are cast as lacking in relation to a naturalized ideal of physical and mental processes.[98] Within what is termed the "medical model" of disability, "the proper approach to disability is to 'treat' the condition and the person with the condition rather than 'treating' the social processes and policies that constrict disabled people's lives." By contrast, in the "political/relational model" adopted in disability studies (also known as "the social model"), as Alison Kafer observes, "the problem of disability no longer resides in the minds or bodies of individuals but in built environments and social patterns that exclude or stigmatize particular kinds of bodies, minds, and ways of being."[99] Such physical and social infrastructures take a particular vision of personhood as the baseline for *normal* bodily and mental functioning, treating that image as expressive of an asocial and ahistorical notion of health. This set of assumptions, in which those cast as disabled are seen as failing to live up to that image, can be described as *ablebodiedness* or *ablenormativity*. The idea that disability equals deficit comes along with the aim to cure such deficits, to eliminate them in the name of health and wellbeing. As Eli Clare suggests, "At the center of cure lies eradication and the many kinds of violence that accompany it." Such medicalized ideologies and interventions are of a piece and work in tandem with a broader range of normalizing conceptions of the body: "The medical-industrial complex is an overwhelming thicket. It has become the reigning authority over our body-minds .... It shapes our understandings of health and well-being, disability and disease. It establishes sex and gender .... It diagnoses, treats, and manages the human life cycle as a series of medical events."[100] More than creating distinctions between the healthy and those deemed "'defective,' 'deviant,' and 'sick'" in ways that "have been used to justify discrimination against people whose bodies, minds, desires, and practices differ from the unmarked norm," such notions of the normal themselves historically emerge out of more explicitly eugenic discourses in which "fears and anxieties about disability" have been embedded in ideas about "reproductive futurity" – "concerns about the future of the 'race' and the future of the nation."[101] In addition to attributing *feeblemindedness* to people of color, linking it to claims about their supposed incapacity to uphold white conceptions of sexual and gender order, as Ryan Lee Cartwright notes, "Eugenicists understood same-sex sexuality, interracial sex, and gender transgression, among other forms of deviance, to be evidence of low intelligence and irresponsibility that afflicted white people" and that, consequently, needed to be contained, disciplined, and prevented from being spread through reproduction.[102] Thus, not only do ideologies of (dis)ability intersect with norms around gender and sexuality, they arise out of a racializing, eugenicist concern about the proper form and future of the species.

People with disabilities also are perceived as having aberrant sexualities and genders. As Anna Mollow and Robert McRuer observe, "the sexuality of disabled people is typically depicted in terms of either tragic deficiency or freakish excess," and efforts to conceptualize and represent disabled people as erotic beings run against the grain of "a liberal conception of disability as squeaky-clean and respectable," one in which disabled persons are not supposed to be sexually desiring.[103] In this vein, Tobin Siebers insists, "The point is to ask how the ideology of ability determines how we think about sex," recognizing the ways that disabled people "represent disability not as a defect that needs to be overcome to have sex but as a complex embodiment that enhances sexual activities and pleasures" – including remapping the "limited erogenous zones" envisioned within "normative sexuality."[104] Moreover, not only have deviant sexuality and gender nonconformity historically been seen as indicative of intellectual disability, but nonnormative desires and genders in disabled people are often seen as merely an effect of their constrained mental dynamics. In their study of autism as a mode of *neuroqueerness*,

Melanie Yergeau insists that they "are unwilling to accept research that would attribute [autistic people's] gender identities to ableist ideas such as 'lacks conceit of self and other.'" Yergeau also observes that autistic practices such as "stimming – repetitive motions that might include body rocking and hand flapping – was (and still is) frequently regarded as masturbatory and sexually perverse," thus needing to be prevented.[105] Part of that process of containment often involves Applied Behavioral Analysis (ABA), which seeks to reorganize autistic physicalities into more normative social patterns. That project also involves the "attempt to straighten" autistic people – and others subjected to the treatment – in ways that "reinforce stereotypical and cis/heteronormative behaviors," a dynamic that is particularly notable given the prominent history and role of ABA in "attempts to defeminize gender-nonconforming children."[106] Moreover, gender normativity itself can prove elusive to disabled people, since "the mannerisms that help define gender – the ways in which people walk, swing their hips, gesture with their hands, move their mouths and eyes as they talk, take up space with their bodies – are all based upon how nondisabled people move." Clare adds, "The construction of gender depends not only upon the male body and female body, but also upon the nondisabled body."[107]

When considered together, queerness, transness, and disability further can extend as well as disorient each other's framings in ways that complicate ideas of embodiment, cure, and critique. Foregrounding disability, for example, helps bring into focus a critique of what Abby Wilkerson has described as "normative sex," the ways understandings of eroticism depend on a range of social presumptions – including ideas of bodily integrity and what actions count as *sex* – that are mediated to a large extent by medical assumptions that depend on "the heteropatriarchal sex/gender binary."[108] In its attention to kinds of felt experience that do not fit available social categories, queer analysis can help in figuring forms of disability that do not fit conventional models of impairment. Discussing efforts to characterize and conceptualize chronic pain, particularly with respect to the difficulty of physically locating it as well as its temporality, Michael Snediker observes that queer theory facilitates a "poetics of phenomenology" due to its habit of addressing "the difficulty posed to thinking by objects about which one doesn't quite know how or what to think" – the dynamics of entities, relations, and sensations that are "neither-quite-subject-nor-object."[109] This effort to articulate the nowhereness/everywhereness of chronic pain also speaks to the multilayered desire for a bodymind free from agony, disease, and debility. Even while raising sustained questions about the ways medicine promises to eliminate disability, "routinely turning body-minds into medical objects and creating lies about *normal* and *natural*," Clare notes the importance of medical technologies in his own transition, indicating the *messiness* of the felt tensions between "my lifelong struggle to live my disabled self exactly as it is with my use of medical technology to reshape my gendered and sexed body-mind."[110] Ideologies of cure, then, are violently normalizing while also pointing toward chemical and surgical interventions that can alleviate (or at least reduce) suffering and at times can create a greater sense of bodily and mental wholeness. Conversely, efforts to distinguish transness from mental illness, especially in the wake of transition, can end up displacing complex ongoing feelings of, in Cameron Awkward-Rich's terms, *maladjustment*. Not only are trans phenomena explicitly excluded from coverage under the Americans with Disabilities Act,[111] but efforts to refuse psychiatric oversight of access to gender-affirming care can end up "reaffirming the sanity/health of trans people" such that public validation of the trans experience can "hinge on whether it can be effectively decoupled from pathology, mental illness, and feeling bad." Awkward-Rich notes that, while "ostensibly meant to open up space for politics," such representation "disavows bad feeling" in ways that leave unaddressed "the task of learning how to live with, through, and despite" such feeling and that create a vision of "the good trans subject" as "one who can *get over it*."[112] Considering transness as a form of debility, Alexandre Baril observes that his own "dysphoria is as psychologically disabling as my other mental disabilities," suggesting how trans experience may point toward forms of disability that are "not merely a consequence of ableism."[113]

Work in queer and trans studies, though, also has emphasized the ways that disability encompasses not only bodyminds that diverge from normative standards but the "unnatural" effects of "war, toxic landfills, childhood abuse, and poverty."[114] Jasbir Puar emphasizes the "promot[ion of] disability empowerment" by the same political and economic systems that create "the precarity of certain bodies and populations precisely through making them available for maiming." She tracks "how the global north holds the key to the liberalization of disability while the global south bears the brunt of its weaponization," in terms of the mechanisms of warfare, imperial occupation, and capitalist extraction.[115] In these ways, disability marks not only the disjunction between normative conceptions of health and a range of lived bodily/mental states, but also the political, economic, and imperial distinctions made between persons and populations cast as subjects of care/rights/state protection and those deemed sacrificable.

Further contesting dominant ideas of the human, scholars have explored how queer and trans analysis can highlight ideas about species difference and the forms of hierarchy built into such ideas. As with Butler's argument that *sex* was *gender* all along, the representation of heterosexuality, monogamous union, and dimorphic sexual difference as all biologically inherent has been shown to depend on historically specific cultural assumptions. Not only does same-sex eroticism occur in hundreds of species, the concept of sex itself is changeable given that numerous species move between "sexes" in terms of their role in reproduction, with members of some species containing multiple "sexes" at the same time.[116] In fact, "the majority of living organisms on this planet would make little sense of the human classification of two sexes," much less of an understanding of transness as "based upon a conceptual separation of nature and culture."[117] Moreover, the sociobiological insistence on heterogendered pairing as the center and motor of evolution can be traced back to early Enlightenment discourses of European gendered hierarchy, in which "the natural right of humans over animals" mirrors "the right of the father in civil society."[118] Presumptions of heterocouplehood have shaped/skewed the interpretation of behavioral data from studies of animals while also contributing to racializing frameworks in which sexual difference and monogamy have been used as tools to measure relative evolutionary advancement among human populations.[119]

Heteronormative and cisnormative dynamics still often are portrayed as themselves a result of evolutionary progress, as signaling the difference from nonhuman animals and marking the superiority of *Homo sapiens* as a species. This employment of sexuality and gender to mark human identity and evolutionary development cannot be severed from the ongoing history of using these same metrics to privilege whiteness as the apex of civilizational advancement. As Mel Chen has argued, an *animacy hierarchy* shapes how "objects, animals, substances, and spaces are assigned constrained zones of possibility and agency." Those distinctions involve attributing lesser ability to affect the world to other entities while claiming a right by ostensibly more animate beings to control, regulate, and own less animate ones. This spectrum has allowed for racialized populations to be cast as less animate, as less fully human and less endowed with natural and acquired capacities for engaging the world, suggesting the role "comparative racisms" play in attributions of relative development – including when gender and sexuality feature as evidence of such (in)capacity. Chen further contends that intellectual strategies of *queering* "can work to blur the tenuous hierarchy of human-animal-vegetable-mineral" by challenging hierarchies attributed to natural development.[120] As Chen and Dana Luciano note, "'full humanity' has never been the only horizon for queer becoming," and queer analysis can draw attention to how "the very possibility of making a distinction between human and nonhuman" historically has depended on modes of (racializing) "dehumanization."[121]

Queer and trans scholarship has sought to open up possibilities that sit beside and trouble homogenizing notions of human exceptionality. For example, rather than viewing forms of gender-affirming bodily modification as the mutilation of natural bodily wholeness, Eva Hayward compares such alterations to a starfish's capacity to remake itself, seeing trans processes of becoming as illustrating "the reach and possibility of our layered experience" in ways that enact a complex "ongoing relationship with the world" that is also transspecies.[122] Additionally, in the face of climate change and what Neel Ahuja refers to as *late-carbon capitalism*, an attention to the queer intimacies produced by "racialized forms of carbon privilege" that shape "social and biological precarity" can challenge Global North narratives of contagion in which both persons (such as migrants) and other species (such as mosquitos) are cast as invasive *parasites*. Instead, queer analysis can offer accounts of the kinds of "interspecies entanglement" produced by fossil fuel consumption and the "casual reproduction of forms of ecological violence" (in which queer and trans people in the Global North also participate).[123]

Conclusion

Looking back at two of the most influential and iconic figures from the 1990s helps provide a sense of the intellectual trajectories of queer and trans studies as they emerged as academic fields. Butler's theorization of "sex" as a function of how gender operates within a heteronormative matrix, insistence on the performativity of sex/gender/sexuality, and attention to the ways humanness emerges through the ways bodies are rendered normatively intelligible and Sedgwick's attention to how sexual identity oscillates between minoritizing and universalizing frames, foregrounding of what doesn't *line up* within extant cultural narratives of sexuality, and tracking of complex affects and bad feelings that don't directly contribute to an oppositional politics still do important work within queer and trans studies. Scholars continue to engage with, build on, and critique Butler's and Sedgwick's formulations and approaches. Their work considers the ongoing processes through which ideas of health, family, embodiment, and proper social roles are constructed, circulated, fused to each other, and naturalized. In doing so, they seek to open room for thinking about and representing sexual and gender minorities in nonpathologizing ways.

While incredibly generative, those intellectual projects also can be somewhat overly optimistic about the inherent radicalness of such (implicitly white) minority positions and can underemphasize the role of other social dynamics – such as racialization and empire – in shaping how gender and sexuality work. Other scholars have traced how race, class, migration, imperialism/colonialism, disability, and species difference can complicate, reorganize, and reimagine Sedgwick's and Butler's frameworks. In addition to challenging what some have seen as the dematerializing of trans lives within queer studies, scholars have raised questions about the ways articulations of gender nonconformity can rely on imperial figurations (or at least can efface the geopolitical implications of how transition is envisioned) and the (racial and colonial) limits of notions of "transgender community," as well as developed structural frameworks for engaging how gender is produced within overlapping administrative systems. Work in queer and trans studies also has explored the historiographic and demographic limits of "the closet," the problems of metronormative methodologies, and the importance of moving beyond positive narratives of pride and transition.

Exploring Butler's and Sedgwick's ideas and their import for later thinkers, conversations, and debates, though, is not the same as presenting them as originary. As Kadji Amin notes, there needs to be "a reckoning with the field's affective haunting by the inaugural moment of the U.S. 1990s." That haunting has to do with an *idealizing* linkage of "understandings of same-sex sexuality," and one might add gender-nonconforming identity, with "social transformation, political futurity, [and] more egalitarian social relations."[124] Even as work over the past twenty years has developed and dissented from Butler's and Sedgwick's *oeuvre* from the 1990s and early 2000s, they remain touchstones of a particular period in which queer and trans studies took shape as such, and their ideas and the issues to which they drew scholarly attention continue to resonate powerfully, in ways both haunting and inspiring.

Chapter 2

Genealogies of Queer and Trans Studies

Queer and trans studies often have been presented as emerging out of previous social and intellectual movements from the 1960s onwards. Over the past couple of decades, queer and trans scholarship has created, circulated, and revised stories about these movements. Those stories have played a range of roles in how queer and trans studies have turned to the more recent past and mobilized it for the present and future. As Clare Hemmings has argued with respect to feminist theory, "the story of its past is consistently told as a series of interlocking narratives of progress, loss, and return that oversimplify this complex history and position feminist subjects as needing to inhabit a theoretical and political cutting edge in the present." This kind of historical narrative, which also appears in its own ways in queer and trans studies, not only positions the present as in some ways transcending or progressing beyond what's come before (or at least aspects of earlier intellectual work and social movements) but tends to offer a highly stereotyped and isolating image of those previous formations and formulations, in particular segmenting them into rather homogenizing decade markers.[1] This kind of story, as Hemmings notes, tends to cast the teller as in the vanguard of change, as the hero/heroine in a process of becoming ever more politically astute, attentive to social difference, and able to develop compelling analysis and advocacy. However, as Ramzi Fawaz observes, "The ease with which we disavow a feminist and queer past, the withering condescension that accompanies our dismissal of women's and gay liberation as a shared history of misguided failures, tells us nothing about those social movements and everything about the impoverishment of our contemporary political imaginations." Instead of this kind of dismissal, which Fawaz argues often has its own unacknowledged and rather rigid notions of identity and politics, he suggests the importance of attending to the *queer forms* generated by previous movements, appreciating how they envision more enabling ways of being "without fetishizing [those social movements'] political demands, assuming they can explain or ameliorate all forms of oppression, or expecting any movement to eternally live on intact from its inception."[2]

Rather than judging these narratives of genealogical connection and influence, trying to establish which one is *right* or developing a new narrative that can be cast as the *truth*, we can survey the variety of ideas, frameworks, and social interventions offered by these earlier movements. This chapter will consider a collection of intellectual and political movements that often have been cited as laying the groundwork for the development of queer and trans studies as scholarly fields, namely gay liberation, lesbian feminism, women of color feminism, the AIDS crisis, and the emergence of the category/concept of transgender.[3] It's also important to remember that these movements were not sealed off from each other and that there was a great deal of overlap among them. As Roderick Ferguson observes, "from 1960 onward, the struggles over race, gender, class, and sexuality were imagined not separately but simultaneously."[4] Recognizing that layered and textured simultaneity also complicates efforts to treat movements as fully distinct or to present any of them in monolithic ways. As against forms of history-telling and memorialization that seek to present past movements as preface to an inclusionary present, Che Gossett insists, "our histories of resistance refuse to be contained within neoliberal packaging or sanitized by homonormative narratives of progress."[5] Or, as in the title of Merle Woo's well-known essay, "Stonewall Was a Riot – Now We Need a Revolution."[6] While offering important critiques of ongoing oppression, though, the political investments of contemporary scholarship can be animated by "the purity of a queer stance in opposition to norms" coupled with "a *utopian longing* that draws hope for the future out of the radical aspects of various pasts."[7] The flip side of that longing and the search for political inspiration in the past is disappointment and denigration when prior movements do not live up to those utopian standards, which themselves also arise out of a social and historical context that shapes them in ways that may not be acknowledged. The turn to prior movements in this chapter, then, is not to redeem, lionize, or condemn them, but to consider them in their internal heterogeneity and to engage with some of the ways that they have been taken up in queer and trans scholarship, contributing to "the constant accumulation of alternative struggles that we can cite and build upon" in all their rich and historically specific invention and messiness.[8]

Gay Liberation

Early in the morning, just after 1 a.m., on Saturday June 28, 1969, police raided the Stonewall Inn, a popular gay bar in Greenwich Village, New York City. Unlike the usual monthly raids, the mafia-affiliated management had not been notified that this one was coming despite their regular payoff to local police of about $3,000 a month. While police were arresting patrons, particularly those deemed gender-nonconforming, some of them fought back, and the raid became a riot. After the previous night's struggle was reported in the New York daily newspapers, the crowd grew the next night, leading to even larger clashes with the police. The last of the riots occurred on Wednesday, July 2.[9] As Martin Duberman, the author of perhaps the most famous history of these events, suggests, "'Stonewall' is *the* emblematic event in modern lesbian and gay history" that "has become synonymous over the years with gay resistance to oppression."[10] Other queer and trans movement-related activity had occurred previously, including the existence since the 1950s of *homophile* organizations (as they were known) like the Mattachine Society and the Daughters of Bilitis and the occurrence of civil disobedience at Cooper Do-Nut in 1959 in Los Angeles, a sit-in at Dewey's lunch counter in Philadelphia in 1965, and the Compton's Cafeteria Riot in 1966 in San Francisco.[11] These earlier developments, though, did not give rise to annual celebrations as did Stonewall. Also, the weeks following Stonewall saw the emergence of an organization whose name and political commitments would help define a movement – the Gay Liberation Front (GLF).[12] The organization itself lasted for only a few years, but it helped give powerful form to a wide-ranging understanding and critique of the intertwined roles played by sexuality and gender in US society.[13] Collecting a range of activists, many of whom had been participants in an array of cross-cutting political struggles (including the New Left, the antiwar movement, Civil Rights, and women's liberation), GLF (and *gay liberation* more broadly as a kind of political imagination) offered a capacious and contentious account of the place of desire and gendered embodiment within the family, capitalism, and US imperialism.[14]

Looking at some of the most important writings of the time, we can see how gay liberationists connected the critique of homophobia and heterosexism to a much broader indictment of dominant institutions, reminiscent in various ways of contemporary work in queer and trans studies. Although originally circulated before Stonewall, Carl Wittman's "A Gay Manifesto" was reproduced widely by gay liberationists and offers a constructivist account of sexuality much like the Foucault-inspired work that would emerge in the late 1980s and early 1990s. Wittman argues, "Nature leaves undefined the object of sexual desire. The gender of that object is imposed socially[;] . . . it is not genetic." He also refuses the image of conjugal couplehood as the ultimate horizon of gay politics, insisting, "To accept that happiness comes through finding a groovy spouse and settling down, showing the world that 're just the same as you' is avoiding the real issues, and is an expression of self-hatred." As against the pursuit of mainstream recognition and rights, Wittman indicates the importance of aligning with other radical struggles including Black liberation that "are under attack by the establishment." Doing so entails "figur[ing] out who our common enemies are," such as "police, city hall, capitalism": "we know the system that we're under now is a direct source of oppression, and it's not a question of getting our share of the pie. The pie is rotten."[15] This wide-ranging analysis situates the oppression of sexual minorities and the pursuit of forms of sexual self-determination within a repudiation of what later would be termed heteronormative institutions, ideologies, and social frameworks, articulating this critique within an expansive vision of solidarity among seemingly disparate movements dominated in differentiated but related ways by "the establishment." In a similar vein, Martha Shelley positions gays and lesbians less as a minoritized group seeking inclusion than a monstrous challenge to notions of the normal. In "Gay Is Good," a title that somewhat disingenuously suggests an anodyne affirmation of homosexual identity, she begins, "Look out straights. Here comes the Gay Liberation Front, springing up like warts all over the bland face of Amerika, causing shudders of indigestion in the delicately balanced bowels of the movement." Speaking of both the mainstream United States and the progressive political struggles of the time that often were spoken of together as *the movement*, Shelley confronts them with their inability to engage queer people and their reliance on conventional heterogendered ideals, asserting, "We want something more now, something more than the tolerance you never gave us." In presenting GLF, and gay liberation generally, as "your worst fears made flesh" and "the nightmare that awakens you," the essay positions *gay*-ness as not so much a kind of identity as itself an effect of an institutionalized system of sexual meanings, roles, and limitations that have been imposed on everyone.

In this vein, "coming out," which prior to this time meant becoming known in gay and lesbian circles (parodying a debutante's coming-out ball), is less about revealing a personal truth than repudiating the larger dynamics of shame and the kinds of categories and hierarchies imposed within existing sexual ideologies.[16] Rather than calling for the acceptance of gays and lesbians, Shelley underlines the ways they are "alien" from the "majority culture" while also indicating, "We want to reach the homosexual entombed in you, to liberate our brothers and sisters, locked in the prison of your skulls."[17] This gesture is not about becoming homosexual, instead of being straight, but about claiming homosexuality or gayness as a challenge to the entire matrix of heteronormative conceptions of gender, desire, and identity. As Allen Young suggests in "Out of the Closets, Into the Streets," "Straights who are threatened by us like to accuse us of separatism – but our understanding of sexism is premised on the idea that in a free society everyone will be gay," or as stated in the "Gay Revolution Party Manifesto," "Gay revolution will produce a world in which all social and sensual relationships will be gay and in which homo- and heterosexuality will be incomprehensible terms."[18] Separating "gay" from "homosexual" allows the former to signify a rejection and transcendence of the binary system of erotic identities represented by the distinction between homo and hetero. *Gay*, therefore, does similar work as *queer* would starting in the 1990s, indicating not a minoritized identity to be accepted within existing systems but a more universalizing critique of how normative discourses and ideologies of sexuality and gender affect everyone.

This vision involves an intersectional analysis of how various oppressions and modes of social control operate in tandem as well as awareness of how forms of domination, exploitation, and structural violence affect people and groups differently. In the introduction to the groundbreaking collection *Out of the Closets: Voices of Gay Liberation*, Karla Jay presents gays and lesbians as involved in a "class struggle" against a society that "has relentlessly persecuted and murdered homosexuals and lesbians." Yet, "ultimately our struggle reflects the struggle of other revolutionary groups and of other oppressed people such as the blacks, [C]hicanos, the American Indians, and women," because "we share their goals and aspirations," even as "straight groups" have failed to "extend their conceits of freedom to all people, especially us." The connections presented are not those of analogy, one group or struggle being *like* another; they are simultaneous and implicated in each other. That very interdependence, though, means that the subjects of gay liberation also participate in other struggles as well as the kinds of discrimination and domination against which those struggles are fought. Jay observes, "we are by no means a homogeneous group. . . . Gay men oppress gay women, white gays oppress black gays, and straight-looking gays oppress transvestites" (one of the terms used at the time, including by those so named, to refer to gender-nonconforming people who did not, or could not, pursue gender-affirming surgery): "We see our struggles in different terms, and each fights the oppression which hits him or her hardest."[19] At its most reflexive, gay liberationist discourse acknowledges such differences and their effects on relations among queer and trans people and how such differences impact the shape of political theorizing and organizing. Within this effort to think in expansive and multi-layered ways about what would come to be called heteronormativity and cisnormativity, gay liberationist intellectuals tended to foreground *sexism* as the explanatory framework for talking about the interwovenness of seemingly disparate norms with respect to desire, gender, embodiment, coupledom, and social reproduction. As Young notes, "Gay liberation, on the surface, is a struggle by homosexuals for dignity and respect – a struggle for civil rights," but this appearance does not capture the scope and force of its aims. Young further indicates that "the movement for a new definition of sexuality does not, and cannot, end there. The definition of sexism, as developed by women's liberation and gay liberation, presupposes a struggle against the main perpetrators of sexism – straight white men – and against the manifestations of sexism as they appear in all people. The revolutionary goals of gay liberation" include "the elimination of capitalism, imperialism[,] and racism."[20]

Part of the critique of sexism as it manifests in "the artificial categories of 'heterosexual' and 'homosexual'" and "the gender programming" that emerges from and organizes the "nuclear family" also involves advocacy for gender-nonconforming people. Young observes, "Transvestites (only some of whom are homosexuals) are frequently arrested for wearing 'the clothing of the opposite sex.' Transvestites find it almost impossible to obtain employment, a situation which often drives them to prostitution. They are frequently arrested for prostitution, impersonation, solicitation, loitering, harassment, disorderly conduct, etc., or are carted off to mental hospitals." In recounting the events of the Stonewall Riots, he also centers trans people's leadership role in them: "The police invaded the bar, forcing people out in to the street. But instead of running away, the gay people, led by transvestites, locked the police inside the bar, [and then] set the place afire."[21] Here we see the articulation of issues of gender self-determination and trans hypervisibility (and its implications for arrest and assault) as a significant part of the gay liberationist critique of sexism. Young offers a robust, if brief, account of the nexus of gendered embodiment, the economics of gender-nonconforming life, and the disciplinary function of systems of criminal punishment, mental health, and social services.[22] The demand for "the right to be gay, any time, any place" and "the right to free physiological change and modification of sex upon demand" also appears in other gay liberationist statements and manifestos of the period.[23] While "the right to be gay" seems like it's about sexual object-choice, it's also quite powerfully about gender expression and embodiment. Part of gay liberation was contesting the gendered ideals that were seen as part of the larger system of sexism that also constricted erotic choice, and what was termed *sexual self-determination* was part of a broader understanding of "the human right to use of one's own body."[24]

Moreover, trans activists who participated in the Stonewall Riots and later founded trans organizations such as Street Transvestites Action Revolutionaries (STAR), used gay as a way of referring to themselves, their political struggles, and their vision for change. As Marsha P. Johnson, an African American trans woman who helped lead STAR, indicated in an interview with Allen Young: "We want to see all gay people have a chance, equal rights, as straight people have in America. We don't want to see gay people picked upon on the streets for things like loitering or having sex or anything like that." She refers to STAR as "a very revolutionary group" for "gay transvestites," adding that she would "like to see the gay revolution get started."[25] Sylvia Rivera, a Puerto Rican trans woman who was both a veteran of Stonewall and a founder of STAR, was a member for years of the Gay Liberation Front as well as the more single-issue-focused Gay Activists Alliance (GAA).[26] She was introduced to GLF in its early months by Johnson, and Rivera attended the Black Panthers' Revolutionary People's Constitutional Convention in 1970 as one of the GLF delegates.[27] Rivera later recalled of Stonewall: "I wanted to do every destructive thing I could think of to get back at those who had hurt us over the years. Letting loose, fighting back, was the only way to get across to straight society and the cops that we weren't going to take their fucking bullshit any more."[28] She casts this protest in terms of a challenge to "straight society" in ways that reflect how "gay" and "transvestite" were connected to each other within the struggle against sexual and gender normativities.

Such participation in gay liberation, though, did not mean that they and other trans activists did not encounter significant pushback, discrimination, and dismissal from others in the movement. As Susan Stryker observes, "Gay liberationists who had little familiarity with transgender issues came to see transgender people as 'not liberated' and lacking in political sophistication, as being still mired in an old-fashioned 'preliberation' engagement with the establishment, as still trying to fit in with the system."[29] While many may have supported forms of what was called "political drag," "undermining gender by mixing its norms" in what would soon come to be called *genderfuck*,[30] some understood "transvestites," particularly trans women, as engaged in a parody of womanhood that mocked what they deemed to be actual women. This sentiment led to Rivera herself being denounced at the 1973 Christopher Street Liberation Day Parade in New York City (now known as Pride), in which Jean O'Leary (a member of GAA who later became cochair of the National Gay and Lesbian Taskforce) tried to stop Rivera from speaking.[31] About this violent silencing, Rivera later said, "We died in 1973, the fourth anniversary of Stonewall. That's when we were told that we were a threat and an embarrassment to women. ... It came down to a brutal battle on the stage that year between me and people I considered my comrades and friends."[32] As Shannon Price Minter observes of the divorcing of gender and sexual deviance from each other within gay politics, "our modern understanding of homosexuality as based on same-sex desire rather than on gender status was a product of white middle-class gay men's embattled efforts to dissociate themselves from the dangerous visibility of working-class gay culture," thereby illustrating "class- and race-based stratifications within the gay movement."[33]

Yet, in remembering this assault on Rivera at Gay Pride and ones like it, we also need to be careful not to tell a story of gay liberation that excludes trans activists that were a vital part of it, to see them solely as oppressed and silenced rather than as active contributors whose political and intellectual work mattered. Finn Enke suggests with regard to memories of trans women's relation to and presence within lesbian feminism (discussed further in the next section), "why, when existing nuanced narratives might invite us to deeper analyses, are stories of exclusion and abjection so magnetic? More to the point, how might we highlight the mixings in the past and simultaneously envision a less polarized present?"[34] Registering the significance of trans women, particularly trans women of color, in gay liberation also refuses a seemingly laudatory narrative that acknowledges their place in the story of Stonewall but cuts them out of movements before and after it. Such tellings present trans people of color as "pre-political subjects who merely provided a stepping stone" to a "single-issue gay politics," as opposed to reckoning with Rivera's own account of she and those around her as "working for so many movements at the time. ... We were all radicals."[35]

Similarly, other kinds of organizing by queer activists of color need to be recognized for the ways they self-consciously engaged and furthered gay liberation while also challenging forms of unacknowledged white privilege.[36] In 1970, Black and Latino New York GLF members created an affinity group, Third World Gay Revolution, and similar organizations also formed elsewhere, including in Chicago and San Francisco. A founding member of the New York group, Néstor Latrónico recalls, "Being gay to us was just one of the things that oppressed us, and not the one we could focus the most on, considering that racism, poverty, hunger, the marks of slavery, dictatorships (supported by the United States) in many of our countries (including mine), political persecution, were the most important in our minds." He notes of GLF, "It was not that GLF didn't deal with racism, but as its members were practically all White, they were not the 'receivers' of racism except in a reflected form."[37] Third World Gay Revolution issued a sixteen-point platform that began with the demand: "We want the right of self-determination for all Third World and gay people, as well as control of the destinies of our communities." Like other gay liberationists, they saw the family as a principal vehicle through which gender, sexuality, and class were managed, calling for "the abolition of the institution of the bourgeois nuclear family" because it "perpetuates the false categories of homosexuality and heterosexuality by creating sex roles, sex definitions and sexual exploitation" and functions as "the basic unit of capitalism." They further call to "abolish the existing judicial system" since "the function of the judicial system under capitalism is to uphold the ruling class and keep the masses under control." The platform also critiques other so-called "revolutionaries," including in organizations of color, who "have failed to deal with their sexist attitudes" and who "cling to male supremacy and therefore to the conditioned role of oppressors," thereby generating "counterrevolutionary struggle to maintain and to force heterosexuality and the nuclear family."[38] They extend this analysis in their statement "The Oppressed Shall Not Become the Oppressor," where they note that "[b]rothers still fight for the privileged position of man-on-the-top. Sisters quickly fall in line behind-their-men," and they argue that racism works to deny men and women of color the privileges of white gender such that people of color should "stop perpetuating in yourselves and your community the white supremacists' notions which are basic to our own oppression."[39] In 1975 in San Francisco, Gay American Indians (GAI) was founded by Randy Burns and Barbara Cameron, partially as a response to gay liberationist representations of "the place gay people had in the Indian culture before the invasion of the white man's values and education" but in ways not connected to contemporary Indigenous peoples and absent solidarity with queer Native people. As Cameron indicated, "Bringing together gay Indians is our most important current task."[40] The analysis of both the whiteness of ideas of sexual and gender normativity and the import of attending to current issues of empire would become incredibly important within queer and trans studies, as will be discussed further in Chapters 4 and 5, but one can see the presence of such concerns within gay liberationist discourse.

Lesbian Feminism

Of all the movements discussed in this chapter, lesbian feminism has received the most criticism within later scholarship.[41] Lesbian feminism often appears in later scholarly work as the emblem of what needs to be repudiated in order to make possible queer and trans imaginaries, particularly inasmuch as it is associated with attacks on forms of desire deemed deviant (such as BDSM) and with the rise of TERFs (trans-exclusionary radical feminists).[42] Such accounts ignore the scope of what Rox Samer has termed *lesbian potentiality*:

the possibility "that gendered and sexual life could and would someday be substantially different, that heteropatriarchy may topple, and that women would be the ones to topple it." Samer adds, "Those who did not conform to normative sexual and gender identities, just as they do now, were working to find the language that fit. Often that was *lesbian*."[43] In addition to contesting sexism among gay men (including within gay liberation) and the heterosexism of many women's liberation organizations (including the effort to weed out the "Lavender Menace" in the National Organization for Women), lesbian feminism offered a profound and multidimensional critique of systems of heteronormativity in all their institutionalized infrastructures and coercions. The foregrounding of the lesbian as a kind of subjectivity sought to challenge and rework the category of *woman* – the ways it has been constructed and sustained through patriarchy (especially via the institution of marriage). Lesbian feminism sought to value women's experiences, emotions, and relationships with each other as sources of individual and collective insight, interpersonal transformation, community-building, and political imagination. It further aimed to push the boundaries of the feminist slogan "the personal is political" to understand the relation between social, political, ideological, and economic dynamics and everyday desire, eroticism, and bodily sensation.

"The Women-Identified Woman" (1970) provides a beginning point for self-consciously lesbian feminist theorizing. Although numerous lesbians were part of the women's liberation movement and were involved in feminist work prior to this point, and Gay Women's Liberation started meeting in San Francisco a year earlier,[44] the drafting and distribution of this essay marks a turning point in explicitly thinking about lesbianism as a matrix of feminist analysis, organizing, and worldmaking. The statement was authored collectively by the group Radicalesbians, which emerged in New York City out of a collection of women in GLF as well as non-GLF-affiliated feminists (some of whom had been part of homophile organizations like the Daughters of Bilitis).[45] The essay begins with the following: "What is a lesbian? A lesbian is the rage of all women condensed to the point of explosion. She is the woman who, often beginning at an early age, acts in accordance with her inner compulsion to be a more complete and freer human being than her society ... cares to allow her." It further observes, "She may not be fully conscious of the political implications of what began as personal necessity, but on some level she has not been able to accept the limitations and oppression laid on her by the most basic role of her society – the female role."[46] Note that *lesbian* here is not about a distinct, minoritized sexual identity or women's desire for women per se; instead, it entails being "woman-identified" in ways that involve "rage" at extant gendered norms, refusal to be bound by them and the forms of *oppression* they generate, and the pursuit of *freedom* from such norms as a *political* project that arises from a deeply *personal* need to be a whole human being. The authors distinguish this set of feelings and the movement to which they give rise from conventional conceptions of lesbianism as female homosexuality. Like many other gay liberationists, they argue that "the categories of homosexuality and heterosexuality" are a result of "a sexist society characterized by rigid sex roles and dominated by male supremacy," and they suggest that "in a society in which men do not oppress women," such categories would "disappear," since the modes of sex differentiation and hierarchy on which those differences depend would be no more.[47]

More than deconstructing existing modes of intertwined sexual and gender classification, though, lesbian feminist analysis illustrates how charges of lesbianism are used to police the boundaries of true womanhood and, thus, why lesbian subjectivity provides a position outside and critical of heteronormative gender, sexuality, and privilege. The Radicalesbians argue, "Lesbian is the word, the label, the condition that holds women in line .... She knows that she has crossed the terrible boundary of her sex role," adding, "For in this sexist society, for a woman to be independent means she *can't* be a *woman* – she *must* be a *dyke*." Woman and lesbian/dyke are socially constructed and contradistinguished categories; to be one is decisively not to be the other. In this sense, *woman* as a social identity gains meaning through a subordinate relationship to men that enables women to gain "social acceptance" and "more privileges within the system."[48] In order to break free from this routinized domination, which also is enacted through intimate relationships that direct "love and value" toward men and "male-defined response patterns," "we must create a new sense of self" that is not the same as "being a woman," since that identity is defined by and in relation to men. The name for that new kind of nonpatriarchal, liberated selfhood is *lesbian*.[49] As Arlene Stein observes, within lesbian feminist discourse, "Lesbians were not 'failed women': they were rebels against the oppressive sex/gender system, the vanguard of women's liberation."[50] To be *woman-identified*, then, as Charlotte Bunch suggests, is to be "a woman whose sense of self and energies, including sexual energies, center around women," thereby "put[ting] women first while the society declares the male supreme." To be lesbian is "a political choice" to "become feminists and fight against woman oppression."[51]

Lesbianism appears as a personal and political choice to repudiate a womanhood defined on heteronormative terms and to (re)orient one's affection, support, and labor away from privileging men as well as from the privileges that come with being linked to men (particularly through marriage). From this perspective emerges the slogan that "feminism is the theory, lesbianism is the practice."[52] Such formulations helped give rise to communal modes of living and what has been described as *separatism* – creating households, building communities, and politically organizing without men. Poet and activist Judy Grahn describes this pattern of "collective lesbian households" as showing "that a 'household' needed to address a number of unmet needs for loving and caring that were social, not individual, in their origin. Extending outward from the base of households, women began to occupy public space in the women-owned bookstores, clinics, and presses ... and much more."[53] As Victoria Brownworth recalls,

> There was no place for men in that lesbian nation because it was men we were trying to escape. Not gay men per se, but men as a gender class, men as the provocateurs of the patriarchy that had turned so many of us into survivors of, at the very least, sexual harassment and second-class status and at the worst, rape and incest and other violence.[54]

If lesbian feminism often has been cast in queer and trans scholarship as an essentializing framework from which later generations of thinkers and activists should distance themselves,[55] it also offered a pointed and wide-ranging analysis of institutionalized heterosexuality and the ways that system has limited our ability to see the variety, intensity, and significance of all manner of relations among women. The concepts of *compulsory heterosexuality* and *the lesbian continuum* developed by Adrienne Rich are incredibly influential examples of such intellectual work. Insisting on the need to see the "connections between our sexual lives and our political institutions" as well as to "understand the assumptions in which we are drenched," Rich explores how the presumption of heterosexuality as a default framework – "unexamined heterocentricity" – erases the ongoing history of the roles marriage and sexism play in shaping the emotional, erotic, and economic opportunities visible and available to women.[56] Such institutionalized and systemic control makes women's access to personal identity, social standing, and economic resources dependent on erotic relations with men, particularly in marriage, meaning that "for women heterosexuality may not be a 'preference' at all but something that has to be imposed, managed, organized, propagandized, and maintained by force."[57] However, if one ceases to see the social matrix of heterosexuality as natural and given, what comes into view is the "lesbian continuum": the "range – through each woman's life and throughout history – of woman-identified experience," which exceeds "consciously desired genital sexual experience" and includes "female friendship and comradeship" in ways that also expand the possibilities for what "the erotic" can entail. Moreover, attending to this continuum opens up the sense of what can count as political struggle, moving beyond patriarchal notions of "concrete revolutionary situations" to address resistance to marriage and motherhood as well as the "*nascent* feminist political content in the act of choosing a woman lover or life partner in the face of institutionalized heterosexuality."[58] In this way, *lesbian* indicates a perspective from which critically to analyze structures of heteronormativity as well as to mark and affirm a wide range of connections among women historically and in the present that may include sexual desire and that do not obey available heteropatriarchal ideologies, interests, and imperatives.[59]

Lesbian feminism often has been characterized as fundamentally white-oriented in its analysis of sexism as the principal cause of oppression.[60] For example, Bunch describes sexism as the origin of all other modes of oppression: "Having secured the domination of women, men continued this pattern of suppressing people, now on the basis of tribe, race, and class."[61] By contrast, in a piece published in the early days of lesbian feminism (1972), Anita Cornwell observes that, as a Black woman, she "was somewhat shocked recently when I realized that most of the white Lesbians I know seem to feel more oppressed *as Lesbians* than I do." Addressing police and state violence against Black people, she insists, "when the shooting starts *any* black is fair game. The bullets don't give a damn whether I sleep with woman or man, their only aim is to put me to sleep forever."[62] Yet, there were also feminists of color for whom the foregrounding of patriarchy facilitated simultaneous engagement with sexism and racism. As Pat Parker notes, "In speaking of the feminist and lesbian-feminist movements, many still say that they are 'white women's movements' – yet I was there and have never been white."[63]

Particular tensions emerged within lesbian feminism around butch/femme identities, sadomasochism, and the presence of trans people in lesbian communities and organizations. Butch/femme often was cast as a retrograde commitment to sex roles, as indicating male-identified thinking, and as simply mimicking the worst of heterosexuality. As Rita Laporte suggests in "The Butch/Femme Question," "The anti-butch/femme contingent tries to make our lives miserable by making fun of what to them is a ridiculous copycat existence. Many young Lesbians therefore find that their own kind can be as vicious as heterosexual society."[64] This kind of ostracism – in which lesbians seen as too masculine, too feminine, or as paired in gender-differentiated ways were subject to ridicule and ousted from lesbian-specific spaces – extended from the 1970s through at least the 1990s.[65] In challenging such dynamics, Joan Nestle, a long-time lesbian feminist and one of the founders of the Lesbian Herstory Archives, argues that the idea that "the personal is political" needs to be supplemented by the realization that "the more personal is historical," that ways of experiencing and expressing desire and gender gain meaning within situated social circumstances that do not fit abstract grids of politically acceptable identifications. She further observes that, "in the 1950s," "Butch-femme was an erotic partnership serving both as a conspicuous flag of rebellion and as an intrinsic exploration of women's sexuality," one that made couples visible and that refused calls, including by other lesbians, for more respectable dress and behavior: "These women presented gender challenges at a time when only deviants questioned gender destiny .... I see and hear the fear of being recognized as a queer every time we use the word *woman* when we know we really mean *Lesbian*." Nestle also highlights the class dynamics of this disparagement, noting the interest in "the butch-femme lives of upper-class women" like Radclyffe Hall and Gertrude Stein while "working butch and femme women are seen as imitative and culturally backward."[66] Gayle Rubin argues that "the wholesale condemnation of butch-femme impoverished our understandings, experiences, and models for lesbian gender," and she understands this denial of intra-lesbian differences as part of certain lesbian feminist tendencies "to impose new but equally rigid limitations" on identity and sexual expression in ways that "create new vulnerable and exploitable populations."[67]

Such impositions include the struggle around proper lesbian forms of desire and sexual engagement. What has come to be known as the "sex wars" started in the late 1970s and largely turned on feminist critiques of pornography and BDSM, which came to include a push for civil and criminal action against those participating in either.[68] Rubin argues that the equation of lesbianism with feminist consciousness "has prevented the lesbian movement from asserting that our lust for women is justified whether or not it derives from feminist political ideology. It has generated a lesbian politic that seems ashamed of lesbian desire and made feminism into a closet in which lesbian sexuality is unacknowledged." She further suggests that this skewed vision of lesbian eroticism privileges femininity in ways that "reinforce traditional gender roles," a perspective she calls "*femininism*."[69] Struggles around how to address lesbian sexuality and its relation to feminism emerged perhaps most spectacularly around the conference "The Scholar and the Feminist IX: Towards a Politics of Sexuality" held at Barnard College in 1982. Although there had been significant conflicts between anti-pornography feminists (who treated lesbian BDSM as particularly problematic) and pro-BDSM lesbians on the West Coast for a few years prior, the controversy exploded into national lesbian consciousness and circulation in light of the coverage that the Barnard conference received, largely shaped by the press releases, accounts, and articles generated by members of Women Against Pornography.[70] In "Thinking Sex," Rubin's field-shaping essay that developed from her presentation at the conference, she argues for the importance of a theory of "benign sexual variation" that refuses the "sex negativity" and "fallacy of misplaced scale" that characterize antiporn discourse. Observing that "[o]ne of the most tenacious ideas about sex is that there is one best way to do it, and that everyone should do it that way," the essay traces how questions of sexual representation and practice take on outsized symbolic significance that far exceeds their ability to shape social life. Instead, Rubin insists on the importance of challenging hierarchies that understand certain consensual sexual desires and acts as inherently more moral than others, which includes rejecting the charge that "the way to make the world safe for women is to get rid of sadomasochism." She argues, "Antiporn literature scapegoats an unpopular sexual minority and its reading material for social problems they do not create," engaging in "a massive exercise of scapegoating" that "criticizes nonroutine acts of love rather than routine acts of oppression."[71] This analysis builds on Rubin's earlier critique of the increasing use of *male-identified* to mean anything associated with masculinity, rather than to suggest a lack of political awareness with regard to patriarchal systems, as well as her linkage of the lesbian feminist crusade against S/M with nineteenth-century purity movements and the McCarthyite targeting of homosexuals in the 1950s.[72]

In her talk at the Barnard conference, Amber Hollibaugh further underlines the dangers of a lesbian feminist conception of sexuality that has "now trapped us into a singularly victimized perspective" that is focused on understandable "rage" and "horror" over the ubiquity of sexual coercion and violence but that "creates a theory from the body of damage done to us." From this perspective, feminists who also seek to challenge "sexual stigma, censorship, and repression" – while fighting "to expand more sexual options for women" – have been cast as "outside feminist standards, political integrity, and moral authority." Hollibaugh asks, "In the struggle against pornography, are we creating new definitions of sexual sickness and deviance? ... Are we creating a political movement that we can no longer belong to if we don't feel our desires for a model of proper feminist sex?"[73] As opposed to theorizing in the abstract about what kinds of lesbian desires and pleasures can count as feminist, Hollibaugh insists on attending to the ways "[w]e live out our class, race, and sex preferences within our desire and map out our unique passions through our varied histories." She insists on the importance of starting from "where we are right now, from the real bodies we live in, the real desires we feel" as the basis for building social analysis and feminist politics.[74]

More than indicating the limits of lesbian feminism as such, though, the *sex wars* illustrate struggles among lesbian feminists from which queer and trans scholarship explicitly and implicitly has drawn in later accounts of BDSM and pornography. As Lynda Hart suggests, presenting lesbianism as the paradigmatic expression of feminism depended on the "foundational fantasy of a 'role-less equality'" that "effectively (re)*eliminated* lesbians from the feminist movement, in the very *name* of constituting their inclusion." Rather than being embodied subjects, lesbians functioned as "a sign of purity"; they were less understood as actually desiring subjects than as a kind of feminist figure through which "to represent the unrepresentable" – namely, an impossible deferral of dynamics of power from the scene of eroticism.[75] By contrast, lesbian sadomasochism, Hart argues, not only explores the roles power plays in erotic imagination and sensation but uses those dynamics as part of investigating and remaking experiences of selfhood. She observes that "the s/m practitioner disarticulates the 'body' as it has been disfiguratively constructed and makes it 'flesh,'" self-reflexively drawing attention through erotic play/performance to how socially constructed ideas about bodily identity are lived in everyday ways – including the dynamics of power that shape such experiences. In this way, sadomasochism does not so much *reproduce* ordinary forms of hierarchy as *thematize* them in potentially illuminating and reconstructive ways.[76] That difference, though, is not a simple distinction between fantasy and reality but a taking up of emotionally and symbolically laden images, clothing, props, and relations in ways that play with their social, political, and historical meanings. In her analysis of Black women's participation in BDSM, particularly in scenes that deploy markers of white supremacy and the history of enslavement, Ariane Cruz observes that such sexual play draws on lived, embodied identities – such as race – that are not merely contained within the BDSM scene. She notes that the "heated debates in the arena of feminist sexual ethics" that comprise the sex wars register tensions "surrounding the historical legacies of violence and the entanglement of violence and pleasure in our intimate lives." These activist and scholarly conversations have largely evaded matters of race: "Race extends the field of play while constraining its potential for subversion." Cruz asks, "How can rituals of domination and subordination in BDSM reveal such positions [of racial difference/hierarchy] as not necessarily unstable but rather as unnatural, socially constructed, continually (re)produced, and hence possibly deconstructed and reconstructed?"[77]

The kinds of feminist arguments made during the sex wars with regard to sexual freedom, self-knowledge, and exploration, as well as the importance of considering economies of sex work in non-moralizing ways, also animate current work on feminist, queer, and trans pornography.[78] As Sophie Pezzuto and Lynn Comella argue, studying pornography "can offer important insights about the larger political, economic, and social organization of a significant domain of cultural production and representation," in which "political and social anxieties are played out" and which serves as "a sector of the economy" that highlights "issues of labor, technology, gender inequality, class distinctions, racial differences, and modes of production and consumption."[79] Such cultural production, and the study of it, "captures the struggle to define, understand, and locate one's sexuality," recognizing "the importance of deferring judgment about the significance of sex in intimate and social relations and of not presuming what sex means for specific people."[80] While acknowledging that commercial pornography is a for-profit business, with particular market imperatives and labor conditions that also operates "within a tiered system of racialized erotic capital," scholars also address the ways pornography offers possibilities for "illicit erotic activism," such as potentially "provid[ing] a space where black women performers can try on roles and stage imaginaries against expectations of decorum and normativity."[81] While much pornography featuring trans performers can reinforce cisnormative assumptions, porn made by and for trans people can enact (re)arrangements and combinations of persons, identities, erotic relations, penetrations, and pleasures that contest existing cultural scripts about proper alignments of bodies, genders, desires, and acts.[82] The policing of sexually-explicit media, including online platforms, also can have magnified effects for trans people. Given the extensive forms of employment discrimination and lack of access to gender-affirming medical care that trans people face, sex work provides a particularly important means of support, and recent efforts to outlaw sex-work-related online content (such as pornography and advertising for escort services) in the name of preventing sex trafficking have done serious damage to these kinds of businesses, pushing people toward other kinds of sex work that tend to be less lucrative and to have more dangerous and coercive working conditions. Moreover, while not technically included in the material banned by sites to comply with these laws, extensive and explicit user-generated information on gender-affirming bodily modification is getting removed as part of the sites' censoring mechanisms.[83]

This discussion, though, returns us to consideration of the place of trans people, particularly trans women, within lesbian feminism. As Finn Enke suggests, "In less than one generation, the 'second wave' became aka 'white feminism' and 'trans-exclusionary feminism,' and now *1970s feminists* is often used as a shorthand genealogy of today's racist and trans-exclusionary feminists (TERFs)," but "we need to know that trans women and men were also the movers and shakers of – indeed integral to – even the most iconic feminisms during the 1970s. It's possible to narrate histories in ways that don't perpetuate the abjection and removal of trans from feminism."[84] There certainly were lesbian feminists who developed a notion of womanhood that excluded and denigrated trans women,[85] and those perspectives definitely affected later feminist movement and community-building, such as the trans-exclusionary "womyn-born-womyn" entry policy adopted in 1991 for the annual Michigan Womyn's Music Festival and maintained through its closure in 2015.[86] However, part of what has created a rather limited and totalizing sense of lesbian feminism is the high archival visibility of anti-trans polemics. Perhaps the most famous and widely reprinted (during the period and afterwards) is Robin Morgan's keynote presentation at the 1973 West Coast Lesbian Conference in Los Angeles. Morgan decries the presence of Beth Elliott, consistently misgendering her, presenting her transness as an act of "drag" comparable to "when whites wear blackface," and casting trans women as "leeching off women who have spent entire lives *as women* in women's bodies."[87] Morgan further casts Elliott's very presence as a form of violence against women and implies that she has a history of committing sexual assault, helping give rise to "the 'transsexual rapist' trope" that circulated for years "in grassroots lesbian networks."[88] However, not only was Elliott one of the central planners for that conference, she also had a following as a lesbian feminist musician, for years wrote for the feminist newspaper *The Lesbian Tide*, and had been a prominent member and officer of the San Francisco chapter of the Daughters of Bilitis (DOB).[89] When Sandy Stone resigned in 1978 from Olivia Records – a lesbian feminist music collective – to prevent further calls for violence and boycotting due to her identity as a trans woman, her fellow collective members issued a statement saying,

> In evaluating whom we will trust ... our focus as political lesbians is on what her actions are now. If she is a person who comes from privilege, has she renounced that which is oppressive in her privilege, and is she sharing with other women that which is useful? ... Is she open to struggle around class, race, and other aspects of lesbian feminist politics? ... We felt that Sandy met those same criteria we apply to any woman.[90]

Moreover, Sara Ahmed suggests "that it is transfeminism today that most recalls the militant spirit of lesbian feminism in part because of the insistence that crafting a life is political work."[91]

Even as attributions of backwardness proliferate within later scholarship, lesbian feminism remains a site of identification in the contemporary moment. It can be thought of as exerting a "gravitational pull" on current "queer" articulations. The *temporal drag* of this return across generations works "to reincarnate the lost, nondominant past in the present and to pass it on with a difference."[92] The investment of younger intellectuals and activists in maintaining and further building the Lesbian Herstory Archives, for example, illustrates how "lesbian feminism is also an ongoing position that generates attachments to the past that have both material and affective implications for the present," including attending to the kinds of community and informational infrastructures lesbian feminists created as part of building extended and multidimensional networks – such as hotlines, indexes, archives, magazines, book publishing, film distribution, conferences, and other organizations.[93] Yet, even in considering the significance of lesbian feminism(s) for the present-day work of scholarship and movement-building, Samer cautions that those of us living now are not the inheritors of the "lesbian futures" projected in the 1970s and 1980s, that "the queer aesthetics of the past do not contain the map to queer futures" but that taking lesbian feminist imaginings seriously can enable "a capacious commitment to the unknowability of the feminist future."[94]

Women of Color Feminism

More than simply indicating nonwhite feminists, women of color feminism (often also known as Third World feminism) might be described as a large and multifaceted body of intellectual and political work that foregrounds *difference* as a central analytic principle.[95] Often, women of color feminism and the highlighting of difference as a central principle gets cast as a development of the 1980s, sometimes described as part of *third wave* feminism (the first being the movement for women's suffrage and the second linked to the women's liberation movement of the 1960s and 1970s, presented de facto as white). However, "the 'wave' model of feminist history" can be seen "as insufficient because the significant events on that time line refer overwhelmingly to white and middle-class feminist history."[96] Moreover, this implicit chronology edits out the ways the presence of feminists of color in the Civil Rights and other movements served as inspiration for early organizers in women's liberation, the important presence of women of color in feminist organizations from the beginning of women's liberation, and the existence of explicitly feminist organizations among women of color from at least the late 1960s onward.[97] Rather than adding kinds of identity together or seeking to include them into ideas and struggles organized around a single-issue focus, women of color feminist thinking and organizing takes the intersecting, interwoven, irreducible, and simultaneous copresence of multiple identities (gender, race, class, sexuality, nationality, religion, etc.) as its frame of reference. As Lisa Kahaleole Hall suggests, "women of color" was a self-consciously fashioned category for conceptualizing together and putting into conversation a range of what otherwise might be considered disparate struggles, generating "a construction of community through shared and unshared difference, solidarity, and contradiction." That foregrounding of difference "allows for the analysis of relations that depend not on identical subjects but on interrelations. It is the ground of possibility for bringing complexity and nuance to forms of both identity and solidarity."[98] Alice Hom observes, "interweaving differences provides a generative opportunity to create solidarity between communities and to open space for even more complex understandings of identities and issues than were imagined previously."[99] In this way, women of color feminism addresses the multiple dimensions of one's own sense of selfhood, the variability of experiences as well as relations of oppression within any given identity group, and the difficulty of working across while also valuing distinctions among groups.[100]

One of the most significant aspects of women of color feminism has been the effort to grapple with how identity is multidimensional and to draw on that multiplicity as the basis for social and political theorizing. Perhaps the most influential and oft-cited example of such work is the 1977 statement of principles by the Combahee River Collective. Named after the military action in 1863 led by Harriet Tubman that freed hundreds of enslaved people, the collective of Black women, mostly lesbians, formed in 1974 in Boston, with Demita Frazier, Barbara Smith, and Beverly Smith serving as the group's core and the authors of the collective's celebrated statement.[101] The statement starts from the premise that "we are actively committed to struggling against racial, sexual, heterosexual, and class oppression, and see as our particular task the development of integrated analysis and practice based upon the fact that the major systems of oppression are interlocking."[102] The "integrated analysis" of how those systems are overlapping and interdependent comes out of an engagement with the particularities of their lives as Black lesbians and the ways what may analytically seem like separate axes of domination – race, gender, sexuality – are embodied and lived in ways that are inseparable and that cannot be broken up into differentiated parts. The collective indicates that their analysis grows out of a desire "to look more deeply into our experiences" in order to develop a "sharing and growing consciousness" from which "to build a politics that will change our lives and inevitably end our oppression." They offer the concept of *identity politics*, a phrase they coined, as a way to name their attention to the integrated character of multiple kinds of oppression in their own lives and their use of those experiences as the basis for materialist analysis and organizing that would address their own oppression(s). They observe, "We believe that the most profound and potentially most radical politics come directly out of our own identity, as opposed to working to end somebody else's oppression." Attending to the details and dynamics of their lives as Black lesbians requires bringing together different kinds of identity to illustrate how they are enmeshed, also meaning that the discriminations and forms of domination they face depend upon the ways those identities are interwoven.[103]

While certainly thinking about larger systems of oppression and how to challenge and dismantle them, other feminists of color focused attention on how attending to the lived relation among multiple identities forced them to engage their own fears, prejudices, and shame in ways that altered their critical and political perspectives. In "La Güera," Cherríe Moraga explores how her experience as a light-skinned Chicana led her to identify with forms of racial and class privilege that also alienated her from parts of herself. She notes that during her childhood "everything about my upbringing, at least what occurred on a conscious level, attempted to bleach me of what color I did have," and her mother supported this process because "to her, on a basic economic level, being Chicana means being less," although this pattern left Moraga feeling "bleached and beached" – cut off from "the brown in me."[104] Moraga's awareness of this loss, and the ways privilege has "worked against" her even as she has "worked it," comes through her acknowledgment of her own lesbianism. She learned "that the joys of looking like a white girl ain't so great since I realized I could be beaten on the street for being a dyke" but also engaging her lesbianism "reawakened" a "profound connection" with her mother: "I had no choice but to enter into the life of my mother. *I had no choice.*"[105] Considering how being a lesbian denies her privilege enables her to address the other parts of herself that she has denied or suppressed in seeking such privilege, simultaneously opening up a woman-centered connection with her mother that foregrounds aspects of Chicana culture, oppression, and community from which she had distanced herself in the implicit pursuit of social advantage (and to avoid the effects of discrimination and oppression). From this perspective, she cautions against the "danger" of "attempting to deal with oppression from a purely theoretical base," rather than engaging and working through the messy, painful ways "we have taken the values of our oppressor into our hearts and turned them against ourselves and one another."[106] Her attention to her own identities allows her to offer a self-reflexive assessment of her investments, conscious and not, in existing institutionalized power arrangements.

In their groundbreaking collection *This Bridge Called My Back: Writings by Radical Women of Color*, Moraga and Gloria Anzaldúa describe this way of approaching how the personal is political as *theory in the flesh*.[107] More than focusing attention on a definite politics or specific projects for change, considering the multiplicity of your own identities allows you to consider your relations with other people, the ways those relations may themselves be structured by dominant hierarchies, and how seeking to avoid engaging your own fears turns you away from the possibility of meaningful solidarity and work toward change and equity. In "Letter to Ma," a contribution to *This Bridge*, Merle Woo insists in response to her mother's disgust at her lesbianism, "Until we can present ourselves to the world in our completeness, as fully and beautifully as we see ourselves naked in our bedrooms, we are not free." Yet, that sense of holistic affirmation also involves exercising "deliberative consciousness" – looking at the parts of herself she has avoided and denied, which point to internalized enmeshments of racism and sexism. Woo observes, "You gave me, physically, what you never had, but there was a spiritual, emotional legacy you passed down which was reinforced by society: self-contempt because of our race, our sex, our sexuality. For deeply ingrained in me, Ma, there has been that strong, compulsive force to sink into self-contempt, passivity, and despair." Acknowledging and embracing those denigrated parts of oneself opens a path not only to marking and challenging the social dynamics that produce such shame (such as racist conceptions of Asian women as properly "passive") but to turning that self-knowledge toward organizing for justice.[108]

Engaging with the multiple forms of identity that come together in one's own sense of selfhood further points toward the ways any given identity group is crosscut by a range of other identities, and women of color feminist work further aims to make visible and address these differences and the tensions they can create in defining ostensibly shared political visions/goals based on that group identity. Audre Lorde is perhaps most associated with the effort to highlight and value such differences, rather than cast them as obstacles or distractions. As Grace Kyungwon Hong suggests, Lorde uses *difference* in a range of ways that enact "a cultural and epistemological practice that holds in suspension (without requiring resolution) contradictory, mutually exclusive, and negating impulses."[109] In "Age, Race, Class, and Sex: Women Redefining Difference," Lorde observes that "we have no patterns for relating across our human difference as equals. As a result, those differences have been misnamed and misused in the service of separation and confusion": "Too often, we pour the energy needed for recognizing and exploring differences into pretending those differences are insurmountable barriers, or that they do not exist at all." In doing so, difference appears as a threat (as "deviance") or an impediment to political organizing and action, instead of "as a springboard for creative change." This tendency arises out of the effort to locate a single cause of oppression through which to define collective identity and struggle. Lorde argues, "Those of us who stand outside that power [of dominant institutions] often identify one way in which we are different, and we assume that to be the primary cause of all oppression, forgetting other distortions around difference, some of which we ourselves may be practicing." Here Lorde is addressing the focus on patriarchy by white women in the women's movement. Elsewhere in the essay, though, she also turns to how singularizing conceptions of blackness can efface the complexities of Black communities and movements. She insists, "Those of us who are Black must see that the reality of our lives and our struggle does not make us immune to the errors of ignoring and misnaming difference. Within Black communities where racism is a living reality, differences among us often seem dangerous and suspect. The need for unity is often misnamed as a need for homogeneity."[110] The idea that belonging to a group in struggle – women, Black people – means sameness within that group and a necessary coming together around a primary, shared experience of domination erases not only the differences within that group but the ways such homogenization actually perpetuates and perpetrates other forms of oppression. Such supposed unity also undermines an ability to value the experiences of everyone in that group, to see how various oppressions intermesh, and to develop inclusive strategies that build a range of overlapping coalitions. As Lorde suggests in "Learning from the 60s," "unity does not mean unanimity," and it also "implies the coming together of elements which are, to begin with, varied and diverse in their particular natures," thereby suggesting that all identities, as Hong notes, "are themselves always already coalitional."[111]

Sexuality stands as a particularly difficult source of tension within projects of forging an expansive sense of collectivity. Addressing other Native people's denigration of her sexuality, Beth Brant talks about them as engaged in a process of "recovery" from "the disease of homophobia. The disease has devastated my Indian family as surely as smallpox." She further describes it as a "chasm" that "has [been] blasted into our Nations." This response is a function of conquest, through which "our sexuality has been colonized, sterilized, whitewashed."[112] In contrast, she refuses to "make distinctions between sexuality and spirituality" and refers to her own experiences of pleasure as "primal ritual" and "physical prayer."[113] The understanding by Native people of homoeroticism as unnatural or deviant, Brant argues, arises out of colonial assessments of Indigenous people as backward and savage, disowning homosexuality as a way of seeking to evade further forms of racist denigration by settlers. She suggests, "I believe what you are really saying is – you embarrass me with your sexuality, therefore you embarrass our people, and *white* people will have even more ammunition to use against us."[114] Paula Gunn Allen notes of these dynamics that they involve a "change in the images of women and gays among American Indians caused by patriarchal propaganda" in ways that are "historical, cultural, and political" and that illustrate "the history of patriarchy on this continent."[115] The attention to submerged or disowned differences with respect to sexuality becomes a vehicle for considering how indigeneity can get defined in ways that normalize nonnative perspectives and frameworks while creating damaging antagonisms among Indigenous people. Similarly, in "The Failure to Transform: Homophobia in the Black Community," Cheryl Clarke argues that Black political projects often have been undermined by their "homophobia": "It is ironic that the Black Power movement could transform the consciousness of an entire generation of black people regarding black self-determination and, at the same time, fail so miserably in understanding the sexual politics of the movement and of black people across the board." Not accounting for the presence of homophobia and of Black queer people "sabotages coalitions, divides would-be comrades, and retards the mental restructuring, essential to revolution, which black people need so desperately."[116] None of these feminists of color seek to cast people of color as more homophobic than whites; rather, they aim to illustrate how heteronormativity closes off possibilities for broad-based organizing and alliance that could challenge racism and colonialism in their complex, multifaceted manifestations – potentials for "transforming the social, political, and economic systems of oppression as they affect all our people."[117]

In addition to critiquing the limits of single-issue politics or the erasures that attend constricted conceptions of group belonging, women of color feminists further have theorized the process of coalition-building across difference in ways that take difference itself as necessary and valuable. As Liza Taylor observes, "For the feminists who developed the analytic of intersectionality, [in which she includes many of the writers discussed in this section,] the corresponding politics was always coalition politics."[118] A distinction, though, needs to be made between *home* and the space of *coalition*. Drawing on Bernice Johnson Reagon's articulation of the politics of coalition, Lisa Kahaleole Hall argues, "Home is where you want to feel safe with others like you; coalition is a deeply painful process during which you come to terms with others who are different in the pursuit of a finite common goal .... If you look for home in a coalition you will always get hurt."[119] In her introduction to the field-shaping collection *Home Girls*, Barbara Smith begins with the following: "There is nothing more important to me than home." When indicating that she "learned about Black feminism from the women in my family," she includes the ways they were "humiliated and crushed" due to the interlocking dynamics of race, gender, and class. She also highlights the importance of attending to "those excruciating places where I have abandoned, and been abandoned by, other women, when our anger about our differences seemed insurmountable."[120] Even though *home* is a space in which one seeks comfort and mutual recognition, it is complicated by the material, emotional, and psychological effects of oppression as well as forms of difference that can be experienced as betrayal. Coalition, then, emerges out of both the need to make common cause against multifaceted modes of dominance and exploitation *and* the awareness of how separatism or single-issue formulations can envision a comforting sense of unity that effaces differences among those at *home*.

In contrast, coalition involves responding to shifting circumstances and developing tactical analyses of those circumstances. Chela Sandoval refers to such an evolving and context-dependent process as *oppositional consciousness*. She argues that if notions of "power" are "frozen" based on schematic identity categories, "it then becomes too easy for us to identify who our friends and who our enemies might be." As against the idea of a "simple unity for feminists of color," Sandoval insists, "We will not naively repeat the same mistakes as the women's movement by erasing our own internal differences through gathering them into one single unity which will then stand against all other categories." She adds, "If society's powers are ever mobile and in flux, as they are, then our oppositional moves must not be ideologically limited to one, single, frozen, 'correct' response."[121] In seeking to illustrate this kind of maneuvering, Sandoval suggests, "As the clutch of a car provides the driver the ability to shift gears, differential consciousness permits the practitioner to choose tactical positions, that is, to self-consciously break and reform ties to ideology, activities which are imperative for the psychological and political practices that permit the achievement of coalition across difference."[122] Coalition must engage with and respect a range of differences, difficult and unpredictable as they may be, because to fail to do so creates an unhelpful and unrealistic vision of stasis that prevents both real connection and meaningful work toward change within present conditions. As Pat Parker famously argues, "revolution" is "not neat or pretty or quick. It is a long dirty process," one that depends on seeing relations among a range of what otherwise may look like disparate struggles. She insists, "Our interest does not lie with being a part of this system, and our tendencies to be co-opted and diverted are lessened by the realization of our oppression."[123] These formulations of antiracist and anti-imperial feminist work illustrate the limits of an appeal to sameness as a basis for political imagination and organizing.

Developing concepts through which to elaborate this capacity for affirming and negotiating shifting forms of multiplicity as a central part of coalition-building, then, has been a significant part of women of color feminist intellectual practice. Gloria Anzaldúa's discussion of *mestiza consciousness* and María Lugones's notion of traveling among worlds offer influential examples of such theorizations of relations amid and across difference. In *Borderlands, La Frontera*, Anzaldúa foregrounds the imperial and racial dynamics of the US–Mexico border, which she describes as "*una herida abierta* [an open wound] where the Third World grates against the first and bleeds. And before a scab forms it hemorrhages again, the lifeblood of two worlds merging to form a third country."[124] Anzaldúa addresses the legacy of the US conquest of Mexican territory in 1848 and the racist institutionalized discourses of border protection from the mid twentieth century onward, considering the mixture of languages, cultures, geographies, and understandings of individual and collective identity at play in the region of that conquest. In doing so, she draws on Chicanx movement discourses that address the relation of oppressed Mexican-descended people to Indigenous peoples, especially through the figure of *mestizaje* – of generations of racial mixture that produces a new people.[125] This "new *mestiza* consciousness," "a consciousness of the Borderlands," can name a broader dynamic through which difference comes to challenge a wide range of borders and binaries. She suggests, "Those who are pounced on the most have it the strongest – the females, the homosexuals of all races, the darkskinned, the outcast, the persecuted, the marginalized, the foreign," and the capacity developed by those so disparaged and dominated is to see beyond existing divisions and distinctions: "It is anything that breaks into one's everyday mode of perception, that causes a break in one's defenses and resistance, anything that takes one from one's habitual grounding, causes the depths to open up, causes a shift in perception." Drawing on the Nahua deity, which she indicates Chicanx people have inherited through their relation to Indian ancestors, Anzaldúa also characterizes this enabling sense of betweenness as "the *Coatlique* state," which "can be a way station or ... a way of life" and which "transforms living in the Borderlands from a nightmare to a numinous experience" – "a path/state to something else."[126] While also at times drawing on the figure of *mestizaje*, Lugones develops the idea of overlapping and intersecting *worlds* as a way of talking about the presence of social differences. She emphasizes how varied frameworks of perception, communication, and engagement with others are "sufficiently self-coherent and sufficiently in contradiction with others to constitute an alternative construction of the social." Such worlds are not fully sealed off from each other, and people move among them all the time, either in the process of what she calls *traveling* – voluntarily seeking to understand other social frameworks, such as among women of color who belong to different groups/communities – or in coercive ways, such as the insistence that "white/Anglo" must serve as the de facto, enforced standard. Theorizing difference and coalition as movement among worlds emphasizes the existence of other ways of seeing and being that exceed existing forms of domination: "the oppressed know themselves in realities in which they are able to form intentions that are not among the alternatives that are possible in the world in which they are brutalized and oppressed."[127]

Rather than offering a picture of ready agreement or easy answers, women of color feminist work speaks to the difficulties and transformative possibilities in acknowledging and engaging difference – the ways it can be painful and draw attention to one's own failings but can also open toward powerful insights, coalitions, and a rejuvenated sense of potentials for change. The varied ways of conceptualizing difference sketched above, then, neither support the idea of a singular vision of justice nor the attempt to cast women of color feminism itself in singular terms. Speaking to the homogenizing circulation of the figure of what she terms the "Black.female.queer" within queer studies, Sharon Holland suggests that "Black.female.queer voices are foundational but not generative, as there is little active engagement with the diversity of this relational voice," further noting that "the call to revere 'women of color feminism' also serves to mask its historical specificity as well as contribute to its unmaking."[128] Similarly, in her study of early Chicana feminist organizing, Maylei Blackwell observes, "we must give our critical attention to how women of color feminisms are different from each other and develop from different genealogies and traditions of political struggle and cross different borders and diasporas."[129] In tracing such important distinctions, though, we also need to be mindful of the ways these feminist intellectuals were in ongoing conversation and layered relation with each other, complicating an effort to too-rigorously attribute concepts and frameworks to a given person. As Barbara Smith suggests, "As for other Third World women usurping 'our' movement, understand that movements are not owned and that ethnocentrism is ethnocentrism no matter whose face it wears."[130]

The AIDS Epidemic

In June 1981, an article in the *Morbidity and Mortality Weekly Report* issued by the US federal Centers for Disease Control and Prevention (CDC) indicated cases of *Pneumocystis carinii* pneumonia (PCP) in otherwise healthy men in Los Angeles, all of whom were identified as "homosexual." This initial mode of official recognition telegraphs much about how the set of opportunistic infections that would come to be named AIDS (acquired immunodeficiency syndrome) in 1982 would be understood going forward.[131] Connected as it was in its initial public representation to homosexual men – the syndrome originally was known as GRID (gay-related immune deficiency) – and to kinds of sexual practice deemed perverse, particularly anal intercourse, AIDS discourses indelibly shaped the analytical orientations of what would emerge as queer studies. Had public attention coalesced around earlier expressions of AIDS in a group not specifically defined by their relation to sexual deviance, such as the presence of "junkie pneumonia" in New York City in the late 1970s, the trajectory of frameworks for understanding and engaging AIDS would likely have been significantly different.[132] The epidemic's initial and ongoing association with homosexuality helped frame intellectual and political critique of governmental, medical, and media responses to AIDS around an engagement with interlocking and cross-referencing notions of sexual (ab)normality from which terms and concepts like *queer* and *heteronormativity* would arise.

After the early public notice of the epidemic, the idea of designating *risk groups* became a way of targeting those thought most likely to develop AIDS (especially prior to the discovery that HIV was what caused the condition) while also distinguishing between those groups and a supposed *general population* seen as insulated in their separation from perverse/degraded practices and populations. As Jan Zita Grover notes, "According to the term's users – the media, public health officials, politicians – 'the general population' is virtuously going about its business … so AIDS hits *its* members as an assault from diseased hedonists upon hard-working innocents."[133] The initial groups categorized as at-risk by the CDC were "the four H's" – homosexuals, heroin addicts (intravenous drug users), Haitians, and hemophiliacs. Although the last of these were seen as "innocent victims," the others were associated with various forms of deviance, including racialized understandings of Haitian sexuality that later would be associated with Africa when countries there started reporting rising AIDS rates and scientists and others started speculating that HIV originally evolved and emerged from the continent.[134] This effort to specify which persons and groups might particularly be in danger of infection suggests a reciprocal effort to indicate those who could be conceived of as a threat to the public at large. As Cindy Patton suggests, one of the scholars to write earliest and most consistently about the epidemic, we need to "interrogate the interests served by the narrative framing AIDS as 'crisis'": "it is important to step back and ask, who declared this an emergency, and for whom, and who benefits from operating under these rules?"[135] In this way, specifying risk groups functions less as a means of seeking to protect them – through, say, putting heightened government resources into prevention and treatment for them – than indicating those who threaten the welfare of the nation, their sickness signifying the dangers inherent in their various forms of unhealthful aberrance. Paula Treichler, another important scholar early in the epidemic, notes of the "4-H list" that it "has structured evidence collection in the intervening years and contributed to the view that the major risk factor in acquiring AIDS is being a particular kind of person rather than doing particular things," illustrating a "commitment to categories based on monolithic identity" in ways that "filters out information."[136] Such *alienizing* conceptions of HIV/AIDS as a danger posed by those who were not true national subjects extended to the US ban on admitting HIV-positive people into the country from the late 1980s through 2010, as well as the infamous quarantine of Haitian asylum seekers at the US base in Guantánamo Bay in the early 1990s.[137] The problems of such "risk" discourse further were extended globally in systems of categorization that not only linked particular routes or profiles of transmission to entire global regions ("Africa" and "Asia") but that also redeployed longstanding colonial narratives built out of racist stereotypes as explanatory frameworks.[138]

The epidemiological attempt to identify and isolate *risk* reproduced existing notions of normality in which a white heteropatriarchal idea of *family* provides the de facto framework for morality, health, and national well-being. Simon Watney, another important figure in early scholarship and critical public discourse on AIDS, notes, "Epidemiology is thus replaced by a moral etiology of disease that can only conceive of homosexual desire within a medicalised model of contagion." In contrast, he argues that "we have to expose 'the family' as a murderous myth, which is responsible for incalculable emotional and psychological damage for everyone involved," otherwise "all those who threaten to expose the brutal, hypocritical, and degrading implications of contemporary 'family values' and 'standards of decency' will undoubtedly continue to be stridently denounced ... as 'enemies of the family.'"[139] Within dominant discourses, commitment to such family values appears as if it were a kind of prophylaxis against HIV infection. This pattern includes the implicit distinction in government-funded safe sex education between "safe people (true heterosexuals) and dangerous people (closeted gay men, bisexuals, IV drug users, prostitutes)."[140] The representation of AIDS as a "plague" implicitly presents infection either as divine judgment or some sort of natural selection in ways that further extended existing dominant associations of homoeroticism and gayness with death.[141] The initial association of HIV/AIDS with homosexuality allowed vectors of transmission to be cast as expressions of perverse identity, intensifying extant connections between heteronormativity and personal/national health and well-being and, conversely, giving greater force and urgency to the critique of those ideologies since the lives of people with HIV/AIDS depended on challenging government inaction and popular apathy legitimized by such notions of the normal/deviant.[142]

The reason why white gay men were the first officially to be cited as having infections that would come to be classified as AIDS is that such effects of immune disorders could be registered as anomalous against a background of what would otherwise be considered normal health, and this fact meant that early definitions of "AIDS" (the kinds of opportunistic infections that were included in the category) were based largely on middle-class male bodies exposed to the virus through sexual intercourse. HIV infection often registered in cis women's bodies differently (including bacterial pneumonia and gynecological problems such as pelvic inflammatory disease, repeated cycles of yeast infection, and cervical cancer), and women often were treated merely as potential vectors of transmission – to men, especially through sex work, and to children through pregnancy – rather than as independent persons whose health and well-being mattered. Much higher rates of tuberculosis also appeared among poorer people with HIV infection. Not registering these phenomena as "AIDS" not only meant that AIDS statistics were vastly undercounting deaths from the epidemic in ways that were deeply gendered, classed, and raced but that individuals with these conditions could not gain access to social security and Medicaid benefits available to people with "AIDS," as well as the state and local programs/benefits that relied on the federal definition.[143]

The framing of the disease and institutional responses to it as centered on ideas about perversity (in both dominant and oppositional accounts) led to what can be described as the "queer paradigm" for thinking about the epidemic.[144] Adam Geary suggests, "Generalizing the initial descriptive conflation of the emerging epidemic with gay men, dominant scientific and public discourses on HIV risk have described those found to be suffering AIDS (even before the discovery of the viral agent) as queers engaged in perverse pleasures, especially perverse sex and drug use."[145] Following this logic, critical commentary on the epidemic largely foregrounded the ways a range of groups were linked in their shared marginalization with regard to sexual normality. In particular, white gay men and Black people, whether in Africa or elsewhere, were linked in their wrong expressions of desire: "Gay men were said to have made of their bodies something of the order of the sewerage system of a Third World city, while 'third world' inhabitants were said to engage in anal sex, an activity coded as 'homosexual' within U.S. culture"; "African (black) heterosexuals were homosexualized through their allegedly greater practice of anal sex – anality being a chief Western symbol of homosexuality" (a putative explanation that was then extended to include Black people elsewhere, such as in the United States).[146] Additionally, despite the fact that sex workers are far more likely to contract HIV from their sexual partners than to transmit it, they repeatedly were and are seen as a public health threat that needs to be managed by the state through mandatory testing and criminalization of those who are HIV-positive (regardless of whether they are performing high-risk or very low-risk sexual acts), while effacing the relation between sex work and economic survival for many people such as migrants and cis and trans women of color.[147] The fact that so much of the discussion of the epidemic turned on issues of desire, pleasure, and the use of the body helped give rise to forms of analysis and critique that treated sexuality and notions of deviance as the nexus through which to connect various groups, oppressions, and struggles for social justice, thereby shaping what would become queer studies.[148]

The conflation of transmission with kinds of persons also helped animate the effort to differentiate acts and identities. As Patton notes, "AIDS activists were increasingly concerned to delink practices and identity, so that for example men-having-sex-with-men could recognize the risks involved without having to reorganize their identity and claim to be gay." Moreover, modes of transmission – such as unprotected intercourse and sharing needles for intravenous drug use or administering of gender-affirming hormones – are embedded "within networks of face-to-face communication and within cultural [dynamics] ... which *cut across* the 'communities' articulated for the purpose of engaging in the political languages of civil rights and claims for apportionment of social resources."[149] However, acts that enabled HIV transmission were presumed to express distinct *lifestyles*, a concept that gains meaning only in contrast to the "underlying assumption of a 'natural' heterosexuality" and proper uses of the body from which deviations can be cast as collective forms of "aberration" in ways that legitimize "any amount of scapegoating and victim-blaming."[150] By contrast, grassroots campaigns by AIDS activists to promote safer sex and to create and decriminalize needle exchanges illustrate the effort to foreground situated practices, instead of presuming that behavior and its meanings could be derived from preconstituted identity categories.[151]

The activist refusal to equate behavior and routes of HIV transmission with identity also was a response to problematic methods for aggregating epidemiological data, which drew on categories like gender and race in deciding the likely path of infection for given persons with AIDS and which would then be incorporated into official tabulations and statistics. As a result, some groups were presumed to be inherently low-risk, such as lesbians.[152] Moreover, trans women often have been categorized as "men who have sex with men" in ways that not only misgender them but that efface the significance of the institutionalized forms of cisnormativity that produce the circumstances which contribute to heightened chances of HIV infection (including the economic necessity of sex work and the lack of access to affordable and safe gender-affirming care).[153] Additionally, given the ways data were gathered nationally, the presence of certain groups within AIDS statistics was not deemed large enough to be significant and so they were displaced under "Other" – such as Asian Americans and Native Americans – thereby conveying the impression that those groups (as opposed to "whites," "African Americans," and "Hispanics") were outside the epidemic.[154] Not only did these confusions and erasures create a false sense of immunity, they rendered invisible the actual presence of people with HIV/AIDS in those groups in ways that further stigmatized them.

The refusal to equate routes of transmission with degraded or spoiled identities and populations can be seen as part of the activist push to represent the epidemic as a result not of various groups' supposedly antisocial predilections but of murderous government indifference and punitive discipline. Such a strategy was central to the most well-known activist group to emerge in response to the epidemic, ACT UP – the AIDS Coalition to Unleash Power.[155] Founded in New York City in 1987, and quickly spreading to other parts of the United States and beyond, it was known in particular for its mass demonstrations and use of civil disobedience, vivid use of graphics and issue-specific slogans, targeting of a range of institutions previously deemed largely nonpolitical, and repudiation of notions of public decorum. ACT UP generated a political sensibility based on challenging the legitimacy of existing institutional categories, processes, and ideologies. Their rhetoric and actions repeatedly charged officials with responsibility for mass death, such as the famous "Silence = Death" logo (originally created by a separate artist collective) against a black background with the pink triangle (a symbol used to mark homosexuals for extermination during the Shoah) and "The Government has Blood on Its Hands, One AIDS Death Every Half Hour" with the image of a bloody handprint.[156] This publicly visible orientation toward critique and broad-based opposition is part of what shaped the reclamation of the term queer in the late 1980s and early 1990s.[157] ACT UP certainly was not the earliest or only form of AIDS activism, and in addition to gay liberation, it powerfully drew from prior and ongoing organizing in women's health and reproductive rights, the Civil Rights movement, Latin American solidarity work, drug treatment and anti-homelessness work, and anti-prison activism, among other movements.[158] The focus of its actions and campaigns included decriminalizing needle exchange, reducing the timeline for and expanding access to drug trials, ending the ban on HIV-positive migrants and the detention of Haitian asylum seekers, creating housing for people with AIDS, addressing HIV/AIDS among imprisoned people, expanding the CDC definition of AIDS, and increasing access to HIV/AIDS medications for people (and countries) that could not otherwise afford them. Although it has taken up an oversized place in histories of AIDS activism, in ways that can crowd out and invisibilize less media-focused efforts, ACT UP's ways of framing discussions of sexuality, articulating political outrage, and situating bodies and pleasures within systems of institutionalized oppression contributed a great deal to the focus, style, and political imagination of early queer studies.[159]

The complex relation between denigrated behaviors and forms of collective identity addressed in HIV prevention efforts and activist/intellectual work can also be seen as at stake in how racialized populations in the United States responded to the epidemic early on, particularly in terms of how they enacted a *politics of respectability* in an effort to protect marginalized groups from further charges of deviance. If AIDS discourses often positioned acts that contributed to HIV transmission as expressive of forms of group identity, racially marginalized groups often sought to distance themselves from the kinds of behavior that would be seen as aberrant, such as homoeroticism and drug use. Cathy Cohen has addressed this pattern in Black communities in the United States in terms of fears of *secondary marginalization*: "Those marginal group members who are close to the edges of dominant power, where access and involvement in decision making actually seem possible, confront incentives to promote and prioritize those issues and members thought to 'enhance' the public image of the group, while controlling and making invisible those issues and members perceived to threaten the status of the community," in doing so "replicating a rhetoric of blame and punishment and directing it at the most vulnerable and stigmatized in their communities."[160] The attempt to distinguish the innocent from the guilty/tainted as part of reiterating claims to respectability can also be seen in the concept of *the down-low* that emerged in the early 2000s – the idea that large and rising rates of HIV infection among Black women are due to closeted gay and bisexual men whose erotic relations with men have been hidden from their wives/girlfriends. This narrative also redeploys existing discourses of Black sexual duplicity – what C. Riley Snorton terms "the glass closet" – in ways that help license increased surveillance and criminalization.[161] As Evelynn Hammonds argues in early commentary on these dynamics, "The black community's relative silence about AIDS is in part also a response to this historical association of blacks, disease, and deviance in American society." She further suggests that "the black community's response to the historical construction of sexually transmitted diseases as the result of bad, inherently uncontrollable behavior of blacks – is sexual conservatism."[162] Similar responses can be seen in Native American communities. Native AIDS activists have had to challenge "the internalization of heteropatriarchy, and the naturalization of sexism, homophobia, and transphobia as traditional to Native peoples," a process that arises from the historical and ongoing representation of Indigenous peoples as backward, savage, and perverse.[163] Andrew Jolivette has characterized this dynamic as part of a "posttraumatic invasion syndrome" that "stems from the specific responses of Indigenous peoples to ongoing settler violence," which he also describes as "colonial haunting."[164] The attempt to disown supposedly deviant HIV-transmitting practices and persons in the interest of preserving a sense of collective morality/normality has been a response to ongoing discourses of racialized aberrance, and the AIDS epidemic has helped highlight these patterns, in ways that have influenced the development of queer and trans of color critique (discussed in Chapter 4).

In challenging the dominant emphasis on biomedical knowledges and solutions as well as the attendant vision of treatment and prevention as an individualized phenomenon, critical analyses of the epidemic also have contested the narrative of "the end of AIDS."[165] With the advent of HAART (highly active antiretroviral therapies), "the AIDS crisis" often has been cast either as a thing of the past (a manageable chronic illness which is avoidable through the use of preexposure prophylaxis (PrEP)) or as a straightforward matter of more broadly extending prevention information and access to pharmaceuticals. In addition to the continued rates of infection and AIDS death among people of color in the United States and globally, intellectuals and activists have pointed out the conjuncture in the mid-1990s of the advent of effective antiretroviral treatments with the development of international trade agreements, driven by the United States, that provided greater patent protections for pharmaceuticals, making gaining affordable access to those very HIV medications far more difficult in much of the world.[166] Moreover, the proliferation of drug-based prophylaxis available now not only depends on implicitly understanding the problem of HIV transmission as itself somewhat intractable (itself due to limited access to HAART) but also makes those using PrEP dependent on Gilead, the drug's manufacturer (which drew on US government officials with investments in the company to facilitate testing on HIV-negative women in Nigeria, even as the product is now too expensive for those outside the Global North and most within it).[167] Citing PrEP as indicative of a movement beyond AIDS, then, continues the pattern of casting the ongoing epidemic in a consumerist mode that foregrounds individual choice rather than systemic vulnerabilities produced by racism and imperialism.

Additionally, an emphasis on generic individual susceptibility to the virus – a focus on personal practices – implicitly helps justify processes of criminalization. The HIV/AIDS epidemic emerged amid a vast expansion of incarceration in the United States, a pattern that preceded but was further animated by the "war on drugs." This reliance on imprisonment as the means of addressing all manner of social conflicts included a significant expansion of the scope and severity of punishment for what are termed "sex crimes." Given the modes of HIV transmission, and their dominant associations with deviance, the criminalization of HIV-positive people occurs at the intersection of these dynamics, while also drawing on the increasing ideological emphasis on supposed *personal responsibility* (versus government responsibility or notions of collective welfare) in all sectors as part of the growth and intensification of neoliberalism (the notion of "the market" as the ultimate basis for policy, ethics, and social organization) from the late 1970s onward. That trend increased within public health discourses around HIV in the early 2000s, "in which the HIV-positive person is portrayed as being individually responsible for ending the epidemic – and, implicitly, the one to blame when things go wrong."[168] The federal law through which HIV/AIDS funding is distributed, the Ryan White CARE Act, itself includes a provision requiring states to verify that their laws are "adequate to prosecute any HIV infected individual" who knowingly exposes someone to HIV.[169] The majority of states in the United States have statutes that define having sex without revealing one's HIV-positive status (and sometimes even having sex as an HIV-positive person) as a crime, and the charge does not depend on there being actual "harm" in the form of HIV transmission or even likely transmission given the particular acts performed. These kinds of statutes are implemented and enforced more intensively against sex workers and trans women, particularly trans women of color, and many of these statutes were passed at the urging of police as a response to what they, often without substantive evidence, took to be the "problem" of HIV-positive sex workers. This way of approaching the spread of HIV further turns public health workers into extensions of the criminal punishment system, positioned as enacting necessary forms of surveillance to make sure people with HIV are complying with these laws. Among the vicious ironies of this pattern of criminalization are that HIV/AIDS discrimination is illegal in civil law (since it is considered a disability under the Americans with Disabilities Act) and that the vast expansion of imprisonment in the United States over the past forty years likely is the cause of a great deal of HIV infection, because of transmission while incarcerated as well as the ways forces of policing and imprisonment massively contribute to the structural precariousness of Black and brown people – with profound effects on overall health and susceptibility to infection.[170]

Critical engagement with the epidemic further has given rise to more expansive considerations of feelings – of care, grief, the affective dynamics of living under precarious conditions, and the emotional bonds that develop within movements for change – that have been influential within queer and trans studies. As Douglas Crimp notes in his influential essay "Mourning and Militancy," one of the hallmarks of AIDS direct action activism was the slogan, "turn your grief to anger," which he suggests "assumes not so much that mourning can be foregone as that the psychic process can simply be converted." This presumption, though, externalizes the violences of the epidemic – the "gross political negligence" that "allowed [the epidemic] to happen" and "the violence of unleashed hatred" – "in 'enemy' institutions and individuals" in ways that "deny its psychic articulation, deny that we are effected, as well as affected, by it."[171] While necessary to counter "the series of untruths that underwrote AIDS research and representation" and to challenge the "deeply hateful view" that "homosexuality = AIDS = death," activism and social/political critique can defer and efface the emotional and psychological implications of living through the epidemic: "Only with a fuller sense of the affective life of politics can one avoid too easy assertions of a 'political' solution to the affective consequences of trauma in which politics becomes a phantasmatic structure that effects its own forms of displacement."[172] It's difficult to represent the scale of loss that queer and trans communities have endured due to AIDS, especially before the advent of HAART. Just prior to the availability of protease inhibitors, over 350,000 people had died of AIDS in the United States and over four million globally.[173] Dagmawi Woubshet characterizes the immensity and intensity of the epidemic as producing a "poetics of compounding loss" in which those most affected were also "'disprized' mourners" – those "who are denied the rites, honor, and dignity of public mourning, and whose losses are instead shrouded in silence, shame, and disgrace."[174] The attempt to avoid addressing such mourning and abjection, or to put them securely in the past tense, also can be seen as animating what has been cast as the turn to homonormativity in the mid- to late 1990s. As Woubshet observes, "Gay liberalism has entailed not only an articulation of neoliberal claims to citizenship, ... but also an erasure of the immediate queer past of immense suffering and loss."[175] Efforts to grapple with that grief and the other complex feelings generated by, around, and beside the epidemic – as well as the kinds and scope of care work in response to it – in many ways inspired and helped shape the engagement with affect in queer and trans studies (as discussed in Chapter 1).

Additionally, part of the mourning produced by AIDS has been for forms of sexual culture that not only were assaulted by public policy but that were depicted by some as responsible for the epidemic. As Crimp observes, "Alongside the dismal toll of death, what many of us have lost is a culture of sexual possibility: back rooms, tea rooms, bookstores, movie houses, and baths ...Sex was everywhere for us."[176] This very sense of possibility – and the kinds of affects, pleasures, and socialites it made possible – has been the subject of early, and ongoing, dismissal by other gay men, such as Larry Kramer's claim in "1,112 and Counting" (his now famous column from March 1983) that "I am sick of guys who moan that giving up careless sex until this blows over is worse than death. How can they value life so little and cocks and asses so much?" or Richard Berkowitz and Michael Callen's earlier polemic against "promiscuity" (1982, also published in the *New York Native*) where they argue that "[w]e have remained silent because we have been unable or unwilling to accept responsibility for the role our own excessiveness has played in our present health crisis. But, deep down, we know who we are and we know why we're sick."[177] In his oft-cited essay "How to Have Promiscuity in an Epidemic," Crimp argues that the very practices and relations decried by others actually made possible gay communities' quick and life-saving responses to the epidemic: "We were able to invent safe sex because we have always known that sex is not, in an epidemic or not, limited to penetrative sex. Our promiscuity taught us many things .... It is that psychic preparation, that experimentation, ... that has allowed many of us to change our sexual behaviors."[178] The loss of the pre-AIDS potentials of promiscuous and public sex also has given rise to study of the relation between public health discourses and processes of gentrification, which have sought to privatize so much of urban space, as well as of the fantasies and desires for stranger sociality that help animate cultures of barebacking (the pursuit of condomless sex).[179]

Engaging with such issues of mourning, militancy, sexuality, and community was key to the renaissance of Black gay writing, cultural production, organization-building, and public self-articulation in the 1980s and 1990s. As Darius Bost observes, "the gendered and sexualized formations of anti-black violence that wiped out a generation of black gay cultural artists in the early era of AIDS also forged the imaginative possibilities for black gay world-making," and describing that period ("*the long 1980s*") and its relation to the present as "*epidemic time*"; Jafari Allen suggests the importance of "valorizing and prioritizing moments of Blackfull vitality and intensity."[180] They locate such potentials within the work of writers, editors, and film-makers like Joseph Beam, Melvin Dixon, Essex Hemphill, Isaac Julien, Marlon Riggs, and Assotto Saint. These cultural producers also understood themselves as building on intellectual and political work by Black feminists over the prior decade.[181] In the introduction to his groundbreaking collection of Black gay male writing *In the Life*, Beam asserts, "We are bringing into the light the lives which we have led in the shadows," adding, "We are even more susceptible to the despair, alienation, and delusion that threatens to engulf the entire Black community."[182] Hemphill similarly decries such silence and alienation in his introduction to *Brother to Brother*: "There was no gay community for black men to come home to in the 1980s. The community we found was as mythical and distant from the realities of black men as was Oz from Kansas." He further notes, "What is most clear for black gay men is this: We have to do for ourselves *now*, and for each other *now*, what no one has ever done for us."[183] These writings present "black gay personhood as a site of possibility, imbued with the potential of creating a more livable black gay social life," and they serve as an "an alternative site of memory" that "push[es] against the interpretation of this period as solely about trauma and loss."[184]

Early Transgender Writing and Activism

As a medical and popular category, transsexuality dates back to the 1950s, but the use of *transgender* as a way of describing a broad range of experiences and embodiments, in which a person's gender does not align with the identity presumed to follow from their sex assigned at birth, emerges into widespread usage in the 1990s. Over time and in different places, there have been any number of ways of categorizing bodily morphology/physiology and drawing on it as a basis for defining social identities, as well as a wide range of ways of understanding felt experiences of embodied selfhood that do not conform to extant social norms of sex/gender (as will be discussed in greater detail in Chapters 3 and 5). The term transgender, then, less refers to a new phenomenon than makes existing kinds of gender nonconformity more visible while grouping them with each other such that they collectively come to signify differently. While used by some in the 1960s as a noun, an alternative to and explicit critique of surgical forms of gender affirmation, transgender came to be used to encompass all manner of what could be understood as deviations from dominant ideas of sex/gender. This usage, though, can privilege conceptions of constructedness, gender queerness, and nonbinary formulations to which many self-identified transsexuals have objected (and continue to do so).[185] The sense that the concept of transgender challenges the dominance of dimorphic, sexed notions of gender and opens room for a much wider range of kinds of gendered embodiment and selfhood proliferates within intellectual and political work in the 1990s, even as such formulations also raise questions about the potentially racialized, classed, and colonial assumptions that can shape such accounts. Sometimes cast as an "umbrella" term covering a wide range of experiences of gendered embodiment and selfhood that do not conform to dominant notions of sex/gender, the concept of transgender as it gained prominence in intellectual and activist work over the 1990s can be understood as engaged in a range of projects that are not always fully consistent with each other, even as they often overlap and intertwine in complex ways. These projects might be categorized as visibility, phenomenology, deconstruction, and coalition.

One of the central goals of early transgender writing was to draw attention to the kinds of personal history, feelings, and desires edited out in medicalized frameworks that regulate transsexuality. Originally developed in the 1960s, the criteria for assessing candidates for gender-affirming surgery included that the person detest the genitals with which they were born (including getting no sexual satisfaction from them), have a desire/intention to live a heterosexual life post-surgery, and illustrate an ability to "pass" in the person's desired gender (as demonstrated by doing so for two years prior to the surgery being authorized by a psychiatrist). Transsexual patients also were counseled not to speak of their pre-transition lives to others, since doing so would undermine the *realness* of their post-surgery gender. As Kate Bornstein observes, transsexuals had "lived their lives hiding deep within a false gender" only to be called on to "spen[d] the rest of their days hiding deep within *another* false gender," in the sense of needing to erase their transsexuality – to present themselves, in contemporary terms, as cisnormative people. Bornstein further notes, "Transsexuality is the only condition for which the therapy is to lie," adding, "we're not allowed, in therapy, the right to think of ourselves as transsexual."[186] Sandy Stone also argues that transsexuals must "erase" their existence in order "to fade into the 'normal' population as soon as possible." In doing so, "What is gained is acceptability in society. What is lost is the ability to authentically represent the complexities and ambiguities of lived experience," such as a potentially pleasurable relation to one's genitals (even while wanting gender-affirming surgery) or an understanding of oneself as having queer desires (instead of wanting post-surgery straightness). Given the clinically imposed demand to narrate transition as "go[ing] from being unambiguous men ... to unambiguous women," or vice versa, Stone suggests that there is no possibility to articulate oneself "*as a transsexual*" within this framework: "How, then, can the transsexual speak? If the transsexual were to speak, what would s/he say?"[187] *Transgender* serves as a way of marking and refusing those erasures, opening room within public discourse to express kinds of feelings, sensations, identifications, and pleasures excised by the dominant therapeutic/medical framework of transition. Although this particular way of formulating transgender may also underestimate the presence and scope of extant communities of gender-nonconforming people who also had no choice about their (hyper)visibility – raising the question of visibility to whom and for what. In this vein, we might think about the positions occupied by queer and trans working-class people and people of color that were, and are, policed for their gender nonconformity.[188]

Rather than seeking to efface the process of transition, these writers drew attention to its supposed unnaturalness in order to challenge gendered ideas of the natural. In her field-shaping essay "My Words to Victor Frankenstein above the Village of Chamounix: Performing Transgender Rage," Susan Stryker indicates "a deep affinity between myself as a transsexual woman and the monster in Mary Shelley's *Frankenstein*." Both, Stryker argues, are "the product of medical science" and involve "flesh torn apart and sewn together again in a shape other than that in which it was born" while also being "exclu[ded] from human community" in ways that provoke "a deep and abiding rage."[189] Asserting such an association with monstrosity refigures attempts to pathologize trans people. In particular, writers in the early to mid-1990s were responding to the influence of Janice Raymond's 1979 transphobic screed *The Transsexual Empire*, which claims that trans women's existence is an insult to women, medical technologies of transition are a patriarchal effort to impose gender stereotypes, and trans women's efforts to participate in women's spaces (particularly lesbian ones) are fundamentally invasive.[190] The title of Stone's immensely influential essay "The *Empire* Strikes Back: A Posttransexual Manifesto" positions it directly as a rejoinder to Raymond. Yet, instead of entirely rejecting Raymond's account of the ideological implications of "sex reassignment" surgery, Stryker, Stone, and others turn its supposed artificialness into an occasion for making visible the broader "*apparatus of production of gender*," emphasizing how even "a deeply conservative attempt to stabilize gendered identity in service of the naturalized heterosexual order" (as medical authorities presented surgical transition) can be directed otherwise.[191] Stryker describes this process as "conditions in which it becomes imperative to take up, for the sake of one's continued survival as a subject, a set of practices that precipitates one's exclusion from a naturalized order of existence": "To encounter a transsexual body, to apprehend transgendered consciousness articulating itself, is to risk a revelation of the constructedness of the natural order."[192] Foregrounding the technologies of transition, they indict the "set of practices" and ideologies that limit possibilities for transition by directing them in normalizing ways. In doing so, these writers highlight the presence of forms of "transgendered consciousness" that do not fit dominant ideas of sexed personhood ("a naturalized order of existence"), thereby pointing to such ideas and the violence they enact by presenting alternative experiences of gender and embodiment as monstrous and inhuman.[193]

In contesting the obviousness of there being only two genders that each are attached to a particular sexed morphology (particularly from birth), the concept of transgender underlines how that framework effaces other ways of living gendered selfhood. We might describe this pattern as an emphasis on the variety of trans phenomenologies – the many ways gender arises from embodied sensation. When working within the medical framework of transsexuality, Stone suggests, "Emergent polyvocalities of lived experience, never represented in the discourse but present at least in potential, disappear," such that "transsexuals for whom gender identity is something different from *and perhaps irrelevant* to physical genitalia are occulted" from "what counts as a culturally intelligible body."[194] Her use of *transsexuals* to refer to persons who do not desire what was called "sex reassignment surgery" illustrates her writing at the cusp of the uptake of the term transgender to refer both to such persons *and* to the proliferation of genders to which Stone gestures. In this vein, Leslie Feinberg observes that "gender is the poetry each of us makes out of the language we are taught."[195] This perspective differs greatly from the narrative of *being in the wrong body* that predominated in discourses of transition, particularly medically mediated processes of gender affirmation. Stone says of the "wrong body" narrative that it is not "an adequate descriptive category" for "the multiple contradictions of individual lived experience," and Bornstein notes, "I'll bet it's more likely an unfortunate metaphor that conveniently conforms to cultural expectations, rather than an honest reflection of our transgendered feelings," earlier indicating that "fluidity" – "the refusal to remain one gender or another" – is also an important aspect of conceptualizing transgender identities.[196] Here we also can see an incipient tension within uses of *transgender*: it can indicate those who do not desire gender-affirming genital surgery (often known as *bottom surgery*) and/or who not see themselves within the "wrong body" narrative; and it also can indicate *all* persons whose gender does not align with the one presumed for their sex assigned at birth, seeing them as "transgressively gendered."[197]

Transgender activism and organizing in the 1990s takes up such challenges to binary notions of gender and to the normalizing authority exerted by experts (and attendant narratives of trans pathology) in administering gender-affirming care. The first Southern Comfort conference, focused on the lives of trans people in the South, was organized in Atlanta in 1991. In 1992, Feinberg published *Transgender Liberation* as a pamphlet, and that year Anne Ogborn founded the first chapter of Transgender Nation in San Francisco. The next year, various Transgender Nation chapters demonstrated at the American Psychiatric Association's (APA) annual conference, calling for a change to the ways gender-nonconforming experiences were categorized and insisting they should not be seen as a form of mental illness. A similar demonstration was launched in 1996 at the APA's conference by the group Transsexual Menace, founded in 1994 by Riki Anne Wilchins, with another demonstration at the APA's national office later that year. The year 1993 also saw protests against the decision by the national organizing committee of the March on Washington for Lesbian, Gay, and Bisexual Equal Rights not to add "transgender" to the event title. A similar decision was made by the organizers of Stonewall 25 the next year, generating protests from transgender groups. Also in 1994, activists created Camp Trans in response to the exclusionary entrance policy for the Michigan Womyn's Music Festival, discussed earlier, and campaigned for inclusion of transgender people and issues of gender identity within the Employment Nondiscrimination Act (focused on lesbian, gay, bisexual rights and matters of sexuality) introduced in Congress. The murder of Brandon Teena in 1993 (which gained greater national prominence through the film *Boys Don't Cry*) also served as a rallying point for transgender activists, who held demonstrations and vigils during the trials of those responsible for his murder in 1995.[198]

While a critique of normative ideas of gender difference and transition and of the imposition of these notions within medicine and psychiatry is shared across most of the intellectual and political uses of transgender in this period, a prominent tension emerges between more explicit efforts to deconstruct the dominant sex/gender system and a more coalitional ethos that sees *transgender* as a way of forging connections among otherwise potentially disparate groups and issues. Bornstein was perhaps the most well-known proponent of the former. Declaring that "it's the gender system – the idea of gender itself – that needs to be done away with," she envisions transgender intellectual work as challenging the ways the sex/gender system creates "a dangerously invisible and pervasive cult-like system."[199] Contesting and undoing this system entails not only refusing to treat certain notions of gender as natural but seeking possibilities for conceptualizing selfhood and embodiment that do not rely on notions of determinate gender.[200] In addition to developing the idea of fluidity, discussed earlier, Bornstein suggests the potential to *transcend* gender by imagining/creating a "third space" – "a space that constantly shifts and changes" in ways that are "outside the binary" of normative ideologies of sex/gender. She associates such possibilities with the figure of "the shaman," presenting nonwestern and Indigenous persons whose identities would not fit within such normative ideas as "ancestors" of contemporary (white?) transgender people in ways that implicitly position the former as of the past while also effacing ongoing colonial and imperial dynamics (including the appropriation of Indigenous identities, knowledges, and cultures by non-Indigenous people).[201] By contrast, Feinberg suggests, "Transgender people are not dismembering the categories of man and woman. We are opening up a world of possibilities in addition." She presents sexism, patriarchy, and heterosexism as oppressive to everyone and argues that "trans liberation" lies in linking together the struggles of "all gender transgressors," thereby "develop[ing] multi-issue coalitions ... for social equality and economic justice."[202] Thus, even as Feinberg recognizes certain shared features of oppression among homosexuals, transsexuals, and other sexual minorities and gender-nonconforming people (observing of Stonewall and similar forms of resistance, for example, "Did we fight back because our love was outlawed? Or because we were gender outlaws? I never thought to ask myself that question .... We closed ranks and fought hard"),[203] she aims less to specify and challenge particular principles and practices that shape the sex/gender system than to champion "the right of all people to self-determination of their own bodies," "to expression of gender, free from criticism or condemnation."[204] Similarly, Patrick Califia observes, "If the concept of gender freedom is to have any meaning, it must be possible for some of us to cling to our biological sex and the gender we were assigned at birth while others wish to adapt the body to their gender of preference, and still others choose to question the very concept of polarized sexes."[205]

Some uses of transgender in the 1990s, then, speak to a broader integrated critique of the ways gender is made and imposed, raising questions about all gender-based categories and identifications, while others use the term to mark the potential for productive alliances and shared organizing among persons whose relation to various forms of gender-based categorization may be quite different, emphasizing individual self-definition over a structural analysis of how such categories of definition take shape.[206] The relations between these modes of trans intellectual and political work from the 1990s – as well as other questions raised in the period through the use of transgender, such as how to understand matters of visibility and how to engage the range and complexity of phenomenologies of gendered experience – remain ongoing concerns in trans studies.

Conclusion

This chapter is less a chronology of movements that have influenced queer and trans studies than an extended consideration of some of the earlier intellectual and political frameworks that are cited, mobilized, and refracted within these areas of study. These movements cannot be situated in waves with respect to each other, in a teleological story of progress. Not only do each of these movements contain differences and disagreements within them, they also overlap, intersect, influence, cross-pollinate, and refract each other in complex ways, creating a rich nonlinear matrix. They do not so much provide a singular genealogy as suggest a mosaic of genealogies (including other influences not discussed here). Considering these various movements and frameworks in their variability and dispersion opens up possibilities for engaging with the intellectual and activist ecology that made queer and trans studies possible, on which scholars continue to draw, and to which their work contributes.

These movements all worked in some way to reframe extant terminologies and intellectual and political strategies in order to attend to broader processes of normalization and institutionalized systems of power and their effects on experiences of selfhood and interpersonal relations. Gay liberation recast *gay* as contesting "the establishment" – the weave between the state, the family, capitalism, and medicine – in order to critique dominant formations of sexism, racism, and imperial power, also at its best opening toward forms of gender nonnormativity. Similarly, lesbian feminism refigured *lesbian* as a challenge to normative conceptions of womanhood, foregrounding the ways personal experience is shaped by heteronormativity and attending to the coercive force of the institution of marriage – and various other state-backed patriarchal policies treated as natural and given – while emphasizing the possibility for a wide range of relations, intimacies, and communities outside of such forms. Women of color feminists generated *identity politics* as a way of talking about the kinds of knowledge and strategy that emerge from considering the multidimensional complexities of one's own experience of oppression, and they also developed rich ways of making visible, valuing, engaging, and productively working across *difference* – among one's own identities and forms of belonging, within marginalized groups, and among varied groups in coalition. AIDS activist and intellectual work highlighted the ways various persons, groups, and behaviors had been linked in being positioned within dominant discourses as perverse and aberrant, and such work developed ways of challenging discourses about identity and health that contributed to the marginalization and abandonment of entire populations. Early transgender writing and activism distinguished transgender from transsexual in ways that increased visibility beyond a medicalized paradigm of transition, drew attention to phenomenologies of gender nonnormativity, sought to deconstruct normalized (hetero)gendered categories, and create coalition across forms of embodied experience in the interest of gender self-determination.

While elements of these movements can and have been understood by later scholars as essentializing or lacking awareness of their own exclusions, they all had a wide range of perspectives rather than a singular line of thought, and all at their best sought to offer broad-based visions for social change. We certainly might fault particular movements or prominent figures within them for their limits (especially in terms of effacing questions of race, class, nationality, empire, etc.), but we also need to reckon with the diversity of those movements and the participants in them as well as their efforts to imagine otherwise. Scholarship in queer and trans studies continues to bring forward ideas/examples from the past, aims to shift our sense of how this history happened, and seeks to articulate what productively can be teased out from the past in ways that can affect the present and help in envisioning the future.

Chapter 3
Histories of Sexuality and Gender Identity

To think historically about something involves thinking about how it manifests over time – the various ways that something appears at different moments, in different places, and the relationships among those patterns. To think historically, though, is *also* to mark conceptual and empirical discontinuities, attending to how the categories used now do not readily map onto the dynamics of past periods or the ways the kinds of identities or phenomena present in the present do not really line up with those of other times. That complex movement between continuity and discontinuity is particularly pressing and vexed for queer and trans studies because of the simultaneous need to insist that forms of desire and embodiment seen as new and strange aren't either of those things while also challenging assumptions about the ahistorical naturalness of heteronormative and cisnormative ideas and ideals. How do you both draw on contemporary concepts, categories, and identities to make sense of the past in ways that are meaningful for the present *and* challenge their apparent obviousness? How do you both trace the structural continuities of forms of power and privilege across time *and* draw attention to other ways of being that have been effaced or supplanted by newer configurations of sexual and gender identity? Furthermore, how do we understand the central role in these processes of forms of identity, power, and privilege that, at first glance, do not seem to be *about* sexuality and gender identity, such as race, religion, class, and citizenship? As Dana Seitler suggests, "the construction of perversity appears as part of a story in which race, gender, physical deformation, sexuality, and many other bodily forms and practices emerge in ... interdependent ways: each interacts dynamically in a process of mutual reinforcement for the very existence of one confirms the perversity and 'peculiarity' of the other."[1]

Michel Foucault's *The History of Sexuality, Vol. 1* has been particularly influential in shaping how scholars think about what it means to offer a history for what are deemed deviant acts, orientations, and identities.[2] As discussed in Chapter 1, he begins by challenging what he terms "the repressive hypothesis" – the idea that in prior periods *sexuality* was repressed in various ways, which he suggests positions the speaker as a voice for liberation. Speaking in the name of freeing sexuality offers an "opportunity to speak out against the powers that be," but he asks whether what seems like a "deliberate transgression" of dominant ideas does not, in fact, reaffirm "the same historical network as the thing it denounces" by treating a thing called "sexuality" as self-evident and just a part of human nature that political regimes accept or deny in particular ways. Instead, Foucault argues that the concept of sexuality is invented over the course of the eighteenth and nineteenth centuries and creates an "artificial unity" among a range of desires, acts, bodily sensations, kinds of emotional intimacy, forms of homemaking, and kinds of family arrangements that have no inherent relation to each other. Treating all of these things as somehow necessarily bound up together naturalizes particular social forms that tie these various kinds of associations and experience together (such as the Euro-American middle-class household and the nuclear family). That dynamic is driven by "the self-affirmation of one class," namely the rise of a middle class as part of the development of European capitalism and that class's depiction of its own forms as inherently good, healthful, and contributing to the welfare of the population.[3] The *artificial unity* enacted by the concept of sexuality further is part of a more expansive historical process through which social phenomena come to be represented and regulated in terms of norms that themselves are organized around biologized notions of health, well-being, and productivity – a longer historical transformation in which "notions of error or sin" are replaced by determinations of "the normal and the pathological." The increasing reliance on *normalization* is part of what he characterizes as the development of *biopolitics* or *biopower*. Measuring "effects and distributions around the norm" provides a different way of justifying law, policy, and administration than relying on the will of the monarch; instead of the divine right of kings, including their right to kill, "power [is] organized around the management of life," including presenting actions by authorities of all kinds as justified due to their ability to promote the health of the population and diminish threats to that supposed health – such as from forms of deviance figured as a kind of disease in the population.[4] Notably, though, in this account Foucault does not address the roles played by colonialism in shaping norms with regard to class, embodiment, desire, and family, nor does he address the ways race centrally shapes ideas of health and pathology, differentiates between those whose welfare matters and those deemed a threat to the *general population*, and provides a principal line of distinction between those made subject to biopolitical regulation and those groups subjected to direct state violence (by the police and/or military).

This chapter will engage these historiographic issues, and the significance of history for queer and trans studies, from several different angles. The first section will address the stakes of centering race and empire, highlighting how doing so shifts the contours and character of queer and trans historical analysis. The next section will consider how scholars have conceptualized eroticism and embodiment in periods before the advent of the concepts of homosexuality and transsexuality. From here, I'll address the methodological difficulties raised by the question of whether particular historical persons and social dynamics should be understood as *queer* or *trans*, and then I'll turn to the emergence from the late nineteenth century through the mid twentieth century of the dominant categories of sexual and gender identity we've inherited from that period, including their racializing and eugenic dynamics. The chapter will close with scholarly articulations of queer and trans temporalities – the effort to rethink how we understand the experience of being-in-time.

Centering Race and Empire

In the context of Euro-American histories, conceptions of desire, pleasure, and gendered embodiment arise within social fields that themselves are shaped in fundamental ways by racial and colonial dynamics. Processes of race-making and empire-making serve as principal sites for the construction of gendered and sexual meanings, identities, and relations. With regard to Europe, the United States, and their spheres of imperial influence and occupation, we might characterize queer and trans histories as always powerfully inflected by dynamics of race and empire. Attending to the ways imperialism has been central to ideologies of sexual and gender normativity highlights how relations with non-European people(s) have been fundamental to Euro-American policy, political economies, and self-articulations.

If Europe and its diasporas often are cast as the origin point for all things modern, including notions of homosexuality and gender transition, what happens if the things taken as expressive of (Eurocentric) modernity are understood as arising as a result of colonial intervention and racialized engagements with those outside Europe (building on the work of women of color feminists, discussed in Chapter 2)? The effort to manage the populations living within the areas claimed as colonies by European powers in the sixteenth through nineteenth centuries gave rise, as Ann Laura Stoler argues, to forms of racialized differentiation based on "home environments, child-rearing practices, and sexual arrangements," the very kinds of relationships and social formations that have been seen as central to discourses of sexuality in Europe and the United States. Middle-class notions of home, family, respectability, and proper modes of desire and gender arose out of regulative efforts in the colonies. Such "middle-class sensibilities" emerged through authorities' attempts to "cultivat[e] ... distinctions from those to be ruled," distinctions that were attributed to racial difference but manifested through the regulation of forms of association, reproduction, and inhabitance.[5] In this way, the "discursive and practical field in which nineteenth-century bourgeois sexuality emerged was situated on an imperial landscape," such that "an implicit racial grammar underwrote the sexual regimes of bourgeois culture."[6] Reciprocally, as Anne McClintock illustrates, "imperialism is not something that happened elsewhere – a disagreeable fact of history external to Western identity." Not only did other parts of the world function as "porno-tropics for the European imagination," onto which "Europe projected its forbidden sexual desires and fears," but the ideologies of proper desire, gender, home, and family generated in order to manage colonized populations and spaces become the basis for social hierarchy and administrative regulation *at home* as well. McClintock observes, "Projecting the family image onto national and imperial progress enabled what was often murderously violent change to be legitimized as the progressive unfolding of natural decree," which involved understanding other social forms (including other arrangements of desire, social reproduction, and gendered embodiment) as less advanced – as indicating an earlier point in a singular timeline of human development ("figured as a prehistoric zone of racial and gender difference").[7] Forms of behavior that did not fit this "family image" were presented as eruptions of racial backwardness in the imperial metropole, such as urban slums repeatedly being analogized to the colonies as part of accounts that drew on "popular images of imperial travel."[8] The "freak show" is another example of this pattern, in which "nondisabled people of color and cognitively disabled people [were thought to embody] the missing link between primates and humans," and in that space, "*white* or *whitened* gender nonconformity and disability [were constituted] as the same kind of difference," in contrast to "freaks of color" who were seen as "representative" of their races in ways that positioned the failure of proper sex/gender among white people as expressive of a disabling degeneration toward nonwhiteness.[9]

Attributions of sexual and gender deviancy were crucial aspects of imperial rule, serving as signs of what was taken to be an underlying racial essence and, thereby, justifying Euro-American intrusions as civilizing projects whose aim was to redeem nonwhite populations from their supposed immorality and savagery. Charges of widespread perversity were routine parts of Euro-colonial governance and discourse from at least the sixteenth century onward.[10] In Hernán Cortés's first letter after he began the project of occupying what would become Mexico in 1519, he asserts, "They are all sodomites"; as Jonathan Goldberg notes, "once made, few reports failed to repeat the charge." However, the reference to *sodomy* has less to do with particular acts or desires on the part of Native people (none are described by Cortés) than the role such allegations have in legitimizing military action against a population by Catholic forces. The Spanish invaders transferred images of deviance derived from representations of Muslims, which were part of the early-modern campaign to *reclaim* Spain for the Catholic monarchy, to the Americas: "Accusations of sodomy, responsible for deaths in the thousands, are transported to the New World. Sodomites 'are' Moors," thereby validating similar action against Indigenous peoples in the Americas as was taken against Islamic populations in Europe. In this way, the charge of "sodomy comes to occupy a place in the ritual of possession and justification."[11] The broader category of "sins against nature" (which included anal intercourse as well as bestiality, masturbation, and certain forms of heresy) served as an important vehicle for asserting Spanish authority throughout the Americas, punishing examples of "excess" and "function[ing] as a means of exerting colonial control over all aspects of the population."[12] Charges of sodomy also centrally related to supposed violations of Spanish gender norms and served as a way of seeking to remake Indigenous peoples' own complex gender systems, including forms of spiritual practice and iconography that involved homoeroticism and gender transitivity.[13] The assertion that evidence of mass perversion among the colonized was contained somewhere in colonial records often provided a way of validating imperial governance, including by distracting from the failures and incoherence of imperial policies. Anjali Arondeker argues with regard to charges of widespread sodomy in India, British colonial reports and court cases often would allude to information supposedly available elsewhere that would substantiate such assertions. Claims about the prevalence of perversity allowed colonial authorities to present themselves as in the know about the goings-on among a degraded population in need of civilizing aid and disciplinary control, rather than as "struggling under the weight of information gathering and reform in a vast region divided by language and religious differences." As Arondeker suggests, "The sin of *le vice* ... hovers strategically over areas of critical British vulnerability."[14]

Images of and references to sodomy and gender nonconformity in colonial records, then, are less evidence of queer and trans forebears ready to be reclaimed by contemporary LGBT people than markers of processes of imperial recoding, in which complex social dynamics are transposed into terms that facilitate the efforts of colonial powers to manage their own unstable regimes. We might think of this work of colonial regimes less as the persecution of queer and trans people than as the development of ideas of proper intimacy, affiliation, and selfhood in which practices seen as threatening to Euro-American political economy are cast as expressive of ingrained racial difference, which needs to be contained, disciplined, and regulated. In this way, "race has operated not as a fig leaf covering the larger, lurking economic substructures of imperialism; racialization instead frequently conditions the very modalities of economic domination."[15] As T. J. Tallie illustrates with regard to British policy in Natal (in what is now South Africa), this reorganization of existing social forms includes the management of marriage and the networks of kinship and alliance it can create. Monogamous couplehood between a man and a woman is positioned in colonial discourses as the sole example of civilized family-making, conversely presenting Indigenous peoples' participation in polygamy as indicative of their *African* propensities while also seeking to prevent white men from taking part in such unions.[16] Reciprocally, polygamy among those otherwise understood as white, such as the Mormons prior to their renunciation of plural marriage in 1890, racializes them in US popular and legal discourses, marking them as like Asian, African, and American Indian peoples and, thus, as degenerating from the civilized pinnacle of middle-class whiteness in their enactment of deviant kinship, desire, and governance.[17] Moreover, the understanding of monogamous hetero-couplehood and the nuclear family household as central to civilized life served as the means of imposing Euro-American kinship and homemaking on Native peoples in the United States and Canada in ways that sought to break up Indigenous modes of governance, social life, and placemaking.[18]

Colonialism generates forms of social distinction that validate and seek to secure Euro-American governance, and the kinds of racial difference produced through that process provide the framework in which *gender* and *sexuality* gain meaning. Queer and trans historical work has shown how forms of racialization – particularly with regard to blackness – function as the background against which (white) gender and sexual identities become visible as such. One cannot overestimate the significance of African enslavement in the making of Europe and the Americas from the early-modern period onward.[19] Black feminist scholarship has demonstrated how enslaved people were *ungendered* by casting them as *flesh*, whose lack of access to dominant gender roles is a key part of defining them as ownable and saleable nonpersons.[20] In this way, blackness takes shape not only in contrast to notions of proper masculinity and femininity but as a lack of gendered differentiation, as a kind of gender unfixedness that serves, by contrast, as the means of giving definition to gender identities that implicitly depend on whiteness. For this reason C. Riley Snorton suggests, "To feel black in the diaspora, then, might be a trans experience," further arguing that "captive flesh figures a critical genealogy for modern transness, as chattel persons gave rise to an understanding of gender as mutable and as an amendable form of being" in which gender is "subject to rearrangement."[21] Thinking of histories of transness as bound up in and dependent on histories of blackness, and their relation to enslavement and its afterlives, draws attention to the ways Black people have been used as resources in the making of white gendered ideals from which they were excluded. For example, Snorton addresses the development of the field of gynecology in the nineteenth-century United States, particularly in the work of James Marion Sims. Sims sought to find a surgical cure for vesticovaginal fistula, and to do so, he experimented on a series of enslaved persons – Anarcha, Betsey, and Lucy as well as "unnamed others"– who "function[ed] as a living laboratory" in which their status as malleable "flesh" inherently available for white use served as "a condition of possibility for the science and symbolics of modern sex." Their status as beings defined by their blackness meant that they would not be extended the kinds of (still deeply patriarchal) respect and consideration reserved for "women," and as a result, they could enable "the possibility of 'being made again a normal woman'" for white patients while such a horizon of care and gendered social belonging "would not be available" to them as enslaved people.[22]

Across the nineteenth and early twentieth centuries, blackness served as a crucible for forging the difference between normal and aberrant genders and sexualities in ways that enabled and legitimized white supremacy. In his discussion of discourses of *amalgamation* in the nineteenth-century United States, Tavia Nyong'o tracks how that concept extended beyond what in the latter half of the century would be termed *miscegenation*. If the latter more strictly indicates procreation between persons legally defined as belonging to different races, particularly Black and white, amalgamation had a much wider field of reference, illustrating how notions of racial reproduction were enmeshed within broader ideologies of racialized social (dis)order. The term invoked the sense of a wide-ranging "racial state of exception" that "produces situations of legal, racial, and political anomaly that cannot be accurately" conveyed through the figures of "mixedness of halfness" used to describe children whose parents are of different races. In this sense, proximity to blackness, in social and sexual terms, indicated an ungovernable kind of chaos that not only deviated from but actively endangered emergent middle-class ideals of selfhood, behavior, and family formation while, simultaneously, providing a demonized counterpoint that helped shape the emergence of those ideals.[23] In the wake of emancipation, formerly enslaved people often were cast in official and popular rhetorics as immanently criminal, their blackness seen as indicating an inability to enact proper forms of gendered personhood, sexual propriety, and domestic organization (including child-rearing). In her study of the incarceration of Black women in Georgia in the post-Reconstruction period, Sarah Haley argues that "the construction of their bodies as monstrous meant not only that their political and economic power would be limited, but also that they would be subject to disproportionate arrest and punishment." Haley further shows how *queer* referred to forms of gender and sexual aberrance with regard to Black people as early as the 1890s, significantly before its documented use as a way of naming same-sex attraction per se; the term served as a way for the "mainstream press to describe perverse black bodies, ideas, and behaviors that could only be interpreted and governed through police and judicial action."[24] This understanding of Black people, particularly Black women, as threatening in their deviance was based not on sexual object-choice or specific kinds of gendered self-presentation but on the very fact of their blackness, a category of (non)personhood which popular, judicial, and medical discourses continued to recreate in ways that made it a sign of irredeemable aberrance in need of policing and state discipline and that, as a result, also enabled Black people to continue to be conscripted into enforced, unpaid labor through incarceration.[25] Moreover, legitimized through discourses of Black sexual and gendered excess and deviance, the violence enacted on Black people, such as "the ubiquitous presence of lynching in the public imagination during the period from 1890 to 1940," "may have informed and helped naturalize the rationale used to support medical castration and asexualization" as part of eugenic campaigns against those deemed feebleminded (often itself a result of their perceived sexual deviance).[26]

The racialization of sexuality further historically operates as a way of managing residency and mobility, within and across national borders. The legal and administrative construction of nonwhiteness (including through the criminalization of marriages between white and nonwhite persons) and the ideological association of it with degeneracy, depravity, and moral disorder shaped social mappings of US space and possibilities for access to political and economic resources. In the early twentieth century, Black people increasingly were pushed into limited and geographically marginal neighborhoods in cities across the country, and those areas also served as vice districts.[27] Police and city officials intentionally sought to contain illegal activities considered immoral – such as gambling, prostitution, and bootlegging (after the onset of Prohibition) – in areas that were known to have substantial numbers of Black residents, which themselves were the result of active residential segregation and white mob violence to keep African Americans out of white neighborhoods. This creation of racialized vice districts, what Kevin Mumford has called *interzones*, not only depended on existing associations of blackness with aberrance but spatially intensified the connections between perversity, nonwhiteness, and criminality while also limiting Black inhabitants' access to income in ways that increased illicit activity (such as more visible forms of sex work, like street walking) and that, therefore, seemed to provide empirical evidence for Black propensities toward deviance.[28] More than a place for containing blackness, these zones also provided a site for tabooed interracial interactions, including same-sex erotic encounters which vice reformers noted as especially prevalent in clubs in Black areas.[29] Addressing the policing of Black girls and young women in urban areas in the early twentieth century, Saidiya Hartman describes their efforts as "carr[ying] on *as if [they] were free*" while being construed as a deviant threat in need of containment. Hartman notes, "What the law designated as crime were the forms of life created by young black women in the city," adding that "segregation was seen as a way to maintain the health and morality of the social body and police power was critical to achieving that goal."[30]

On the West Coast of the United States, prohibitions with regard to marriage, property, and residency played central roles in constructing Asianness as a racial category. From the 1870s to the 1940s, a series of US national laws and administrative policies increasingly denied entry to persons from East, Southeast, and South Asia, with different countries and populations at various points coming to be defined as not white and, therefore, ineligible for naturalization as US citizens.[31] While separate from federal law as such, state policies helped drive this process of racialization, including through acts forbidding white–Asian marriage and alien property laws that prevented those ineligible for citizenship from owning land (which also could prevent "attempts to transfer property between parents and children").[32] As Nayan Shah argues, such "racial bounding of marriage and inheritance rights" produced and sustained a "racial cartel" that sought to police the boundaries of whiteness while giving those deemed white almost exclusive control over major sectors of the agricultural economy.[33] This racial limitation on legally recognized family combined with the prevention of immigration by Asian women, who were viewed as likely to be prostitutes,[34] to create communities of largely migrant male laborers whose forms of sociality were then cast by officials as perverse and disruptive – such as in the repeated image of South Asian men as more prone to engaging in sodomy, thereby licensing further surveillance and discipline, regardless of actual behavior.[35] As Eithne Luibhéid illustrates, across US history, "the immigration control apparatus" (and associated national, state, and local laws) has served "as a key site for the production and reproduction of sexual categories, identities, and norms within relations of inequality," which can include homoeroticism and nonnormative gender identity but which also understands the signs of those patterns – and perversity and pathology more broadly – in deeply racializing ways that are irreducible to sexual object-choice and gender expression.[36]

Foregrounding the roles played by race and empire in histories of sexuality and gender identity draws attention to how the latter do not operate separately from the former. Not only do many dominant ways of understanding sexual and gender (ab)normality emerge from situations of colonization and settlement, but the ideas/ideals that arise out of efforts to institute and sustain imperial governance come to shape life in the metropole. Moreover, notions of health, well-being, and belonging that attach to ideologies of sexual and gender normality often depend on distinctions between whiteness and various kinds of racialization, usually characterized in terms of their own kinds of deviance – like savagery, criminality, and inassimilable alienness. These accounts of ingrained aberrance legitimize and help give form to official modes of racial distinction that regulate access to citizenship, resources, residence, placemaking, and mobility.

Terms, Norms, and "Nature"

When using words like *queer* and *trans* to talk about earlier historical periods, what do these terms mean? Do they refer to particular kinds of persons, sorts of bodily experience, specific desires or acts? If these terms function as *analytics*, as frameworks for interpretation rather than pointing to identities that people had in the past, those frameworks gain meaning in relation to the present. We look back from the heteronormative and cisnormative assumptions at play now and think about other possibilities and social structures that existed then. In Carolyn Dinshaw's terms, we *touch* the past in ways meaningful for the current moment.[37] However, the social forms and dynamics of our time don't necessarily fit those back then. Scholars have addressed these continuities and discontinuities in a range of ways, including exploring the unfamiliar meanings and implications of terms we think we know and addressing how notions of the normal or the natural are historically shifting.

Attending to what's unfamiliar about the past can, somewhat paradoxically, help highlight how it resembles the present, albeit in ways that further raise questions about taken-for-granted ideas of desire, embodiment, and identity (building on Eve Sedgwick's point about the absence of a singular "Great Paradigm Shift," discussed in Chapter 1). For example, tracing how people lived gendered lives that did not follow from the sex they were labeled at birth challenges ongoing claims that trans experiences are *new* (and, therefore, threatening or unnatural). Such assertions of newness have been "consistently used to undermine the legitimacy of nonbinary genders, trans people[;] activists and scholars have had to fight to claim the historicity of trans lives," including by showing how "narratives about gender transition and gender confirmation were told long before any of those terms came into being."[38] In this vein, we can approach historical study through the idea, in Valerie Traub's terms, of "*cycles of salience*" in which "perennial axes of social definition ... become particularly resonant or acute at different historical moments."[39] Or, as Greta LaFleur suggests, we can hold onto "the possibility of transhistorical similarities *as distinct from* continuities," noting such similarities in ways that allow us to think about them together – relating the past and the present – without assuming that they "share all or even very much ideological territory."[40] We can see how the resemblance of prior social phenomena, relations, and identities to those now might open up intellectual possibilities (challenging the idea of history either as a teleological unfolding implicitly directed toward the evolution of some better, more developed form or an increasing awareness of the *real* dynamics of gender, sex, and sexuality). At the same time, we can mark differences among historically distinct social configurations that have their own potentials and limits and cannot simply be equated to each other. As Rachel Hope Cleves observes, "Rather than simply add nonbinary people and stir, we need to reexamine our core categories."[41]

At the level of basic terminology, the words we have to refer to bodies, felt experiences, desires, and intimacies do not necessarily travel well across time. Attending to the varied configurations of meaning and social significance in earlier periods can help in seeing aspects of present ideas that we might take for granted. As Jeffrey Masten notes, looking to the past "may bring into view for us" how "even our most apparently clinical ways of describing 'sexual' practices ... must remain subject to queer-philological scrutiny."[42] Philology is the study of the history of how words and phrases are used, and Masten suggests that "the word *sexual*, transparent as it may now seem to us, itself requires our serious historicizing, philological attention," coming to refer to kinds of genital pleasure only in the late eighteenth century and early nineteenth century.⁴³ Traub notes that "[m]any of the terms that we now regularly use to describe sex assumed their sexual connotations or were coined ... much later," including terms like *coitus* and *sexual intercourse*.⁴⁴ With regard to trans histories, such philological concerns open up possibilities for connecting matters of gender to a wide range of social relations. Joseph Gamble observes the proliferation in the seventeenth century of a series of *trans* terms that address forms of gender variability but also "transitions that reached far beyond the bounds of gender."⁴⁵ Similarly, Marjorie Rubright points toward the "transgender capacity of words and phrases," suggesting the potential of "speculative philology" – considering the multiplicity of ways that words might mean in a given context – to enact a "hermeneutics of cispicion": "to be suspicious" of the presumption that persons are "necessarily cisgender" unless proven otherwise.⁴⁶

Scholars have illustrated how paying attention to those earlier contexts can increase our sense of the multiplicity of ways that what we now largely refer to as gender and sexuality gain social meaning, including the role in that process of other aspects of personhood – such as class, race, religion, and nationality – that are not reducible to someone's "sex." Terms used in earlier periods like *sodomy/sodomite*, *tribade*, and *hermaphrodite* can indicate how what we might consider to be different kinds of identity or status were mutually defined, although in ways that largely supported privileged social institutions (like marriage, the Christian Church, and the power of the monarchical/imperial state).⁴⁷

Sodomy in current terms usually means anal intercourse, particularly between two men. If one looks historically, though, the term sodomy neither represents a kind of sexual identity (a stand-in for homosexuality) nor is reducible to anal pleasure of any kind. It appears as part of the English criminal law starting in the 1530s. At that point, as Mario DiGangi suggests, the concept underwent a "historical shift from the understanding of sodomy as an offense against God to the understanding of sodomy as an offense committed within and against social institutions."⁴⁸ While the sixteenth-century English legal definition focused on anal penetration between men, sodomy had a range of meanings that did not simply evaporate but continued to exceed that of the single male–male sexual act. These associations include its linkage to idolatry and Catholicism, so that public discourses and accusations of *sodomy* had a much wider field of reference and were shaped by ideas about religious practice and belonging.⁴⁹ In the medieval period, sodomy "inhabits the zone of sexual acts *contra naturam* that includes other heterosexual acts, such as women on top during heterosexual intercourse," and it also could include erotic relations among women, masturbation, and bestiality.⁵⁰ While forms of vaginal and anal penetration among persons labeled as female were not legally categorized as sodomy in England, they were elsewhere in Europe, including France, Spain, and the Netherlands,[51] and even when not criminalized, such relations could be part of the term's web of meanings. More broadly, as Goldberg argues, the implications of *sodomy* actually depend on the ways "the term remains incapable of exact definition," incorporating a variety of challenges to extant "social order." Up through the eighteenth century, whatever violated "the structures of social hierarchy" could be deemed sodomitical, especially inasmuch as such actions were counter to the gendered, racialized, and class relations organizing marriage (itself the principal social unit for propertyholding, inheritance, and social reproduction).[52] Conversely, the shadow of sodomy haunts the importance of "validated, condoned homoaffection" among men that was central "to domestic arrangements, educational structures, [and] the rhetoric of male friendship."[53] Michael Warner observes with regard to Puritan accounts of settling in the Americas, "The new colony threatened to resemble Sodom not only because of its global notoriety but also because of the intensity of its affective bonds among males," which were envisioned as crucial to "sustain[ing] a disciplined public body."[54] Sodomy, then, represents the disruption of social hierarchies organized around marriage and Christianity as well as the potential for an outbreak of perversity within horizontal relations of fellowship between privileged men. As a figure that "everything bad sticks to," sodomy also could connote other kinds of social ills and excesses, including "pride, idleness, and gluttony."[55] Moreover, it further gained power as a sign of aberrance and threat from being associated with racialized foreignness, particularly Islam: "no geographical domain onto which the Anglo-European gaze has fixed its sometimes imperial, sometimes covetous, sometimes simply curious eye has been so associated with the specter of male-male sexuality over the centuries" as "the Muslim world."[56] The Islamicate presence in Europe (prior to the Reconquista and during the height of Ottoman expansion) and as a horizon of European engagement (during the Crusades as well as through circulation of Arab texts in translation, expansive travel literature, and trade) helped fuel the portrayal of Muslims as having sodomitical tendencies while, reciprocally, tinting charges of sodomy with a sense of dangerous – and also potentially alluring – alienness.[57]

Tribadism and *hermaphroditism* further illustrate how gendered understandings of proper embodiment and eroticism were suffused with racial and religious significance. These two terms are largely no longer in use, the latter because it's come to be seen as an offensive way of referring to intersexed persons. However, both these words – tribade and hermaphrodite – did important work in making sense of bodies, desires, and social relations.

Most simply, the tribade is a woman who gains pleasure through genital rubbing, particularly clitoral stimulation. More than indicating a generic capacity of female bodies, though, such pleasure was seen prior to the eighteenth century "as imitative of masculine prerogatives and hence monstrous," particularly in terms of women's erotic relations with each other.[58] Derived from ancient texts, many of which had been translated from Greek to Arabic and then centuries later from Arabic to Latin (in which form they were disseminated through Europe), the figure of the tribade is envisioned as playing a penetrative role, with the clitoris serving a phallic function. In this way, the term interweaves a kind of desire, a form of embodiment, and a gendered role. The balance among these elements, though, was shifting and indistinct. Were both participants in such erotic relations tribades? Did the term refer only to persons with a particularly elongated clitoris (seen as having penetrative potential), or was it a potential for all women? Was penetration purely clitoral, or was the use of implements (including dildos) also tribadic? Was the term tribade indicative of erotic attention to women specifically, or was it suggestive of excessive forms of desire unconstrained by patriarchy that were present – or at least latent – in many, perhaps all, women?[59] This ensemble of meanings and potentials further was shaped by racializing conceptions of women from Africa and India who were believed to have excessively large clitorises. The association of physical, erotic, and gendered dynamics with peoples beyond Europe also linked the term tribade with the figure of the Amazons, who were located by various writers at different points in Africa, India, and in the Americas and seen as a limit figure of European Christianity and heteropatriarchal whiteness.[60]

The multifaceted nexus of body, pleasure, desire, and race that *tribade* indexes overlaps conceptually and referentially with *hermaphrodite*.[61] In the Middle Ages, that term, along with *androgyne*, expressed and cut across a range of kinds of social difference. As Leah DeVun argues, "nonbinary sex participated in a staggering range of ... intellectual, political, and social contexts," "play[ing] a pivotal role in the formation of categories and definitions fundamental to the European Christian tradition."[62] Various kinds of religious identification inside and outside of Europe were made "corporeally distinct from the residents of Christendom" through their description as hermaphroditical, including Muslims and Jews.[63] While speaking to what often were understood to be physical qualities of bodies (including the idea that Jewish men menstruated from their anuses), such categorization also included the ways the practices of those racialized groups were thought to violate the "natural" order, in terms of gendered roles, sexual behavior, forms of marriage and childrearing, and political structure. Thus, *hermaphrodite* historically solders gender, sex, religion, and race together.[64] In this way, references to hermaphroditism gesture toward kinds of bodies cast as anomalous, but that anomaly often was not simply a matter of what now usually would be described as a person's *sex*. Instead, various dimensions of social identification and difference were seen as pointing or related to gendered embodiment. The layered and shifting meanings connected to terms like sodomy, tribade, and hermaphrodite suggest the difficulty of seeking to pin down specific types of bodies, behaviors, and identifications across time but also the possibilities for the present in considering the complex and multi-vectored ways *gender, sex,* and *sexuality* gain meaning – the range of their meanings and how they are shaped through multidimensional relations to each other and to other kinds of social experience.

More than considering the historically changing and multivalent terms we use to speak and think about erotics and embodiment, we also need to be wary, scholars have suggested, of assuming that dominant ideas in one place and period necessarily stretch to others. Treating contemporary sexual and gender norms as if they themselves do not have histories not only de facto presents them as unchanging and, therefore, unchangeable but also assumes we automatically know the ways desires, practices, and lived experience line up. As Karma Lochrie suggests, we are "seriously distorting our historical recuperations of past sexualities when we position them against a reigning heterosexual norm, since heterosexuality as a norm did not exist before the twentieth century."[65] She argues that the very idea of *the normal* (as both a statistical average and an ideal of health and well-being) emerged in the nineteenth century; earlier cultural "anxieties" about eroticism, including between people of different sexes, were less about what was considered *abnormal* than expressed a generally "desiro-skeptical" attitude that was "deeply suspicious of the mobility, disruptiveness, and affiliations of all forms of desire."[66] Moreover, a concept like heterosexual conjoins eroticism and a notion of in-born orientation with a particular model of family and household. However, as Susan Lanser notes, "where marriage is a compulsory institution especially for women ... heterosexual consummation proves nothing about affective affiliation or sexual desire."[67] Conversely, the assumption of a unified heterosexuality/heteronormativity leads to "limited definitions of queerness" based on the "tacit sense that cross-sex desires and practices are coherent, predictable, and normal," thereby leaving aside "pleasures and intimacies" such as "polygamy, group sex, zoophilia, and masochism."[68] In this vein, Valerie Traub cautions, "Some forms of female eroticism are neither subsumed under marital exigencies nor performed in defiance of them," thereby exceeding analytic frameworks organized around "patriarchal ideology *or* its transgression." On this basis, she indicates the need for a *"historicized theory of sexual variation."*[69]

Presuming that the dominant ideas of *now* applied to *then* homogenizes both the present and the past, overlooking how prior systems of power and privilege worked as well as the possibilities that lay within other configurations of bodies, pleasures, and institutional forms. Speaking of the American colonies and the early US republic, Cleves insists, "We cannot and should not shoehorn early American history into an assumed binary rigidity that flatters the present but misapprehends the past." In a similar vein, the editors of the collection *Trans Historical* observe that the "past may hold a space for forms of transness that have not yet been fully articulated or imagined, a past that, in the future, may unfold forms of alterity unknown to us at present."[70] Historical work, then, can open up the sense of what domination and opposition look like but also of potentials for living that readily fit neither.

Perhaps the most seemingly obvious concept at play in notions of gender and sexual normality is *nature*, but over time, ideas of the natural have fluctuated widely and wildly. In the Middle Ages, rather than indicating something having to do with biology or physical processes, it largely referred to a vision of God's will, which could be at odds with bodily or environmental phenomena known to be relatively common: "The Nature of medieval theologians was a prelapsarian one that represented all that was good and perfect" as opposed to "the corrupted nature that was necessitated by the Fall."[71] A range of things were thought to be "against nature" that had little to do with bodily relations per se, including "heresy" and "treachery,"[72] and bodies that did not necessarily fit a model of binary sex/gender were seen as having a "morphological defect" (comparable to "dwarfism, obesity, [and] physical disability") that "reflected the broken nature of this world."[73] Yet, male and female were not themselves fully distinguished as physical types. Up through the late eighteenth century, a one-body model of sex predominated. Drawn largely from the second-century writings of the Greek physician Galen, this vision of embodiment posited a "structural" identity of "the male and female reproductive organs," in which women's lack of "heat" meant that they had on the inside what men had on the outside.[74] As Thomas Laqueur demonstrates, "doctors understood there to be only one sex" but two "social sexes with radically different rights and obligations"; during the Renaissance, for example, despite the growth of human anatomical studies, the modern terms for "female reproductive anatomy" – such as "vagina, uterus, vulva, labia, Fallopian tubes" – did not exist and do not really have period-specific equivalents.[75]

While a binary model of bodily sex gained prominence during the eighteenth century, ideas about what constituted sex as an erotic practice also changed considerably. Building on earlier work by Henry Abelove, Tim Hitchcock traces the "sexual revolution" in which "people engaged in heterosexual activity increasingly restricted their behavior to forms of phallocentric, penetrative sex which could be countenanced as procreative," a shift endorsed by medical experts and evidenced by the vast growth in population in Great Britain during the 1700s "as a result of changes in fertility, rather than mortality" – including a population increase of about 70 percent and a fall in the number of unmarried adults from about 22 percent to less than 5 percent of the populace.[76] This reduction of sex to vaginal intercourse with male orgasm (women's orgasms ceased to be thought of as important for conception while women increasingly were considered "sexually passive" rather than "actively lascivious") displaced the previous prominence of non-penetrative forms of eroticism.[77] As Valerie Traub suggests, "we might speculate that nonprocreative, nonmissionary, and even nonprivate sex in the early modern period seems to have been *what most people actually did*."[78]

At various points, "nature" also included the ways particular environments influenced bodies, desires, and practices. Addressing "*the sexual politics of racial difference*," Greta LaFleur illustrates the presence in the long eighteenth century of "a large-scale cultural faith in the power of one's social, natural, physical or architectural, climatic, or gustatory environment to affect one's body, temperament, and character," such as the understanding of "Turks" as "sodomites" as a function of the "climate" in which they live.[79] Instances of what we might term perversity, then, depend less on individual orientations than environmental conditions that shape entire (racialized) populations. Similarly, Kyla Wazana Tompkins has addressed the ways that ideas about diet and eating practices were linked to notions of proper embodiment, eroticism, and racialized understandings of nationhood in the nineteenth-century United States due to the ways eating is part of how "an organism yields and opens to the outer world ...[,] reveal[ing] the self to be reliant upon that which is beyond its epidermal limits." Tompkins describes what were seen as wrong forms of consumption as *queer alimentarity*, "a form of sensuality, *in and of itself*" that "disrupt[s] both the individual body and the social order" by "indulging in the senses at the expense of virtuous behaviors oriented toward upholding orderly systems of feeling, being, and acting."[80] These examples point to varying contexts and frameworks in which what we might consider to be commonsensical ideologies about biology, embodiment, eroticism, and morality did not obtain in the past – or, at least, were configured in ways quite different than what seem to be dominant ideas in most

Euro-American societies currently. What *queer* or *trans* might mean in those different contexts, then, is also an open question.

Part of considering such possibilities, and not presuming that today's *normal* can simply be extended into the past (or that the past can be plotted on a timeline of progress), lies in addressing the potentials for erotic and gender agency that were available in other historical moments in ways that may not look like contemporary identities and practices. As Peter Coviello suggests with regard to considering forms of embodiment, eroticism, and identification prior to the consolidation of *sexuality* and *sexual identity* in the late nineteenth century, the goal "is less to make clear the routes by which presexological forms of intimate relation came to arrive at what we now recognize as modern habitations of sexuality than to trace, in as much detail as we can, the outlines of any number of broken-off, uncreated futures, futures that would not come to be," ones whose "errancy" allow us now to think about the possibility of other feelings, objects, and orientations beyond current identity categories.[81] Such potentials, though, themselves often are shaped by forms of class, racial, and imperial privilege. Earlier, I noted the longstanding European association of Muslim men with sodomy, and while such linkages arise out of a series of racializing and Orientalizing narratives that seriously misconstrue Islamicate societies, they do point toward the presence of homoerotic dynamics, particularly within artistic production – such as male poets addressing the attractiveness and desirability of young men in the ghazal tradition and tales of women's erotic relation (most prominently in *One Thousand and One Nights*).[82] Although, while Euro-American scholars have seen the presence of these works (as well as European travelers' accounts of the prevalence of homoeroticism) as evidence of a greater erotic permissiveness among Islamic peoples in earlier periods, that perspective can undersell the criminalization of male anal intercourse (on terms much like across Europe) and its outlawing under Islamic law, albeit with great variation with respect to how and whether sexual practices among men were prosecuted and how such desires and practices were interpreted within Islamic theologies.[83] The figure of the harem also has provided inspiration for European visions of the possibilities for significant and sustained erotic connections among women, contributing to the literary genre of what scholars have called the *feminotopia* – in which "women thrive without men and find pleasure in living together without rancor and dissent" – even as polygamy (among the Ottomans and elsewhere) also served as a sign of patriarchal barbarism that was taken to signal the (racialized) backwardness of non-Europeans.[84]

At various points, what often has been termed "romantic friendship" among women also gained public prominence as a way of addressing a range of kinds of affectional, erotic, and household relations. In the eighteenth and nineteenth centuries, women living together in what were recognized as long-term partnerships was a matter of public knowledge. From the Ladies of Llangollen (upper-class Irish women living in Wales and visited by numerous luminaries in British literary and political culture) to the "Boston marriages" of the late nineteenth century (women setting up households together, largely in the US Northeast), these were usually elite women who were known in prominent social circles, more or less treated as couples, and who were often seen as models of decorum and of the possibilities for egalitarian relationships that could provide a more equitable vision of couplehood than the gender hierarchies of legal marriage.[85] Such relationships among upper-class white women gained legitimacy by being implicitly distinguished from a range of others deemed perverse, such as "sensuous barbaric Turks, simple but savage Africans, sexually aberrant Indians, [and] slaves."[86] Beyond such partnerships, the language of friendship enabled a range of kinds of connections among white women, more or less erotic and more or less publicly celebrated or satirized at various points depending on situated circumstances (although not following anything like a consistent pattern across time) – at times presented as ameliorating or evading marriage and at times appearing as a crucial supplement to it.[87] The role of race in shaping those discourses of friendship, though, can be seen in the 1810 case of Jane Pirie and Marianne Woods. They co-ran a school in Scotland and sued the grandmother of a student, Jane Cumming, who had been withdrawn due to the supposedly "lewd and indecent behavior" of the teachers with each other that Cumming had witnessed, a claim the grandmother then publicly circulated. The teachers won the case based on the absence of evidence of a dildo (given the judges' inability to imagine sexual activity among women absent such an implement or an enlarged, penetrative clitoris) and the fact that Cumming's status as a "Hindoo" born in India would make her aware of, in the words of one of the judges, such "imputed vice [which] has been hitherto unknown in Britain."[88] *Indecency* and *lewdness* appear as a function of the presence of racialized alienness, rather than attaching to respectable, white, English womanhood.[89]

Non-elite modes of white transmasculinity were recognized publicly through the figure of *the female husband*. The phrase was used to describe people assigned female who publicly were known as men and who lived as married couples with women (sometimes actually having gotten legally married). It was coined in 1682 but gained prominence when used as a title by Henry Fielding for a fictionalized account of the real story of Charles Hamilton, and the phrase was used in public discourse (especially newspapers) until the late nineteenth century.[90] While not allowed to continue living as men once their assigned sex became public, those designated as female husbands largely were not depicted in pathologizing or even necessarily denigrating terms. Instead, as Jen Manion notes with regard to the coverage of James Howe, a tavern owner in London's East End who became perhaps the most famous female husband, such accounts often were "marked by an emphasis on hard work, respectability, [and] powerful depiction of a husband who embraced civic duty," and in such public narratives, "being married to a woman affirmed one's manhood."[91]

Prior to the passage of laws that sought to outlaw what has been called *cross-dressing*, various forms of transfemininity and transmasculinity were fairly common throughout the US West.[92] Such gender expressions were highly "visible and ... a part of daily life in the nineteenth-century West"; in addition, "news article after news article" about transmasculine persons "both near and far circulated constantly in the region's newspapers," as well as about transfeminine behavior.[93] Peter Boag argues that the portrayal of various kinds of *inversion* (including homoeroticism and trans genders – as will be discussed in a later section) "as an unfortunate by-product of modernization" led to their retrospective erasure from the space of the "frontier," which is then seen as having been "unimpaired by all the troubles of the modern period."[94] Similar kinds of metronormative associations of queerness and transness with the urban have helped entrench that erasure.[95] This example helps highlight the ways importing current terms, norms, and interpretive frameworks into the past can close down our sense of the specific configurations of desire, embodiment, and social roles in given times and places, leaving us with a rather thin sense of their textures and density as well as the implications those other formations might have for thinking of possibilities now and for the future.

Queer vs. Trans

In seeking to engage the past in ways attentive to its complexity, and how the past both resonates with the present and is distinct from it, one significant methodological issue that arises is whether to understand historical persons and relations as *queer* or as *trans*. While certainly not mutually exclusive as categories or analytical approaches, the effort to read someone as one can seem to preclude or erase the possibility of the other. Valerie Traub, for example, conceptualizes "lesbian historiography" as "analyzing recurring patterns across large spans of time in the identification, social statuses, behaviors, and meanings of women who erotically desired other women," and Susan Lansing approaches her analysis of "sapphic subjects" (and the ways representation of them shaped political discourses from the sixteenth through the nineteenth centuries) as about "intimacies between women," including "tribade" and "hermaphrodite" in a list of "labels" that address "homoerotic desires and behaviors" and beginning her first chapter with an example from 1566 of a "woman's act of dressing as a man."[96] To what extent do the critical terms *lesbian* and *homoerotic* implicitly assert the womanness of persons who may not have understood themselves as such?[97] To what degree does a *lesbian* or *sapphic* historiographic framework close down engagement with how people in the past *transed* gender? Manion defines transing by drawing on Susan Stryker's earlier definition of transgender as "people who move away from the gender they were assigned at birth," which Manion suggests offers a way of analyzing historical persons, processes, and practices "without claiming to understand what it meant to that person or asserting any kind of fixed identity on them."[98] Thinking back to the discussion of Judith Butler in Chapter 1, how can we trace multifaceted genealogies of gender construction without implicitly presuming the coherence and stability of the category *woman*?

Jack Halberstam offers *female masculinity* as a way of complicating ideas of shared womanness while also refusing a clear man/woman binary in favor of the idea of variable kinds of masculinity. He suggests that we need "to think in fractal terms about gender geometries," considering how masculinity as expressed by persons labeled female at birth "is actually a multiplicity of masculinities": "because so many women whom one may study under the heading 'female masculinity' identify only partially or problematically[, or not at all,] with the category 'woman,' relations between women and same-sex relations are poor descriptive terms for the physical relations between masculine women and their lovers."[99] Even "female masculinity," though, can fall into the difficulty Manion addresses of conflating "two distinct relationships to gender: first, a gender nonconforming person who was still perceived by others as a woman; second, a person assigned female who lived . . . as a man in their society."[100] This set of conceptual issues is complicated further by the ways the same terms – such as *tribade* and *hermaphrodite* – were used to address a wide range of practices, relations, and erotics that differed from extant maritally-organized modes of patriarchal authority.[101] Moreover, scholars have indicated the importance of also allowing historical persons "the freedom *not* to 'be' transgender" as well as recognizing how someone's gender expressions may be mutable – "ephemeral" or "fleeting" – across their lifetime.[102]

More than simply potentially miscategorizing persons from the past, especially given the historical changeability of and overlap between categories for what we might term *gender* and *sexuality*, what's at issue in framing persons, social patterns, and diachronic dynamics as queer or trans is the intellectual and political projects toward which they are mobilized (such as in the question of the place of gender nonconformity and transness within gay liberation and lesbian feminism, discussed in Chapter 2). Lansing, for example, seeks to address how "sexual representations" are not simply affected by but significantly influence "larger discursive frameworks," particularly the role accounts of eroticism centered on "the sign *woman*" play in shaping and contesting notions of political order, subjectivity, and personhood.[103] This focus on the making and undoing of dominant social forms (arguably the principal aim of *queering*), though, differs from a focus on proliferating possibilities for envisioning livable lives (arguably a central goal of *transing*). That tension can be seen in discussions of Eleanor Rykener, a person assigned male at birth who was arrested for prostitution and sodomy in late-fourteenth-century London. Carolyn Dinshaw describes them as "a man dressed as a woman," even though she almost immediately notes that Rykener "is taught by women how to behave, indeed live, [as] a woman." Dinshaw interprets Rykener as illustrating "queer desires or queer truths about the inessentiality of gender, the inadequacy of binary gender categories of heterosexuality, and the resistance of bodies to their official gender constitution and categorization."[104] By contrast, M. W. Bychowski understands Rykener as "a trans woman sex worker," and rather than seeking to indicate a polymorphous queerness that contests dominant heteronorms, Bychowski aims to challenge "the supposed neutrality of cisgender subject positions and the compulsory cisgender assignment of history and historical figures": "both premodern writers and modern subjects have made medieval transgender identity unutterable by speaking of potential trans subjects almost exclusively under the terms of sodomy and queer identity."[105] We might read this argument as less about locating transgender identity per se in other times than, drawing on Rubright's work discussed earlier, seeking to indicate the *trans capacities* toward which Rykener's life points – possibilities for selfhood, community, and agency that may be subordinated or displaced in the rush to queerness.

A different issue arises if one considers the relation between *molly* and *sodomite* in the eighteenth and nineteenth centuries. Across the long eighteenth century, the term molly was used to describe particular clubs and ale houses, and those that frequented them, in which people assigned male often would dress in women's clothing, take part in behavior deemed feminine, and/or engage in erotic relations with each other. In a somewhat conventional description of molly houses, Tim Hitchcock characterizes them as the site for "the first recognizable homosexual identity," further suggesting they represented "the London homosexual community" and were places where "homosexual men could develop a unique attitude to their society and to themselves."[106] Yet, he also notes the role of women's clothing and accessories among mollies, a dynamic which, drawing on Emma Heaney's work, we might characterize as *transfeminine*.[107] While the molly houses were subject to a series of raids from 1698 to 1810 sponsored by moral reform societies, by the 1820s public concern, in terms of newspaper coverage and arrests, had shifted away from molly houses to acts of sodomy or "attempted sodomy" in public places by otherwise gender-normative men.[108] Conflating the molly with the sodomite (those legally charged for such sexual behavior), and both with *the homosexual*, not only effaces the significant differences between the two in terms of gender expression and class status (the former largely working class, the latter largely middle class and elite) but creates a sense of a cohesive homosexuality always in the process of emerging rather than a multidimensional array of gendered eroticisms and social dynamics that become sites of popular visibility and legal discipline at different points, in ways not really amenable to a unified narrative of historical development.

Beyond the potential enfolding of transness into queerness in ways that can muddle our sense of gender and erotic relations, trans histories face the challenge of determining who can constitute trans subjects and the available ways of recognizing them as such. In this vein, C. Jacob Hale warns of "necrophagic fights over dead bodies" and reminds us that placing someone within a given identity category involves "hav[ing] reliable, relevant information about those people over whose dead bodies we fight: about how they actually lived their lives and about how they actually thought about themselves."[109] Further, as Scott Larson observes, that process is complicated by the ways evidence of a person's eligibility for inclusion in trans history often depends on moments of violation in which the person was "arrested, stripped, prodded, palpated, photographed, interrogated, and cross-examined": "This raises the critical ethical question of how students of gender histories might engage these pasts without restaging these violations," including thinking of trans history as one of "gender in motion and variation" that is not solely about persons who are envisioned as in some way *verifiably* "trans and gender-variant."[110] Moreover, as previously suggested (and as will be developed further in Chapters 4 and 5), non-Euro-American social systems, including those of Indigenous peoples, are enfolded into Western gendered frameworks or viewed as "a utopian, precolonial past," thereby "consigning Native [and other nonwestern] peoples to a past that is seemingly irreconcilable with the present."[111] Either way, the modes of embodiment and self-understandings of people of color can come to serve as a site of identification for contemporary white trans people in ways that reinforce forms of racial and colonial violence.

Inversion and Its Afterlives

In the late nineteenth century and early twentieth century, matters that later would be understood as separately belonging to sexual or gender identity largely were seen as expressive of a version of the same condition – *inversion*. At base, this concept judged modes of eroticism, gender expression, and felt experiences of embodiment in relation to a model in which there were two biological sexes whose properties inherently shaped distinct gendered social identities and in which those two sexes were inherently attracted to each other. Persons who deviated from this model were categorized in varied ways as taking on qualities, sensations, and desires that properly belonged to the other sex – as *inverting* the paradigmatic biological order of things. This diagnostic framework, and the field of medicine called sexology from which it emerged, provided the context out of which the concepts of *homosexuality* and *transsexuality* would arise.[112]

In sexological discourse, characteristics, desires, and actions cast as abnormal increasingly were presented as expressive of a kind of person, the invert, whose selfhood was seen as defined in substantive ways by gender and/or sexual deviance. As Halberstam observes, "Medical experts ... tried to force multiple expressions of sexual and gender deviance into a very narrow range of categories and tried to explain a huge array of physicalities in relation to the binary system of sexual difference that they were absolutely committed to bolstering and preserving."[113] This understanding of nonnormative sexual attraction and gendered embodiment as part and parcel of the same medical condition can be traced as far back as the 1860s in the German scientist Karl Ulrichs's formulation of "desire between men" as having, in his terms, "a woman's soul in a man's body." The term homosexual, actually, first emerges in an 1868 letter to Ulrichs in which the writer sought to distinguish same-sex desire by masculine men from those whose gender expression appeared inverted.[114] Scholars have noted that even as normative gender expression and cross-gendered desire are cast as primary and natural, conceptions of aberrance and perversity in this period historically tend to precede terms for the normal states from which they deviate (such as the term homosexuality being publicly circulated before heterosexuality), making normality somewhat belated even while it is presented as prior and given.[115] With regard to sexological narratives of the cause of sexual and gender aberrance, Benjamin Kahan observes that "congenitally and acquisition stand on equal footing into the 1930s": biological inheritance stands alongside "habit and addiction" as ways of interpreting how such patterns take shape and become rooted in the body.[116] Richard von Krafft-Ebing, another German scientist writing after Ulrichs whose work (primarily through numerous editions of *Psychopathia Sexualis*) would become central to sexological study across Europe and the United States, offered the notion of a primary bisexuality where sexual difference increasingly emerged due to human evolution and the attendant advancement of civilization: "the higher the anthropological development of the race, the stronger the contrasts between man and woman." In this way, as Mel Storr suggests, Krafft-Ebing manages the "unstable distinction between what is 'primitive' and what is 'civilized'" while also producing a "model of 'gradation' or continuum" among kinds of desires, genders, and bodily sensations that "is able to contain the disruptive potential of all this diversity."[117] Serving as a container for everything that did not fit emergent heteronormative and cisnormative ideals, inversion was a flexible, multivalent, and somewhat unstable (set of) medical discourse(s) that presented sex, gender, and desire as intimately biologically intertwined even as it also implicitly illustrated the ways that supposed unity could not really describe the complexities of social reality nor hold steady the distinctions and hierarchies on which that idea of the natural was based.[118]

Although agreeing that medical discourses did not capture the range of ordinary understandings and categories of eroticism, desire, and gendered embodiment used by people outside of sexological circles, scholars disagree on the extent to which medical formulations successfully effaced or replaced other formulations, especially among those who would have been labeled as inverts in medical terms.[119] For example, Heaney observes that "[i]n the late nineteenth century, trans femininity emerged in sexological understanding as an extreme expression of [an] inverted condition," one modeled on the notion of *a woman trapped in a man's body* rather than accepting trans women's understanding of themselves – and their recognition by many other women – as women. For this reason, Heaney distinguishes between "the expert trans feminine" and "the vernacular trans feminine," arguing that sexological discourses remake transfemininity as an *allegory* of inversion that becomes increasingly psychologized through the mid twentieth century.[120] Sexological texts, though, seem to have circulated somewhat freely among middle-class and elite networks of those who would be deemed inverts,[121] and that dissemination helped give rise to forms of what Stephanie Foote has called "vernacular sexology," in which "laypeople contest, define, and revise sexual subjectivity in relation to more official modes of sexology."[122] Prior to the emergence of Freudian psychoanalysis as the privileged public frame for interpreting homoeroticism, a number of men and women inverts, who also described themselves in these terms, drew on sexology to critique popular and official narratives of them as pathological, including through novels like Radclyffe Hall's *The Well of Loneliness*.[123] In addition, the most famous works by sexologists, such as Kraft-Ebing's *Psychopathia Sexualis* and Havelock Ellis's *Studies in the Psychology of Sex*, contained numerous case studies that "allow[ed patients'] voices to be heard without intrusive commentary," thereby "challenging and even overturning certain widely held beliefs about inversion."[124] As Will Fisher has shown, several of the most prominent participants in public discourse around sexology in Great Britain, including John Addington Symonds and Ellis, were also publishing well-known books that helped shape the idea of "the Renaissance." Historical figures associated with homoeroticism – like Michelangelo and Christopher Marlowe – appear as exemplary of artistic expression and the potentials unleashed by the supposed rediscovery of classical learning, which "had the effect of associating homosexuality with civilization itself."[125] These class-, gender-, and race-inflected ways of engaging sexology illustrate how certain social subjects were able to inhabit or redirect discourses of inversion to argue for the legitimacy of some forms of sexual desire and gender expression that differed from an emergent heterosexual standard.

Medical accounts of the kinds of attraction, identity, and orientation that eventually would coalesce in the category of homosexuality (itself still uneven and contradictory, as in Sedgwick's analysis discussed in Chapter 1) also drew on representations present in newspapers and novels. Focusing on the trial of Alice Mitchell, a woman in Memphis who in 1892 killed her lover Freda Ward for planning to marry a man, Lisa Duggan traces the proliferation in the press of the genre of the "lesbian love murder story," illustrating how Mitchell is made into a recognizable type through her depiction as "like a man" and mentally unstable. Duggan also illustrates the profound distinctions between the coverage of Mitchell's crime – and emergent narratives of pathological and gender-inverted (white) desire – and press accounts of the lynching of Black men, famously also occurring in Memphis that same year (leading to Ida B. Wells's career as an anti-lynching advocate) and at their height nationally.[126] That distinction, Duggan argues, shows how the press helped medicalize white erotic and gender deviance while casting what was presented as antisocial Black desire as in need of remediation through extra-legal but state-backed murder. The 1895 trial and conviction of Oscar Wilde in Great Britain for committing "gross indecency" with other men provides another example of such popular influence. As Ed Cohen demonstrates, the legal category of "gross indecency" was largely undefined, having replaced the charge of "sodomy" in British law in 1885, but due to concerns of public propriety, the newspapers would not *"describe or even explicitly refer to the sexual charges made against Wilde."*[127] As a result, they developed ways of implying homoeroticism without directly naming it, portraying Wilde as a sort of person that would engage in such conduct. Among the most prominent of those strategies was highlighting the differences between Wilde and some of his known associates, "younger, (usually unemployed) working-class men," implying "that his 'friendships' with them could not be 'proper' because they were marked by gross disparities in class, age, position, and social and educational background" such that "these relationships could not have taken place within the sphere of 'normal' behavior."[128] In this way, in newspaper accounts the crossing of class difference serves as a sign not simply of a specific set of sexual acts but of aberrant tendencies toward something like *indecency*. Similarly, Natasha Hurley illustrates how novels and short stories over the latter half of the nineteenth century built up stock depictions of character types that then helped give shape to the notion of the homosexual as a distinct kind of person. A figure like that of the "old maid" as it appears across a range of kinds of fiction begins to accrue more expansive and specific characteristics: "Types are perhaps discernible once enough detail has accumulated around them" in ways that can "mark a transition in the narration of sexuality from outer to inner life."[129] We can think of the figure of the old maid as *becoming* a lesbian – as coming to be seen as bearing that identity – through the building up of a social type by connecting a range of attributes and relations to each other such that they are seen, in their frequent combination, as all pointing to a distinct sort of personhood. In these ways, popular forms helped coalesce the kinds of characterizations that would gain medical authority in the figure of *the invert*.

The effort to categorize certain kinds of sexual and gender behavior as expressive of a biological type that differs from normal personhood was part of a broader Euro-American concern with maximizing the civilizational advancement of white people, as against the unhealthful, backward, and brutish tendencies of nonwhites and those whites who were seen as regressively enacting primitive attitudes and orientations.[130] The intellectual and administrative work of sexology takes place against the backdrop of the growing prominence in Great Britain and the United States of notions of *degeneration* – a civilizational backsliding of which gender and sexual deviancy were seen as clear examples as well as being symptoms of a broader crisis. Sexologists built their models of distinct kinds of inverted bodies out of available frameworks for describing the differences among racialized bodies, such as comparative anatomy and extant discussions of the perils of miscegenation, and such work further drew on existing Darwinian notions of human evolution in which "sexual characteristics" – and gendered distinctions between men and women – were seen "as indicators of evolutionary progress toward civilization."[131] Julian Carter illustrates how the rise of the notion of *normality* in the early to mid twentieth century as a way of designating supposedly generic ideas of human health and well-being replaces what previously had been more explicit references to whiteness and "civilization": "normality discourse [as presented in a wide range of popular scientific guides] appeared to be politically neutral in large part because it so often framed its racially loaded dreams for the reproduction of white civilization in the language of romantic and familial love." This "depoliticization of white dominance" meant that "aligning oneself with normal heterosexuality had the effect of performing one's alignment with ideal whiteness" in the absence of any direct mention of race or associated figures of Euro-American cultural evolution.[132]

Notions of sexual deviance emerge within a wider field of racializing ideologies and theories of *eugenics* – the attempt to cleanse the (white) population of diseased and degenerative persons who due to their ingrained nature create social disorder. These campaigns of social hygiene linked together sexuality, gender nonconformity, disability, and race and included dozens of states adopting laws allowing for the sterilization of persons deemed likely to transmit their antisocial tendencies through reproduction.[133] Siobhan Somerville illustrates the ways that major participants in sexological public discourse explicitly expressed concerns about a slide into *primitiveness*. For example, Ellis suggests that "the question of sex – with the racial questions that rest on it – stands before the coming generations as the chief problem for solution," elsewhere indicating, "I shall do what I can to insinuate the eugenic attitude."[134] Discussions by investigators and prison officials of eroticism among people who were incarcerated took part in this developmental narrative, as the supposed "primitivism of prison sex was often cast in classed and racialized terms." Connecting homoeroticism to criminality, seeing both as expressive of ingrained tendencies toward immoral action, not only linked same-sex desire to (racial) degeneration but the focus on sex in prison "led to some of the first efforts in the United States to understand and codify deviant sexual types and practices," which, then, appeared as tied to the deviant and socially disruptive behavior for which prisoners putatively had been convicted.[135] Relationships across forms of racial difference in the United States also were seen as indicative of perverse orientations given the presumption of racial separation in the Jim Crow era (why interact if not for sex?) and the ways cross-racial intimacy already was coded as deviant given the commonness of anti-miscegenation laws across the country.[136]

In grappling with how to locate (white) gender and sexual nonnormativity in relation to notions of civilizational advancement, various discourses of inversion also took up older European narratives of gender and sexual difference among Indigenous peoples in the Americas as part of evidencing patterns of human variation and generating taxonomies of (Euro-American) abnormality. Will Roscoe notes that "accounts of [Indigenous] North American gender diversity were cited in ongoing discourses on gender and sexual difference," helping "g[i]ve rise to the modern conception of homosexuals as a category of persons." He adds, "The construction of the medical model of inversion ... *required* historical and cross-cultural examples" in order to indicate, somewhat paradoxically, that the psychological and behavioral patterns labeled as inversion were neither historical nor cultural but facets of human biological variation, albeit ones that were more notable and visible among Euro-Americans due to their supposed advancement as illustrated by the predominance among them of middle-class marital and gender norms.[137] Reciprocally, those classified as inverts drew on narratives of Native peoples in order to validate their existence and generate a sense of themselves as having a history (as discussed in Chapters 1 and 2). This "foundling imagination," in Christopher Nealon's terms, helps explain the longstanding reference to belonging to "the tribe" as a way of describing gay and lesbian identity.[138] Indigenous forms of social life and personhood are appropriated as a resource for both medical discourses of inversion and as a strategy for self-definition by Euro-Americans categorized as aberrant within such discourses, without engaging with the ongoing presence of Native peoples or the colonial forces to which they continued to be subject (including such appropriations of them for Euro-American ends).

If discourses of inversion tended to conflate gender expression and (homo)sexual desire, the emergence of transsexuality as a distinct category in the mid twentieth century might be seen as resolving this confusion and as ceasing to position trans experience as evidence of degeneration or a mode of aberrance within whiteness. However, scholars have suggested that not only can notions of medicalized diagnosis be seen as an extension of ideologies of inversion but ideas about the need for surgical and hormonal intervention may arise from and remain immersed in racialized notions of bodily and social order. Transsexuality as a term first was coined in 1949 by an English sexologist named David O. Cauldwell to refer to the desire for surgical intervention to alter one's physical sex by a person who otherwise is considered biologically "normal" (not intersexed).[139] He described transsexuals as "individuals who are physically of one sex and apparently psychologically of the other sex," recommending "psychological rather than physical adjustment."[140] Gender-affirming surgeries of various kinds had been regularly conducted in Europe (particularly in Denmark and Germany) starting in the 1910s, receiving somewhat sensational newspaper coverage in the United States.[141] Up through the mid-twentieth century, the desire to change sex, as distinct from correcting what were seen as ambiguous or mixed-sexed physical characteristics (or presumed physical defects that created aberrant hormonal profiles), largely was understood in Euro-American terms as a perverse or antisocial psychological state in need of mental treatment. Deviations from normative gender and hetero-desire were all seen as due to a similar set of fundamentally psychological causes but also expressive of a psychologically abnormal relation to one's *real* sexed body. As Heaney argues, the experiences of transfeminine people were derealized and remade as a figure for a range of perverse genders and sexualities, "install[ing...] a social type *as* metaphor" such that "female identification" appeared as "a symptom of homosexuality and not an identity or desire in itself."[142] Trans experiences and embodiments from this perspective are imagined rather than lived, "suggesting that trans women and men were not already women and men (as their lives frequently testified) but that they somehow *aspired* to become women and men" – a notion "that trans people *need* medical knowledge" in order to "name or understand" themselves.[143] The emergence of transfemininities and transmasculinities as a psychological *problem* that needs to be remedied through medical intervention, then, depends on a denial of trans people's articulations of their own existing experience of gender (in which gender-affirming care would not *make* them a given gender but would complement an already present sense of self and embodiment). As Heaney suggests, this medicalizing narrative also emphasizes a class-inflected vision that does the following: focuses on the "needs of bourgeois patients who didn't have easy access to the working-class queer milieu in which trans women lived without the necessity of medical diagnosis"; conceptually isolates trans people from the communities in which they lived in which their genders were recognized; and effaces the popular awareness of such persons and communities.[144]

Furthermore, ideas about the mutability of the body with regard to "sex" (*changing* it or *correcting* it for intersexed people, particularly children), as well as the development of medical knowledge and procedures to do so, arise in the context of the broader cultural conversations about degeneration, evolution, civilization, and eugenics discussed above. As Kadji Amin suggests, "access to the medical technologies of transition is always also access to the medical management of populations and rationalization of health and productivity."[145] In the late nineteenth century through the mid-twentieth century, the scientific question of how bodies acquire physical sexed characteristics was never separate from explaining how, and ensuring that, (white) persons come to live appropriately gender-differentiated and heteronormative social lives.[146] Medical intervention to understand and achieve sexual difference, via endocrinology and then increasingly more reconstructive kinds of surgery, depended on the idea of two determinate sexes as physical types; yet, as Jules Gill-Peterson shows, scientists were well aware that not all bodies fit this dimorphic model, leading to investigation of those supposed anomalies in order to trace the process of sexual development in terms of both human evolution (envisioned as tending toward more civilized forms of sex/gender distinction) and forms of individual maturation. Intersexed children served as key in connecting these various intellectual concerns, providing a set of experimental subjects on which to test theories and procedures. As Gill-Peterson observes, "medicine promised to capitalize on their plasticity to produce a binary," with doctors and scientists "promulgating a developmental framework that made gender identity the endpoint of a teleology of growth out of plasticity" – a teleology that was intertwined with racialized notions of civilizational progress.[147]

The concept of *gender* itself came out of the effort to preserve that evolutionary trajectory. Coined in the 1950s by John Money, one of the founders of the Johns Hopkins Gender Identity Clinic, the idea of gender did not so much displace discussion of physical sexual difference as seek "to *save* the sex binary from imminent collapse by offering a new developmental justification for coercive and normalizing medical intervention into intersex children's bodies."[148] The concepts of "gender role" and then "gender identity" created by Money and his colleagues less aimed to open possibilities for a range of kinds of socially acceptable experiences of embodiment and senses of self than sought to privilege a heteronormative and cisnormative vision of sexed selfhood in line with racialized and classed ideals of proper personhood, understood, though, as simply the healthy endpoint of natural development (even if such development required medical intervention and ongoing monitoring by doctors).[149] Through the 1960s, trans people routinely were refused gender-affirming care, since they were seen as having psychological problems (as some version of invert) rather than as having a physical condition in need of correction (as with intersexed children). This dynamic is why many people who desired gender-affirming surgery or who were able to secure it, such as Christine Jorgensen (perhaps the most famous of trans celebrities, who was featured in US national news starting in the early 1950s), presented themselves as having intersexed conditions. Even after access to gender-affirming healthcare came to be seen as medically legitimate, although still cast as requiring psychological diagnosis and treatment, trans patients needed to disavow any sexual desire for persons of the sex to which they were transitioning, thereby presenting transition as inherently shaped around the gendered norms of straightness.[150] Moreover, Black trans people routinely were diagnosed as schizophrenic and institutionalized or were seen as an issue for the criminal punishment system.[151] Thus, even as the history of transsexuality includes increased access to gender-affirming modes of care for some, it also illustrates how such medical interventions and the diagnostic apparatus around them were shaped by the pathologizing legacies of discourses of inversion, including the ways related notions of development and healthful personhood are implicitly oriented around the norms of middle-class whiteness. As Halberstam notes, rhetorics of solving "wrong embodiment" by "moving to the right body ... may as easily depend on whiteness or class privilege as it does on being regendered."[152]

Queer and Trans Temporalities

More than addressing ideas, persons, and dynamics *in* history, considering how we access and narrate desires and embodiments from the past, scholars have taken up the question of what it means to think about time – and our experiences of being-in-time – in queer and trans ways. In this vein, they've developed ideas about what might be called *cis time* and *straight time*. For the former, one might include assumptions about the consistency of selfhood, drawing on "the temporal dislocations necessary for self-narrativizing" across processes of transition to point to the ways identity may shift and change across a lifetime.[153] Conversely, as Jacob Lau suggests, we might focus on how institutions seek to preserve an enduring sense of unity and coherence in forms of identity and selfhood: "I think about the ways state documents such as birth certificates, social security cards, travel visas, and death certificates provide a linear narrative of a gendered, racialized, and classed life."[154] The everyday of trans experience, then, can open into alternative ways of understanding dynamics of being and becoming that differ from conventional accounts of personal and historical development. In a similar vein, queerness can unsettle the "middle-class logic of reproductive temporality"; it is disjunct from "socially shared, normative periodicities" and potentially "uninvested in lineage as a temporal paradigm."[155] As José Muñoz observes, "Straight time tells us that there is no future" except "that of reproductive majoritarian heterosexuality," which he also describes as "normative white reproductive futurity."[156] Queer and trans approaches to time, then, can contest presumptions about maturation, inheritance, and legacy at multiple scales – personal, collective, and national. What shape is a life supposed to take? What institutionalized cisnormative and heteronormative expectations guide how individual development is supposed to unfold? How do those ideologies shape the relations between generations? In what ways do they affect how we conceptualize the relations among the past, present, and future? Elizabeth Freeman's notion of *chrononormativity* speaks to these issues – how "[m]anipulations of time convert historically specific regimes of asymmetrical power into seemingly ordinary bodily tempos and regimes, which in turn organize the value and meaning of time."[157] Historically contingent social structures and dynamics are cast as if they were expressions of the natural/given dynamics of the body, and thus an inherent part of the unfolding of time itself, rather than specific ways of constructing, regulating, and maintaining available social forms and kinds of personhood.

From this perspective, the present is neither identical to itself nor is the past necessarily cordoned off from the present, instead multidimensionally inhabiting it. While *now* may seem self-evident, we can see it as permeated by a range of times in at least two senses. First, as Dinshaw observes, we might attend to "forms of desirous, embodied being that are out of sync with the ordinarily linear measurements of everyday life," opening "ordinary time frames" to "the multiplicities within."[158] Second, as discussed in the first section, narratives of progress and development tend to cast practices that do not fit dominant patterns as holdovers from a properly superseded past, such as the imperial representation of non-Euro-American peoples as backward (which McClintock has described as a vision of "anachronistic space") or of forms of desire that don't fit a strict hetero/homo binary as premodern.[159] Carla Freccero characterizes the present as "haunted" – "the way the past or the future presses upon us with a kind of insistence or demand" – suggesting that the apparent solidity of *now* remains perforated by the presence of feelings, memories, and identifications with other times.[160] The past and present, then, can be considered linked, but less in the linear sense of inheritance, succession, decline, or progress than in achronological connections across time.[161] Freeman has theorized such relations in terms of what she calls *temporal drag*. While most literally referring to dressing in the clothing of another era, it more broadly encompasses the felt presence of the past in the present, the "cultural debris" from "incomplete, partial, or otherwise failed transformations of the social field"; forms of generational difference and seemingly outmoded kinds of "collective political fantasy"; and encounters with places, persons, and objects that conjure past pleasures (what Freeman terms *erotohistoriography*).[162] The sense of an intimate proximity between then and now may be even more pressing with respect to trans identifications. As noted earlier, trans subjectivities and embodiments consistently get cast as unprecedented and new in ways that collude with their depiction as unnatural, monstrous, and dangerous. In this way, connecting trans pasts and presents "might save lives," "tell[ing] the story of trans lives" in earlier historical moments with the aim of "building a future for trans lives now."[163] Reciprocally, such narration of the past for the trans present can offer social and political frameworks for trans youth that exceed the horizon of the nuclear families that Halberstam contends increasingly provide the somewhat individualizing and privatizing context for initial gender affirmation.[164]

Such ideas of contact between the past and the present, or sorts of continuity that are not the same as the causal unfolding of time (the passing away of a moment as it shapes the next), put pressure on the notion of the past as an alien space: "Why has it come to pass that we apprehend the past in the mode of difference? How has 'history' come to equal 'alterity'?"[165] As Valerie Rohy notes, "Historical alterity is, after all, a recent invention," an idea not necessarily consistent with notions of time at play in the past. This way of viewing the relation between the present and the past, Freccero argues, can replay in a different mode assumptions from "cultural anthropology," but instead of seeing peoples in other places as living in anachronistic ways, "temporality is spatialized as cultural difference," with the past envisioned, the saying goes, as another country.[166]

In this vein, considering the ways racialized groups get cast as of the past, scholars have addressed how attending to that dynamic offers ways of rethinking the present and future. In particular, Indigenous peoples consistently are envisioned as holdovers from a bygone era, in the process of disappearing. As Lou Cornum notes, "In the colonial imaginary, indigenous life is not only separate from the present but also out of place in the future, a time defined by the progress of distinctively western technology," but by contrast, "indigenous futurism is centered on bringing traditions to distant, future locations rather than abandoning them as relics."[167] Moreover, while mainstream discourses tend to envision a coming apocalypse, Indigenous peoples "have already survived the apocalypse – this, right here, is a dystopian present."[168] Thus, rather than presenting non-Indigenous peoples as the inheritors of Indigenous knowledges (including with regard to sexuality and gender diversity),[169] Indigenous peoples themselves connect the past to the future, both indicating the apocalyptic violence of the past half-millennium and carrying forward lived formations of peoplehood. Moreover, those continuities across time cannot simply be written off as heteronormative inheritance. Considering the problems of equating "reproduction" per se with "heter-ofuturity," Alexis Lothian observes that the labor of parenting must be performed by someone and that "biological and social reproduction" cannot be seen as merely "a byproduct of patriarchy": "there are many reproductive futures, often in conflict and contradiction with one another" – including the ways racializing and eugenic accounts of particular populations (such as Black and Native people) present them as unworthy of reproducing due to the drag they supposedly produce on a future envisioned in dominant Euro-American terms.[170]

From the perspective of such a dominant image of the future, other kinds of futures may seem "like no future at all." For this reason, to the extent that queerness represents a challenge to the ongoing production of white heteronormativity, it can serve "as an ally in building the antifragility of [Black] freedom dreams." If indigeneity gets associated with a barbaric past, blackness often is presented as an anarchic antisocial disruption, not the basis for a livable future. However, as Kara Keeling argues, that "cut of Black existence," if viewed from a queer angle, "might cleave an opening in the present order of meaning and being through which another structure, another world, perhaps might be" seen and made.[171] In this vein, Lau observes that "progress narratives" are "dependent on those [who are deemed] temporally abject," particularly people of color: "cis time functions by trans (particularly of color) bodies 'doing time,'" including within "the medical and prison industrial complexes."[172] As Muñoz suggests, "Theories of queer temporality that fail to factor in the relational relevance of race or class merely reproduce a crypto-universal white gay subject that is weirdly atemporal." Instead of offering an alternative vision of the future that affirms its continuity with non-dominant pasts or dreams of a freedom to come, though, Muñoz insists on the value of the ephemeral. For him, queerness represents possibilities that are "not yet here," and forms of what he describes as "utopian" potential appear in fleeting moments that provide "an anticipatory illumination of a queer world, a sign of an actually existing queer reality, a kernel of possibility within a stultifyingly heterosexual present."[173] In these ways, queering and transing can enable us to consider how race shapes normative ideas of reproduction, inheritance, and generationality while also engaging pasts and futures that do not fit the story of Euro-American progress, especially given its reliance on ongoing histories of settler colonialism and racial capitalism.

Conclusion

Turning to the past is less about knowing how we got here – how the present emerges out of a line of development – than considering other possibilities for being in the world. Those possibilities may not necessarily be desirable, but their difference from how things are now challenges the sense of the inevitability of what currently is. Moreover, queer and trans engagements with history prompt questions about how well we know what supposedly is. Historical study does not just reveal something about *then* but can enable us to look more carefully at the ways prominent (or perhaps dominant) ideas about and categories for gender, sexuality, eroticism, and embodiment do not capture the variability, layeredness, and complexity of *now*. The sense of a mutable relation between the past, present, and future – which is neither self-evidently one of inheritance nor transcendence of what came before, but, instead, far more slippery relations of desire, longing, haunting, multiplicity, ephemerality, utopian dreaming, and drags of all kinds across time – is the stuff of queer and trans temporalities. As against notions of *straight time* and *cis time*, queer and trans studies have sought to address kinds of feeling and relation that do not fit a sense of linear unfolding, especially as shaped around normative conceptions of maturation, milestones, marital reproductivity, and gendered self-sameness.

Not only can one identify with past figures and movements in ways that can facilitate envisioning more livable lives in the present, queer and trans historical work also traces largely acknowledged dimensions of contemporary phenomena, such as the ways that notions of normality, health, perversion, and immorality are braided around longstanding racial and imperial dynamics and vice versa. We can see this dynamic through examining the ways that ideas about sexuality and gender emerge within and help give shape to imperial expansion and occupation, enslavement, and the projects of racialization that accompany both. We can see how the social forms and experiences of embodiment among various peoples and populations get translated within colonial ideologies, giving rise to racialized narratives of backwardness and deviancy while also providing the basis for developing universalizing narratives of proper human desire, corporeality, homemaking, and reproduction (as well as providing examples of other cultural frameworks that problematically are appropriated by Euro-American gender and sexual minorities as evidence of the transhistorical existence of their own identities). Historical work in queer and trans studies further considers the ways attention to enslavement and its aftermaths highlights how the *ungendering* of Black flesh provides a crucial background for conceptions of queerness and gender mutability and how the regulation of the sexuality and gender of people of color has been crucial to the organization of space, both in terms of policing US national borders and managing various groups' relation to place within "domestic" space. Additionally, the discourse of inversion, out of which dominant frameworks for naming sexuality and gender have developed, was enmeshed in evolutionary conceptions of degeneration and reproductive fitness that themselves depended on a series of racializing and imperial assumptions about human development and progress.

Queer and trans historiography also raise the question of the stakes of understanding persons and movements in the past as *queer* or *trans*. Not only do *queering* and *transing* tend to point in different directions, the one emphasizing an undermining of straightness (or assumptions about straightness) and the other the presence of a range of possibilities for gendered embodiment in a given period, but many of the same historical figures may be read within either framework, giving rise to debates about what aspects of their lives are highlighted or erased in the process and what such (in)visibility means to the ways the past gets narrated in and for the present. Moreover, many of the terms from earlier periods used to address what were taken to be nonnormative desires, bodies, and social relations (such as sodomy, tribade, and hermaphrodite) do not nestle easily into a distinction between sexuality and gender, were themselves also complexly cross-hatched with various other kinds of identities, and were measured against notions of *the natural* quite different from that concept's current connotations. Likewise, possibilities for forms of erotic and embodied experience in the past do not necessarily fit within current expectations about how to define sexuality and gender, suggesting the presence of practices and forms of agency that do not necessarily map well onto forms of current queer and trans identity.

Chapter 4

Queer/Trans of Color and Indigenous Critique

In *Aberrations in Black*, Roderick Ferguson offers what has been seen as the earliest articulation of *queer of color critique*. He suggests that "[q]ueer of color analysis extends women of color feminism by investigating how intersecting racial, gender, and sexual practices antagonize and/or conspire with the normative investments of nation-states and capital."[1] As discussed in previous chapters, by virtue of their nonwhiteness, people of color historically and currently are cast as aberrant in their sexualities, genders, and family and household formations. Movements for inclusion and rights – to be seen as deserving of recognition as full legal persons and social subjects – thus involve seeking to distance those who are *respectable* from persons who may more obviously appear as examples of sexual and gender perversity within dominant (white) norms.[2] Yet, as queer of color critique illustrates, that bid for belonging tends to overlook how people of color may be "heterosexual but never heteronormative," how they may be defined as *normal* in terms of categories of sexual and gender identity (not homosexual, not trans) but will still be marked as deviant as well as being policed and disciplined in their racialization as nonwhite.[3] As Ferguson and Grace Kyungwon Hong suggest, drawing on the work of Cherríe Moraga, queer of color scholarship's "response to this uneven devaluation of racialized life is decidedly not the opposite reaction of *valuing* life, of seeking comfort in the pockets of safety where certain forms of racialized life escape such devaluation."[4] Queer and trans of color analysis highlights how seeking the protections of the state and civil society can involve investing in racialized ideals in ways that perpetuate white norms of gender and sexuality.

Certain kinds of queers who reaffirm the supposed goodness and justice of the nation-state are seen as properly rights-bearing subjects even as the state extends and intensifies racializing forms of discrimination and domination. As Chandan Reddy argues, "In our current moment, it seems that every movement to validate a claim of social freedom produces a disparate and adversarial claim by the state elsewhere against what it determines to be irrational cultures and practices," a dynamic he characterizes as "freedom with violence," rather than freedom *from* violence.⁵ Queer and trans of color critique, then, traces how gender and sexuality operate as part of historical and ongoing projects of racialization while also refusing to see inclusion into existing political and economic systems as a way of remediating ongoing forms of state-enabled violence. As Jian Neo Chen observes, most of the early social service and advocacy organizations ostensibly focused on transgender needs "were founded and accessed by white transgender people," and they tended to privilege the "narratives of identity and bodily *transition ... in alignment with the white gender binary under the management of psychomedical professionals.*"⁶ The resistance to such inclusion also involves a wariness toward explicitly or implicitly white-centered intellectual frameworks in queer and trans studies. Hong and Ferguson explain that they "narrate queer of color critique as emerging from women of color feminism rather than deriving from a white Euro-American gay, lesbian, and queer theory tradition."⁷ The editors of "We Got Issues: Toward a Black/Trans* Studies" note that "the institutionalization of transgender studies as a discipline functions as a scene of subjection for blackness," treating the "Black subject as a springboard to move toward other things, presumably white things" while also "configur[ing] the trans-of-color subject as the always belated arrival to the (white) archive."⁸

Developed primarily with reference to the United States, queer and trans of color scholarly work cuts across conventional racial distinctions, understanding those very distinctions as a function of the ideological and institutional dynamics that are the object of analysis and critique. In this chapter, though, I've opted to discuss Indigenous, Black, Latinx, and Asian American studies separately. The reason is not because these areas of study are utterly discrepant or mutually exclusive (in terms of the issues at play in them, the intellectual frameworks they employ, and persons belonging to more than one of these groups), but, instead, because the processes of racialization and attendant histories of domination that created these distinctions have led to differences in experiences of oppression, collective identity, and traditions of thought and organizing. While not wanting to overemphasize or reify those differences, I also do not want to ignore them and the ways those differences have affected knowledge-production in queer and trans studies.

Native American and Indigenous Studies

Work in Native American and Indigenous studies raises an additional set of conceptual and political concerns often not addressed in – and at times at odds with – other kinds of queer and trans of color critique. Native people are racialized as *Indians* in ways that resonate with the issues at play for various racialized populations in the United States, including the roles played by gender, sexuality, and notions of deviance in shaping how such racialization works. However, Native people are also part of Indigenous peoples, self-governing political entities whose relation to the lands and waters that comprise the United States precedes the existence of the (settler-)state and whose presence as peoples continually challenges the legitimacy of the existence of the United States in ways that must be colonially disavowed, managed, and assaulted. Indigenous peoples precede the existence of the states that claim jurisdiction over them and their territories. *Settler-states* like the United States and Canada are created through the seizure of Native lands and the assertion of a right to exert authority over them, a colonial process of invasion, theft, imposition, and expropriation through which the supposedly *domestic* space of the nation-state is created and maintained. Joanne Barker characterizes Indigenous peoples' authority, which precedes and exceeds claims by the colonizing state, as "*the polity of the Indigenous* – the unique governance, territory, and culture of Indigenous peoples in unique and related systems of (non)human relationships and responsibilities to one another."[9] If *sovereignty* is often seen as an expression of state oppressions in queer and trans studies, for Native peoples it often operates as a way of acknowledging their rightful governance over themselves and their territories, serving as a way of contesting state-legitimized modes of dispossession even as Euro-American political forms do not capture many Indigenous ways of understanding networks of relation, respect, and accountability. Rather than being *excluded* from belonging in the nation-state, Native people(s) are subjected to colonial violence through their forced *inclusion* in it, as racialized domestic subjects – as *Indians*. Queer and trans work in Native American and Indigenous studies traces the roles played by heteronormativity and cisnormativity in settler colonialism while also addressing Indigenous eroticisms, social roles, and modes of embodiment that do not fit Euro-American models.

While many Indigenous peoples on lands claimed by the United States and Canada take part in legal and political relations with the national government, the terms of such state recognition largely hinge on heteropatriarchal assumptions that reinforce the legitimacy of settler frameworks and work to replace Indigenous modes of self-understanding and forms of social organization.[10] As Jennifer Denetdale observes, colonial policy "has reconfigured tribal nations as heterosexual patriarchies": "modern settler nations such as the United States value only those aspects of Indigenous knowledge, culture, and practice that do not threaten the structure of heteronormative patriarchy."[11] That process historically has involved treating Native modes of social organization and governance as primitive and perverse in their supposed failure to emulate Euro-American models of home, family, property, and gendered personhood. That putative deficiency has helped legitimize massive and sustained interventions by the state into all aspects of Indigenous life, casting Native peoples as uncivilized and unable to govern themselves and, thus, validating the expropriation of their lands and their forced assimilation. Leanne Betasamosake Simpson suggests that "heteropatriarchy isn't just about exclusion of certain Indigenous bodies" – of persons deemed deviant in Euro-American terms due to their desires or ways they embody their gender – but "is about the destruction of the intimate relationships that make up our nations."[12] As Marie Laing suggests, "to destroy our ways of doing gender is to destroy our ways of being together – in effect, to destroy our nations," and Sarah Hunt observes, "The near-total erasure of two-spirit and trans people that was accomplished through the imposition of the gender binary is integrally related with the hierarchy that continues to perpetuate the violent marginalization of Indigenous girls and women."[13] Among other ways, that destruction occurs through transforming Indigenous modes of social reproduction by insisting that they need to look like the nuclear family, treating political forms based on networks of genealogical connection – like clans – as not really governance (because they don't resemble the supposedly impersonal bureaucracies of state institutions), supporting gendered modes of production and authority that subordinate women, and targeting what appear to Euro-Americans as expressions of sexual and gender nonnormativity for criminalization and state-sanctioned assault (a process that Deborah Miranda has described as "gendercide").[14] In this way, heteropatriarchy "is a *foundational dispossession force* because it is a direct attack on Indigenous bodies as political orders," the ways Indigenous "bodies and ... constructions of gender, sexuality, and intimate relationships" serve as the building blocks for "Indigenous orders of government," which threaten the asserted sovereignty of the state over Native people and lands.[15] We can see this work as building on the arguments offered by earlier queer Native feminists, such as Beth Brant and Paula Gunn Allen (discussed in Chapter 2). Kim TallBear observes, "We must collectively oppose a system of compulsory settler sexuality and family that continues building a nation upon Indigenous genocide and that marks Indigenous and other marginalized relations as deviant."[16] In contrast, scholars have emphasized the importance of Indigenous systems of kinship. Joseph Pierce has characterized such dynamics as creating *kinstillations* that speak to "how to negotiate our beings-with and beings-in-relation as a form of ongoing enactments of Indigenous sovereignty, mutuality, and care."[17]

Native peoples have at times themselves adopted forms of hetero- and cisnormativity within their own governing institutions as part of efforts to be seen as civilized. With respect to the US effort to eliminate polygamy among the Navajos, Denetdale notes, "The uprising at Beautiful Mountain provides an example of how federal Indian policies are intended to eliminate the Diné as Diné by transforming the Navajo nation into a heterosexual patriarchy."[18] The forceful intervention into Diné social forms gets narrated in both US and official Navajo history, though, as "a movement from 'traditional' to 'modern'" (which includes the Navajo Tribal Council in 1940 passing a resolution "which defined marriage as between one man and one woman").[19] Denetdale argues that efforts to "minimize the level of violence and coercion that was used to transform Navajos into American citizens," such as in the criminalization of Diné marital and familial forms, can also entail Diné people "internal[izing] colonial values" (like monogamous couplehood) as well as institutionalizing them as part of tribal law and policy.[20] Addressing nineteenth-century Hawai'i (prior to US annexation in 1898), J. Kehaulani Kauanui illustrates how the "major reorganization of social forms as a strategy to fight Western racism through independent nationhood" depended on the performance of civilizedness. The effort to get European countries and the United States to see Hawai'i as "a competent modern nation of people capable of self-governance rested on the rejection, repression, and restraint of sexual practices deemed savage within a new Christian order that cannot be separated from colonial forces."[21] These measures included instituting Euro-American *marriage* (monogamous, lifelong, hetero-romantic couplehood) as the legal norm as opposed to the much more fluid and expansive sets of sexual and genealogical relations that had shaped kinship networks, connection to lands, and political authority. These changes included requiring that married women take their husband's name, mandating that inheritance be based on *legitimacy* (descent from a proper marriage), and pathologizing same-sex intimate connections (known as *aikāne*).[22] In this way, "the linkages between sexuality and sovereignty cannot be overstated": "Hawaiian chiefs enacted forms of colonial biopolitics in order to secure sovereign recognition" by Euro-American states.[23]

Such colonial efforts to interpellate Indigenous peoples within Euro-American norms and Indigenous efforts to seek such recognition efface the sexual and gender diversity and expansiveness at play in Indigenous languages, histories, philosophies, cultural expressions, and practices. With respect to Native peoples in what currently is southern California, Deborah

Miranda has tracked the ways the precontact social role of *'aqi* (in Chumash), characterized by Spanish soldiers as "Indian men ... observed in the dress, clothing, and character of women" and ritually responsible for caretaking the deceased, has survived in the archive under the Spanish term *joya*. In use from early in the Spanish conquest of the region, by the mid-1770s this term registers the continuing presence of such persons in Indigenous societies throughout the period of missionization into the 1830s, when baptisms of people listed as *joyas* were still being recorded.[24] Miranda also suggests how information on such persons, deemed *hermaphrodites* and *sodomites* in the accounts of soldiers and priests (see the discussion of these terms in Chapter 3), came to appear in the accounts of early-twentieth-century anthropologists, including speculating that one of J. P. Harrington's informants – Kitsepawit Fernando Librado – may themself have belonged to this category.[25] Similarly, Kai Pyle explores the *trans*temporal kinship* between contemporary queer and trans Native people and nineteenth-century Ojibwe and Plains Cree persons who were seen as gender nonnormative by Euro-American traders, missionaries, and officials in the Great Lakes region.[26] Pyle addresses the presence of terms that may have been used to indicate such persons, including *ayakwao/ayekkwe*, but they also indicate that "the Cree language does not use gendered pronouns," suggesting greater potential for acknowledging gender variability.[27] The kinds of archival and lexical work in which Miranda and Pyle are engaged open up not only possibilities for registering the diversity of Indigenous genders historically but of positioning that historical evidence as a vital part of projects of resurgence and self-determination in the present.

In addition to documenting terms and roles on which contemporary Indigenous people might and do draw, work in queer and trans Indigenous studies attends to the broader potentials in Indigenous philosophies for thinking beyond Euro-American conceptions of identity, intimacy, and embodiment. Writing about peoples in what is currently the US Southeast, Daniel Heath Justice suggests that they possess an affirmative sense of *anomaly* that can speak to forms of queer indigeneity. Justice turns to shared regional conceptions – articulations "of difference drawn from Mississippian cosmology and iconography." Rather than designating a particular kind of sexual/gender identity or practice, anomaly refers to "beings *and states of being*" that belong to or cross among otherwise distinct social categories.[28] The anomalous and the normal are less antagonistic, with the former disruptively displacing the latter and therefore needing to be policed, than operate in productive and ultimately balanced tension that defines them both. As opposed to ideas of *perversity* or *aberrance*, anomaly suggests the importance of difference, a way of thinking that exceeds queerness and transness but that can provide Indigenous conceptual resources for valuing them. In a different vein, Jamaica Heolimeleikalani Osorio shows how Kānaka Maoli (Native Hawaiian) stories connect all manner of interpersonal intimacies, desires, and sensory experiences to deep and ongoing relations to their lands and waters. Drawing on the *mo'olelo* (story/chant) of Hi'iakaikapoliopele (a powerful ancestral figure in the movement to the lands of Hawai'i), Osorio illustrates how *aloha 'āina* (love for and responsibility to the land) comprises a "diverse and vibrant collection of multibodied relationships between Kānaka Maoli, our ancestors, peers, descendants, and the environment," "an internal love for place and community so strong that it cannot be overcome." That network of love includes erotic relationships and pleasure, including how the mo'olelo Osorio interprets features a "spectrum of sexualities" and forms of desire. Those connections, though, "come from the 'āina [land]; it is our pilina [bonds/connections] to it that we share between us, that makes pleasure possible": "Being intimate and pili with our *'āina* teaches us how to be intimate and *pili* to each other."[29] Across a range of Indigenous modes of self-expression, as Lisa Tatonetti demonstrates, we can see forms of "gender expansiveness" and "an erotics of responsibility."[30] She defines "the Indigenous erotic" as "a topography of desire that includes a felt relationship between bodies and landscape," and she shows how various Native authors, themselves queer and not (such as Louise Erdrich), present nonnormative expressions of gender and desire "as part of the everyday fabric of Native communities," including representations of "non-cis genders."[31]

The term *Two-Spirit* has gained prominence as a way of signifying Indigenous genders and sexualities in ways that distinguish them both from histories of sexology (see Chapter 3) and identity categories that tend de facto to center white experiences – like *gay* and *transgender*. The term Two-Spirit emerged from the 1990 meeting of the Third International Gathering of American Indian and First Nations Gays and Lesbians held in Winnipeg, and it was coined by a Cree community member and scholar named Myra Laramee.[32] In various usages, it can indicate historical persons whose identities among their peoples do not map onto Euro-American concepts of gender and sexuality, contemporary persons in those Indigenous roles/statuses, and Native persons who otherwise (and sometimes simultaneously) might be seen or see themselves as LGBTQ but who want to foreground their indigeneity. In this way, "the term cannot be drawn along an analytical distinction between 'traditional' and 'nontraditional,'" and the concept of Two-Spirit "may be an especially fruitful way to challenge assertions of a radical disconnect between the Indigenous past and present without resorting to overly romanticized or atemporal ideas about the past."³³ Pyle observes that the term Two-Spirit speaks to the "need to find ways to talk about LGBTQ Indigenous life among Indigenous people in a way that makes cultural sense to other community members."³⁴ The concept's multiplicity and complexity, which is its strength, also can produce a desire for clarification that can be oppressive. In her study of self-definition among queer, trans, and Two-Spirit youth in Toronto, Laing indicates that "many of them noted that they are frequently coerced into educating people ... on what two-spirit does and does not mean," a pedagogical demand that can leave them without, in one participant's terms, "opportunities to philosophize" that (range of) meaning(s) for themselves. Laing characterizes the concept and its community of usage as "a container that can hold multiple truths," one that "holistically links Indigeneity with the ways in which people experience their gender, their roles in community, and their sexuality."³⁵ Also, while recognizing the frequent association of Two-Spirit with specific spiritual dynamics or roles in ceremony, Pyle warns of how presuming that connection can impose "exclusionary" notions of "traditionalism" that limit recognition for a variety of kinds of contemporary Indigenous gendered being, and Hunt cautions, "in recounting pre-colonial gender roles, it is important to avoid generalized statements that idealize pre-contact Indigenous societies as uniformly balanced, accepting, and appreciative of non-gender-conforming individuals."³⁶

As acknowledgment of Indigenous queer, trans, and Two-Spirt presence has grown in academic and activist contexts, scholars have been attentive to a potential disconnect between apparent acceptance of such presence and continuing indifference to the lives and well-being of queer, trans, and Two-Spirit people. While noting the uptick in the phrase "women and 2spirits" in discussions of "gendered violence and heteropatriarchy in indigenous communities," Pyle observes that this repetition tends to efface rather than engage the multidimensional experiences of Two-Spirit people, while also leaving intact ongoing forms of denigration. Moreover, prominent ideas about Indigenous activism – conceived of as "large anti-state agitation" – tend not to address the strategies of mutual care adopted within queer, trans, and Two-Spirit communities.³⁷ With regard to the role of *sovereignty* and modes of Indigenous collectivity within Native American and Indigenous Studies, Billy-Ray Belcourt has suggested that the notions of Native subjectivity in the field (what he terms "Native Studies' Native") appear as given while also not engaging forms of Indigenous queer, trans, and Two-Spirit everyday feeling and experience.³⁸ Those ordinary modes of living – and the pleasures, vulnerabilities, and quotidian interdependencies that shape them – are, in Belcourt's terms, *stomped out* by "the genre and form of politics speak"; those kinds of emotions and sensations, including forms of negative feeling, seem to have no place in discourses of clear and self-assured collective political identity, which "cherry-picks feelings that will get held up as national sentiments."[39] Discussing writings by Native lesbians, Janice Gould observes, "I am aware that in speaking about a lesbian American Indian erotics, and even more in speaking about lesbian love, I am being disloyal and disobedient to the patriarchal injunction that demands our silence and invisibility," further noting that her own lesbianism, which she refers to as "disobedience," "led ... to my being emotionally and psychically cast out from my family, cast away from the most intimate affectional bonds I knew."[40] Discussing writings by self-identified Native lesbians, Craig Womack notes that "a significant reality for these working-class writers has to do with the fact that out Native lesbians do not receive approval from the Native literary mainstream." Womack characterizes the effort to locate same-sex desire within Native writings, especially when the author has not publicly identified themself as queer, as an interpretive act of *suspicioning*: "A suspicioner brings up taboos, secrets, impolite observations normally off-limits in states of self-assurance and control. Suspicioning takes advantage of doubt to go out on a limb and blurt out or whisper."[41]

The presumption of an inherent alignment between indigeneity and queerness and/or gender nonnormativity can vacate the possibility of engaging with queer and trans Native persons by presenting them as always-already included. Jodi Byrd argues that "critiques of heteropatriarchy [within Indigenous feminisms] have queered all Indigenous peoples and have flattened Indigenous women's bodies into land." In doing so, such analyses present Indigenous "embodied materiality as always already decolonial" in ways that portray such embodiment *as queer* while "den[ying] any ground for the difference queer [and one could add trans] might make." In contrast to Black feminisms, which Byrd suggests engage the queering of Black bodies "within racial capitalism ... without ever losing the material and lived particularities of" Black queer and trans bodies, "Indigenous queer bodies go missing" in Native American and Indigenous Studies, raising questions about the work done by apparently critical/radical indications of queerness.[42] Thus, while attending to the ways heteronormativity and cisnormativity have shaped settler interventions into Indigenous governance and collective life, and addressing alternative conceptions of desire, sociality, embodiment, and personhood present in Native practices and philosophies, scholars in Indigenous studies also need to be wary of turning *queer* and *trans* into metaphors that help coalesce Indigenous sovereignties at the expense of effacing actual queer, trans, and Two-Spirit persons.

Black Studies

The understanding of blackness as expressive of deviance has been a crucial part of ideologies of sexuality and gender in the Americas and beyond. As Roderick Ferguson notes, "African American communal and corporeal difference became the symbol of the nonheteronormative perversions of industrializing and urbanizing economies."[43] Demonstrations of Black "compliance with heteropatriarchal cultural standards," though, served "as a way of claiming access to state and civil society," including in the formation of Black studies in the 1960s and 1970s, which enacted "an exclusionary agenda that effectively cordoned off all identity categories that were not primarily based on race."[44] Sidestepping questions of sexual and gender nonnormativity, then, was part of a broader institutionalized politics of respectability but also a result of the specific cultural and political implications of engaging Black women's sexuality. As Evelyn Hammonds observes, even Black feminists tended to enact a "silence about sexuality" in order to avoid the "racist sexual terms" used to characterize all Black women, a threat both individually and "to the race as a whole," making Black women's erotics into something of a "black hole" – not visible in conventional ways but still felt in their effects.[45] In contrast to such ostensibly tactical evasions, work in Black queer and trans studies has sought to read for such deviance – the ways blackness is constructed as aberrant and the significance of the lived and felt patterns of desire, expression, and association presented as deviant within dominant (white) norms. Cathy Cohen has argued for a Black "politics of deviance" that takes up behaviors and relations deemed not *respectable* and draws on their "transformative potential" in shifting existing normative ideals, including those that have been internalized by Black people.[46] In a similar vein, Marshall Green offers trans method as an important complement to and extension of the ways Black feminism has opened up "multiple possibilities of gender within the category 'woman,'" further capacitating scholarship "attuned to difference rather than sameness."[47] Such intellectual projects enact what Patrick Johnson has described as *quare* studies, a "vernacular" mode of theorizing that attends to everyday life as well as the possibilities and difficulties at play in finding and occupying a Black "homeplace."[48] This section will explore these issues by focusing on discussions of the contemporary implications of the history of enslavement, the specificity of Black genders, and the relations between blackness and pleasure.

The history of enslavement, including its afterlives in ongoing structures of racial capitalism and antiblackness, can be seen as fundamentally shaping the ways Black people are cast as aberrant and, therefore, disruptive, dangerous, and criminal. Stephen Dillon argues that "the whiteness of heterosexuality came into being through its parasitic relationship to the fabrication of racialized inhumanity. 'Forced queering' is a name for the way the state and capital produce nonnormative genders and sexualities through racial violence."[49] Similarly, Aliyyah I. Abdur-Rahman suggests that enslaved people's availability for sexual use and violation – "the violence, the illegitimacy, and the inchoateness of rape that produced the body, the status, and the (non)identity of the slave" – makes "the slave ... not simply the product of sexual criminality but its very *incarnation*."[50] Not only are enslaved people fatherless, in the sense of being denied access to legally recognized paternity and being placed outside of the framework of the (white) heteropatriarchal family, but, in freedom, Black people continue to be represented and disciplined as failing to inhabit proper erotics, embodiment, and domesticity.[51] In discussing efforts to elude containment, intervention, assault, and criminalization, Dillon presents "the fugitive" as "a queer figure who is the site of a dramatic reimagining of freedom," suggesting that "the forces that create difference do not determine its future. Something takes flight and escapes even as capture is always immanent." He draws on Audre Lorde's notion of "the erotic" to name "an unrecognized, unnamed force that is prior to the powers of white supremacy, capital, and heteropatriarchy" that engenders such possibility for queer Black fugitivity in the face of the enforced queering of blackness.[52]

Historical and ongoing processes of being *made deviant*, though, can lead to narrating Black histories in ways that edit out desires and kinds of embodied expression that are treated as perverse anomalies. Treva Ellison has tracked the double dynamic by which Black queer and trans people have been effaced in Black history while being incorporated/appropriated in a deracialized and whitened LGBT history. For example, the story of the arrest of "three young Black femmes" in 1950 in Los Angeles can be included in a Los Angeles Public Library collection focused on LGBT *pride* in ways that leave aside how that arrest (and its linkage of gender nonconformity with criminality) was part of the expansion of the role of policing in intensifying geographies of segregation. Conversely, "depictions and discussions of Black gender and sexual deviance in *Jet* and *Ebony* during the 1950s" reaffirm the disorderliness of Black queer and trans presence.[53] Similarly, the prosecution of the Black performer Sir Lady Jay in 1950s Los Angeles for violating police commission rules about impersonating the "costume or dress [of] a person of the opposite sex" can get folded into "genealogies of male-to-female transgender activism" in ways that efface the role of antiblackness in her arrest and her protests. However, such police action also dovetailed with attempts by

Black middle-class reformers to push out and punish what they saw as seedy elements in their communities, adopting "a script of gender and sexual conformity as a method of building class power."[54] In response to the straightening of Black histories, lesbian writers have offered their own fictional rewritings of history that "offer reference toward history and push back against it through rebellious narratives" that do not accept "the familiar heterosexual and normatively gendered story of the past," instead "creating anachronism centering queers who 'don't belong' in the historical narratives as they are currently known."[55] As Matt Richardson illustrates, such projects of reclamation and invention include depictions of pleasurable same-sex eroticism within conditions of enslavement, the emergence of possibilities for greater Black gender expression and fluidity in the movement to urban spaces from the South, the presence of queer relations and West African spiritual practice in the spaces of the South, and complex queer and trans networks of relation across the Black diaspora.[56]

While tying the present to the past of enslavement – and to African belonging prior to enslavement – envisions forms of generational and ancestral relation, some scholars have suggested it can also reinforce a deeply heteronormative logic of reproductive inheritance. Diaspora often is represented in Black studies through "hetero-genealogy" and "hetero-futurity" that posit something like a line of descent from "Mother Africa" that continues to bind together Black people.[57] As against this somewhat reproductive rendering of belonging, Keguro Macharia argues for conceptualizing "black diaspora as proximity and rubbing rather than descent." He observes that "focusing on the erotic as the meeting place for Africa and Afro-diaspora ... interrupt[s] the scholarly tendency to frame this meeting place through tropes of hetero-kinship," instead attending to how that meeting is shaped by "mourning [for] the loss of erotic diversity because of the disruptions of colonial modernity." Foregrounding the role of Euro-American discourses of sexuality in "histories of unhumaning," including enslavement and the colonization of Africa, underlines both "the ruptures of the black diaspora" and the role of embodied experiences of contact, movement, and relation in shaping felt senses of blackness.[58] Offering perhaps the strongest version of the argument against historical continuity, Stephen Best suggests that "a shared queerness" emerges from "shared blackness" in a running "sense of alienation" that also undoes "conceptions of black collectivity and community across time." In "extending the queer acknowledgment of non-relationality between the past and the present," Best critiques *melancholy historicism* – "the idea that the slave past provides a ready prism for understanding and apprehending the black political present." Instead, attending more directly to the queerness of blackness, Best argues, highlights forms of *unbelonging* and displaces "the need for it to all add up to something in terms of collective identity."[59]

Queer and trans engagements with diasporic blackness highlight how it troubles notions of genealogical connection and racial sameness. As Jafari S. Allen notes, "To follow the route of black/queer/diaspora is to interrogate dynamic, unsettled subjects whose bodies, desires, and texts *move*."[60] More than simply or solely indicating forms of dislocation and flight, that movement itself suggests a desire to encounter forms of difference – people, places, and experiences that do not coalesce into an easy sense of home or belonging. Nadia Ellis characterizes diaspora as "the urgent sensation of a pull from elsewhere" in which "places and people of black identification" are felt as "horizons of possibility." Ellis links this sense of diasporic blackness to queerness, which she, drawing on José Esteban Muñoz, describes as "*that thing that lets us feel that the world is not enough*" and that enables forms of affect that work against the need for "compulsory sameness."[61] Similarly, Rinaldo Walcott argues that blackness in the Americas cannot "be conditioned by a search for an authentic African sexuality but rather might concern itself with the 'new' and recombined sexualities of the Black diaspora." Doing so enacts what Walcott calls a *homopoetics* that also refuses to insert Black genders and sexualities into a developmental narrative of "normative queer history" that posits the rights-bearing citizen-subject of the liberal nation-state as the inherently desirable model and goal – a vision of blackness that erases the complex "refusals of heterosexual monogamy" at play across the diaspora, particularly in the Caribbean.[62]

Much of the queer and trans scholarship in Black studies can be traced back in some fashion to the work of Hortense J. Spillers, whose essay "Mama's Baby, Papa's Maybe: An American Grammar Book" has profoundly influenced discussions of enslavement and its aftermaths. Spillers describes the distinction between the *body* and the *flesh* as "the central one between captive and liberated subject-positions." If the *body* indicates institutionalized social conceptions of embodiment for those who count as persons, including forms of patriarchal gender differentiation, the *flesh* speaks to the "ungendered" understanding of enslaved beings as quantifiable objects equally available for white use (including sexual objectification and violence, which Spillers registers through the notion of the *pornotrope*). Those enfleshed beings further are alienated from "notions of the domestic" and are denied any legally recognized familial bonds – what Spillers terms *kinlessness*. Within this frame, blackness entails a "*loss* of gender," which is a crucial part of how Black people are cast outside of personhood. However, rather than arguing for inclusion into (white) gender norms, and their accompanying ideologies of home and family, Spillers indicates, "we are less interested in joining the ranks of gendered femaleness" than "*claiming* the monstrosity" of experiences of embodiment within blackness.[63] She suggests, then, that *flesh* is not simply the absence of gender and its legal forms but may entail ways of being in the world beyond the normative framework of the *body*.[64]

This analysis helps give rise to scholarship that addresses how Black modes of gender expression and identity are overdetermined by historical and ongoing forms of antiblack imposition, regulation, and consumption. For example, within US popular culture, Black drag queens often serve as supplements whose aid helps secure *heteroperpetuity* – the idea that "(white and middle class) heteronorms are desirable, natural, essential, and eternal." Black gender nonnormativity can then be circulated and consumed as a happy spectacle in the service of a white cisnormative future.[65] These dynamics of racialized gender, though, are not simply part of public discourse and dominant ideologies but can come to be lived as part of Black self-understanding and self-representation. The marginalization of Black *sissiness* provides an example of this process. Marlon B. Ross has illustrated how the figure of the sissy – the effeminate man – has come to be seen as an indication of "unfit black manliness" and often has been read, including by queer critics, as a sign of hidden "homosexual subjectivity." However, emphasizing the idea of *conduct* over notions of ingrained sexual and gender identity, Ross traces the ways the forms of gendered behavior tied to the sissy – and the disdain often expressed toward them – gain meaning within the history of white supremacy due to the gendering of Black service (particularly in domestic spaces) as contrary to "white hegemonic masculinity," which itself "has been haunted by and constructed on the unstable category of multiply marginalized black sissiness."[66] He also shows how the enactment of nonnormative gender and the disavowal of it have been significant in the history of the Black church (which "nurtures sissy character and conduct" while expressing a deeply "patriarchal doctrine") and to gay Black men's assertion of public presence (such as the use in multiple media of the phrase "Brother to Brother" rather than, say, "Sissy to Sissy").[67]

In response to the ways oppressive social forms shape the possibilities for Black gender, some scholars have issued calls to move beyond gender entirely. Connecting to other abolitionist movements, such as with respect to police and the prison system, these efforts envision the potential for ways of being, individual and collective, not organized around the matrix of social roles and forms of embodiment that currently operate as *gender*. In this vein, Marquis Bey argues that "Black trans feminism cannot abide such classificatory violences, so it urges us to abolish the categories we may love." They add, "I am in the business of dissolving borders and boundaries," including those that shape the terms of racial and gender identity: "My commitment to the nonnormative is thus a commitment to what has not been permitted to appear on the scene. The nonnormative must be carefully distinguished from the 'counter' or the 'oppositional' inasmuch as these, to me, express a reaction to what has been established." From this perspective, "the nonnormative" is "not predicated on legitimizing identities, knowledges, or sense-making apparatuses already in place" for understanding, categorizing, and regulating bodies and the ways they move through the world. Bey presents this movement beyond extant frameworks of identity and selfhood, which affect everyday kinds of perception and interaction, as a project of "gender radicality" that is also a process of "fugitive un/gendering."[68]

Other scholars, though, point to existing Black genders that offer possibilities for generating livable presents and futures. Kara Keeling addresses what she terms *the Black femme function*, which she argues gets denigrated and displaced in conventional conceptions of Black collectivity and political movements. Within them, "a notion of femininity" appears to "designat[e] passivity or receptivity to sensations from the outside and one's currency as an object for desire": "Masculinity and its affectations and accoutrements appear as the terms adequate to Black Liberation." Within this masculinist vision of blackness, the Black femme, Keeling suggests, remains present but "out-of-field" – outside extant ways of representing Black collective identity. Black femme-ness encapsulates the "invisible affective labor [that] ensures the survival of forms of sociality that were never meant to survive."[69] In this way, the Black femme less complements masculinity than indicates practices and relations of care and protection necessary for everyday Black flourishing, which get gendered as feminine and seen as less valuable or even as a hindrance to more supposedly revolutionary action. Extending Keeling's analysis, Omise'eke Natasha Tinsley illustrates how enacting forms of femininity defies "commonsense expectations of butchness for black queer ciswomen" – "the persistent masculinization of black lesbians." She argues that non-trans forms of Black lesbian femininity also should be seen "as fundamentally troubling binaries of gender and sexuality," although in ways that are different from yet allied with expressions of transfemininity.[70] Tinsley, though, approaches such gender through engagement with "Caribbean authors" whose "vision of creative genders and sexualities" draws on the figure of Ezili – a *lwa*, or powerful ancestral spirit, within Haitian Vodou. Such portrayals and experiences of Black gender, then, emerge out of a cultural development in the Americas that "also enacts resistance to slavery and its aftermath."[71] Focusing on another form of creative adaptation, Marlon M. Bailey attends to how Ballroom culture provides ways to "perform gender, create kinship, and forge community" amid varied dynamics of "marginalization." Highlighting how experiences of antiblackness are intensified through forms of family and community rejection due to being queer and trans, Bailey presents the Ballroom community as a network that provides members "a means of altering their ways of *being* in the world and of creating an *alternative world* together." The *balls* are events where people from different *houses* – teams that also serve as part of alternative kinship relations beyond legal/biological families – compete in specified categories to see who can best achieve *realness* in that category. The categories themselves are gendered – such as Butch Queens (gay men), Butches (transmasculine), Femme Queens (transfeminine) – but not in ways that readily map onto heteronormative and cisnormative ideals: "Ballroom members ... view categories of sex as open and unfinished, just as they do gender. Akin to their notions of gender and sexuality, the sex of a body is the result of an ongoing process or activity as opposed [to] being a biological fact." These complex gendered relations also affect ordinary life outside the balls through the houses, which "challenge conventional notions of marriage, family, and kinship by revising gender relations and redefining gendered labor within the kin unit."[72] Thus, while marking the force of interwoven racial and gender norms, scholars show how existing Black genders contribute to possibilities for everyday thriving.

As discussed previously, a politics of respectability can shape discussions of Black life in ways that disallow discussion of erotic life and that displace the sense of deviance that attaches to blackness onto non-straight and non-cis subjects. Robert Reid-Pharr suggests that in anti-queer Black discourses, such as certain strains of Black nationalist writing, "the homosexual stands in for the fear of crisis and chaos," serving as a figure for "that which is unauthentic, base, and perverse in order to adequately define the borders of black 'realness.'"[73] In the face of such disavowal, scholars emphasize the importance of turning toward forms of Black embodiment, pleasure, and desire that do not fit within the parameters of bourgeois visions of family, work, and morality. L. H. Stallings describes such kinds of pleasure that likely would be seen as perverted, hypersexual, or criminal as *funky erotixxx*, which she argues "provides alternative knowledge about imagination and sexuality." Focusing on *funk* – "radical configurations of family, love, and relationships where monogamy and marriage are not situated as the ideal praxis" – opens possibilities for engaging sex and erotic relations in ways that refuse both pathologizing narratives of Black deviance and desexualizing narratives of Black normativity.[74]

Black studies scholars, though, also have critiqued the tendency in queer studies to cast desire as inherently liberatory, rather than as itself potentially animated by race in ways that reinforce the givenness of racial difference. Dwight McBride notes that "the realm of desire for queer theorists seems ever to represent the possibility for a kind of idealized freedom and liberality," and he contrasts this portrait with the powerful roles played by racialized imagination and hierarchy within the "gay marketplace of desire."[75] The story that eroticism can transcend existing social relations, critics have argued, works in the service of consolidating whiteness as the invisible norm. As Sharon Holland argues, "we can't have our erotic life – a desiring life – without involving ourselves in the messy terrain of racist practice."[76] Holland suggests that the celebration of desire and pleasure in queer studies, as well as in some earlier Black feminist formulations (such as Audre Lorde's notion of the erotic), "works its magic because it functions in a very neat nonreproductive zone."[77] Queer studies, then, de facto can treat racial identities, like blackness, as given rather than addressing the ways they are (re)created through forms of sexual contact that bear racial meanings for all involved. As both Holland and Reid-Pharr illustrate, the Black body does not simply immanently bear its blackness but is attributed blackness as an identity due to understandings of the sexual union out of which that body comes, and the ongoing process of naturalizing the blackness of that body includes normalizing the social institution of *the Black family* as the self-evident crucible from which blackness generationally emerges.[78] Without attending to the racial significance and sentiments that animate forms of desire, race as an identity and a history of domination appears to attach to some bodies and not others in ways that efface how race as an ideology is embedded in everyday interactions and intimacies – including queer ones – that continue to generate the color-line and blackness itself.

If eroticism does not operate outside of or beyond forms of racialization, how do we understand the workings of pleasure within Black lives, particularly Black queer and trans lives? How can Black pleasure be addressed in ways that engage the role of existing racial and racist dynamics in shaping erotic subjectivity and experience without only seeing Black desire, sensation, and ecstasy in terms of the effects of ongoing antiblackness? One way of addressing these questions is through consideration of forms of Black kink – Black people's participation in forms of eroticism that do not fit conventional notions of romance, intimacy, and coupledom. Beyond contesting limiting ideas of respectability, these kinds of sexual play can involve staging fantasies that tap into modes of racial hierarchy and objectification. Talking about porn made by Black lesbians, Jennifer Declue observes, "Rather than working to free black lesbian sexuality from the legacy of sexual violence and trauma, the films ... engage with loss, trauma, and unspoken violence by creating scenarios in which black lesbian characters explore sexual domination and submission, pleasure and pain, as ecstatic modes that can release the trauma of sexual violence and racial oppression." She adds, "The perception that black and brown bodies do not engage in kinky queer sex culture avoids having to contend with the messiness of racialized power dynamics within sexuality."[79] Thinking in broader terms about what she calls *brown jouissance*, Amber Jamilla Musser considers the ways that Black fleshliness (in Hortense Spillers's sense discussed earlier) has a "sensuous materiality that brings together pleasure and pain" and that "takes joy and pain in the gesture of radical openness toward otherness," which is irreducible to "only woundedness and pain."[80] Connecting desire and erotic sensation to histories of racial objectification opens up the complex relays among "abjection, pleasure, and pleasure in abjection" that do not transcend ongoing forms of racism but that also are more than merely acquiescence to those forms, instead indicating a living within and working through of such histories as part of "project[s] of recovery and survival" that refuse to take dominant notions of selfhood as given.[81]

Everyday attempts to find joy and pleasure within existing circumstances of antiblackness themselves require forms of individual and collective labor. Considering Black queer women's participation in Chicago nightlife, Kemi Adeyemi situates their efforts to *feel right* within existing urban economies in which "the value of financial profit is bound to the accumulation of *certain kinds* of good feeling for *certain kinds* of people in *certain kinds* of places," feelings "made possible only by removing certain people to the margins of the city's zones of profitability." Working to find pleasure within these dynamics of displacement and erasure, Black queer women "interrupt, manage, and redirect the racialized territorialization of feeling in the neoliberal city toward the production of sustainable black queer community in its midst." In the words of one of Adeyemi's interviewees, the pursuit of Black joy "exists in connection to us being oppressed *and* living." Adeyemi insists on the importance of the everyday and a scholarly focus on people's efforts to feel *normal*, not in the sense of conforming to dominant ideas of proper personhood but of being left to live one's life without being seen as a spectacle or subjected to violence. Instead of searching for topics and subjects that seem to "model how to be better, more radical, or more ethical" and that are imagined as pointing to ways of being beyond current oppressive conditions, what she characterizes as *the event–potentiality matrix*, Adeyemi argues for the importance of considering "the lived materiality of black queer life" in all its complex ordinariness.[82]

Latinx Studies

Latinx may be the most geopolitically and conceptually dense of the kinds of racialization/minoritization considered in this chapter.[83] It encompasses persons from territories that now are part of US domestic space, made so in varied moments of conquest, as well as people who come from other countries in the Spanish-speaking and Portuguese-speaking Americas. This category also is quite complex in terms of its relation to whiteness. While all racial identities are crosscut by others (with people, families, and communities that belong to more than one), Latinx emerges at the intersection of racial frameworks derived from Spanish and Portuguese colonialisms as they are transposed into frames largely inherited from English law and colonialism. That conversion (or translation) means that persons who may be white in one imperial formation are not in another – or sometimes are, or at certain times and places are while being not at other times. Moreover, while the African slave trade was a significant part of Spanish Caribbean and Latin American histories, and many people of African descent live in and trace their genealogies to these spaces, Latinx identity often is discussed as if it were not substantially constituted by blackness and Black people. In this way, *Latinx* less indicates a unified perspective or identity than a shifting array of diasporas, displacements, and identifications in which the complexity of relations across the Americas and Caribbean are at play. The United States has colonized territories and exerted ongoing imperial influence in ways that produce patterns of mobility and border-crossing (both moving across national borders and having such borders shift around you). While highlighting such effects of US intervention and policy, queer and trans frameworks also challenge normalized ideas of national identity organized around heteronormative and cisgendered notions of family, purity, and belonging.

The notion of an encompassing *latinidad* can indicate continuities of experience and shared goals while also effacing profound disjunctions among those persons and groups collected together through this category. Even at the level of terminology, pato, bugarrón, marícon, loca, cuir, travesti, joto/a, tortillera, and marimacha, among many other terms, all can indicate kinds of nonnormative gender and sexuality. Their meanings and usage, though, vary greatly among different groups, and the ideas and associations they convey also do not necessarily translate easily into English terms/concepts like *gay* and *trans*.[84] In this vein, Cole Rizki uses "the term *Latin/x America* to mark both Latinx and Latin American contributions and to insist on the entanglements of 'US' and 'Latin America' as geopolitical categories, underscoring their inherent instabilities" and refusing the idea of an easy distinction between the "Global North" and the "Global South," especially one in which the former is seen as leading the way for the latter's development.[85] Similarly, the editors of "*Cuir*/Queer Américas" seek to emphasize the "tensions, resonances, and contradictions" at play in seeking to think about relations, identities, and movements across the Americas with regard to gender and sexuality, an aim that they describe as "the *contrapunte* [contrapuntal] *cuir*... a process of encuentros [meetings/encounters] and desencuentros [disagreements] that constitutes a forum for decolonizing knowledge."[86] In mapping these multiple, dense, and intersecting kinds of imperial relations, queer and trans scholars in Latinx Studies have challenged the ways other scholarly work and political discourses invoke a supposed "Latin culture" to address expressions of gender, sexuality, and collective identity. From this perspective, the oppression of queer and trans people is due to the privileging of supposedly distinctly *Latin* cultural forms of heteropatriarchal masculinity, while positioning US culture (de facto seen as white and Anglo) as inherently more progressive and inclusive. As Lionel Cantú notes, appeals to a supposedly shared culture as a way of explaining Latinx identities, social patterns, and movements are "reified and monolithic (Latino culture is defined as static regardless of location)" while such culture "is also called on as the explanation of the 'symptoms' of social inequalities" among Latinx people and in Latin American and Caribbean places.[87]

Within queer and trans Latinx Studies, attending to hemispheric networks, mobilities, and differences occurs against the background of US imperialism and its increasingly draconian forms of immigration control. As Verónica Mandujano suggests of the most recent waves of undocumented migration to the southern US border, "Immigrants from Central America are fleeing their homelands due to deteriorating living conditions that are the aftermath of years of U.S. intervention in the region," including a seven-fold increase in asylum seekers largely from El Salvador, Nicaragua, and Honduras.[88] These refugees include "caravans of LGBTQ people," which itself is "not a new phenomenon,"[89] but when they reach the US border, they are subject to processes of racialization, criminalization, and containment that do not recognize their claims to having been oppressed, often subject trans women to misgendering and sexual assault, and even when acknowledging refugees' claims cast the countries from which they come as backward rather than as destabilized due in many ways to US policies and actions.[90] This pattern builds on a long history in which migrants from the south are both racialized as a threat to and/or burden on the United States and in which normative conceptions of gender, sexuality, and family serve as the basis for deciding who could be considered to be a healthy potential citizen. Such policy has included barring persons deemed immoral due to their sexuality (expressing "sexual deviation" or "moral turpitude" – a restriction not changed until 1990) and, as of 1965, pegging legal entry for most people to "family reunification," based on a heteronuclear model of family that some mainstream LGBT organizations have sought to expand to include same-sex and trans couples but in ways that do not undo the broader "normalizing visions of which families, relationships, and individuals 'deserve' protection and incorporation."[91] The *undocuqueer* movement emerged over the course of the 2010s as a way of challenging the calls to give citizenship status to currently undocumented migrant youth based on various criteria and hierarchies of *worthiness*, including educational performance and the absence of a record in the criminal punishment system.[92]

While decades of US imperial intervention in Latin America and the Caribbean and subsequent patterns of migration appear more prominently in public discourse, the US annexation of Mexican and Spanish territories in the nineteenth century continues to shape the lives of Latinx people. About half of Mexico's territory was seized by the United States in the Mexican–American War (1846–1848), and while the Treaty of Guadalupe Hidalgo that ended the war promised citizenship to Mexican nationals now in US domestic space, the prominent racialization of them as nonwhite and disregard for their legal geographies and property claims vitiated that promise. This control over once-Mexican space and populations involved managing political, economic, and social relations at multiple scales: not just, in Mary Pat Brady's terms, "monumental spaces like the border" but extending to "microspatial practices that weave together to form the [everyday] norms of gender and sexuality."[93] The history and continuing implications of the conquest further are effaced in the demonization of "Mexican" people as a foreign intrusion. As Cantú observes, the power the United States exerts that "legitimizes migration across its borders depends on its ability to differentiate the citizen from the foreigner," a distinction that itself relies on "normative discourses of race/ethnicity, gender, class, and sexuality."[94] Puerto Rico was claimed by the United States in the Spanish–American War (1898), and while Puerto Ricans are US citizens who can move freely between the island and the continental United States, Puerto Rico officially remains an *unincorporated territory* subject to direct federal oversight in ways that produce intervention, underdevelopment, and an expansive diaspora, with almost two-thirds of Puerto Ricans living elsewhere in the United States: "Our stay in the United States, permanent or not, is a curiously continuous experience that produces cultural anxiety precisely because of its ambiguities."[95] For non-straight and non-cis Puerto Ricans, these effects have been even more intensive, including federally-led efforts to *modernize* Puerto Rico in the mid-twentieth century (including seeking to discipline Puerto Ricans into dominant Anglo forms of family, gender, and sexuality and attendant Puerto Rican government efforts to push those who were not compliant to leave the island) and twenty-first-century efforts to increase white gay tourism to Puerto Rico while continuing to discriminate against queer and trans Puerto Ricans and to see them as deviant subjects who have failed to embody Puerto Rican values/nationalism.[96]

Latinx Studies scholars highlight how queer and trans mobilities illustrate patterns of diaspora that are influenced by transnational political and economic dynamics, and such scholarly work also shows how queer and trans diasporic networks challenge dominant visions of nationalism. Migration by queer and trans people is not just one-way, nor does it necessarily indicate a desire to "come out" within dominant US notions of sexual and gender identity. As Frances Negrón-Muntaner argues, moving to the United States for some Puerto Ricans may be a response to a nationalist ideal organized around the white heteropatriarchal family: "Where do those expelled from the nation – the poor, the mulattoes and blacks, the sexiles – go?" Forms of Puerto Rican nationalism, though, emerge within the context of a longstanding "subjection to American colonialism" that profoundly influences such self-articulations, especially in response to racializing US narratives of Puerto Rican backwardness.[97] Yet, the movement into diaspora also took "the nation with it," expanding the boundaries of Puerto Rican identity. Negrón-Muntaner also emphasizes "Puerto Ricans' constant and circular migratory patterns," indicating that Puerto Rican sexual and gender identities on-island and off have been influenced greatly by engagement with discourses and social formations in the continental United States, and vice-versa.[98] Lawrence La Fountain-Stokes has referred to such movements and reciprocal influence as *translocality* in which "persons in diverse geographic locations, whether in the country of origin or in the diaspora, ... are in complex and constant daily, weekly, or yearly contact, be it through travel, migration, communications, or other forms of exchange," and he sees what he calls *transloca* performance (drawing on the association of *loca* with madness, femininity, gender nonconformity, and deviant sexuality as a way of speaking about "drag and trans embodiments") as helping "create, challenge, and disorganize" such expansive networks and relations.[99] Similarly, in his study of immigrant Dominican men who have sex with men, Carlos Ulises Decena describes New York City as "another part of a Dominican world," with migration as part of "the multiplication of sites for 'being' Dominican" in ways that make places like New York less "a final destination" than "another site for relationships that are multisited."[100]

Feminist accounts of Latinx genders and sexualities illustrate how everyday feeling and desire opens up toward other kinds of relationships, networks, and possibilities for collective self-organization that are not defined by inclusion into the nation, whether the United States or that of a "home" country. Juana María Rodríguez draws on the concept of *gesture* as a way of thinking about how ordinary forms of feeling, fantasy, and pleasure can be seen as the basis for kinds of community-building and political imagination that do not depend on naturalizing dominant notions of family, gender, and sexuality. She suggests that for Latinx people, "Our racialized excess is already read as queer, outside norms of what is useful or productive." As part of that supposed excess, the habit of gesturing *too much* serves for Rodríguez as a way of "metaphorically" linking the violation of Anglo-American ideas of order and proper bodily comportment with "activist interventions that push, jam, open, block, and twist social forces": "As a mode of critique, gesture emphasizes how a cascade of everyday actions is capable of altering political life," as against the notion that "in order to enter the fold of collectivity, be it familial or revolutionary, we must first be liberated of our sexual deviance and our politically incorrect desires."[101] Considering how rhetorics of national revolution tend to consolidate a heteropatriarchal image of who and what the nation is, and how such rhetorics get taken up in later social and political movements (including Latinx and Chicanx ones), Emma Pérez argues for the importance of a *decolonial imaginary* that can attend to forms of Latinx collectivity and consciousness that do not replicate "uncompromising nationalist movements in which feminisms are dismissed as bourgeois" and in which "queer voices are scoffed at as a white thing." She defines such an imaginary as looking for "borderlands" and "interstices" that "introduce the possibility of a postcolonial, postnational consciousness," addressing the ways people move within, across, and among national spaces even as they seek to transform them (with scholars often drawing on Gloria Anzaldúa's work in doing so, discussed in Chapter 2).[102] Focusing specifically on trans of color political movements and mobilities, micha cárdenas draws on figures from programming – such as algorithms, cutting, and stitching – to consider how ordinary trans embodiment is tied to reimagining relations across the Americas. Cárdenas highlights possibilities for alternative ways of networking persons and groups than those based on nation-state identities and the capitalist and imperial political economies through which they are linked. She notes that "stitching" refers to "the mechanism for holding variables together in lines of code, grouping instructions into cohesive units," but cárdenas suggests it can be connected to the stitching involved in the gender-affirming remolding of bodily form, thinking of them together as ways of recoding possibilities for personal identity and community formation that open potentials for connection across language difference and national boundaries. As she notes, "Solidarity is an act of stitching."[103]

Although much work in queer and trans Latinx studies seeks to challenge national ideals and identities that are tied to constructing and policing borders, there are also forms of minority and oppositional nationalism that seek to make visible and counter the absorption of Latinx lands and populations into US national space. In particular, Chicanx nationalism emerged out of movements in the 1960s and 1970s to reconceptualize Mexican American identity and politics in what is now the US Southwest, drawing attention to the violence of the US conquest of the region, emphasizing Mexican American people's longstanding connection to those lands, and highlighting forms of US racism and extractivism.[104] These efforts coalesced around the idea of the Southwest as the conquered nation of Aztlán, drawing on Aztec (Nahua) terminology and imagery to present Mexican Americans – renamed as Chicanos/as – as indigenous with regard to this national homeland. This vision of semi-national identity, though, has tended to be articulated through patriarchal imagery in ways that also are tied to a heteronormative vision of *la familia*. As Alicia Gaspar de Alba suggests, "In Aztlán aesthetics, ... we could say that *familia* becomes the primary signifier for place of origin, and place of origin often amalgamates mother's womb, barrio or neighborhood, and regional landscape – all of which constitute the list and living homeland in the Chicago imagination."[105] Furthermore, as Catrióna Rueda Esquiel argues, "It's crucial to recognize that the first articulations of feminist goals and struggles within the Chicano/a movement were marked by a homophobic backlash in which all Chicana feminists were subject to lesbian-baiting, at both personal and professional levels."[106] Reciprocally, gay men also challenge notions of nationalist continuity and inheritance, given both the "cultural and historical deployments" of "*la familia* ... as an organizing principle" and the equation of being sexually penetrated with a "nonfertile" sexuality that "signals the end of reproduction" as well as the refusal of the "patriarchal authority" that shapes "the naturalized family."[107] Yet, rather than simply refusing nationalist conceptions of community and related ideas, such as the notion of Aztlán and *mestizaje* (collective identity as mestizo/a), Chicanx intellectuals and artists often appropriate and reconfigure them. These include recasting homeland in terms of the female/lesbian body, embracing and recasting in queer-friendly ways iconic Mexican and Chicanx figures such as La Virgen de Guadalupe and the Aztec Princess Ixtacihuatl, finding and inventing narratives of queer and trans Chicanx people in the more distant past of what is now the US West, and taking up the nationalist language of brotherhood as signaling both homoerotic connection and alternative forms of kinship to dominant notions of *la familia*.[108]

The question of how to understand Latinx identity within the United States is complicated not only by the differences among the various groups that fall into this category, but the ways those people, populations, and social forms are racialized. Even while Latino/a is officially considered an *ethnicity* rather than a *race*, such as in the US census, *latinidad* partially gains meaning through its distinction from the cultural dominance of whiteness. As Rámon H. Rivera-Servera observes, "Being Latina/o in the United States" involves "negotiating the assumption of criminality not just in terms of citizenship status but in reference to myriad other xenophobic, racist, and classist stereotypes." Work in queer studies, though, has tended "to subsume all *latinidades* into one abstract class category," assuming "a primarily working-class aesthetics as a challenge to the codes and conventions of a homonormative whiteness" in ways that can efface, among other things, how forms of "tropicalization" – stereotypical ideas about "ethnoracial difference" – can circulate *among* queer Latinx people.[109] There's a need to attend to how Latinx people are racialized for their "culture, color, language, class, legal status, religion, and sexual practices" while also addressing how latinidad "contains within it the complexities and contradictions of immigration, (post) (neo)colonialism, race, color, legal status, class, nation, and the politics of location."[110] In this vein, one might consider the ways that all Latinx people are affected by forms of "racialized sexuality." Discussing Chicanx cultural production, Sandra K. Soto indicates the value of "reading like a queer," by which she means looking for "the unpredictable, polymorphous, and often contradictory representations of the mutual constitution of racialization and sexuality" in ways that are neither about finding and affirming same-sex eroticism nor necessarily looking for the ways Chicanx desires and feelings directly contribute to some clear political project or movement.[111]

José Esteban Muñoz explores these tensions through his development of the concept of *brownness*. Unlike other colors used to indicate forms of racial identity (such as white, black, red, and yellow), brown does not refer to what is imagined as a clearly defined group; instead, it gestures toward a more amorphous nonwhiteness, which attaches to Latinx people but not them alone. Muñoz suggests, "I want to think about how different kinds of brownness touch but do not fuse. Brownness as a grounded experience, for a brown commons, is often borne out of what we could call a shared sense of harm." That harm comes from being seen as in some sense failing to enact dominant ideas of decorum, respectability, propriety, and morality that are associated with whiteness – a perceived "inability to act properly within majoritarian scripts and scenarios" by being "over-the-top subjects" and, thereby, "failing to conform to the affective protocols of normative cultural citizenship." However, even as such brownness may extend across Latinx groups, that shared racialization does not produce sameness or inherent agreement: "To be of the brown commons is not to be in sync, or to be lined up; conflict and disagreement are central to the commons."[112] Francisco J. Galarte builds on this sense of brownness, addressing how "transness and brownness work in proximity to each other": "representation[s] of brown trans subjects ... are framed by sensational and formulaic narratives," as in public accounts of the murders of trans Latinas, in ways that aim to make "trans bodies, narratives, and embodiments intelligible to nontrans audiences." For example, he illustrates how the effort by the district attorney supposedly to *seek justice* for the killing of Gwen Amber Rose Araujo – a seventeen-year-old trans Latina murdered in 2002 in Newark, California – contributed to the national push for hate crimes legislation. However, while the conviction of Araujo's killers "should signal that the system is more inclusive, the outcome is instead an enhancement of prosecutorial, police, and immigration enforcement in the area."[113] Instead of pursuing claims to rights and respectability in the face of racialization and criminalization, then, queer and trans work in Latinx studies turns toward those persons, practices, behaviors, and spaces seen as "lewd, obscene, offensive," an analytic orientation Deborah Vargas calls *"lo sucio,"* drawing on a popular Latinx term for "dirty, nasty, and filthy." In this vein, Eddy Francisco Alvarez, Jr., argues for "finding sequins in the rubble," looking for forms of "aesthetics, worldmaking, and self-fashioning" that occur amid ongoing forms of displacement, police harassment, and personal and collective trauma.[114]

Asian American Studies

Asian American is perhaps the racial category least often treated as one. Anti-Asian sentiment and policy has been a staple across the longue durée of US history – from the forms of legal exclusion and denial of citizenship in the late nineteenth through the mid-twentieth centuries, to the animus against Korean and Vietnamese people in the midst and wake of US wars in those countries, Japanese internment during World War II, and the meteoric rise of the figure of the Islamic/Middle Eastern terrorist in the early 2000s. David Eng has characterized Asian Americans as "a group alternately seen as the most foreign, racialized, and unassimilable in the era of exclusion (the myth of the yellow peril) and the most invisible, colorless, and compliant in the post-1965 era (the model minority myth)."[115] Despite the ways Asian Americans continue to be treated as foreigners, seen as perpetually alien to the nation, Asian American identity tends not to be understood as marked in powerful ways by institutionalized and ongoing dynamics of racism. As against what Dana Takagi has referred to as a "counting practice," in which sexuality and gender expression are simply "additive" with regard to matters of Asian American race and class, queer and trans work within Asian American studies not only marks the ways heteronormativity and cisnormativity affect Asian Americans but how notions of nonnormative sexuality and gender are central to the various ways that persons and groups are racialized as *Asian*.[116] In addition to tracing the importance of sexuality and gender as analytical frames through which to conceptualize Asian American identities, histories, political movements, and forms of everyday experience, this scholarship explores how notions of diaspora can in varied ways both contest and reinforce dominant ideas about nationality, belonging, and cultural authenticity.

In their groundbreaking collection *Q & A: Queer in Asian America*, David Eng and Alice Hom indicate

> the need for Asian American studies scholars to understand that legal and cultural discourses on "deviant" sexuality do not affect only those contemporary Asian American subjects who readily self-identify as queer, lesbian, gay, bisexual, or transgendered; they affect a much larger Asian American constituency as well – regardless of sexual identity or identifications – whose disavowed status as legitimate or proper subjects of the U.S. nation-state render them abnormal as such.[117]

That process of being rendered deviant dovetails historically with the defining of particular groups as inabsorbably alien and, thus, dangerous to the health and welfare of the nation. Such legal measures include the following: the Page Act (1875), a supposed ban on prostitutes that effectively prevented immigration by most East Asian, particularly Chinese, women; the Chinese Exclusion Act (1882) that sought to bar entry of Chinese laborers into the United States; the Gentleman's Agreement (1907) in which Japan agreed to limit the immigration to the United States of its citizens; a 1907 congressional act that stripped citizenship from US women who married foreign nationals; the creation of the "Asiatic Barred Zone" by congressional act (1917); the Immigration Act of 1924, which eliminated lawful immigration from Asia; the internment of Japanese Americans starting in 1942; and the passage of numerous state laws banning interracial marriage as well as alien land laws that prevented property ownership by those ineligible for naturalization.[118]

Cumulatively, these policies sought to prevent the formation of nuclear families – denying entry to Asian women, penalizing marriage to white women, denying access to property and inheritance – and to cast Asian people(s) as threats due to the kinds of immorality, perversity, and degeneration attached to their racial difference. They are made *abnormal*, in Eng's and Hom's terms, through attributions of sexual and gender disorder, in which the conditions produced by US policy (such as the presence of bachelor communities) are seen as expressions of their ingrained deviant inclinations and in which such supposed tendencies are portrayed as expressions of their dangerously foreign cultures. In this way, "queerness comes to affect and encompass a much larger Asian American constituency – whatever their sexual identities or practices – whose historically disavowed status as U.S. citizen-subjects under punitive immigration and exclusion laws renders them 'queer' as such."[119]

While Filipinos have had a different relation to the US state than other "Asians," it has equally been shaped by racial ideologies of sexual normality. As Martin Joseph Ponce suggests, engagement with the Philippines requires a framework that "begins with the notion not of immigration but of imperialism" as "the point of departure."[120] The history of the Philippines has been described as "*Three hundred and fifty years in a convent, fifty years in Hollywood.*"[121] The United States occupied the Philippines from 1898 to 1946, truncating the Philippine movement to gain independence from Spain (which had held the territory for several centuries) and conducting a genocidal counterinsurgency against the population to establish acquiescence to US imperial rule.[122] Such governance was presented as a temporary and tutelary, until Filipinos had developed the civilized capacity to govern themselves: "No matter how much evidence was presented before Congress 'proving' the Filipinos' capacity for self-rule, the colonial rulers held the power to recognize or not recognize those appeals."[123] For most of that time, Filipinos were designated as US nationals, not citizens, which did give them the ability to live, attend school, and work in the United States despite existing bans on Asian immigration. They were, in the words of the US Supreme Court, "foreign in a domestic sense," a status shared with other colonized but not incorporated territories such as Puerto Rico: "Filipino America is a simultaneously inassimilable *and* assimilable entity in the 'house' of the American empire," in ways that make "Filipinos structurally queer to the United States."[124] Moreover, US imperial governance was justified through narratives of Filipino racial perversity: "if colonialism was likened to marriage, even hastened by it, what possible affirmations about sexuality did U.S. colonialism's 'white love' for the Philippines make?"[125] Such modes of, in Victor

Román Mendoza's terms, *colonialnormativity* included the policing of Filipino sexual acts through charges of "vagrancy" ("to regulate, on local and national levels, a range of nonnormative, unproductive, and habitually immoral bodies").[126] Ongoing US influence in the Philippines, including support for the decades-long dictatorship of Ferdinand Marcos and continued military intervention since that time in the name of counterterrorism, has helped engender large-scale immigration of Filipinos to the United States, alongside the Philippine government's investment in promoting labor migration to other countries to support the economy through remittances from abroad.[127] Thus, as Martin Manalansan observes, "the Filipino gay immigrant arrives in the United States not to begin a process of Americanization but rather to continue and transform the ongoing engagement with America."[128] That process confronts the foregrounding of heteronormative and cisnormative conceptions of family in representations of both US and Philippine national identity.

In the wake of the major shift in US immigration law in 1965, which ended national quotas and inaugurated the privileging of professional contributions and family reunion as the framework for lawful immigration, the number of emigrants and refugees from places of US military intervention, such as Korea, Vietnam, and Cambodia, increased exponentially. While people of Asian descent continued to be seen as racially and culturally alien, this policy change helped give rise to a transformation in dominant ideas about Asian presence, from a narrative of the United States as likely to be overwhelmed by foreign hordes to one of grateful families finding a better life in the United States – in ways that were contrasted implicitly and explicitly both to African American unrest and illegal Latinx border-crossing. This larger story, though, can mask how various Asian groups were contrasted with each other at different moments (such as flip-flopping assessments of Chinese and Japanese savagery and civility, cast in terms of forms of sexual and gender self-regulation and decorum)[129] and how the same group could be viewed in very different terms at different times (South Asian men seen as backward, perverse British colonial subjects versus as upstanding, respectable, and entrepreneurial patriarchs).[130]

While conceptions of deviance and dangerousness have attached to varied Asian populations in ways that have shifted historically, the ascription of model minority status seems to promise an entry into normalized citizenship, one that leaves aside the racialized queerings of the past. This desire for national inclusion has animated "the rather static cultural nationalist conception of racial identity around which Asian American studies was originally formed (the assumed but unspoken subject of the field was male, heterosexual, working class, American born, and English speaking)."[131] Eng further suggests the value of reading for the sexual and gender dynamics at play in the "expensive psychological toll" (which he refers to as "internal exile") exacted by model minority discourse, due to the way it effaces the historical and continuing effects of Asian racialization and anti-Asian racism – forms of "everyday exclusion and disenfranchisement, material and psychic," that live on despite "changes to immigration law" and the ending of explicit, official forms of anti-Asian exclusion.[132] Those same ideals, though, also can be (re)cast as Asian cultural values, presenting queer and trans people as inauthentic outsiders within their communities. As Karin Aguilar-San Juan says with regard to Asian American gays and lesbians being out within their families, "Many of us simply cannot do so, at least not openly, because of the intolerance of parents, relatives, or friends who bristle at our 'lifestyles'": "It seems that for many Asian Americans home is a place where 'Asianness' originates, a place made more compelling by the negation of an Asian American presence elsewhere."[133] Thus, even as notions of *home* may be shaped by Euro-American discourses and institutions, they often are enacted as expressions of Asian realness in ways that reaffirm their centrality to articulations of Asian American identity. Examining contemporary Asian North American novels (from the United States and Canada), Stephen Hong Sohn highlights how "queerness endangers the next generation of model minorities . . ., polluting the narrative of progress," and he traces forms of *inscrutable belonging* through which queer characters establish networks of connection and support for themselves, which exceed the nuclear family and "are unrecognized by larger cultural and legislative entities."[134]

Work in queer and trans studies specifically has considered the ways *Asianness* is positioned outside of dominant conceptions of (white) heteromasculinity. Addressing the feminization of Asian American men and the prevailing portrayal of gay Asian men as sexually passive and penetrated, almost always by white men, Richard Fung argues in his much-cited article "Looking for My Penis," "antiracist strategies that fail to subvert the race-gender status quo are of seriously limited value . . . . Race is a factor in even our most intimate relationships," and he adds that although "established racial hierarchies may be experienced as oppressive, we are not necessarily moved to scrutinize our own desire," including the psychological effects of Asian people being understood as "undersexed" and "assigning the Asian the role of bottom."[135] As Eng notes, if "the Asian American male is both materially and psychically feminized within the context of a larger US cultural imaginary," the answer is not seeking access to "the dominant heterosexist and racist structures through which the Asian American male is historically feminized and rendered self-hating in the first place."[136]

Foregrounding feminization and bottomhood, other scholars have explored the potentials at play within such gendered discourses of Asian deviance. In *A View from the Bottom*, Tan Hoang Nguyen argues "for a politics of bottomhood that opposes racism and heteronormativity without scapegoating femininity," one that "accounts for the sense of vulnerability, intimacy, and shame" associated with supposed sexual passivity/receptivity.[137] He sees in portrayals of feminized submission a model of Asian American subjectivity and relationality not based on an investment in normative masculinist ideas about assertive, autonomous selfhood. As opposed to largely white gay male efforts to rescue bottomhood from its association with femininity, illustrating a "continuing investment in phallic masculinity," Nguyen seeks to "make space for a plurality of gender expressions" while also opening possibilities for exploring "the ways negative affects – such as shame, loss, grief, and anger – underline our social alliances and political identifications."[138] If Asian bottomhood often is associated with the figure of the "rice queen," white gay men who are attracted to a feminized vision of Asianness, some have suggested "sticky rice" pairings – gay Asian men having erotic/romantic relationships with each other – as the answer to forms of gay racial objectification. Rather than emerging only recently as a rejoinder to white exoticization within queer discourses and dynamics, eroticized Asian–Asian male pairings long have served as a way of negotiating various forms of difference and privilege among Asian American men. Cynthia Wu argues, "the reason this figuration of same-sex contact remains alluring is precisely because the halves of these pairs are *not* equal even as they seem to be." Such pairings, then, register the difficulties "for a population that has often struggled with coalition building."[139] Even as Asianness may appear as racial sameness, it incorporates a range of groups who have complex, shifting, and often fraught relations among themselves and with each other, such that *Asian American* as a category is less simply descriptive than itself a political project – "aspirations" toward "collectivity and to a fragile yet crucial coalition of multiple communities."[140] *Sticky rice* figurations, then, can point toward such desires for alliance across difference while also registering the difficulties and failures of such aspirations: "It is having these hierarchies in place, no matter how hard we pretend they are not there, that makes the figure of a set of intraracially paired men so attractive as a metaphor."[141]

The prominence of considerations of bottomhood and male homoeroticism, though, can leave aside the implications of racialized femininity for Asian American women – cis, lesbian, and trans. As Vivian L. Huang shows, dominant representations of Asian femininity convey the idea of it as an inscrutable surface in which women are ornaments, self-effacing hosts and helpmates, and endlessly available for erotic service. That very sense of inscrutability, though, Huang argues, also serves as a basis for queer and trans aesthetics. Emphasizing relationality, the power of silence, and the dynamism of apparent impassivity, such aesthetics move away from the understanding of "Asian forms" as "spectacular surfaces with mysterious interiors to penetrate or cut into" – "an anti-woman ontology of 'Asia' premised on forceful penetration." Instead, Huang suggests that a queer and trans vision of inscrutability displaces such models of racialized hetero-masculinist dominance with the potentials of surface relations, such as the pleasurable tactility of skin-to-skin contact and the ways "feeling distant" enables layered emotional work that acknowledges forms of difference.[142]

If certain notions of Asianness constellate around feminized passivity, particularly with regard to East Asia, others take shape around images of perverse barbarism associated with the figure of the terrorist. Talking about "the consolidation of new racial populations" targeting "Arabs, Muslims, and South Asians," which has characterized the post-9/11 "War on Terror," Jasbir Puar illustrates how the "racialized queernesses" attributed to such populations are differentiated from the performance of home and family by the "good straight ethnic."[143] Drawing on much older exoticizing discourses that present sexual and gender deviance as endemic to the Middle East and South Asia (see Chapter 3), a set of ideas often characterized as *Orientalism*,[144] the depiction of the terrorist relies on racializing ideas of sexual depravity. Such "Orientalist constructions of 'Muslim sexuality'" depend on creating a kind of racial identity in which "Muslim = Islam = Arab" and in which aberrant modes of gender and desire are thought to give rise to irrational, uncivilized, and uncontrollable impulses, including violence, thereby constructing the *terrorist* as a social type – "a body almost *too perverse to be read as queer*."[145] Such efforts to "produce a coherent idea of the 'Muslim enemy Other' from disparate populations of Arabs, Middle Easterners, and South Asians" is part of the ideological and institutional process of legitimizing what Ronak K. Kapadia has characterized as the *forever war*, the post-9/11 forms of US assault abroad (including expansive use of drone strikes) and systems of racial profiling that build on "a longer history of US imperialism that has been erased or evaded."[146] The racialized image of *the terrorist* relies on conceptions of sexual and gender nonnormativity in ways that construct persons and populations as deviant threats to the civilized order ostensibly represented by the United States, thereby licensing various forms of surveillance, invasion, discrimination, and detention by distinguishing terrorist-producing groups from those seen as viable citizens or participants in the rule of law.

Citizenship and national belonging, however, are not the goal for much Asian Americanist scholarship, instead addressing the significance of diasporic networks and identities. Addressing Korean American identity and genealogy, JeeYeun Lee asks, "How do I claim a past that seems both mine and not mine? How do I negotiate a history located in another continent in another tongue?" The notion of diaspora, she suggests, aims to undermine the prevalent narrative of immigration in which "the so-called Third World is an inherently bad and undesirable place to live," particularly for queer and trans people, "and the United States and the rest of the West are the fount of all opportunity and good."[147] Instead, a focus on diaspora highlights ongoing relations among places, including the ways (as noted previously) migration to the United States often results from forms of US military, political, and economic intervention and support for authoritarian regimes abroad. As Lu Thuy Nguyen asks specifically with regard to Vietnamese American refugees and their children, "what do we make of the many worlds supposedly ended, whose inhabitants must go on, even when their legacy and memory are of trauma and war debris?"[148] This emphasis on the racialized political economies that help produce dislocation unsettles discourses of "cultural authenticity" among migrants that emphasize their status as "model minorities" committed to "self-help, the sanctity of marriage, and intact families," in which sexual and gender nonnormativity appear as a culturally inauthentic adoption of white forms of deviance.[149] As Lee observes, "Diasporic queers cannot inscribe themselves into an imagined or real homeland without radically changing its terms, since many forms of nationalism are constructed around assumptions of normative heterosexuality."[150]

Attending to such dislocations and claims to authenticity from a queer critical perspective also involves raising questions about how diasporic relations with the *homeland* can reinforce sexual and gender norms in both. Gayatri Gopinath observes the value of "foreground[ing] notions of impurity," drawing attention to how, for example, "Hindu nationalist organizations in India are able to effectively mobilize and harness diasporic longing for authenticity and 'tradition' and convert this longing into material linkages between the diaspora and (home) nation," particularly in terms of "nationalist framings of women's sexuality." In response, she suggests that aligning *queer* and *diaspora* "recuperates those desires, practices, and subjectivities that are rendered impossible and unimaginable within conventional diasporic and nationalist imaginaries."[151] She further observes that "the aesthetic practices of queer diaspora make apparent how all spaces of 'home' and dwelling are shot through with contradictions and fissures, there is … no return to an unsullied past, no secure space of safety."[152] From that point of view, diaspora is not a dyad – the abandoned "home" country and the new one in which full inclusion is sought – but a web of shifting inhabitances and movements.[153] Eng-Beng Lim argues for "an inter-Asian diasporic framework that produces new models of cross-cultural understanding about queer sexuality" that also "imagine alternative ways of conceptualizing traditions, affiliations, kinship, genealogies, and citizenship," moving away from defining "transnational Asian queerness [and transness] . . . in contradistinction to Western epistemic categories." Referring to this kind of analysis as *glocalqueering*, connecting the global and local in ways not necessarily routed through national identities and nationalist ideologies, Lim suggests that it can "shift the discourse from one about complicity, resistance, or subversion to one about comparativity, lateral relationality, and coalition," and within this framework, "the United States is a nodal point rather than the center of the world."[154] In this vein, Gopinath offers "a queer regional imaginary" as an alternative to one fixated on the scale of the nation-state, offering "the possibility of tracing lines of connection and commonality" in a "South-South relationality" – one that is not the same as "a metronormative 'global gay' imaginary" in which there is a singular, US-centric vision of modern sexual identity.[155]

The sexual and gendered subjectivities and sensibilities of such networks, however, do not necessarily translate well into Euro-American categories, and such differences, scholars argue, cannot be understood in terms of a developmental timeline – as simply on the way to taking proper shape as LGBT identity. Discussing how forms of queer desire circulate transnationally, particularly in the reception of Bollywood films, Gopinath suggests that "looking for 'lesbians' in Bollywood . . . would falsely presume that queer representation . . . rests on the same logic of visibility as do dominant Euro-American constructions"; instead, it less involves "characters who are explicitly marked as sexual or gender deviants" than moments and scenes that "exploit the slippages between homosociality and homoeroticism that occur in representations of gender-segregated spaces."[156] In his study of "Filipino immigrant gay men," Martin F. Manalansan highlights the discrepancy between *bakla* and gay: "*Bakla* is the Tagalog term that encompasses homosexuality, [being intersex], cross-dressing, and effeminacy." This concept and its modes of social relation differ notably from dominant notions of gayness in being marked definitionally by a pronounced sense of gender nonnormativity, not conforming to a vision of "coming out" (an idea "premised on the idea of a truer inner self"), and being shaped by a collective performative ethos of "transformation" (rather than as revealing an aspect of individual selfhood).[157] As these examples suggest, attending to the complexities of diaspora entails an engagement with modes of pleasure, identity, and gender expression that neither can be measured against a Euro-American standard nor can be viewed as expressive of a kind of cultural essence from the supposed home country.

Conclusion

Queer of color and Indigenous critique refuses the lure of recognition and inclusion as upstanding, respectable citizens. Instead, such work addresses the complex and multifaceted subjectivities, kinds of embodiment, identifications and forms of belonging, placemaking, and mobilities generated by ongoing histories of racialization, imperialism, and colonial occupation. This work helps map out the ways the United States is both itself a colonial formation (through its status as a settler-state and its expansions and annexations) and is transected by geographies of diaspora, imperial investment and intervention, and networks of capital. In doing do, these scholars also show how sexuality and gender are inextricable from racial differentiation, hierarchy, regulation, and forms of everyday felt experience. As Kyla Wazana Tompkins notes, queer of color work has argued that "the state, the nation, and citizenship" are "articulated as universals that are normatively heterosexual and white, both producing and obscuring populations of color as always and already non-heteronormative and sexually deviant," and for such scholarship "the nation-state emerges as more of a problem than as a site for solutions."[158] Although there may be overlaps among forms of racialization, those forms are not equivalent, and different kinds of racist conceptions attach to different populations. While not presenting racial groups as hermetically sealed off from each other, queer and trans scholarship grapples with these differences, their effects on how varied groups are interpellated within dominant ideologies of sexuality and gender, and the diverse ways that such groups may contest those ideologies and envision possibilities for freedom, justice, and self-determination. Moreover, work in queer and trans studies illustrates the range of conceptual and cultural frames groups have for naming the matrix of desire, pleasure, gender expression, and social belonging, as well as the ways such frames do and don't transit to other places and people(s). In these ways, Indigenous, Black, Latinx, and Asian American studies draw on allied sets of questions, concerns, and methodologies but remain distinct in important ways that reflect complex and multifaceted ongoing histories of racialization and empire.

Chapter 5
Global Dynamics, Refusals, and Reorientations

When thinking about the world outside of "the West" (the United States, northern and western Europe, and predominantly white settler-states like Canada and Australia), scholarship can fall into generalizing frameworks in which comparison with the West predominates or in which the world is divided up into *areas* that are treated as self-identical blocks, also de facto portrayed as more or less sealed off from each other. The presence of such patterns raises a series of questions: how can we reckon with the effects and ongoing histories of imperialism and occupation, uneven transnational dynamics of exploitation and extraction, and racial capitalism while not understanding those subjected to oppression and domination as merely passive in the face of those processes? How do we engage with forms of difference while understanding them as multidimensional, permeable, and changing, rather than freezing them in ahistorical and essentialized accounts of local/national/regional culture? How do we attend to forms of place-based specificity (at whatever scale) while engaging the heterogeneity and diversity of the area/country/population under discussion and while also addressing dynamic relations with other peoples and places – both chosen and coerced? Moreover, how do we decenter "the West" without recentering it in that very process (as the thing whose negation ends up defining the shape and character of our studies)?

Those conceptual and political questions, though, are not new within queer and trans studies.[1] One of the central matters that has concerned these fields is the stakes of using terms and identities largely developed within English-speaking contexts to talk about phenomena in other places and languages. As David Gramling and Aniruddha Dutta observe, "the rise and hegemonic consolidation of English as a default lingua franca of transnationalism means that translation both to and from anglophone discourses has become an imperative that structures daily life as well as academic and activist practice in many postcolonies."[2] Further, queer and trans conceptual and analytical frameworks emerging out of the United States often are taken as the intellectual matrix into which social formations elsewhere are incorporated as a distinct content. Anjali Arondeker and Geeta Patel note that "the citational underpinnings that provide the theoretical conduit for such explorations were and continue to be resolutely contemporary and drawn primarily from the United States; that is, geopolitics provides the exemplars, but rarely the epistemologies."[3] This question of how to address and understand what might be seen as concerns of sexuality and gender expression arises in particularly pointed ways in international fora and declarations. With respect to employing terms like *lesbian* and *feminist*, Katie King suggests, "Using them in global terms is a political act. Refusing them as global terms is also a political act."[4] There is the problem of seeking to speak across geopolitical differences in ways that allow for solidarity, meaningful transnational organizing, and mobilization of human rights discourses and institutions, while, on the other hand, there is the danger of those very formulations being treated as simply the obvious and incontestable way through which to make universalizing claims.[5]

In struggles over how to articulate, categorize, and interpret across languages and geopolitical formations, topics that concern sexuality and gender are especially fraught. Rejecting what are taken to be nonnormative forms of desire and embodiment, or insisting that there are none of *those* persons in a given place, can serve as a way of bolstering nationalist projects centered around ideas of purity/heritage and of rooting out contaminating foreign/ imperialist influences. Conversely, however, the claiming of "progressive" stances on LGBT issues can also be taken as a sign – or metric – of a country's proper enactment of human rights principles (as determined by those elsewhere), which may be significant for access to aid, investment, or admittance to international institutions of various kinds. As Arnoldo Cruz-Malavé and Martin Manalansan observe, "queer sexualities and cultures have often been deployed negatively to allay anxieties about 'authentic' national belonging in our massively migratory contemporary world ... and positively by nation-states in order to project an image of global modernness consistent with capitalist market exchange."[6] Such asymmetries emerge out of and continue racializing colonial narratives "in which the United States and Europe are figured as modern ..., while other parts of the world are presumed to be traditional, especially in regard to sexuality," asserting a "cosmopolitanism [that] emerges over and against [for example] rural, African, and Islamic 'barbarism.'"[7]

In light of the difficulties of such nationalist consolidations and transnational pressures, scholars can position *the local* as an autonomous space of difference that refuses both. However, queer and trans work also has sought to complicate this sense of localized identities and practices as either fully insulated from the national/global or as simply derived from them. As Elizabeth Povinelli and George Chauncey argue, "The question that scholars of globalization face is how to conceptualize these delicate and dramatic figurations and refigurations of local embodiments, identities, and imaginaries."[8] Another concern is positioning the *local* "as working against or in resistance to the global" in ways that position "queer [and trans] subjects" as "always already avant-garde for all times and places," rather than considering them as diverse communities and individuals participating in multidimensional ways within situated social circumstances.[9] In this way, work in queer and trans studies has sought to draw on "the kind of thick, linguistic, cultural detail" that historically has been part of methodologies in area studies while eschewing the presumed "stability and continuity of culture areas and their diverse populations" that has predominated in those fields, which themselves were formed out of Cold War political geographies.[10] This kind of intellectual work, studying sexuality and gender within a transnational frame in ways that do not depend on static notions of scale or culture (or of *sexuality* and *gender*, for that matter), involves addressing distinctions without treating them as absolute while also tracking how ideas, terms, practices, and institutional forms transit globally in complex ways.

In considering how queer and trans studies has taken up these various intellectual and methodological challenges, the chapter is organized into three sections. The first considers critiques of imperialist and capitalist influence as well as critiques of those critiques, due to what other scholars have suggested can be their homogenizing tendencies. The second section focuses on articulations of national/local differences and how to understand them in relation to layered histories and contemporary transnational mobilities and influences. The final section will address such circulations and exchanges, particularly as they generate forms of regional interrelation – connections that themselves do not simply follow from Western/Global North formulations and frameworks, despite the latter's presumed dominance.[11]

Imperial and Capitalist Expansion/Intervention

In challenging naturalized assumptions about gender and sexuality, part of the work of queer and trans studies has involved registering the presence of other social arrangements of desire, embodiment, and identity than those inherited from Euro-American sexology (as discussed in Chapter 3). In doing so, these fields also have tracked how such templates have been imposed elsewhere as part of Western political and economic interventions. Reorganizing modes of pleasure, kinship, gender difference, and conceptions of corporeality and selfhood has been an important part of exerting authority over nonwhite populations (under the banner of inculcating *civilization*), thereby creating social infrastructures seen as more conducive to imperial forms of governance, exploitation, and extraction (discussed in Chapters 3 and 4). As a result, existing social configurations and experiences of personhood in a given place are cast as backward, savage, and in need of renovation to engage fully in modern life. In addition, the insertion of spaces into global capitalist production, commodification, and financialization can bring with it normalizing forms of gender and sexuality that largely are not imposed as such but whose givenness is treated as part and parcel of participation in global markets and consumption, while also being cast as expressions of what it means to participate in global modernity. Such patterns can also occur with regard to medicine and other forms of knowledge-production, where the global political and economic influence of certain countries/regions allows for ideas and frameworks from there to be treated as if they were universally true and desirable. However, even while recognizing these dynamics, scholars also have suggested that emphasis on imperial and capitalist intervention/influence can efface local agency and set up a binary between "sexual Westernization" and reified "traditional" cultures, "framing non-Western societies as repositories of presumptively authentic, local sexual identities."[12] This dynamic can end up denigrating the adoption of what are presented as foreign forms and problematically can present those engaged in such practices as inauthentic and alienated, thereby denying possibilities for difference and diversity within nonwestern spaces.

Postcolonial nations (which have gained independence from European or US direct colonial control and are now their own distinct states) often continue to seek to be recognized by colonizing countries and other Western powers as having achieved the capacity for full self-governance, as having overcome the racialized backwardness attributed to them within colonial discourses. As scholars have shown, that process often involves embedding heteronormative and cisnormative dynamics in national legal and administrative structures in ways that deny possibilities for queer and/or trans belonging within the nation. Trinidad and Tobago and the Bahamas, for example, stage national civility/autonomy through a repetition of colonial ideologies that also, somewhat paradoxically, facilitates the openness of the nation to ongoing and expanding imperial economic influence. M. Jacqui Alexander observes with regard to countries in the Caribbean, "The state's authority to rule is currently under siege; the ideological moorings of nationalism have been dislodged, partly because of major international political economic incursions that have in turn provoked an internal crisis of authority," even as states solicit such intervention (largely organized around tourism industries) in order to shore up national economies left without infrastructural resources due to the exploitative systems under colonial rule and further extractive relations to richer nations in its wake (including via "structural adjustment" programs instituted by international development institutions, like the International Monetary Fund and World Bank, that largely are dominated by such wealthier nations).[13] In addressing these compromised dynamics of postcolonial Caribbean sovereignty, states present the "sexual decadence" of their ostensible citizens as the reason for the failures of the nation, seeking to remedy the "legitimation crisis" created by structural dependence on foreign capital "by recouping heterosexuality through legislation" – such as the Sexual Offences Act of 1986 in Trinidad and Tobago (overturned by the High Court of Justice in 2018), which criminalized same-sex eroticism alongside what were cast as aberrant/violent forms of straightness.[14] In this way, Alexander suggests, "the law forges continuity between white imperial heteropatriarchy ... and black heteropatriarchy," while "mak[ing] borders permeable for the entry of multinational capital" and "actively socializ[ing] loyal heterosexual citizens into tourism ... by sexualizing them and by positioning them as commodities."[15]

These kinds of contemporary statutes supposedly aimed at demonstrating and insuring Caribbean national decency are themselves legacies of colonial-era legislation, such as the reliance of anti-sodomy statutes in Trinidad and Tobago and other British colonies in the Caribbean on the 1861 Offences against the Person Act.[16] In this way, the legal status of forms of sexual expression within the postcolonial state takes part within a much longer colonial history, in which supposed tendencies toward depravity and bestiality in nonwhite populations were seen as making them unable to achieve civilized self-governance. As Andil Gosine argues, "The end of slavery in the Caribbean [in the 1830s for areas under British control] created a new conundrum in the colonies: how to make the previously animalized, enslaved person human?" He adds, "Across the postemancipation Caribbean, a commitment to disciplined heterosexuality was foundational to becoming characterized as human, not animal, and thus established in law."[17] The contemporary "heterosexualization of the state," then, replays the "racializing and sexualizing [of] the population" that was a key part of justifying European rule for centuries, although this time as part of a performance of national respectability that substitutes for meaningful national autonomy.[18] As Kamala Kempadoo observes, "sexuality appears as the modality through which race is made and refashioned in specific ways" in the Caribbean, and, reciprocally, sexuality appears as "the avenue through which race could be reconfigured and 'civilization' obtained."[19]

The production of straight states in this way, though, can also lead Western commentators to see such countries and their populations as especially homophobic, effacing the effects of ongoing colonial legacies and doubling down on the racializing dehumanization enacted by those legacies. Gosine observes, "policy makers, politicians, businesses, and local and international activists together co-constitute the nonwhite homophobe as an animal," thereby "tak[ing] up missions as new civilizing agents" who will teach nonwhite people how to be human(e) and modern in their attitudes toward sexual and gender minorities.[20] This pattern is abetted by asylum procedures in countries like the United States that "demand the production of claimants' home states as violently homophobic" in order to regulate immigration (also discussed in Chapter 4). Such narratives themselves overlook the presence of forms of queer and trans activism across the Caribbean, and in other majority nonwhite nations, that seek less to be legally acknowledged as visible minority subjects with specifically protected rights than "to be recognized as part of the national family."[21] Not only does the racializing castigation of homophobia/ transphobia elsewhere tend to repeat colonial figures of backwardness (a version of *they* are not as advanced or forward-thinking as *us*), it also displaces discussion of how the very actions that are being critiqued themselves can be understood as "resistance to perceived and real encroachments on neocolonial national sovereignty" by countries of the Global North.[22] Discussing the role of southern African bishops in the 1998 vote within the Anglican conference to deny membership to "non-celibate homosexual clergy" and to prevent clergy from officiating "same-sex unions," Neville Hoad notes that these actions "can be seen as responses to . . . prior attributions of primitiveness" that affirm "the bourgeois nuclear family" as "the proper intimate form of modernity."[23] Moreover, what can be read (and can function) as affirmations of straightness or as regressive resistance to gay and/or trans rights, as Hoad and others suggest, can also be read (and function) as affirmations of postcolonial national and regional autonomy against an international human rights regime that often serves as an extension of the policy goals and ideologies of Western and Global North nations, as well as against the ways AIDS/HIV has been linked to Africa (see Chapter 2). Hoad points toward "the international homosexual rights movement's complicity in developmental and universalist depictions of third world sexual mores," part of the centuries' long imperial project of "dictating what Africans should and should not do with their bodies."[24]

In one of the most forceful and influential critiques of the ways Western social actors and institutions seek to set the terms through which sexuality is conceptualized globally, Joseph Massad has referred to this assemblage as *the Gay International*, but other scholars have suggested that while this formulation, and ones like it, capture something of the relation between Western discourses of sexuality and ongoing imperialism, that analysis comes at the expense of and effaces the politics, advocacy, and self-articulations of queer and trans people in the Global South, particularly in the Arab regions Massad addresses. Massad foregrounds how nationalist modes of Arab historiography from the early twentieth century onward have worked to marginalize and erase evidence of prominent forms of homoeroticism in Arab cultures, such as in love poetry from older to younger men (see Chapter 3), by casting such discourse as aberrant and/or alien (for example, attributing them to Persian influence). Massad notes, "some modern Arab nationalists wanted to safeguard the 'pure' Arab civilization of the past as a basis for the modern Arab nation," in the process discarding "all that they considered unsavory in Arab civilization as a foreign import."[25] Yet while challenging this limited and Western-influenced articulation of Arab pasts and presents, Massad himself decries the importation of a gay human rights frame as a continuation of imperial ideologies. In its naturalization of sexual identity and the hetero/homo binary, the Gay International "produces homosexuals, as well as gays and lesbians, where they do not exist, and represses same-sex desires and practices that refuse to be assimilated into its sexual epistemology," interpellating Arab modes of desire and notions of gendered personhood into Euro-American terms that are cast as generically human.[26] This argument can be understood as part of a broader conversation about what has been termed *pinkwashing*, which involves countries seeking to redirect attention away from their own racist and colonial policies and actions by presenting themselves as significantly supporting LGBT rights in contrast to nonwhite nations and populations. The term particularly has been used to describe Israel's public discourse. As Sa'ed Atshan notes, "rather than improve its global standing by providing Palestinians with basic human rights, the Israeli state, and its supporters, increasingly moving to the right, seek to market Israel as a state that supports LGBTQ individuals and communities," especially as implicitly or often explicitly contrasted with Palestinian communities and neighboring Arab states.[27] Within this frame, supporters of Israeli state narratives present themselves as "saving brown homosexuals from brown heterosexuals," fusing Euro-American conceptions of sexuality and minority identity to imperial ideologies of racial/civilizational superiority in ways that resonate with Massad's analysis.[28]

However, other scholars have drawn attention to how Massad's argument and the discourse of pinkwashing can provide a thin and skewed account of sexual and gender subjectivities and politics among Arab people, particularly Palestinians. Massad contends that "middle- and upper-class native informants and diasporic members of the national group" are *colluding* with "Western human rights groups and organizations" in the promotion of "a Eurocentric culture that is being universalized," suggesting that Arabs who formulate their own human rights claims with regard to sexuality and gender expression are more or less mouthpieces for a Euro-American imperial agenda. Furthermore, the actions by Arab governments presented as homophobic are *"incited* by Gay International discourse," such that "the Gay International" is "largely responsible for the intensity" of antigay actions by those governments.[29] This argument suggests a seamless weave between international institutions and a Western conception of LGBT identities and rights. However, that account leaves aside how international aid and human rights institutions both can advocate for protection for women (envisioned in biological terms) and adopt Christian organizations' emphasis on the heteronuclear family as the basis of moral social order in ways that are deeply antagonistic to erotic and gender diversity. As Josephine Ho illustrates with regard to the work of UN-backed women's and Christian NGOs across East Asia, these organizations deeply influence national law and policy, "mobilizing and transforming conservative vigilance into an active surveillance network that thrives on fanning sex panic," putatively in the interest of protecting vulnerable populations from being corrupted and exploited (such as in sex trafficking). Apparently "enhancing protection for women and children," in line with what seem like the demands of UN covenants/principles, serves "as proof of responsible government" that can be "presented to the international community as evidence of democratic progress toward a rational 'rule of law,'" albeit one in which nonnormative sexualities and genders have no place.[30] This discussion of the work of human rights institutions and discourses raises questions about the cohesion of the elements supposedly fused to each other in Massad's notion of the Gay International.

Moreover, specifically with respect to Arab peoples, formulations like Massad's present "the Arab world" as the "passive victim" of "U.S. and other Western needs" while portraying "those Arabs who identify as homosexual" as "betray[ing] their authentic Arab culture," due to uncritically adopting Euro-American notions of *gayness*.[31] Not only does such an approach radically limit possibilities for engaging the diversity of sexual subjectivities among Arab people, it dismisses queer and trans critique of Arab nationalisms as, at best, marginal/irrelevant and, at worst, inherently complicitous with Euro-American racisms and imperialism. With regard to Palestinian political discourses and movements, Atshan refers to this delegitimization of queer and trans issues as *the empire of critique*.[32] He argues that "some leftist critics demand that queer Palestinians subordinate resistance to Palestinian homophobia to a Palestinian nationalist struggle that fails to acknowledge them," while also presenting the terms used by queer Palestinians in critiques of their erasure – such as "*gay* and *lesbian*" – as merely "by-products of Israel and the West's colonial agenda," such as in Massad's account of Arab "native informants" (which Atshan rejects, especially with regard to Palestinian queer organizations such as Al-Qaws).[33] The discourse of pinkwashing itself can contribute to this problem by portraying the role of queer and trans analysis and advocacy with regard to Israel/Palestine as primarily, or even exclusively, criticizing Zionism and the actions of the Israeli state (and its Western supporters, like the United States): "the fact that pinkwatching [attending to and calling out forms of pinkwashing] has become a central paradigm of the global solidarity movement has effectively elevated Zionism over concerns about antiqueer oppression."[34] In an effort to link specific ways of naming and formulating sexual and gender identity with racializing and colonial projects, scholarly work can end up de facto disqualifying the self-articulations, interests, and political formations of the persons and groups who take up those supposedly alien forms, also closing down discussion of forms of gender and sexual oppression among colonized and nonwestern populations and within the Global South.

Western medical and public health frameworks can play a significant role in such intranational dynamics, particularly around what constitute institutionally legible forms of gender identity and expression. As Aniruddha Dutta and Raina Roy observe, "the attempted universalization of transgender as a transnational umbrella term by the development (nongovernmental) sector, the state, and their funders tends to subsume South Asian discourses and practices of gender/sexual variance as merely 'local' expressions of transgender identity." Doing so not only interpellates gender-variant persons and communities – such as *hijras* in India (discussed further below) – into an ostensibly global, commonsensical framework but makes the adoption of that frame into the condition of possibility for accessing national resources, creating "a constrained rubric of representation for gaining funds and recognition."[35] The issue is not so much that a category like *transgender* is supposedly foreign but that it is treated as if it were able seamlessly to incorporate South Asian and other genders into itself: "while 'transgender' is not indubitably foreign or colonizing, its hegemonic position in discourses of activism and funding reflects inequalities within the hierarchical political economy of social movements and the nonprofit sector, even as the category may be appropriated or translated in ways that subvert these hierarchies."[36] Moreover, the category has been institutionalized by the Indian state, including as part of HIV prevention efforts, in ways that make it the privileged mode for engaging with government discourses and institutions.[37] In similar ways, Brazilian law and policy has adopted a model of medical gender transition that effaces the self-understanding and desires of *travestis*, "individuals who are assigned the male sex at birth, who feminize their bodies through the use of hormones and silicone injections, and who prefer female names and pronouns. Travestis have no desire for sex-reassignment surgery, but they might require other forms of medical treatment such as hormone therapy or breast implants."[38] However, although Brazil's universal healthcare system covers the cost of gender-affirming surgery, the guidelines define the issue as one of gender dysphoria, addressed through movement from one biologized sex to another, and the hospitals authorized to offer gender-affirming care insist that such care must entail this full set of surgical interventions.[39] Access to medical technologies for gender affirmation are being pinned to a particular model of gender identity disorder and transition that emerges out of Euro-American institutions but that then is mobilized by the Brazilian state and medical establishment in ways that work to foreclose extant modes of gender embodiment – particularly those of travestis – that are cast as degraded, low-class, and socially disruptive/disreputable.[40]

A further twist in considering the stakes of how Western models of gender and sexuality circulate in nonwestern spaces lies in the ways the changes brought by global capitalism can enable identifications, practices, and forms of association for gender and sexual minorities outside the West. As opposed to depictions of *the third-world queer* as "an embodiment of alterity that sits at the losing end of cultures of domination," queer persons in nonwestern spaces can be considered as "not just the other but an other that makes its own others."[41] As the editors of the volume *AsiaPacifiQueer* ask, "how can we further theorize the popular appropriation of the image of the global gay in Asia as the desire for sameness without simply reducing it to a homogenizing effect of global queering?"[42] In this vein, Bobby Benedicto addresses the ways relatively privileged men who participate in the self-consciously *gay* scene in the Philippines take part in an aspirational imaginative "trajectory that directs gay life in Manila outward toward the global, forward toward modernity, and upward toward higher states of class privilege," a vision of the *global* and *modern* shaped around a desire to belong within circuits of transnational capitalism that also is shared by others of "Manila's urban elites."[43] Commercial spaces and entrepreneurial forms of self-fashioning can also provide a means of generating queer and trans possibilities in states with conflicted and ambivalent ways of engaging nonnormative genders and sexualities. Prior to 2022, Singapore, for example, criminalized same-sex sodomy between men while also helping subsidize the emergence of queer businesses in and around Chinatown (envisioned largely as promoting gay tourism), and from 1973 onward, the government funded gender-affirming surgery (for many years making Singapore a principal Asian site for medical tourism) while in the 1980s it also tore down and *redeveloped* Bugis Street, infamous for its transgender street culture, which was condemned by officials as a degrading legacy of the colonial era. Amid these cross-currents, "queer commerce" flourished, enabling "dance clubs, public parties, karaoke bars, and saunas" in areas targeted for such economic development, places that facilitated the emergence and consolidation of forms of queer subjectivity and community. These dynamics are part of a "disjunctive queer modernity" in which participation in capitalism offers potentials for gender and sexual expression and worldmaking different than those directly endorsed by the state.[44] Similarly, the Thai government's commitment in urban areas to creating commercial spaces, such as malls, rather than setting aside public space for recreation and leisure enabled the growth of "a new cross-class consumer culture that facilitates different sexual and gender positions, including the role of tomboy, or tom" – a term adapted from English to characterize forms of female masculinity. As Ara Wilson argues, "Shopping complexes allow a venue away from home or school that provides a space of freedom for youth with disposable income, and, in this way, hosts a variety of expressions of identity."[45] Malls provide both work opportunities for toms (as opposed to the strict gender presentation requirements of civil service positions) and places for same-sex sociality separate from the family homes in which most unmarried women continue to reside.[46] In various ways, then, "the infrastructure, discourses, and operations of the capitalist market economy" help engender possibilities for a range of eroticisms, gender expressions, and forms of queer and trans community formation.[47] As with the ongoing legacies of colonialism and the operation of international institutions, scholars both have examined the extractive and imperial force of global capitalism with regard to sexuality and gender and have shown how engagement with capitalist dynamics cannot be reduced to an easy distinction between alien and homegrown/authentic social forms.

Specificity beyond Authenticity/Nativism

Appeals to local, national, and/or regional authenticity – especially as contrasted with supposedly foreign forms associated with the West – often offer an ahistorical view while also insisting on a rigid binary between intrusive change and what is cast as the solidity of tradition, creating a vision of collective purity that sometimes is referred to as *nativism*. How can we talk about forms of specificity (of movements, kinds of self-identification, social conjunctures) without falling into the conceptual and political trap of de facto positing kinds of timeless difference? If queer and trans studies have traced modes of colonial/capitalist imposition *and* challenged essentialist and homogenizing notions of nonwestern identity, what strategies have these fields generated for attending to the particularities of specific areas (at various scales) without slipping into the binary of authenticity versus contamination? Scholars have sought to address the layered and shifting complexities of everyday modes of desire, embodiment, identification, and association as well as the possibilities for political organizing and articulation within particular national and regional structures. They have also engaged the use of gender and sexual regulation by various political regimes, in ways that cannot simply be reduced to Western influence, and, reciprocally, scholarship also has addressed how such regimes can enable possibilities for queer and trans worldmaking.

Attending to the particularity of nonwestern spaces and populations requires setting aside universalizing notions of coming out, gay and lesbian identity, and progress. In her study of sexual relations among Black working-class women in Suriname (many of whom are descended from maroon communities), Gloria Wekker discusses how such erotic relationships are understood less as an expression of an innate identity than as participation in "the *mati* work," as particular "behaviors and actions" – described "in terms of verbs" rather than nouns. As she notes, "In the mati work no real, authentic, fixed self is claimed," although there often is "a gendered role division" among same-sex lovers, partially due to the ways engaging in the *mati* work is understood in Winti spirituality as a manifestation of the presence of gendered non-human entities and dimensions of the soul.[48] These relationships also provide possibilities for gaining resources and generating extensive kinship networks that can help sustain largely women-led households, even as many of the women, at one point or another, also have had sexual relationships with men. Wekker further argues that the particular shape of Black women's homoeroticism in Suriname (including in the frequent migrations between the country and the Netherlands, from which Suriname achieved independence in 1975) embodies "West African 'grammatical' principles in the domain of subjectivity and sexuality," illustrating "a notion of personhood in which the secular and the spiritual are intertwined" and "the full sexual subjectivity of women" is acknowledged which, she suggests, extends across the diaspora produced by transatlantic enslavement.[49] In this case, there is not a minoritized sexual identity to be made visible or around which to organize a sense of community, separate from other existing processes of household formation, social reproduction, and postcolonial migrancy. By contrast, Ghassan Moussawi addresses how issues of queerness in Beirut are less about creating forms of connection (with sexual partners, among households, with spiritual entities) than managing a situation of perennial sociopolitical instability. The after-effects of the Lebanese civil war (1975–1990) combined with the ongoing threat of war, economic crises, and growing numbers of refugees from neighboring countries (especially Palestinians and Syrians) create what people in Beirut euphemistically call *al-wad'*, or "the situation" – a term that speaks to "the complexity of everyday violence, disruptions, and lack of basic services." In this context, for people engaging in nonnormative eroticisms and forms of gender expression, visibility is not so much about "outness or closeting" as "complex strategies of maneuvering" in order to avoid harassment or assault (including based on gender deviance or racializing assumptions about predatory migrant perversity) or to maintain important relationships (such as preventing one's family from being ostracized or shamed by other family members in their communities).[50] While potentially related to forms of sexuality and gender, though, such negotiations about how one is seen, by whom, and where, Moussawi argues, are far more widespread and index more pervasive social antagonisms and instabilities, ones that aren't addressed through identification with or organizing around notions of LGBT community. These everyday difficulties and disjunctions persist even as Beirut is presented – both by outsiders and, at times, by officials seeking to attract tourism and foreign investment – as exceptional in its gay-friendly "openness," "tolerance," and "cosmopolitanism in opposition to traditional Muslim Arab values," offering a homonormative image that aims to separate Beirut not only from other Arab countries in the region but even from other parts of Lebanon.[51] Not only do conventional conceptions of outness not address the issues at play in navigating ordinary life, that image of gayness is used by those both outside and inside Lebanon in ways that efface the politics of everyday disruptions and how experiences of gender and sexuality are intimately enmeshed with family, class, religion, race, and migrancy.

Ways of figuring desire, identity, and visibility also shift generationally, taking on different meanings over time. That uneven and layered process, though, is not the same as progress, or the notion of an inevitable turn toward supposedly enlightened ways of thinking, even as some people may present such developments as becoming more *modern*, whether for good or ill.

Changing conceptions of sexuality in Mexico can help illustrate these dynamics. Guadalajara, the capital of the Mexican state of Jalisco, for example, is known as "one of the most conservative and traditional [cities] in Mexico" while also being "regarded as being the most homosexual city in Mexico." As Héctor Carrillo notes, though, "the location of the boundary between traditional and modern varied considerably from person to person."[52] Notions of normality are suspended between two different formulations: "one set of categories of classification" is "based on gender/sex roles" while the other is "based on object choice," and a man in the former could retain a claim to normality as long as he is the penetrator in sexual relations (*activo*) while, in the latter formulation, any same-sex eroticism would make him *homosexual*.[53] Yet, even as those who drew on a heterosexual/homosexual binary tended to be younger and often understood themselves (whether straight or queer) as more modern and worldly, supposedly generationally outmoded gender frames would return, such as heterosexuals using *homosexual* only when referring to "the receptive partner in anal sex between men" or gay men who distance themselves from effeminacy in order to "pass as *normal*."[54] Moreover, cross-generational commitments to familial belonging, including unmarried people continuing to live with their parents, cut across other apparent differences in attitudes toward sexuality, indicating a widespread investment "in finding ways to make their desires for change consistent with family life."[55] Such involvement, though, also tends to diminish the desirability of forms of *coming out*, given that public political visibility is often linked by middle-class gays and lesbians with gender nonnormative working-class efforts to gain access to forms of reputation and respect.[56] In the wake of the legalization of same-sex marriage in Mexico City and inclusion of protection for "sexual preferences" in the Mexican constitution,[57] women in *el ambiente* (literally the atmosphere but referring to queer spaces and networks) have been more vocal about exploring a greater range of possibilities for eroticism and intimacy than the couple form, with "monogamy and marriage" often being seen as connected to "the private property of goods" and as part of state strategies "to control bodies, minds, feelings."[58] Yet, "for women who had participated in el ambiente for several decades, polyamory as a revolutionary theoretical proposal was not a novelty," even though the terms had changed, and sex with multiple partners was less discussed in explicitly feminist terms than it once had been.[59] Seemingly new, modern modes of eroticism and connection – seen by some as a response to political changes in the legal status of homosexuality in Mexico and as an alternative to the erotophobia engendered by the AIDS epidemic – can, from another angle, be seen as a reinflection, and also effacement, of earlier forms.

In trying to conceptualize relations between the past and present (as well as the native and the foreign) while avoiding essentializing notions of tradition and authenticity, scholars have developed a range of ways of engaging how new ideas and practices with regard to gender and sexuality are recast within existing situated social forms, but also how the past gets reframed, often making it less heterogeneous, unruly, and open to a variety of eroticisms and embodiments than it was. Focusing on the emergence of sexological notions of female homoeroticism in China in the early twentieth century, Tze-lan D. Sang describes China as experiencing a "translated modernity" that is "shot through with colonial, imperial, transnational, cosmopolitan, global – whatever we call it – presence and valence," which is not "an inferior copy" of the West but which gives rise to "an alternative modern discourse of homosexuality."[60] Tracing the ways that Euro-American sexology enters into Chinese medical and popular discourses through translations of Japanese terminology and sources,[61] Sang illustrates how this new vocabulary and paradigm for understanding desire circulates in ways that discipline emergent forms of women's autonomy and generate a pathologized counterpoint to a new familial norm, although the idea of same-sex desire as "an extraordinary homosexual nature confined to a small percentage of the population" did not supplant a conception of "same-sex love as relational and situational."[62] Tom Boellstorff characterizes such dynamics of cross-cultural borrowing as "dubbing culture," a way of framing how the once alien is made familiar but also transformed/translated in the process. Addressing *lesbi* and *gay* identities in Indonesia, he tells the story of the decision in 1997 by the authoritarian Suharto regime (which ruled from 1967 to 1998) to forbid the dubbing of foreign TV shows into Indonesian for fear of "foreign values" becoming "Indonesianized," thereby putatively diluting or degenerating national culture.[63] Boellstorff suggests that foreign conceptions are *dubbed* into the Indonesian context and are remade through that process. He further notes that lesbi and gay Indonesians draw on the national discourse of a united archipelago in order to present queer subjects/communities as also linked "islands." This vision of Indonesian identity, though, itself "is not a timeless cultural archetype but is quintessentially modern, a key structuring principle of the nation-building project" in the wake of independence from the Netherlands in 1945.[64] In a similar vein, Todd A. Henry observes how contemporary Korean media portray "present manifestations of non-normative practices of gender and sexuality in terms of past traditions, especially by highlighting the purported lack thereof," and this widespread narrative erases, among other historical dynamics, the prevalence of "same-sex unions, particularly among working-class women," from the 1950s to the

1980s.⁶⁵ Moreover, responses to what we might call queerness and transness also are shaped by the fear of "guilt by association," "a system of collective culpability that was used both before and after the Korean War (1950–1953) to punish family members of alleged communists" that now "refers to a similar stigma that marginalizes sexual minorities and, by extension, their kin."⁶⁶ These instances suggest how the narration of the past and its connection to the present is less a matter of simply comparing and contrasting the one to the other than of forging a sense of what was (including ideas of tradition) in the context of present exigencies, including state-backed nationalisms.

Citations of *tradition*, though, also can provide openings to queer social forms. In the townships of Cape Town and Johannesburg in South Africa, for example, women are partaking in customary forms of marriage, including working out a bridewealth agreement among their families, rather than pursuing state-recognized same-sex marriage which is available as part of the constitutional recognition of gay and lesbian rights. As Phoebe Kisubi Mbasalaki observes, through such dynamics "black township lesbians resist everyday heterosexism and homophobia, while simultaneously creating spaces of belonging in the performance of everyday life." In doing so, couples present themselves as a gender-differentiated pair (butch/femme) in ways that fit "within the prevailing binary that endorses localized township masculinities and femininities" and that generate "spaces for belonging for black lesbians in these predominantly heterosexual practices and constituencies," thereby also reworking and reconstructing the meanings of *customary* governance in the townships.⁶⁷ Discussing appeals to *culture* within African feminist theorizing and advocacy, Sylvia Tamale observes, "culture [or, arguably, tradition] is a double-edged sword that can be wielded creatively and resourcefully to enhance women's access to sexual justice."⁶⁸ Considering the specificity of nonwestern spaces with regard to gender and sexuality, then, less involves a particular relation to the past or to change than requires attending to the situated ways people negotiate the layered meanings associated with these ideas, often in relation to shifting notions of family, personal identity, and the nation.

Considering the extent to which Euro-American notions can be employed to understand dynamics elsewhere, queer and trans studies work also raises questions about using conventional notions of *gender identity* in engaging experiences of embodiment, self-understanding, and community-making outside the West. Gender identity usually refers to an individual's sense of the relation between bodily form (and the meanings attributed to that form) and gendered social role, usually thought of as belonging to one of two available gender options. Such identity tends to be seen as both deeply ingrained (present consistently from a very early age) and separate from sexual identity (the kinds of persons with whom one wants to engage in erotic activity). This framework, though, does not really speak to a wide range of experiences of gendered embodiment around the globe. Rather than distinguishing between mass-mediated images of femininity and intimate experiences of lived gender, Marcia Ochoa suggests that a range of femininities in Venezuela – including those of *misses* (beauty pageant contestants) and *transformistas* (a person assigned male at birth "who from an early age" aims to "make herself a woman") – all draw on what she terms *spectacular femininity*, "conventions related to mass mediation" that "are available for not just citation or miming but for all kinds of everyday performance."[69] These performances of femininity, though, are less considered artificial or put-on than *sacar el cuerpo* (bringing out the body) – a process through which one's femininity can come to light, such as in the use of plastic surgery or hormones.[70] As with Brazilian travestis (discussed in the previous section), for transformistas bringing out their feminine body usually does not involve gender-affirming genital surgery, thus largely placing them outside what many Venezuelan medical and psychiatric professionals consider to be the proper treatment for what they diagnose as gender dysphoria.[71] The emphasis on performance, the somewhat explicit role of mass-mediated images/ideals in fashioning gendered selfhood, and the troubling of assumptions about authentic identity – as well as about the means and goals of transition – suggest a different conception of gender than one that fits within either a notion of minoritized trans identity or of conventional gender realness (simply *being* the gender one ostensibly is).

Although one of the most often-cited examples used to illustrate the cross-cultural presence of transness, *hijra* social dynamics further put in doubt the assumptions at play in that characterization. Their relations to various aspects of life in South Asia cannot readily be gathered under the notion of gender identity and do not really fit conventional conceptions of transition. Gayatri Reddy observes, "For the most part, hijras are phenotypic men who wear female clothing and, ideally, renounce sexual desire and practice by undergoing a sacrificial emasculation ... dedicated to the goddess Behraj Mata. Subsequently they are believed to be endowed with the power to confer fertility on newlyweds or newborn children."[72] They usually draw on cultural symbols associated with femininity (although sometimes combined with masculine forms), often class themselves as *koti* with other persons understood as male and who are penetrated in anal sex with men (distinguished from *pantis*, masculine men who penetrate during anal or vaginal sex, and *narans*, women categorized as female at birth), engage in men's and women's ritual practice, and can vote as women in national elections in India.[73] Part of what typifies everyday life for hijras is engaging in sex work as partners to pantis, even as such commercial and erotic relations are cast as inauthentic or degraded by other hijras (particularly those who are older and now serving as *gurus* and *nayaks*, heads of hijra households whom others serve as disciples, or *celas*).[74] More than merely a means of economically sustaining themselves, though, such sexual activity in its difference from marriage and coupledom, Vaibhav Saria argues, helps position hijras as vital supplements to "social and familial reproduction," both in fulfilling certain men's desires while returning them to "the world of domesticity ... more fortified to meet" its demands and generating funds that can help in caring for relatives (since married men in the family would largely be committed to their wives, children, and lineage, rather than parents or siblings).[75] Such possibilities, however, also speak to differences among hijras: urban hijras tend to break off ties with birth families to live in hijra households and kinship networks, while rural hijras continue to live in their families' homes or on land inherited from birth families.[76] Hijras also indicate important regional spiritual dynamics, including both their connection (of themselves and by others) to broader patterns and philosophies of asceticism and in the ways they mix and merge aspects of Islam and Hinduism: "the everyday lived reality of South Asia is characterized by the interweaving of Islamic and Hindu ideas and concepts. Hijras stand as particular examples of such interweaving," mostly identifying and practicing "as Muslims but simultaneously deriv[ing] their power and social legitimacy from a Hindu goddess."[77] In terms of hijras' relation to the category of trans, Saria notes, "Hijras, with their long-documented history, are not a local or cultural instantiation of the global category of trans, and neither is this a new question of how to recognize in hijras some universal pattern," referring back to British colonial efforts to manage them as a distinct, pathologized, and criminalized category.[78] Such denigration persists into the present, with trans and associated terms allowing for people to signal greater class status and "to differentiate themselves from the form of life that hijras inhabit, such as begging, prostitution, and community membership."[79] In Pakistan, this distinction also has taken shape through the use of *khwajasara* ("operat[ing] interchangeably" with "transgender") rather than hijra, reviving an older term (now dislocated from its historical meanings) that has become standard in Urdu media and that "promises social mobility" and "a long-desired register of respect" while also not entailing ritual and other responsibilities within particular hijra networks. In this way, not only is hijra more than simply a local version of trans, but "a rights discourse around the identifier *transgender* is able to remit class anxieties" that would come with identifying as hijra, or similar "locally defined" terms.[80]

The line between trans and queer experiences/identities – as well as the ability of either fully to convey nonwestern social forms – becomes even more blurred if one turns to Southeast Asia. Across the region, popular discourses and practices tend not to distinguish physical morphology, social role, and sexual desire from each other as separate aspects of lived personhood. To be categorized as male is to engage in masculine activities and to desire women, and for those labeled as female at birth, expressing masculine gender and having erotic relationships with women, since the 1970s and 1980s, have been linked to each other and designated through the use of versions of the English term tomboy – such as *tom* in Thailand and *tomboi* in Indonesia. As Megan Sinnott observes, "A *tom* is a *tom* by virtue of her self-assumed masculinity, and sexual attraction to women is an assumed extension of being masculine."[81] Unlike people designated male at birth who live feminine genders (*kathoey* in Thailand and *waria* in Indonesia), toms and tombois tend not to seek bodily alteration through hormones or other gender-affirming medical care.[82] Rather than themselves being marked as deviant, the romantic partners of toms/tombois largely are thought of as women whose attraction to female masculinity is an extension of their gender-consistent attraction to men/masculinity more broadly. Evelyn Blackwood notes, "In their attraction to tombois, girlfriends could be interpreted as desiring female bodies as well as male bodies, but they understand their own sexuality as consistently oriented toward men."[83] The general expectation is that these women eventually will marry men and have children, even if while they are with toms/tombois they are known as *dees* (Thailand) or as part of *lesbi* social life (Indonesia). Even when their masculine self-presentation is accepted by their families, toms and tombois don't stop being seen as women in terms of familial responsibility nor stop relying on familial resources, although they may be allowed more personal freedom and unchaperoned mobility (and access to men's spaces). Relationships between toms/tombois and their girlfriends is facilitated by the prevalence of same-sex sociality and the tendency not to see women's intimacies with each other as sexual per se, but instead as encompassed within friendship. In this way, the underlying presumption of toms'/tombois' womanness facilitates possibilities for erotic relation.[84] For those labeled male at birth, there is more of a distinction between queer and trans in the sense that those who identify as *gay* tend to enact forms of masculinity, are erotically interested in others who are gay, and often seek to distance themselves from the gender nonnormativity of waria/kathoey (and similar identities elsewhere in Southeast Asia). Further, warias/kathoeys tend to engage in relationships where, as with toms/tombois, gendered difference from their male romantic and erotic partners is a central organizing feature.[85]

In another sense, though, sexuality and gender are not differentiated, since both kinds of categories or relations are at play in defining gay and waria/kathoey identities (including distinguishing them from each other – gender normative vs. gender nonnormative; desiring the gendered same vs. desiring the differently gendered).

Even as Southeast Asia historically has had a wide range of socially legitimized modes of gender variance, especially in terms of participation as specialists in politically significant kinds of spiritual/ritual practice, contemporary expressions of gender and sexual (non)normativity take shape against the background of nationalist projects that arise alongside and in the wake of European colonialisms.[86] Over the course of the twentieth century, even though Thailand was never formally colonized, it engaged "in an active process of 'modernization' in which Western forms of government and administration have been appropriated and transformed into 'Thai' forms," including instituting "Western laws on family and citizenship" and criminalizing "unnatural sex."[87] Under the Suharto regime in Indonesia, known as the New Order, policy was directed toward "the creation of properly gendered, reproductive citizens situated within heterosexual nuclear families."[88] While popular understandings of gender expression and same-sex desire are not reducible to national politics, they are influenced by the latter, and outside urban and more educated activist circles, which tend to promote accounts of differentiated lesbian and transgender identities more consistent with Euro-American formulations,[89] everyday discourses surrounding toms/tombois and their girlfriends illustrate a Southeast Asian modernity that differs in significant ways from dominant Western political/identity frameworks. Although forms of sexual and gender nonnormativity in Southeast Asia often are attributed to forms of *tradition*, contemporary articulations – such as tom, tomboi, kathoey, waria, gay, lesbi – are a function of changes over the course of the twentieth century and also illustrate engagements with the dynamics of extant nationalisms.[90]

Attending to nonwestern political regimes reveals a range of possibilities for public voice and organizing by queer and trans activists and movements, although such political work may be shaped around different philosophies and priorities than much of LGBT politics in the West. Scholars indicate the importance of attending to the background political frameworks that guide forms of what we might call queer and trans analysis. Despite the view of China in the last few decades as postsocialist, Peter Liu argues that Marxism has remained an animating feature of Chinese and Taiwanese modes of queer analysis and critique. Of Marxism, he observes that it "is not just a critique of capitalism" but "is also a philosophy of the totality of the social world" and "a critique of the bourgeois conception of rights," "contain[ing] a critique of the sovereign subject and identity-based claims in a fashion that anticipates queer theory."[91] Marxist analytical approaches, he suggests, can be seen in the use of the term *tongzhi* (which "is identical to the function of queer in English" but literally means comrade), the development of a "sex-positive feminism" that is explicitly allied "with labor movements" (including campaigns around sex work), and the prevalence of appeals to a notion of human rights which is not a version of bourgeois individualism (instead drawing on what Liu suggests is the *moral equivalence* of all persons within the Marxist labor theory of value).[92] Within the context of a different history of socialist cultural and political change, Nicaraguan activists' formulations and strategies are shaped by the history of the Sandinista revolution, which overthrew a US-backed authoritarian regime, ruled from 1979 to 1990 (undermined by US-funded counterinsurgency efforts), was voted out, but then was voted back into power in 2006 (becoming more socially conservative in order to gain greater support from Catholic and evangelical publics).[93] Public articulations of the politics of sexuality in Nicaragua, as Cymene Howe notes, tend to present "the struggle for sexual rights" and the "revolutionary commitments" of the broader Sandinista project of equitable distribution of resources and broad-based social support as "intimately linked processes." Approaching queer activism through this prism, though, involves less seeking recognition from the state for the specific rights of sexual and gender minorities than "promot[ing] sexual tolerance and cultivat[ing] the understanding that sexuality is something that is embodied in, and of interest to, all Nicaraguans," offering a "democratizing and human rights-based narrative that reflects the country's broader political climate."[94]

The form of queer and trans politics also has been affected greatly by the rise of nongovernmental organizations (NGOs). NGOs have become normalized transnationally as a principal vehicle for framing social problems and channeling resources for redressing them. International funders, including organizations like the World Bank and International Monetary Fund, increasingly have turned to NGOs, seeing them as "more efficient, accountable, and less corrupt than national governments" while national governments increasingly have "receded from welfare provision." Within feminist organizing within India, this dynamic has meant that "pleasure and desire ... could only amount to a distraction from more serious – structural and not subjective – concerns," an orientation also consistent with the Indian Women's Movement's longstanding ways of formulating gendered oppression.[95] Moreover, as defined within NGO funding patterns, the *real* subjects of advocacy/rescue are seen as "grassroots" subjects (rural, impoverished, and of lower castes) with eroticism either positioned in these terms or presented as of lesser concern: "Queer feminist activism was haunted by its failure to penetrate the grass roots, a powerful and enduring construct that historically worked to delegitimize the politics of sexuality vis-à-vis the politics of poverty in the postcolony."[96] In South Africa and Namibia, the widespread representation of LGBT issues as un-African (despite the presence of gay and lesbian rights in the South African constitution) means that organizations can have difficulty receiving state support and often need to turn to funding from the Global North. This dynamic has "contributed to the *NGO-ization* of LGBT organizing" and can "set in motion ... a self-reinforcing cycle of prioritizing Northern donors as the organization's primary target audience," even as such investments make possible the existence of organizations that can create safe space for vulnerable groups and, at other times, can increase visibility for marginalized sexual and gender minorities.[97] However, even while presenting problems, NGO structures neither can be presented as merely externally imposed on national politics nor can they be dispensed with easily as frames and vehicles for organizing in situated circumstances.

In this vein, although queer and trans modes of critique can tend to present forms of state recognition as normalizing, scholarship focused on specific circumstances and conjunctions in nonwestern nations has addressed how people make use of political and legal openings that may not be ideal. Put another way, such work illustrates how queer and trans politics, organizing, and advocacy take place in located ways, enmeshed within extant institutional networks rather than existing in a purified space outside/beyond them. Discussing the Gender Identity Law enacted in Argentina in 2012, Martín De Mauro Rucovsky notes that certain trans intellectuals have depicted the law as enforcing a gender binary that erases the existence of travestis and others who do not fit or "want to maintain the man–woman norm." He observes, though, that the law does not require surgical alteration or hormone usage for someone to change their legal gender designation while, conversely, "the law guarantees obligatory access to the medical system" and covers gender-affirming treatments under the national Compulsory Medical Plan. Moreover, the law does not require an identity change after such treatment and does not limit the number of times one can change one's legal gender identity, and in this way, it "functions as a mechanism of expansion and disruption of identitarian recognition and its matrices," "open[ing] new configurations of sexed bodies, subaltern and popular subjects, and their political strategies."[98] One might also consider the judicial inclusion of trans people in India within the category of *caste*. As Rahul Rao indicates, "In India, where 'backwardness' is understood principally in terms of caste, the struggles of those deemed backward have produced a legal and political framework committed to the amelioration of backwardness," thereby explaining the efficacy of "analogising a particular kind of gender identity to caste" in ways that both collapse trans into hijra and conflate the history of hijra communities with that of the Hindu system of distinct and hierarchical castes (itself codified and institutionalized under British rule, even as the colonial government presented itself as opposed to such distinctions). Yet, these elisions function as a vehicle for seeking greater access to public resources and representation, "in solidarity and identification with those at the bottom of a caste hierarchy in the destruction of which they might be coparticipants."[99] Beyond drawing on the law and its categories as a means of gaining access to social and political resources, participation in the electoral system as candidates is also a means of seeking to reorganize existing gendered and sexual ideologies. In the Philippines, bakla candidates have run for office, as captured in the film *Out Run*, on the ticket of Ladlad, the LGBT political party. In doing so, they tie spaces of ordinary life like "beauty pageants and beauty parlors" to the political system, "acknowledge[ing] the role that these spaces play in fostering diverse solidarities across class difference" while also refusing proper (cis)gendered respectability as a condition of public visibility – either in terms of political institutions or queer efforts to enter them.[100] In all these instances, situated subjects inhabit existing legal, political, and administrative systems in ways that immanently seek to transform the ideological and material terrain – engaging extant institutionalities and seeking to make use of their capacities in ways that cannot be dismissed simply as assimilation or homo/transnormativity.

Attending to the specificity of nonwestern regimes further puts pressure on the equation of oppression with Western colonialism/intervention. In his analysis of responses to the Ugandan government's proposed (and later enacted) anti-homosexual legislation, Rao uses the term *homoromanticisim* to describe attempts to explain such statutes and the ideologies that support them as merely a legacy of European colonialism. This perspective "views Ugandans as blameless pawns in an essentially Western 'culture war' that has been displaced onto Africa" and "fails to account for the embrace and resignification of colonial laws by postcolonial elites or indeed the promulgation of new laws," such as in the case of Uganda. Rao adds, "Even if homophobia were 'imported' into Uganda from elsewhere, we need to ask why it found fertile soil in which to thrive there."[101] In this way, he engages the legacy of colonialism (including Great Britain's lopsided and patronizing 2018 apology for introducing anti-sodomy laws to its colonies, such as Uganda) while highlighting the need to consider "a political economy of homophobia" that is not merely derivable from that legacy.[102] Furthermore, the critique of forms of prejudice in the West cannot simply be extended in trying to understand political forms elsewhere. Discussing the current Islamist regime in Turkey, Evren Savci illustrates how efforts in queer studies to critique Islamophobia in Euro-American contexts do not provide a useful frame for analyzing what he terms *neoliberal Islam*:

> Turkey throws a particular wrench in the ongoing reproduction of the colonized East/colonial West divide as the descendant of an empire as well as thanks to its current imperial aspirations as exemplified in its military invasion of Syria. With a history of repressive secularism and its present of repressive Sunni Islamism, the republic interrupts the representation of Islam as the victim other of the imperial West.

The conceptual tools used to consider queer and trans politics and movements, then, need to consider "neoliberalism as experienced in a Muslim-majority country, under an authoritarian rule that heavily relies on Islam as its moralizing discourse," while attending to the specific articulations with capitalism that help sustain such rule.[103] This particular Islamist and neoliberal combination of repression and governmentality, though, gives rise to modes of public protest in which political alliances and meaning-making take a different form than what tends to be privileged in Euro-American queer and trans intellectual work. Mobilizations against the restrictions and privations of the Turkish state, as Savci shows, have often centered affective relations over rights claims as such, including critiques of forms of cruelty engendered by state policy (against Muslim women wearing headscarves as well as queers), the circulation of love (*aşk*) and humor as a popular political vernacular through which to connect strangers and produce solidarity, and trans women's pursuit of a hate crime law in order to register how hate functions "as a structural element of oppressive systems."[104] These forms of governance, and of resistance to that governance, both differ from Euro-American models and remain irreducible to Western influence.

Additionally, the commonplace equation of Western governance with possibilities for LGBT people brackets the ways regimes otherwise seen as repressive can open potentials for queer and trans self-identification and worldmaking. Under Suharto's New Order in Indonesia, administrative officials created and circulated the term waria (seeking to replace the disparaging *banci*). In doing so, they not only gave greater state recognition and respectability to those we might characterize as trans women but positioned them as in certain ways exemplifying principles of gendered expression and self-development, framing "the temporary yet daily practices that make up dédong [styling oneself] as a waria ... as a way to accomplish national belonging": "waria drew on [and were linked with] the centrality of self-improvement to the state's narrative of development" as part of its own claims to modernness.[105] After the Islamic Revolution in Iran in 1979, a similar project of gender normalization opened up potentials for both trans and queer self-expression. A *fatwa* (legal ruling) from Ayatollah Khomeini in the mid-1980s enabling state-supported forms of gender-affirming treatment, including surgery, allowed people desiring such treatment to seek authorization from the Legal Medicine Organization of Iran for certification as transsexuals (mostly for trans women), which would give them access to health insurance, financial assistance, and exemption from military service as well as provide documentation to prevent arrest or harassment by police and other officials.[106] The idea is to allow Iranian citizens to be able to achieve *congruence* between their bodies and genders, preserving a heterogendered system in which (male) homosexuality is considered abject (*kuni* – literally anal) and in which those seeking transsexual legal status must distinguish themselves from homosexuals (as has also been true in Western medical regimes, as discussed in Chapters 1 and 3), who are seen as deviant and associated with criminality.[107] However, rather than simply being imposed from above, Khomeini's fatwa was the result of extensive trans organizing and lobbying, based on presenting themselves as a vulnerable population in need of government aid (versus as a marginalized group asserting rights).[108] Moreover, this institutional process "has opened up the space for acquiring the certificate of transsexuality without being required to go through hormonal or somatic changes," and even as it largely is premised on pathologizing homosexuality, "it also has allowed some *gays*, in particular, to have a more semi-open life by going under the mantle of *trans*."[109] With respect to contemporary China, there is widespread acceptance of the idea that "Maoism deferred China's ability to reach modernity by impeding Chinese people's ability to express their gendered human natures," a narrative that seems to naturalize heteronormative social patterns. Yet, the idea of innate gendered desires does not so much preclude homosexuality as suggest its universal presence: "Sexual desire has come to represent naturalness par excellence," even as not all sexual desire is "seen as healthy for the nation" – especially in terms of upholding the primacy of the family to both national identity and Chinese culture itself.[110] The presence of ingrained forms of desire, including homosexuality, though, serves as part of articulations of Chinese *cultural citizenship*, since "the desiring subject is portrayed as a new human being who will help usher in a new era in China."[111] These examples illustrate a range of possibilities for how sexuality and gender may articulate with state ideologies, policies, and administrative frameworks in ways that can enable queer and trans lifeworlds and public self-expression.

Mobility, Circulation, and Regionality

Vocabularies, conceptual frameworks, cultural productions, and social and institutional forms don't just stay in one place. They move. They arise out of ideas, discourse, and practices that come from elsewhere; they emerge out of political relationships and partnerships across national borders; and they take shape through circuits of ongoing exchange within and across regions and among geographically disparate populations, especially those using the same language. What intellectual and interpretive possibilities open up if we see such transits and ongoing interaction not solely as the effect of Western imperialisms but as a product of regular flows among peoples and places as well as intentional forms of alliance-building and diasporic connection? This shift away from a singular, Western-centered model of influence/domination allows for investigation of how modes of governance, opposition, forms of representation, and everyday relations with regard to what we might characterize as sexuality and gender expression depend on ongoing networks of connection that may extend beyond a given locale, nation, or global "area." The scholarship discussed in the previous section foregrounds the particularity of given places, even as those places are understood as affected by various outside influences and as subject to internal differences and change over time. Work in queer and trans studies focused on forms of mobility enlarges the scale for understanding various phenomena, challenges the sense that particular spaces can be treated as insulated units of analysis, and thinks about movement and circulation as central dynamics in social life (rather than primarily in terms of invasive intrusion or dislocation).

Just as forms of political control can emerge in ways not predetermined by Western interests and influence (as discussed in the previous section), relationships among nonwestern nations can enable the proliferation of kinds of governance that seek to manage what are taken to be socially disruptive sexualities and genders. Much of the discussion of contemporary political and economic structures that circulate globally focuses on forms of neoliberalism (market-based ideologies), the actions of international economic institutions (like the World Bank and International Monetary Fund), human rights-based interventions (often funded by nations in the Global North), and anti-terrorism initiatives. The invention and implementation of these forms and dynamics usually is attributed to the West. However, nations of the Global South have been developing relationships with each other and experimenting with modes of governance that both are not equivalent to these other models and that also have started taking hold in the Global North. Such linkages include the increasing transnational connections between South America and the Middle East, including Brazil's membership in the Arab League in 2003 and its hosting of the first Summit of South American-Arab Countries in 2005.[112] As Paul Amar argues, such partnerships express and help incubate a growing commitment to what he refers to as "a human-security governance regime" focused on "rescuing sexuality and morally-identified subjects of humanity as well as cultivating militarized projects for securing cultural heritage and development infrastructure."[113] This vision of state policy is dedicated to preserving national safety and heritage by casting the national public as needing to be protected from external impurity and corruption – from "perversions of globalization" and "cosmopolitan networks of debauchers" – and presenting militarized police forces, largely exempted from due process restrictions, as the vehicle for insuring such humanitarian rescue and preserving both the nation's past and that past's availability for wholesome tourist consumption (such as Egypt's *cleaning-up* of places that had been used for homoerotic contact on the Nile or Brazil's efforts to control supposed gangs of travestis in the favelas of Rio de Janeiro).[114] Amar suggests that "this framework is based on tactics of extending moral tutelage into the population, whose members are seen as suspects and as victims to be rescued and detained, regardless of their consent."[115] Somewhat ironically, this conception of preserving national identity and security by policing deviant sexuality and gender (ostensibly as evidence of external corruption) gains traction as a result of countries' participation in transnational networks, but ones that principally are among nations of the Global South.

The effects of the circulation of models of governance and political legitimacy on the internal policy of nonwestern nations also can be seen in efforts to (de)criminalize particular kinds of sexual activity. As Jyoti Puri argues, "governing sexuality helps sustain the illusion that states are a normal feature of social life ... and indispensable to maintaining social order," adding that "states are constituted partly by the mandate to contain sexuality's putative threat to the social order."[116] While certain aspects of the legal regulation of erotic activity may originally have become part of public policy due to colonial imposition (such as the outlawing of sodomy within the Indian Penal Code starting in 1860, which was exported to other British-held territories such as those in the Caribbean, as discussed earlier), the continued existence of these kinds of statutes in formerly colonized countries, like India, can suggest more than merely the persistence of colonial history.[117] Instead, they can indicate a broader transnational template on which states draw in justifying their own existence as such, presenting the institutional apparatus that enacts and enforces such laws as necessary for the smooth and successful continuance of "lineage and inheritance, marriage and family, work productivity, the socialization of children and their conduct, [and] life and health" that supposedly are threatened by unregulated forms of sexual activity.[118] The legal management of sexual activity by the national government, then, is part of the transnational dissemination and validation of the nation-state as an institutional form, even as the particular meanings attributed to deviance may differ (such as, as Puri illustrates, the racializing association of perversion and criminality in India with Muslims and members of lower castes, among which hijras are included).

Forms of queerness also can circulate transnationally in ways that reinforce kinds of nationalism and normativity. Considering how the early-twentieth-century Chilean educator and Nobel Prize-winning poet Gabriela Mistral became an icon across Latin America, Licia Fiol-Matta observes that her queerness was central to the ways she served as a figure for a widely diffused and popularly endorsed vision of national identity. Beginning as a teacher in Chile, Mistral went on to work as a prominent educational reformer in several countries, including Mexico, and as a diplomat, and Fiol-Matta highlights the apparent contrast between Mistral's message as "mythic mother,"[119] in which she endorsed a vision of heterogendered families as key to the success and progress of Latin American nations, and her own gender and sexual nonnormativity in her visually evident masculinity and barely closeted lesbianism. More than an odd contradiction to the maternalism and conventional domesticity she often advocated as part of a transnational discourse of proper national development, Mistral's queerness, Fiol-Matta suggests, allowed her to appear "as so married to the national cause that she had sacrificed her most personal fulfillment to the good" of the nation's, and nations', citizens. In addition, "queer sexuality in Latin America cannot be divorced from the primacy of whiteness in the national social hierarchy," and in visibly implying a nonreproductive selfhood, Mistral could function as the whitewashed symbol of "a racialized form of maternal nationalism" that invoked *mestizaje* (European–Indian mixture) as a Latin American (trans)national ideal while separating it from the image of actual interracial desire and kinship.[120] While not expressive of officially endorsed notions of nationhood, other kinds of queer transnational networks can take shape around a capitalist and class-inflected image of gayness that is experienced as participation within a global cosmopolitanism. Alvin K. Wong describes such connections as "minor-to-minor networks" that enact and circulate a *queer vernacularism*.[121] This sensibility, which he traces across the Sinophone diaspora (including Hong Kong and Singapore), is not specifically endorsed by the state and does not contribute to nationalism as such. Instead, it implicitly defines itself in somewhat opposing terms as part of a cultural formation that transcends the boundaries and provincialism of the nation: "The expressive culture of queer vernacularism ... implies that the imaginative threshold of modernity can be embodied by non-Western yet obviously global subjects," especially those in urban centers like Hong Kong, being "local and global at once" in ways that perform "a translocal hybridity" outside of "the hegemony of Eurocentric queer modernity."[122] Wong notes, though, that this mode of transnational relation relies on forms of spectacular consumption, cultural capital, upward mobility, and racialized distinctions among those who can be seen as such cosmopolitan gay subjects and those who cannot (like privileging those of Chinese ethnicity in contrast to, say, those of Indonesian background).[123] As these examples indicate, forging transnational connections and imaginaries around queerness does not inherently generate liberatory frameworks and, rather, can facilitate forms of propaganda, representation, and imagination that are invested in perpetuating gendered, racial, and capitalist forms of inequity.

Movements of media and genres among countries and regions can also be more mixed in their effects, promoting normative social forms while also opening possibilities for other affective dynamics. This double-sidedness can be seen in the transit of ideas and images within regions and among diasporic publics. For example, among Sinophone publics across the twentieth and twenty-first centuries, homoerotic relations among women persistently have been figured in multiple media as a schoolgirl or young adult dynamic. Within this memorializing frame, such desires of youth are envisioned as abandoned as one enters proper adulthood. As Fran Martin observes, "sexual relations between women are culturally imaginable only in youth; therefore same-sex sexual relations may appear in adult femininity's past, very rarely in its present, and never in its future." Moreover, these relationships – depicted in novels, movies, and television in Taiwan, Hong Kong, and mainland China – consist of "passionate love between young women cherished and then abandoned due to forces beyond their control," but the prominence and familiarity of that story "does not equate in any concrete way to heightened 'tolerance' for lesbian relations between adult women in the societies in question."[124] Yet while seeming simply to underline the inevitability of hetero-marriage and normative family-making, the homoerotic romances of youth "are without exception represented ... as being recollected with mournful nostalgia from the viewpoint of the present": "the memorial mode is mobilized here to suggest that far from representing a satisfying conclusion, externally imposed heterosexuality frustrates the proper narrative and sexual progression of the central same-sex romance story."[125] While not conforming to the trajectory of the *coming-out* story or a movement for LGBT rights, this longstanding, popular, and widely circulating narrative type offers viewers modes of identification and foregrounds kinds of feelings that challenge the self-evident desirability of hetero-homemaking while also, in more recent versions, creating possibilities for seeing forms of female masculinity as attractive (these texts "authorize, foreground, and revel in the particular pleasures of the tomboy-attracted feminine woman").[126]

The ability of transnationally circulating nonwestern media to do ambivalent kinds of cultural work can also be seen in the depictions of queerness within African cinema. Many West African nations have thriving film industries, including Senegal, Ghana, and Nigeria (whose particularly expansive movie production has earned the nickname *Nollywood*), and representation of homoeroticism has been a prominent feature across them. In the vast majority of instances, especially in Anglophone contexts, such portrayals present queer desire "as spiritually and morally dangerous to the heterosexual family" and as "synonymous with debauchery and criminality," reflecting widely held popular attitudes but also due to the intervention of national film boards that refuse to authorize queer-affirmative narratives for public circulation.[127] There are examples of what Lindsey B. Green-Simms calls *Afri-queer fugitivity* in films designed to make space for depicting queer lives (often sponsored by human rights groups, like the Initiative for Equal Rights in Nigeria), using strategies that negotiate with rather than simply decry popular sentiments. Other queer potentials appear even in those films in which homoeroticism is cast as corrupting and productive of social disorder.[128] For example, not only do some films associate queer desire, particularly women's, with a challenge to corrupt state practices (largely in Francophone cinema), but the association of homoeroticism in various films with the water spirit most widely known as Mami Wata and the dissemination online of explicit homoerotic film scenes decontextualized from their narrative contexts suggest possibilities for viewing, identification, and meaning-making by variously situated viewers that exceed the moralizing frames that aim to cast queerness as un-African.[129]

One way that scholars have sought to theorize modes of connection and identification that extend beyond the boundaries of the nation-state is through the concept of *queer diaspora*. Queer diaspora indicates kinds of connection, exchange, migration, and affective attachment that do not take the nation-state and national belonging as their frame of reference, "allow[ing] for other histories of global affiliation and affinity to emerge." In this way, as Gayatri Gopinath suggests, queerness serves "as an optic and reading practice that brings alternative modes of affiliation and relationality into focus," foregrounding not just "nonnormative sexual practices, desires, affiliations and gender embodiments," but also "ways of seeing (and sensing) space, scale, and temporality" that neither accord with nation-state mappings nor the modes of hetero-conjugal life and family-making often endorsed by states.[130] Such analysis further attends to how relations among disparate spaces, and the cultural and political forms that emerge from those relations, are shaped by layered and intersecting histories of migrancy, dispossession, and exploitation, including intergenerational marginality across multiple sites. These "histories of dislocation and expulsion may in fact open new ways of imagining collectivity beyond the horizon of decolonization and civil rights." Engaging these histories involves developing intellectual tools that can address "a palimpsestic landscape marked by the promiscuous intimacies of ... dispossession and containment, diaspora and dwelling."[131] In this vein, Arabness can be thought of as such a transnational formation, and doing so aids in "unseating Orientalist and nationalist renditions of Arab identity that produce essential, authentic Arab subjects," including understanding such subjects as decidedly not queer. Mejudulene Bernard Shomali refers to that vision of identity endorsed by Arab states as *heteronational*, an effort "to restore an authentic Arab subject fit for the postcolonial nation."[132] As against this kind of normalizing national imaginary, she highlights both implicit kinds of homoerotic cultural production (like belly dancing and women's homosocial relations in Golden Era Egyptian film, "locat[ing] queer possibility in these seemingly normative representations of Arab women") and portrayals by "queer subjects who are living and organizing in the present," such as queer women novelists writing in Arabic in Lebanon and Syria and anthologies of non-fiction by Palestinian and Lebanese queer women's organizations – which have been dispersed transnationally through Arab diasporas.[133] Bernard Shomali uses the term *sahq* to address and conceptualize these wide-ranging and shifting networks: "a medieval term that refers to same-sex acts between women," which literally "refers to the friction between a mortar and pestle" in "grinding spices" but that, in its "vulgarity," rejects the "respectability politics" of seeking to fit into forms of proper (hetero)gendered and national subjectivity while also signaling the ways maintaining transnational forms of possibility, imagination, and alliance-building is "a grind, work."[134] In these ways, as an analytical frame, queer diaspora draws attention to how movements and attachments that exceed state borders indicate the vitality of transnational webs of relation that sustain alternative geographies of desire, fantasy, association, and organizing conducive to worldmaking beyond heteronational structures and their visions of authenticity.

In what might be thought of as an allied move, Howard Chiang refigures queer diaspora as *transtopia*. He moves away from the sense of trans as designating a kind of marginalized identity and toward marking how gendered embodiments take on shifting meanings in the movement of ideas and discourses through "a network of places ... outside China and on the margins of China and Chineseness" – transiting across the Sinophone diaspora.[135] Such alterations and accretions as concepts move along diasporic circuits include the historical linkage of gender nonconformity to the human–animal distinction and disability through the term *renyao* (originally meaning "human monster" or "human prodigy" and now signifying transgender) and the ways tongzhi has not only changed from meaning "comrade" to indicating queerness but has picked up a strong sense of gender diversity as well (particularly in Taiwan).[136]

Another way of engaging queer diaspora, as Gopinath suggests, is through a focus on regional formations, and queer and trans work has attended to how the transit of cultural and political frameworks within regions contributes to the envisioning of alternative kinds of social life. If postcolonial states often depict their sovereignty and autonomy through the appeal to heteronormative visions of the nation and its citizenry, a regional focus can reveal queer dynamics that counter such narratives of national straightness. Jarrod Hayes has traced the ways novels across the Maghreb (former French colonies in North Africa – Algeria, Tunisia, and Morocco) "serve a political purpose by deploying sexuality in a critique of the prevailing sociopolitical order in postindependence Maghrebian societies." In these texts, nonnormative sexualities point toward alternatives to dominant accounts of the nation's origins and character, "challeng[ing the] official version of national history" by addressing what has been elided and erased in order to sustain that story and the similarity of those patterns across multiple countries. In particular, the depiction of "sexual nonconformity functions politically as part of a struggle against the power and privilege of postindependence elites," contesting the image of health, well-being, and morality that they present as legitimizing their control over the resources and governance of these decolonized countries. Moreover, as Hayes argues, the novels often connect their portrayal of marginalized sexualities to forms of regional ethnic difference that also are effaced – or recast as threat – in the narration of a secure and singular national identity.[137] These patterns in North Africa complement dynamics further south that illustrate what has been called "the *African queer customary.*"¹³⁸ *Customary law* is the term used to address forms of local self-rule in sub-Saharan Africa prior to and outside European colonial governance, but in perhaps one of the bitterest ironies of colonial rule, this very concept was invented by colonial institutions as a mode of what was called *indirect rule*, in which such institutions produced racialized forms of political difference and codified what they claimed were Indigenous traditions in ways that served the aims of the colonial regime.¹³⁹ Such semi-imposed forms of authenticity persist as a feature of postindependence governance, and they can be "particularly oppressive with regard to nonconforming genders and sexualities," especially given the emphasis on patriarchal lineages as the basis for landholding and inheritance.¹⁴⁰ As a regional imaginary, the notion of the African queer customary refers to "those practices and desires ... that reference (while inhabiting and inflecting) the heteronormativity of customary categories." As Kirk Fiereck, Neville Hoad, and Danai Mupotsa articulate it, this conception of the customary connects multiple sites while opening up how various embodiments and eroticisms might be part of everyday African pasts and presents.¹⁴¹

The ways nonnormative genders and sexualities exceed conventional political structures also can be seen at play in South Asia and Latin America. The association of hijra communities with India overlooks their cross-border, regional dimensions. While sometimes known by varied names, these communities extend across India and into Bangladesh, Nepal, and Pakistan, and members of these communities themselves routinely cross borders as part of ongoing association among communities, migration among them, and participation in underground economies – movements that largely go unchallenged by state authorities (often letting hijras cross without a visa or passport).¹⁴² If relations among hijra communities transect national borders in ways that challenge their association with specific national spaces and traditions, *travesti* increasingly has emerged as a way of framing Latin American intersectional gender analysis and organizing in ways that speak less to literal cross-border connections than to the possibilities opened by a regional imaginary. More than simply designating a kind of gendered embodiment, or necessarily indicating groups specific to particular nations, travesti offers "an identification, a critical analytic, and an embodied mode of politics," one that is responsive to the constitutive interdependence of "hierarchies of race, class, ability, and other forms of difference." As opposed to state-endorsed discourses that emphasize movement between biologized, medicalized binary genders, foregrounding the travesti "subverts both normative expectations of femininity and trans politics structured around assimilation and respectability."¹⁴³ Instead of seeking to fit within (trans)gendered conceptions of model citizenship, travesti-centered intellectual and political work can attend to broader patterns, such as femicide (including trans women and travestis as part of such violence) and antiblackness (given the number of travestis who are of African descent and the relative erasure of blackness in Latin American nationalist narratives), while contesting the reduction of feminist politics to the supposedly self-evident category of *woman* within transnational human rights discourses.[144] As these examples suggest, a regional approach can bring into focus patterns, networks, and movements that extend beyond a national frame as well as put pressure on the heteronormative and cisnormative ideologies many states employ.

Conclusion

While I close the chapter with discussion of queer diaspora, I don't mean to present that approach as more appropriate or advanced than the other approaches I've discussed. Critiques of (neo)colonialism and global capitalism, attention to local and national contexts, and mappings of the circulation of ideas and frameworks all provide useful modes of analysis. These approaches can offer perspectives and insights that are at odds with each other (and scholars that I've cited writing about the same countries and regions often disagree with each other). However, rather than seeking to resolve such tensions, this chapter has sought to turn toward them, emphasizing the conceptual and methodological range of queer and trans work while also highlighting points of debate and disagreement – as with the other chapters. Doing so not only illustrates the intellectual ferment of these fields but positively values such differences and disagreements as a source of strength.

The concerns of this chapter resonate with issues I've been addressing across the book as a whole. Attending to the ways that colonialism, imperialism, and capitalism affect social formations globally brings us back to questions posed throughout about the ways sexuality and gender – whatever we might take those terms to mean – are animated by a range of political, economic, and institutional dynamics. These include the implications of taking the closet as a queer paradigm and ways of figuring transition as migration, the roles racial and class difference play in conceptualizing gay and feminist opposition/revolution/coalition/liberation, the associations of sodomy and gender deviance with "unnatural" religious and racial difference across the history of Europe and in US slavery and settlement, and the ways queer and trans of color scholarship has insisted on the distinction between being seen as persons and peoples whose life is valued (rather than being cast as backward or alien obstructions to national well-being). Considering the specificity of situated nonwestern ideologies and practices of eroticism, embodiment, and personhood connects to earlier discussion of the limits of notions of universal (hetero)patriarchy, the importance of addressing desires for ordinariness and the presence of bad feelings (in contrast to limiting, idealized notions of resistance and what counts as politically meaningful action), the presence of a range of (sometimes competing) ideas about subjectivity and desirable futures in social movements (and those movements' effects on each other), the ways terms and principles for understanding bodies and desires shift over time and space (while also not being singular in any given time and place), and the importance of recognizing the particular political and intellectual genealogies for varied groups of color (without presenting them as either interchangeable or as sealed off from each other). Mobility, transit, and diaspora point toward the continual movement of persons, images and texts, commodities, institutions, and intellectual and political frameworks and their implications for shifting arrangements of gender and sexuality, such as the ways ideas from earlier writings and movements are taken up by and refracted in later ones, Christian Europe's centuries-long engagement with Islam and trade with Asia, the African slave trade and the emergence of forms of diasporic blackness, and the interchange of people and ideas among social and political movements in the United States.

Rather than seeking to provide an integrated account of queer and trans studies, the book has aimed to foreground their multiplicity and messiness. That sense of layered complexity includes attending to the ways queer and trans studies are themselves distinct fields, if adjacent and often overlapping. Queer critique of (hetero)normalization can rub up against the insistence on centering trans experience, even as what can and should constitute *trans* remains an open question. Queer histories and analyses also can absorb gender-nonconforming behavior and self-articulation by treating them as expressive of homoeroticism or by miscasting the enforcement of gender norms as an effort to regulate modes of desire and sexual intimacy. However, those dynamics also can occur at the same time, can be interdependent, can be immensely difficult to distinguish from each other, and can be indicative of social formations where conventional/dominant contemporary Euro-American notions of *gender* and *sexuality* simply cannot capture the social and interpersonal relations, modes of power, and conceptual frameworks that are at stake. Furthermore, the attempt to move away from identity – a determinate, coherent group of queer or trans persons who are seen as the subject of attention and advocacy – can be in the service of better addressing otherwise taken-for-granted social systems (configurations of home, kinship, privacy, citizenship, legal and administrative authority, what-have-you), but it also can result in a seeming subjectlessness whose de facto subject remains white, male, cis, able-bodied, etc. All of these issues, cautions, and disagreements remain very much at play in contemporary intellectual discussion and debate. Queer and trans scholarship, to me, seems most vital when it can hold onto these questions and be galvanized by these frictions while still getting on with the difficult work of saying something meaningful about desire, embodiment, and social life then, now, and for the future.

Given my previously discussed, somewhat recalcitrant '90s proclivities, I'd like to close by returning to Eve Sedgwick. In her later work, she develops the idea of a *reparative* orientation toward our intellectual projects. The effort to offer somewhat totalizing accounts of how forms of domination work, she argues, is driven by a desire not to be implicated in them, to position yourself as fully outside them. That kind of knowledge-production is less about having a clear sense of "the reality or gravity of . . . oppression" than an implicit need not to be taken by surprise by the appearance of oppression. As against this desire to know beforehand, to insert phenomena into a prearranged analytical structure, Sedgwick emphasizes the importance of "queer possibility," not knowing beforehand exactly how things will line up and, therefore, valuing "the force of contingency" itself in how we relate to the stuff of our scholarship.[145] That reparative sense of possibility – the openness to the ways relations in the world may differ from what we expect and the ways we may differ from ourselves – strikes me as an incredibly generative principle on which queer and trans studies have and will continue to draw.

Notes

Introduction

1. de Lauretis, "Queer Theory." In order initially to help readers locate some of these discussions in time, I have provided dates for the pieces I cite in the introduction.
2. The critical popularization of the concept of cisgender often has been attributed to Julia Serano. See Serano, *Whipping Girl*.
3. Cohen, "Punks," 439, 440, 452.
4. Cohen, "Punks," 447–448, 453.
5. Koyama, "Whose Feminism," 702, 703.
6. As a critical term, intersectionality usually is credited to two articles by Kimberlé Crenshaw, "Demarginalizing the Intersection of Race and Sex" and "Mapping the Margins." See also Carastathis, *Intersectionality*; Hancock, *Intersectionality*; Nash, *Black Feminism*.
7. de Lauretis, "Queer Theory," iii, x.
8. Harper et al., "Queer Transexions," 1.
9. Eng et al., "What's Queer," 8.
10. Eng et al., "What's Queer," 1.
11. Stryker and Aizura, "Introduction," 8.
12. Stryker, "(De)Subjugated," 14.
13. Stryker and Aizura, "Introduction," 9.
14. Stryker, "(De)Subjugated," 4.
15. Stryker, "(De)Subjugated," 9.
16. Stryker, "(De)Subjugated," 3.
17. Stryker and Aizura, "Introduction," 7.
18. Eng and Puar, "Introduction," 3.
19. Jagose, *Queer Theory*, 17.
20. Sullivan, *A Critical Introduction*, 51.
21. Fuss, "Inside/Out," 3. Jonathan Ned Katz observes, "The intimidating notion that heterosexuality refers to everything differently sexed and gendered and eroticized is, it turns out, one of the conceptual dodges that keeps heterosexuality from becoming the focus of sustained, critical analysis" (*The Invention*, 13).
22. Foucault, *History of Sexuality*, 43.
23. Sullivan, *A Critical Introduction*, 136, 138; Jagose, *Queer Theory*, 126.

24. Jagose, *Queer Theory*, 82.
25. Jagose, *Queer Theory*, 79. For some important queer and trans engagements with psychoanalytic theory, see Butler, *Gender Trouble*; Butler, *Bodies That Matter*; Dean, *Unlimited*; de Lauretis, *The Practice of Love*; Edelman, *No Future*; Eng, *Feeling*; Hart, *Between the Body and the Flesh*; Musser, *Sensual Excess*; Prosser, *Second Skins*; Salamon, *Assuming*; Scott, *Extravagant Abjection*.
26. Stryker, "(De)Subjugated," 12.
27. Warner, "Introduction," xi, xii–xiii, xxvi.
28. Berlant and Warner, "Sex in Public," 553.
29. Eng et al., "What's Queer," 3; Eng and Puar, "Introduction," 5.
30. Byrd, "What's Normative"; Holland, *Erotic Life*; Rodríguez, *Sexual Futures*.
31. Sullivan, *A Critical Introduction*, vi; Somerville, "Introduction," 2.
32. Wiegman and Wilson, "Introduction," 9; Enke, "Introduction," 4–5. As Stryker notes, "transgender phenomen[a]" also challenge heteronormativity, in ways often effaced by queer studies ("(De)Subjugated," 7).
33. Eng et al., "What's Queer," 11. See Duggan, "The New Homonormativity."
34. Eng and Puar, "Introduction," 3.
35. See Puar, *Terrorist*.
36. Snorton and Haritaworn, "Trans Necropolitics," 67. The term's first usage usually is credited to Austin H. Johnson.
37. Jagose, *Queer Theory*, 98; Wiegman and Wilson, "Introduction," 1.
38. Wiegman and Wilson, "Introduction," 11, 12.
39. Fuss, "Inside/Out," 5.
40. Stryker et al., "Introduction: Trans-," 12, 14. Stryker observes, "Transgender studies helps demonstrate the extent to which soma, the body as a culturally intelligible construct, and techne, the techniques in and through which bodies are transformed and positioned, are in fact inextricably interpenetrated" ("(De)Subjugated," 12).

Chapter 1

1. Butler, *Gender Trouble*, 5.
2. Butler, *Gender Trouble*, 8. On the emergence of the concept of gender in the 1960s as part of efforts to preserve conventional notions of sexual difference, see Gill-Peterson, *Histories*. I'll return to this topic in Chapter 3.
3. Butler, *Gender Trouble*, 9, 154.
4. Butler, *Gender Trouble*, 10.
5. Butler, *Gender Trouble*, 31.
6. Butler, *Gender Trouble*, 104, 169.
7. Butler largely develops this analysis through careful and extended discussions of work by French intellectuals, particularly three prominent feminists (Simone de

Beauvoir, Luce Irigaray, and Monique Wittig), two important mid-twentieth-century structuralist thinkers (Claude Levi-Strauss and Jacques Lacan), and Michel Foucault (whose writings on sexuality, state discipline, and biopower have been particularly important within queer studies). I won't elaborate in any detail the readings Butler offers of them, but want to note these figures as important touchstones in the development of Butler's work.

8. Butler, *Gender Trouble*, 14.
9. Butler, *Gender Trouble*, 151, 161–162.
10. Butler, *Bodies That Matter*, 30.
11. Butler, *Bodies That Matter*, 34–35, 65.
12. Butler, *Gender Trouble*, 34, 152.
13. Butler, *Bodies That Matter*, 15.
14. Butler, *Bodies That Matter*, 107, 225.
15. Butler, *Bodies That Matter*, 123.
16. Butler, *Gender Trouble*, 42, 189.
17. Butler, *Gender Trouble*, 169, 187. Here Butler implicitly builds on Esther Newton's earlier work. See Newton, *Mother Camp*.
18. Butler, *Bodies That Matter*, 18.
19. Butler, *Bodies That Matter*, 182. Although, Butler usually raises the issue of race when speaking about nonwhite people in ways that tend to leave their discussion of sex/gender as de facto "white sexual difference." They explore these dynamics particularly through an extended reading of Nella Larsen's novel *Passing*, attending to how racial boundaries are maintained through the regulation of miscegenation – and what can count as lawful modes of couplehood and kinship – as well as how notions of nonwhite respectability (deferring the perversity attributed to people of color) depend on support for forms of heteropatriarchy. See Butler, *Bodies That Matter*, 167–186.
20. Butler, *Bodies That Matter*, 111, 227.
21. Butler, *Bodies That Matter*, 131.
22. Butler, *Bodies That Matter*, 133. On the balls, see Bailey, *Butch Queens*.
23. Butler, *Undoing Gender*, 2.
24. Butler, *Undoing Gender*, 213.
25. Butler, *Undoing Gender*, 3, 8, 218.
26. Butler, *Undoing Gender*, 117.
27. Namaste, *Invisible Lives*, 31, 9.
28. Namaste, *Invisible Lives*, 55, 58.
29. Prosser, *Second Skins*, 5, 14. See also Lavery, "Egg."
30. Rubin, *Self-Made Men*, 3.
31. Serano, *Whipping Girl*, 26, 10.
32. Serano, *Whipping Girl*, 87. See also Prosser, *Second Skins*, 171–206.
33. Ahmed, "An Affinity," 29.
34. Prosser, *Second Skins*, 40, 64. Trans people often indicate "the perception of a core self" that is male or female, and surgical intervention to affirm that selfhood is

described using "the language of reconstruction .... For example, instead of 'mastectomy,' they say they had a 'chest reconstruction surgery'": "They are not transforming themselves .... They are repairing the link between their bodies and gender identities" (Rubin, *Self-Made Men*, 11, 60, 144). Serano describes her own sense of sexed selfhood as an "*intrinsic inclination*" that does not arise from social processes of gendering (*Whipping Girl*, 99).

35. Serano, *Whipping Girl*, 33, 162, 208. On the potential problems and binaries at play in using notions of *cis*-identity, see Enke, "The Education." On the ways Serano's own account leaves aside how race and class affect the ways transmisogyny operates, see Krell, "Is Transmisogyny Killing."
36. Keegan, "Getting Disciplined," 389; Bettcher, "Trapped," 398. See also Koyama, "Transfeminist Manifesto."
37. Keegan, "Getting Disciplined," 387; Bettcher, "Trapped," 389–390, 396. On the effort to use film to capture trans realities in ways that defy conventional gendered codes and modes of perception, see Keegan, *Lana and Lily*; Steinbock, *Shimmering Images*.
38. Wilchins, *Read My Lips*, 25, 57.
39. Salamon, *Assuming*, 3, 29, 30, 77.
40. Salamon, *Assuming*, 91. On the ways trans phenomenologies occur within community circumstances, and can provide a model for thinking about gender socialization, see Gleeson, "How Do Gender Transitions"; Zazanis, "Social Reproduction."
41. West, *Transforming Citizenship*, 17, 94, 177.
42. Bhanji, "Trans/scriptions," 520.
43. Aizura, *Mobile Subjects*, 2, 166.
44. O'Brien, "Tracing This Body," 63, 64.
45. Towle and Morgan, "Romancing," 471, 492. See also Besnier and Alexeyeff, "Gender on the Edge."
46. Snorton and Haritaworn, "Trans Necropolitics," 74.
47. We might understand the recent spate of state "bathroom bills" that seek to prevent people from using bathrooms other than those designated for their legal sex in these terms. As Toby Beauchamp observes,

    in the era of formal Jim Crow, while bathrooms marked for white people were typically separated into men's and women's spaces, those labeled "colored" were often unmarked by gender at all, a practice that aligns with civilizational discourse. If we understand the overt racial segregation of bathrooms in this period to also inherently produce and maintain hierarchies of gender – in which only white people are civilized enough to warrant distinctly gendered spaces, and those gender distinctions likewise cast white people *as* civilized – then we must also consider how today's gendered bathrooms continue to rely on racist conceptions of a modern, civilized society, even if these spaces are no longer formally segregated by race. (*Going Stealth*, 85)

48. binaohan, *decolonizing*, 4, 18.

49. Chen, *Trans Exploits*, 5.
50. Valentine, *Imagining Transgender*, 98.
51. Jack Halberstam describes such an approach as "looking not for trans people (or people who have legally changed their sex) but for a politics of transitivity" (*Trans**, xiii).
52. Spade, *Normal Life*, 11. For a similar focus on the different kinds of work that sex classification does in particular administrative systems, see Currah, *Sex Is*.
53. Ritchie, *Invisible No More*, 55, 135. See also Faye, *Transgender Issue*.
54. Spade, *Normal Life*, 6.
55. Sedgwick, *Epistemology of the Closet*, 12, 22, 23, 25.
56. Sedgwick, *Epistemology of the Closet*, 40, 44.
57. This issue will be discussed in greater detail in Chapter 3.
58. Sedgwick, *Epistemology of the Closet*, 45, 47.
59. Sedgwick, *Epistemology of the Closet*, 1–2.
60. Sedgwick, *Epistemology of the Closet*, 100, 246. Sedgwick opens the book with her famous polemical assertion that "an understanding of virtually any aspect of modern Western culture must be, not merely incomplete, but damaged ... to the degree that it does not incorporate a critical analysis of modern homo/heterosexual definition" (*Epistemology of the Closet*, 1).
61. Sedgwick, *Tendencies*, 3.
62. Sedgwick, *Tendencies*, 9, 6, 8.
63. Sedgwick, *Tendencies*, 117, 126.
64. Sedgwick, *Tendencies*, 6, 72.
65. Sedgwick, *Tendencies*, 63.
66. See Foucault, *History of Sexuality*.
67. Sedgwick, *Touching Feeling*, 12–13.
68. Sedgwick, *Touching Feeling*, 8.
69. Sedgwick, *Touching Feeling*, 106.
70. Sedgwick, *Touching Feeling*, 63. On the importance of earlier sociological studies of deviance and stigma to queer studies conceptions of affect, see Love, *Underdogs*.
71. Sedgwick, *Touching Feeling*, 21. The distinction she makes between *paranoid* and *reparative* modes of analysis is an extension of this point (*Touching Feeling*, 123–152).
72. Muñoz, *Disidentifications*, 4, 11, 31.
73. Muñoz, *Disidentifications*, 196.
74. Ahmed, *Queer Phenomenology*, 16, 66, 80.
75. Ahmed, *Queer Phenomenology*, 121–122.
76. Thomas, *Sexual Demon*, 4, 9.
77. Ross, "Beyond the Closet," 168, 173.
78. Pérez, *A Taste*, 33, 64.
79. Haritaworn, *Queer Lovers*, 40, 28, 126. On the broader pattern of racializing migrants in Europe, even after generations of residency, see El-Tayeb, *European Others*.

80. Morgensen, *Spaces between Us*, 43, 45.
81. Morgensen, *Spaces between Us*, 136, 167.
82. Halberstam, *In a Queer Time*, 36–37. For discussion and critique of this narrative, see also Weston, *Long Slow Burn*, 29–56.
83. Herring, *Another Country*, 15.
84. Clare, *Exile and Pride*, 35, 61.
85. See Hanhardt, *Safe Space*; Manalansan, "Race, Violence, and Neoliberal Spatial Politics"; Stanley, "The Affective Commons."
86. Gray, *Out in the Country*, 4, 96. See also Howard, *Men Like That*; Johnson, *Just Queer Folks*.
87. Tongson, *Relocations*, 88.
88. Tongson, *Relocations*, 134.
89. Cvetkovich, *Depression*, 115, 200.
90. Cvetkovich, *An Archive of Feelings*, 63.
91. Scott, *Extravagant Abjection*, 245, 29.
92. Scott, *Extravagant Abjection*, 98, 129.
93. Love, *Feeling Backward*, 3; Malatino, *Side Affects*, 2.
94. Love, *Feeling Backward*, 10, 27.
95. Malatino, *Side Affects*, 8, 67.
96. Malatino, *Side Affects*, 121, 159.
97. Stanley, "The Affective Commons," 492, 496, 503.
98. On the concept of bodyminds, see Schalk, *Bodyminds*.
99. Kafer, *Feminist*, 5, 6.
100. Clare, *Brilliant*, 26, 69.
101. Kafer, *Feminist*, 17, 30.
102. Cartwright, *Peculiar Places*, 40–41. See also Awkward-Rich, *Terrible We*; Clare, *Brilliant*; Samuels, *Fantasies*. I'll return to this history in Chapter 3.
103. Mollow and McRuer, "Introduction," 1, 17.
104. Siebers, "A Sexual Culture," 40, 47.
105. Yergeau, *Authoring Autism*, 71, 184.
106. Yergeau, *Authoring Autism*, 26, 29, 100.
107. Clare, *Exile and Pride*, 130.
108. Wilkerson, "Normate Sex," 190.
109. Snediker, *Contingent Figure*, 135, 184.
110. Clare, *Brilliant*, 26, 177.
111. Puar, *Right to Maim*, 37.
112. Awkward-Rich, *Terrible We*, 3, 4, 147.
113. Baril, "Transness," 71, 65.
114. Clare, *Brilliant*, 53.
115. Puar, *Right to Maim*, xvii, 66.
116. Hird, "Animal Trans," 159.
117. Hird, "Animal Trans," 160.
118. Nurka, "Animal Techne," 212.

119. See Willey, *Undoing Monogamy*.
120. Chen, *Animacies*, 13, 15, 98.
121. Luciano and Chen, "Has the Queer," 188, 195.
122. Hayward, "Lessons," 183, 184. See also Colebrook, "What Is It Like."
123. Ahuja, "Intimate Atmospheres," 367, 372.
124. Amin, *Disturbing Attachments*, 177, 36.

Chapter 2

1. Hemmings, *Why Stories Matter*, 3.
2. Fawaz, *Queer Forms*, 365, 343.
3. While these movements and intellectual formations have been discussed extensively as helping generate the conditions for queer and trans studies, there certainly are other intellectual forms that played a role that have not been valorized in the same way. For example, on the influence of sociological studies of deviance from the 1950s and 1960s, see Love, *Underdogs*.
4. Ferguson, *One-Dimensional Queer*, 20.
5. Gossett, "Silhouettes of Defiance," 581.
6. See Woo, "Stonewall."
7. Amin, *Disturbing Attachments*, 175, 185.
8. Ferguson, *One-Dimensional Queer*, 151. I should note that I have chosen not to quote from what might be considered creative work – including poetry and fiction – in favor of more expository writings. However, such work holds great importance for all of the movements discussed in this chapter.
9. See Duberman, *Stonewall*.
10. Duberman, *Stonewall*, xix. On the complexity of dissemination of gay/homosexual liberation movements, challenging a *diffusionist* model centered on the United States and Stonewall, see Garrido, "The World."
11. On the homophile organizations, see D'Emilio, *Sexual Politics*. On the prior demonstrations and riots, see Stryker, *Transgender History*, 81–93.
12. GLF emerged out of the need to create an affinity organization, separate from the New York City Mattachine Society, through which to demonstrate in a solidarity action with the Black Panthers. See Duberman, *Stonewall*, 268; Kissack, "Freaking Fag Revolutionaries."
13. On the history of GLF, see Duberman, *Stonewall*; Ferguson, *One-Dimensional Queer*; Hobson, *Lavender and Red*; Kissack, "Freaking Fag Revolutionaries."
14. On the ways broadly leftist analyses like those developed within gay liberation extended in activist thinking and organizing through the 1980s, rather than simply disappearing by the mid-1970s, see Hobson, *Lavender and Red*.
15. Wittman, "A Gay Manifesto," 331, 333, 340.
16. On this history of the notion of "coming out," and the public visibility of a range of queer cultures in the early twentieth century, see Chauncey, *Gay New York*.

On the broader implications of coming out as a mode of public address and sociality, see Fawaz, *Queer Forms*, 197–245.
17. Shelley, "Gay Is Good," 31, 32, 33, 34.
18. Young, "Out of the Closets," 29; "Gay Revolutionary Party Manifesto," 344.
19. Jay, "Introduction," lxi.
20. Young, "Out of the Closets," 10.
21. Young, "Out of the Closets," 14, 25, 29.
22. I follow Dean Spade in using the phrase criminal punishment system instead of the more common "criminal justice," thereby raising questions about whether that system actually produces anything resembling justice. Another option is "criminal legal system" (Mogul et al., *Queer (In)Justice*).
23. "Statement of the Male Homosexual Workshop," 402; Third World Gay Revolution, "What We Want, What We Believe," 364.
24. Chicago Gay Liberation, "Working Paper," 346.
25. "Rapping with a Street Transvestite Revolutionary," 113, 118. On the relation between "gay"-ness and street queens in the period, see also Newton, *Mother Camp*.
26. GAA was formed in December 1969 in New York City, and it included those members of GLF, as well as some of the people from previous homophile organizations who had not joined GLF, who thought that activism needed to be focused on issues specifically of concern to homosexuals (rather narrowly conceived). While there were some people of color in the various GAAs in different cities, the organization did not understand engaging with issues of racism and imperialism as part of its mandate, ranging from solidarity for the Black Panthers, opposition to the war in Vietnam, or even discrimination against queer and trans people of color within gay institutions (such as being denied entry to or thrown out of gay clubs). See Bell, "The Radicalqueens"; Duberman, *Stonewall*, 285–286; Ferguson, *One-Dimensional Queer*, 73–74; Kissack, "Freaking Fag Revolutionaries"; Roberts, "Pre-Now."
27. Duberman, *Stonewall*, 289–318. On Johnson and Rivera, see also Feinberg, *Trans Liberation*, 106–109; Galarte, *Brown Trans Figurations*; Gan, "Still"; Gill-Peterson, "Trans of Color"; Kissack, "Freaking Fag Revolutionaries"; Lau, "Between the Times"; Pitts, "Sylvia Rivera."
28. Duberman, *Stonewall*, 250.
29. Stryker, *Transgender History*, 127.
30. Hobson, *Lavender and Red*, 27.
31. Duberman, *Stonewall*, 291; Gan, "Still," 296.
32. Ferguson, *One-Dimensional Queer*, 43.
33. Price Minter, "Do Transsexuals," 149.
34. Enke, "Collective Memory," 10.
35. Ferguson, *One-Dimensional Queer*, 21, 18. See also Bell, "The Radicalqueens"; Lewis, "Trans History"; Stryker, *Transgender History*, 110–111.

36. In addition to the sources cited below, see Ferguson, *One-Dimensional Queer*, 31–43; Hobson, *Lavender and Red*, 39–40, 69–96; Roque Ramírez, "That's *My* Place."
37. Latrónico, "My Memories," 50, 51.
38. Third World Gay Revolution, "What We Want, What We Believe," 364, 365, 367. The critique of the police and the criminal punishment system – in terms of the criminalization of nonnormative gender expression, erotic activity, sex work, and harassment of queer and trans people on the street and in spaces where they were known to congregate – was a significant issue across gay liberationist writings. The resonance of this analysis of the normalizing work of criminal punishment can be seen in contemporary critiques of the policing of gender and sexual deviance. See Mogul et al., *Queer (In)Justice*; Richie, *Arrested Justice*; Ritchie, *Invisible No More*; Stanley and Smith, *Captive Genders*.
39. Third World Gay Revolution, "The Oppressed," 400.
40. Katz, *Gay American History*, 332, 333. A similar organization, We Wah and Bar Chee Ampe, was founded in New York City (Hom, "Unifying Differences," 67, 120, 159). See also Morgensen, *Spaces between Us*, 93–99, 118–125.
41. See Fawaz, *Queer Forms*; Freeman, *Time Binds*; Garber, *Identity Poetics*; Hemmings, *Why Stories Matter*; Hesford, *Feeling*.
42. "BDSM" refers to consensual, mutually negotiated erotic play that involves bondage, discipline, role playing, and/or sadomasochism and that is based on intentionally staged scenes of hierarchy, dominance, and the exertion of power. It also is known as SM and S/M.
43. Samer, *Lesbian Potentiality*, 4, 184. See also Hesford, *Feeling*.
44. See Hobson, *Lavender and Red*, 49–50.
45. It began as an organizing committee to plan women's dances, instead of the male-dominated dances put on by GLF, and was called GLF Women. After meeting as a consciousness raising group for several months, participants decided it should be its own group, and they organized a *zap* of the NOW-sponsored Second Congress to Unite Women, which included circulating their manifesto "The Woman-Identified Woman" to challenge NOW's previous efforts to expel lesbians from women's liberation. See Kissack, "Freaking Fag Revolutionaries"; Radicalesbians, "Leaving the Gay Men Behind"; Shumsky, "The Radicalesbian Story".
46. Radicalesbians, "The Woman-Identified Woman," 172.
47. Radicalesbians, "The Woman-Identified Woman," 172–173.
48. Radicalesbians, "The Woman-Identified Woman," 173, 174.
49. Radicalesbians, "The Woman-Identified Woman," 174, 175, 176.
50. Stein, *Sex and Sensibility*, 24.
51. Bunch, "Lesbians in Revolt," 420, 421. Stein notes, "same-sex *desire* became secondary to same-sex *identification*," creating tensions among those who might identify as *lesbian*: "'Old gay' women, who had come out before the arrival of feminism, imagined that the products of lesbian and feminist movements weren't really gay at all – at least in terms of membership in a tightly bounded gay subculture organized around homosexual desire" (*Sex and Sensibility*, 38, 97).

52. This phrase is attributed to Ti-Grace Atkinson, who actually said "feminism is a theory, lesbianism is a practice" (Hobson, *Lavender and Red*, 47). See also Hesford, *Feeling*, 144–145; Samer, *Lesbian Potentiality*, 13.
53. Grahn, *A Simple Revolution*, 268. See also Fawaz, *Queer Forms*, 104–158; Hobson, *Lavender and Red*, 43–51; Shugar, *Separatism*; Taylor and Rupp, "Women's Culture"; Valentine, "Making Space"; Valk, "Living."
54. Brownworth, "Living Lesbian Nation," 105.
55. See Hemmings, *Why Stories Matter*. The story of lesbian feminism as essentialist has facilitated a progress narrative that both casts queer studies as more sophisticated and that effaces the heterogeneity of the kinds of worldmaking that occurred within and through the category *lesbian*. See also Garber, *Identity Poetics*; Martin, *Femininity*; Smyth, *Lesbians*. On the ways lesbian sexuality repeatedly is cast as derivative in relation to models of male homosexuality, see Jagose, *Inconsequence*.
56. Rich, "When We Dead Awaken," 167; Rich, "Compulsory Heterosexuality," 203.
57. Rich, "Compulsory Heterosexuality," 216.
58. Rich, "Compulsory Heterosexuality," 217, 218, 220, 223. On thinking Rich's notion of the lesbian continuum in relation to trans identities/relations, see Cole and Cate, "Compulsory Gender."
59. Rich's analysis, and the broader understanding of *lesbian* as beyond the heteronormative framing of *woman*, resonates with arguments that largely entered the US academy through the work of French feminists such as Luce Irigaray and Monique Wittig. On early queer theoretical engagement with this work, see Butler, *Gender Trouble*.
60. Victoria Hesford argues that the image of the *feminist-as-lesbian* and that image's presumptive whiteness and middle-classness has less to do with actual lesbian feminist intellectual or political projects than the ways popular discourses sought to contain the challenge posed by women's liberation by generating "a boundary figure between white respectability and class and racial otherness" (*Feeling*, 73).
61. Bunch, "Lesbians in Revolt," 421. Rita Mae Brown suggests, "Imperialism, racism and the attendant disregard for human life (change that to all forms of life) spring from sexism," further arguing that learning how to address lesbianism within feminism and among women will inherently provide "the tools to deal" with racial and class differences and domination ("Hanoi to Hoboken," 197, 200). Both Bunch and Brown were part of the lesbian feminist Washington, DC-based collective the Furies. On the Furies, see Valk, "Living."
62. Cornwell, "From a Soul Sister's Notebook," 365, 366.
63. Parker, "1987," 275. See also Clarke, "Lesbianism." On Parker's participation in early lesbian feminist political and community work, see Hobson, *Lavender and Red*, 49–51. On the role of white antiracism within lesbian feminist movements, see Thompson, "Multiracial Feminism."
64. Laporte, "Butch/Femme," 356.

65. See Hollibaugh, *My Dangerous Desires*, 256–266; Morgan, "Butch-Femme"; Nestle, *A Restricted Country*.
66. Nestle, *A Restricted Country*, 10, 101, 112, 107. This sentiment is repeated even in some defenses of butch/femme, such as Laporte's condemnation of "the bars" frequented by "the lower socio-economic stratum" where "one encounters a genuine copying of heterosexual sex roles" ("Butch/Femme," 356). For a careful study of butch/femme community dynamics before Stonewall, based on oral history, see Kennedy and Davis, *Boots of Leather*.
67. Rubin, "Of Catamites and Kings," 252–253. On the complex relation between butch lesbians and transmasculine persons, see also Hale, "Consuming the Living."
68. See Duggan, "Censorship"; Duggan et al., "False Promises"; Hunter, "Contextualizing"; Rubin, "Blood under the Bridge"; Rubin, "The Leather Menace." Sometimes the "sex wars" are cast as an internecine debate among white women, but prominent women of color theorists also actively participated within such discussions. For examples, see Hollibaugh and Moraga, "What We're Rollin'"; Lorde, "Sadomasochism"; Moraga, "A Long Line of Vendidas."
69. Rubin, "The Leather Menace," 125–126. In a similar vein, Patrick Califia quips, "I didn't join the feminist movement to live inside a Hallmark greeting card" ("Feminism and Sadomasochism," 527).
70. On the conference, see Rubin, "Blood under the Bridge."
71. Rubin, "Thinking Sex," 148, 154, 169, 172.
72. Rubin, "The Leather Menace." In this vein, Joan Nestle charges the antipornography movement with "creat[ing] a new McCarthy period in the Lesbian community," in which "[s]ome lesbians are more acceptable than others" and are "told we are not feminists" due to having endorsed supposedly "patriarchal" notions of "submission and dominance" that simply reproduce heterosexual norms. She compares this dynamic to calling in "the vice squad" to rid the community of "undesirables" in ways that seek to separate out "the respectable deviant" who can uphold feminist ideals from those persons, associations, and activities that are simply "obscene" (*A Restricted Country*, 149, 116, 123).
73. Hollibaugh, *My Dangerous Desires*, 94, 95–96, 99.
74. Hollibaugh, *My Dangerous Desires*, 97, 102.
75. Hart, *Between the Body and the Flesh*, 37, 43, 52, 54. See also de Lauretis, *The Practice of Love*, 149–202.
76. Hart, *Between the Body and the Flesh*, 81, 178–179. On the ways BDSM enables reconceptualization of genders in relation to sexual desire and experiences of embodiment, see Bauer, "Transgressive."
77. Cruz, *Color of Kink*, 37, 41, 66. On the ways existing organized BDSM communities can cast themselves as sexual outlaws while being shaped by class and racial privilege, see Weiss, *Techniques of Pleasure*.
78. On lesbians and sex work, see Hollibaugh, *My Dangerous Desires*; Nestle, *A Restricted Country*.

79. Pezzutto and Comella, "Trans Pornography," 156.
80. Penley et al., *Feminist Porn Book*, 15.
81. Miller-Young, "Interventions," 107, 111, 115.
82. See Hill-Meyer, "Where"; Noble, "Knowing Dick"; Steinbock, *Shimmering Images*; Strub, "Trans Porn."
83. See Bronstein, "Pornography"; Faye, *Transgender Issue*; Mia, "Failures"; Pezzutto and Comella, "Trans Pornography." Also, a number of the feminist activists who were prominent in antiporn campaigns have moved into advocacy against sex trafficking (Rubin, "Blood under the Bridge," 214). The affinity between these movements may help explain the antiporn dimensions of anti-trafficking legislation such as SESTA/FOSTA.
84. Enke, "Collective Memory," 10, 11. See also Heaney, "Women-Identified Women"; Samer, *Lesbian Potentiality*, 181–215; Stryker, *Transgender History*, 129–132; and Williams, "Radical Inclusion."
85. Bobby Noble has referred to this line of thought as "feminist fundamentalism." See Noble, "Trans. Panic."
86. See Koyama, "Whose Feminism"; Rubin, "Of Catamites and Kings"; Stryker, *Transgender History*.
87. Morgan, "Lesbianism," 429.
88. Stryker, *Transgender History*, 132. On the longer history of associations of gender-transitivity with murder, see Cartwright, *Peculiar Places*.
89. Enke, "Collective Memory," 19. Elliott's status as a woman was affirmed by her fellow conference organizers, and members of the San Francisco DOB insisted, "It is wrong to say that a lesbian woman in a male body is 'passing as a lesbian woman.' You don't 'pass' for something you ARE" (Heaney, "Women-Identified Women," 140).
90. Enke, "Collective Memory," 23. On Stone, see also Williams, "Radical Inclusion." Stone's crucial work in early discourse around transgender identity will be discussed in the last section of this chapter.
91. Ahmed, *Living a Feminist Life*, 227.
92. Freeman, *Time Binds*, 62, 72. In a similar vein, Sara Ahmed has noted that within later intellectual and political formations the lesbian feminist "is without question a killjoy figure," adding that in "some queer literatures" lesbian feminism "appears as a miserable scene that we had to get through, or pass through, before we could embrace the happier possibility of becoming queer" (*Living a Feminist Life*, 222).
93. McKinney, *Information Activism*, 3–7, 163. See also Samer, *Lesbian Potentiality*.
94. Samer, *Lesbian Potentiality*, 5–6, 7, 184.
95. The use of the phrase "Third World" emerges from the Bandung Conference in 1955 that brought together representatives from Asian and African countries that were not aligned with either the United States or the Soviet Union, offering a *third* option for envisioning global geopolitics that attended to histories of European colonization and the situation faced by newly decolonized nations. See Getachew, *Worldmaking after Empire*. The concept then was taken up as a way of referring

to the struggles of racialized peoples against racism, colonialism, and imperialism, and in the context of the United States in the 1960s and 1970s, it largely was used to indicate relations among nonwhite populations in the United States with some sense of commitment to a larger set of international struggles, although such commitments at times could be broadly gestural rather than specifically articulated. See Higashida, *Black Internationalist*; Hom, "Unifying Differences"; Young, *Soul Power*.

96. Tompkins et al., *Keywords for Gender*, 3.
97. See Blackwell, *Chicana Power*; Breines, *Trouble between Us*; Hom, "Unifying Differences"; Springer, *Living*; Thompson, "Multiracial Feminism."
98. Hall, "Difference," 71, 73.
99. Hom, "Unifying Differences," 8.
100. While I have distinguished women of color feminism from lesbian feminism for the purposes of discussing and (at least in part) differentiating some of their major figures and intellectual strategies, I should note that most of the intellectuals discussed in this section would have defined themselves as lesbian feminists, at least during the 1970s and early 1980s. In this sense, this section in many ways serves as a continuation (or maybe reinflection) of the previous section, here engaging intellectuals who explicitly addressed matters of race in what would come to be described as *intersectional* ways. Also, while I discussed Sylvia Rivera and Marsha Johnson in the section on gay liberation, they too should be recognized as women of color feminists.
101. It started as a chapter of the National Black Feminist Organization, but then broke away to become its own entity. In the later 1970s, the collective was central to organizing efforts in Boston to investigate a series of murders of Black women, and it had a series of intellectual retreats attended by Black women from outside Boston, including Audre Lorde and Cheryl Clarke. On the history of the Combahee River Collective, see Breines, *Trouble between Us*; Springer, *Living*; Taylor, *How We Get Free*.
102. Combahee, "Combahee River," 15.
103. Combahee, "Combahee River," 17–18, 19. The statement also famously declares, "If Black women were free, it would mean that everyone else would have to be free since our freedom would necessitate the destruction of all the systems of oppression" ("Combahee River," 22–23).
104. Moraga, "La Güera," 43, 47, 50. On Moraga's work, see Yarbro-Bejarano, *Wounded Heart*.
105. Moraga, "La Güera, 44, 50.
106. Moraga, "La Güera," 44, 49.
107. Moraga and Anzaldúa, *This Bridge*, 21. On the enormous influence this collection has had, see Alarcón, "The Theoretical Subject(s)"; Anzaldúa, "(Un)natural Bridges"; Keating, "Introduction"; Taylor, *Feminism in Coalition*.
108. Woo, "Letter to Ma," 156, 157. On the significance of Woo's intellectual and cultural work, see Huang, "Wither Asian American."

109. Hong, *Death beyond Disavowal*, 7. For examples of engagement with Lorde's work, see also Corbman, "Tool Optimism"; Higashida, *Black Internationalist*; Musser, *Sensual Excess*; Taylor, *Feminism in Coalition*.
110. Lorde, *Sister Outsider*, 115, 116, 119.
111. Lorde, *Sister Outsider*, 136; Hong, *Death Beyond Disavowal*, 4. Lorde further observes, "There is no such thing as a single-issue struggle because we do not live single-issue lives" (*Sister Outsider*, 133).
112. Brant, *Writing as Witness*, 44, 58, 59–60.
113. Brant, *Writing as Witness*, 47, 55.
114. Brant, *Writing as Witness*, 76.
115. Allen, *The Sacred Hoop*, 203.
116. Clarke, "Failure," 192, 193.
117. Clarke, "Failure," 201.
118. Taylor, *Feminism in Coalition*, 14.
119. Hall, "Bitches in Solitude," 224. Also, see Reagon. Hall's and Liza Taylor's arguments in many ways inspired and shaped this discussion of coalition in women of color feminism.
120. Smith, "Introduction," xxi, xxiv, xl.
121. Sandoval, "Feminism and Racism," 65, 66. Although single-authored and consistent with the terms of Sandoval's later work, this piece was written in her role as secretary of the National Third World Women's Alliance.
122. Sandoval, "U.S. Third World Feminism," 15. For use of this framework to discuss queer migrant politics, see Chávez, *Queer Migration*.
123. Parker, "Revolution," 269, 270.
124. Anzaldúa, *Borderlands*, 25. On Anzaldúa's work, see Keating, "Introduction"; Taylor, *Feminism in Coalition*.
125. I address such movement discourses in greater detail in Chapter 4. For a more critical take on the relation of figures of mestizaje to Indigenous peoples, historically and in the present, see Blackwell et al., "Introduction"; Guidotti-Hernández, *Unspeakable Violence*; Saldaña-Portillo, *Revolutionary Imagination*.
126. Anzaldúa, *Borderlands*, 60, 61, 68, 95, 99.
127. Lugones, *Pilgrimages*, 20, 59, 77–78.
128. Holland, *The Erotic Life*, 81, 84.
129. Blackwell, *Chicana Power*, 18.
130. Smith, "Introduction," xliii. Jennifer Nash has asked with respect to the effort to claim the notion of *intersectionality* for Black feminism/feminists, "What does it mean when an anticaptivity project like black feminist theory claims ownership as a primary model for conducting black feminist inquiry?" From this perspective, "the task of black feminism is to expose the theft and to reclaim proper ownership," which Nash argues "forecloses" other kinds of "radical dreaming" while also enabling "the toxicity of defensiveness" against theft (*Black Feminism*, 26, 43, 138).
131. AIDS was linked in 1983 to HIV, which is transmitted primarily through blood and semen and reproduces through destroying cells in the immune system.

132. Crimp, *Melancholia and Moralism*, 60; Schulman, *Let the Record Show*, 17. As Jennifer Brier notes with respect to the earliest cases of AIDS in San Francisco,

> In three of the first nine cases, public health workers overlooked intravenous drug use as a risk factor in favor of naming homosexual identity as the likely cause of illness.... In addition to using gay identity to overdetermine risk, public health workers also disregarded the fact that seven of the nine men lived close to or at the poverty line, economic circumstances that severely compromised their health as well. (*Infectious Ideas*, 51)

133. Grover, "AIDS," 23. See also Yingling, "AIDS in America."
134. See Farmer, *AIDS and Accusation*.
135. Patton, *Inventing AIDS*, 1, 107.
136. Treichler, *How to Have*, 20.
137. See Chávez, *The Borders of AIDS*.
138. See Patton, *Globalizing AIDS*; Tamale, "Researching"; Treichler, *How to Have*; Watney, *Practices of Freedom*.
139. Watney, *Practices of Freedom*, 44, 48, 58.
140. Patton, *Inventing AIDS*, 47.
141. See Bersani, "Is the Rectum"; Crimp, *Melancholia and Moralism*; Nunokawa, "All the Sad." This rhetoric is also associated with the description of infected persons as "AIDS victims," a label rejected in favor of "people with AIDS" by the National Association of People with AIDS and asserted in the Denver Principles adopted at their conference in 1983. See People With AIDS/ARC, "The Denver Principles."
142. It's also important to remember that "sodomy" in many states was illegal until the US Supreme Court decision in *Lawrence v. Texas* (2003). The legality of state anti-sodomy laws was affirmed in the case of *Bowers v. Hardwick* (1986), which further legitimized and gave additional force to homophobic and AIDS-phobic policies. On the role of the latter court decision in helping generate mass direct action AIDS activism, see Gould, *Moving Politics*, 121–180.
143. Due to a years-long activist campaign to change the CDC definition, largely led by ACT UP, it was modified in January 1993 to include cervical cancer, endocarditis, and bacterial pneumonia as well as anyone with a T cell count (immunity-securing white blood cells) below 200. See ACT UP/NY Women and AIDS Book Group, *Women*; Schulman, *Let the Record Show*, 227–269; Stoller, *Lessons from the Damned*, 5–27.
144. Geary, *Antiblack Racism*, 9. This formulation draws on Cindy Patton's work.
145. Geary, *Antiblack Racism*, 14.
146. Patton, *Inventing AIDS*, 61, 91.
147. See Berger, *Workable Sisterhood*; Chávez, *The Borders of AIDS*; Gossett and Hayward, "Monica Jones"; Hollibaugh, *My Dangerous Desires*; Hoppe, *Punishing Disease*, 110–116; Leonard and Thistlethwaite, "Prostitution and HIV Infection";

O'Brien, "Trans Work"; Stoller, *Lessons from the Damned*, 81–96. On the ways the representation of HIV/AIDS and sex work builds on earlier narratives of syphilis, see Gilman, "AIDS and Syphilis." On how this association is part of mischaracterizing routes of transmission (particularly in accounts of the epidemic in sub-Saharan Africa), see Patton, *Globalizing AIDS*; Tamale, "Researching"; Treichler, *How to Have*.

148. The notion of the epidemic as about individual bodies and their generic exposure to the virus "individualize[s] risk by treating it as a consequence of personal behaviors," a function simply of exposure to HIV through certain practices, but as Geary observes, "epidemics generally require kinds of population-level vulnerability that comes from political, economic, and environmental immiseration" (*Antiblack Racism*, 3, 8). Explaining the astronomical rates of HIV infection among Black people in the United States (currently almost 40 percent of new cases, while being only 12 percent of the US population), as well as in other parts of the world that are subject to ongoing structural racism and the ongoing effects of colonialism and global extractivism, then, requires moving beyond aggregates of individual behavior (rates of exposure). Instead, what must be attended to are the population-level political and economic dynamics that produce broad-based ill-health, suppressed/stressed immuno-systems, and greater vulnerability to all manner of physical ailments as well as the ways conceptualizing and modeling "health" for the purposes of epidemiological analysis itself tends to presume conditions found among the privileged. See also Bailey et al., "Souls Forum"; Fink, *Forget Burial*; Geary, "Paradigmatic"; Ghosh, "The Costs"; Jolivette, *Indian Blood*; Jordan-Zachary, "Safe, Soulful Sex"; Patton, *Globalizing AIDS*; Vernon, *Native Americans*. On structural forms of debilitation, see Puar, *Right to Maim*.

149. Patton, *Inventing AIDS*, 8.

150. Watney, *Practices of Freedom*, 136–137. We can see this concern about the relationship between practices and marginalized identities as animating early queer studies work not specifically focused on the AIDS epidemic. Sedgwick's analysis of the complex oscillations between universalizing and minoritizing notions of sexuality and Butler's emphasis on the role of repeated performance in shaping experiences of embodiment and selfhood (discussed in Chapter 1) both can be understood as deeply influenced by the effort to theorize the shifting and multidimensional connections among behavior, subjectivity, and existing social categories that was a central feature of activist and critical intellectual work in response to AIDS.

151. See Brier, *Infectious Ideas*; Crimp, *Melancholia and Moralism*; Patton, *Inventing AIDS*; Schulman, *Let the Record Show*, 281–311; Stoller, *Lessons from the Damned*, 97–112.

152. See Hollibaugh, *My Dangerous Desires*, 187–218; Leonard, "Lesbians"; Stoller, *Lessons from the Damned*, 9–32.

153. See Fink, *Forget Burial*; Geary, "Paradigmatic"; Gossett, "We Will Not Rest in Peace"; Gossett and Hayward, "Monica Jones."

154. See Asetoyer, "First"; Ports, "Many Cultures"; Stoller, *Lessons from the Damned*, 63–80; Vernon, *Native Americans*; Wat, *Love Your Asian Body*.
155. On ACT UP, see Blasius and Phelan, *We Are Everywhere*, 622–641; Brier, *Infectious Ideas*; Cohen, "Punks"; Crimp and Rolston, *AIDS DemoGraphics*; Cvetkovich, *An Archive of Feelings*; Gossett, "We Will Not Rest in Peace"; Gould, *Moving Politics*; Royles, *To Make*; Schulman, *Let the Record Show*; Shahani, "How to Survive"; and Stoller, *Lessons from the Damned*, 113–134.
156. Crimp and Ralston, *AIDS DemoGraphics*, 30, 80.
157. On connections between AIDS activism and the popular/activist mobilization of the term queer, see Berlant and Freeman, "Queer Nationality"; Gould, *Moving Politics*; "Queers Read This; I Hate Straights."
158. See Berger, *Workable Sisterhood*; Hobson, *Lavender and Red*; McKinney, "Crisis Infrastructures"; Roane, "Black Harm Reduction"; Román, *Acts of Intervention*; Royles, *To Make*; Wat, *Love Your Asian Body*.
159. On the ways AIDS discourses and activism also aided in bringing gay men and lesbians together as political allies, see Hobson, *Lavender and Red*; Schulman, *Let the Record Show*; Smyth, *Lesbians*.
160. Cohen, *Boundaries of Blackness*, 27. On African American AIDS activisms, see Royles, *To Make*.
161. Snorton, *Nobody Is Supposed to Know*.
162. Hammonds, "Race, Sex, AIDS," 29, 33.
163. Morgensen, *Spaces between Us*, 196.
164. Jolivette, *Indian Blood*, 6, 48.
165. See Cheng et al., *AIDS*; Geary, *Antiblack Racism*; Gossett, "We Will Not Rest in Peace"; Gossett and Hayward, "Trans"; Harper, *Private Affairs*, 89–124; Jolivette, *Indian Blood*; O'Daniel, *Holding On*; Shahani, "How to Survive."
166. See Shahani, "How to Survive."
167. "Dispatches on the Globalization of AIDS," 40, 45.
168. Hoppe, *Punishing Disease*, 44.
169. Hoppe, *Punishing Disease*, 204.
170. On these dynamics, see Fink, *Forget Burial*; Geary, *Antiblack Racism*; Gossett, "We Will Not Rest in Peace"; Gossett and Hayward, "Trans"; Gossett and Hayward, "Monica Jones"; Hoppe, *Punishing Disease*.
171. Crimp, *Melancholia and Moralism*, 133, 137, 147.
172. Woubshet, *Calendar of Loss*, 24; Cvetkovich, *An Archive of Feelings*, 157. On the use of vigils and political funerals as part of AIDS activism, see Román, *Acts of Intervention*, 26–29; Schulman, *Let the Record Show*; Woubshet, *Calendar of Loss*, 1–3. On the affective dynamics of AIDS activism, see also Gould, *Moving Politics*.
173. Román, *Acts of Intervention*, 268.
174. Woubshet, *Calendar of Loss*, 3, 4.
175. Woubshet, *Calendar of Loss*, 23.
176. Crimp, *Melancholia and Moralism*, 140.

177. Kramer, "1,112," 584; Berkowitz and Callen, "We Know," 564. On Kramer's sex-negativity before the epidemic and its persistence across the 1980s and 1990s, including in his play *The Normal Heart*, see Crimp, *Melancholia and Moralism*, 45–82; Román, *Acts of Intervention*, 61–65.
178. Crimp, *Melancholia and Moralism*, 64. The title of the essay is taken from Berkowitz and Callen's 1983 pamphlet "How to Have Sex in an Epidemic," credited as being the first guide to safe sex.
179. See Dean, *Unlimited*; Delany, *Times Square Red*; Manalansan, "Race, Violence, and Neoliberal Spatial Politics"; Warner, *The Trouble with Normal*.
180. Bost, *Evidence of Being*, 17; Allen, *There's a Disco Ball*, 25, 30–31.
181. Beam, "Brother to Brother," 180; Hemphill, "Introduction," xxvii. On the ways this movement was perhaps less anticapitalist and broadly structurally-minded than Black feminism, see Allen, *There's a Disco Ball*, 50.
182. Beam, "Introduction," xxii.
183. Hemphill, "Introduction," xix, xx.
184. Bost, *Evidence of Being*, 4, 16, 21.
185. See Rawson and Williams, "*Transgender**"; Stryker and Currah, "Introduction."
186. Bornstein, *Gender Outlaw*, 12–13, 62.
187. Stone, "The *Empire* Strikes Back," 156, 164.
188. See Ellison, "Black Femme"; Kennedy and Davis, *Boots of Leather*; Nestle, *A Restricted Country*; Ritchie, *Invisible No More*; Stanley and Smith, *Captive Genders*; Valentine, *Imagining Transgender*.
189. Stryker, "My Words," 238.
190. See Califia, *Sex Changes*, 86–119. Raymond also significantly contributed to a 1981 report that served as the basis for a decision denying medical coverage on public insurance for gender-affirming surgery that lasted through 2013 (Awkward-Rich, *Terrible We*, 76).
191. Stone, "The *Empire* Strikes Back," 160; Stryker, "My Words," 242. On the dominant medical representation of gender-affirmative surgeries, see Califia, *Sex Changes*, 52–85; Gill-Peterson, *Histories*. This topic will be addressed further in Chapter 3.
192. Stryker, "My Words," 249, 250.
193. On the continuing role of the figure of the monster in critical trans discourses, see Preciado, *Can the Monster Speak*.
194. Stone, "The *Empire* Strikes Back," 163, 167.
195. Feinberg, *Trans Liberation*, 10.
196. Stone, "The *Empire* Strikes Back," 166; Bornstein, *Gender Outlaw*, 66, 51–52. The history of the "wrong body" narrative and its relation to discourses of *inversion* will be discussed further in Chapter 3.
197. Bornstein, *Gender Outlaw*, 134–135.
198. See Califia, *Sex Changes*, 221–244; Stryker, *Transgender History*, 151–194. On the complex racial and class dynamics surrounding Brandon Teena's murder, including the erasure of the murder of Philip DeVine alongside Teena, see Cartwright,

Peculiar Places; Halberstam, *In a Queer Time*; Snorton, *Black on Both Sides*. On the complexity of Brandon Teena's own gender identifications, including the question of using that name to refer to them, see Hale, "Consuming the Living."
199. Bornstein, *Gender Outlaw*, 106, 114.
200. This analysis also resonates with Riki Wilchins views: "I am not personally interested in being a transgender activist – even less a transsexual activist. What I am interested in is fighting a liberatory struggle against gender-based oppression – all the ways in which culture seeks to regulate, confine, and punish bodies, gender, and desire" (Califia, *Sex Changes*, 243). See also Wilchins, *Read My Lips*, 134.
201. Bornstein, *Gender Outlaw*, 97, 158, 164. For a similar dynamic, see also Feinberg, *Transgender Warriors*. On the colonial dimensions of such claiming, see Morgensen, *Spaces between Us*; Towle and Morgan, "Romancing." In the afterword to the second addition of *Gender Outlaw*, Bornstein apologizes for this move (*Gender Outlaw*, 242).
202. Feinberg, *Trans Liberation*, 58, 98.
203. Feinberg, *Trans Liberation*, 96.
204. Feinberg, *Trans Liberation*, 19, 133.
205. Califia, *Sex Changes*, 275. In a similar vein, C. Jacob Hale's insists, "Border zones [between categories of identity, specifically butch and trans-masculine] need not be battle zones, but they must be demilitarized" ("Consuming the Living," 337), such that varied conceptions and experiences of gendered embodiment can coexist without delegitimizing each other.
206. For examples of efforts to synthesize these positions, see Koyama, "Transfeminist Manifesto"; Spade, *Normal Life*. Cameron Awkward-Rich characterizes this tension in this way: "whereas the gender freedom model affirms trans speech on the basis that all gender expression ought to be affirmed the queer trans model affirms trans speech *because* it denaturalizes the logic of the binary sex/gender system" (*Terrible We*, 122).

Chapter 3

1. Seitler, "Queer Physiognomies," 74.
2. For discussion of the historiography of sexuality prior to Foucault (and his translation into English), see Katz, *The Invention*, 1–18.
3. Foucault, *History of Sexuality*, 6, 7, 10, 123, 154.
4. Foucault, *History of Sexuality*, 67, 144, 147.
5. Stoler, *Race*, 97, 98–99.
6. Stoler, *Race*, 5, 8.
7. McClintock, *Imperial Leather*, 5, 25, 30, 45.
8. McClintock, *Imperial Leather*, 120–121.

9. Clare, *Exile and Pride*, 95; Awkward-Rich, *Terrible We*, 42.
10. On European discourses of race in the medieval and early-modern periods, see Hall, *Things of Darkness*; Heng, *Invention of Race*; Kim, "Before Intersectionality"; Morgan, *Reckoning*; Ndaiye, *Scripts of Blackness*.
11. Goldberg, *Sodometries*, 193, 195, 200. See also Horswell, *Decolonizing*; Sigal, *Infamous Desire*.
12. Tortorici, *Sins*, 2, 32, 142.
13. See Horswell, *Decolonizing*; Sigal, "Gendered Power"; Stavig, "Political." On the continuance of Indigenous gender forms in contemporary Mexico, see Mirandé, *Behind the Mask*.
14. Arondeker, *For the Record*, 35, 42. On British efforts to eliminate hijras in northern India, see Hinchy, *Governing Gender*.
15. Tallie, *Queering Colonial Natal*, 188.
16. Tallie observes that "allegations against Zulu masculinity can also be read as means of warning *white* settler men about their own appropriate sexual behavior," and English colonial authorities "worked to shore up their own matrimonial and social formations in contradistinction to the indigenous peoples who surrounded them" (*Queering Colonial Natal*, 24, 43).
17. See Coviello, *Make Yourselves Gods*.
18. See Denetdale, "Return"; Kauanui, *Paradoxes*; Rifkin, *When Did Indians*; Simpson, *As We Have Always Done*; TallBear, "Making Love."
19. The British were invested significantly in slave-trading in Africa from the 1550s onward. See Hall, *Things of Darkness*, 3–19. See also Morgan, *Reckoning*.
20. See Spillers, "Mama's Baby."
21. Snorton, *Black on Both Sides*, 8, 57.
22. Snorton, *Black on Both Sides*, 18, 20, 25, 30.
23. Nyong'o, *Amalgamation*, 52. On the historical cross-referencing of notions of privacy and property in ways that exclude blackness and miscegenation, see Harper, *Private Affairs*, 1–32.
24. Haley, *No Mercy Here*, 26, 40.
25. On the imposition of heteronormative conceptions of marriage on Black people in the wake of emancipation, see Franke, *Wedlocked*.
26. Jarman, "Dismembering," 92.
27. Similar dynamics occurred with respect to the construction of Chinatowns in the US West, for which there were "slumming" tours conducted in San Francisco. See Sears, *Arresting Dress*, 113–118.
28. See Hartman, *Wayward Lives*; Mumford, *Interzones*.
29. Mumford, *Interzones*, 73–92.
30. Hartman, *Wayward Lives*, 65, 236, 248.
31. From 1790 onward, the United States limited naturalization to "white" persons, adding Black persons as well in the wake of emancipation but continuing to forbid naturalization to other racial groups. See Luibhéid, *Entry Denied*; Shah, *Stranger Intimacy*; Wong, *Racial Reconstruction*.

32. Shah, *Stranger Intimacy*, 123.
33. Shah, *Stranger Intimacy*, 124.
34. Luibhéid, *Entry Denied*, 31–54.
35. Shah, *Stranger Intimacy*, 76–82, 145–150.
36. Luibhéid, *Entry Denied*, x.
37. Dinshaw, *Getting Medieval*.
38. LaFleur et al., "Introduction," 4. See also Chess et al., "Introduction"; Gill-Peterson, *Histories*.
39. Traub, *Thinking Sex*, 85.
40. LaFleur, "Sex and 'Unsex,'" 473, 495.
41. Cleves, "Beyond the Binaries," 463.
42. Masten, *Queer Philologies*, 100.
43. Masten, *Queer Philologies*, 100–101.
44. Traub, *Thinking Sex*, 147.
45. Gamble, "Towards," 27, 29.
46. Rubright, "Transgender Capacity," 47, 49. Rubright is building on David Getsy's work (Getsy, "Capacity").
47. We might read such philological insights as in some sense drawing on the ways earlier movements refigured seemingly evident terms such as *gay*, *lesbian*, and *woman* (as discussed in Chapter 2).
48. DiGangi, *Sexual Types*, 22.
49. DiGangi, *Sexual Types*, 53; Dinshaw, *Getting Medieval*, 60–64, 84.
50. Dinshaw, *Getting Medieval*, 8; Lochrie, *Heterosyncracies*, xvi; Warner, "New English Sodom," 23.
51. See Amer, "Cross-Dressing"; De Souza, "Elenx de Céspedes"; Lanser, *Sexuality*; Wahl, *Invisible Relations*.
52. Goldberg, *Sodometries*, 18, 19, 120.
53. Masten, *Queer Philologies*, 95.
54. Warner, "New English Sodom," 28, 34. See also Sanchez, *Shakespeare*, 57–83.
55. Dinshaw, *Getting Medieval*, 67; DiGangi, *Sexual Types*, 32.
56. Boone, *Homoerotics*, x.
57. See Arvas, "Performing and Desiring"; Boone, *Homoerotics*; Epps, "Comparison"; Heng, *Invention of Race*, 110–180; Rouhi, "A Handsome Boy"; Wahl, *Invisible Relations*. On understandings and depictions of homoeroticism in the Ottoman period, see El-Rouayheb, *Before Homosexuality*; Ze'evi, *Producing Desire*. On the erasure of histories of racializing religious difference in Europe (particularly Islam) and the implications of this pattern for current Europeans of color, see El-Tayeb, *European Others*.
58. Traub, "Renaissance of Lesbianism," 258. Alongside the *tribade*, there's also the question of the *sapphic*, which refers to the historical Greek poet Sappho. While references to her have a long history, they did not come to be primarily associated with sexual contact between women until the eighteenth century. See Halperin, *How to Do*, 50–52.

59. See DiGangi, *Sexual Types*, 62-79; Lochrie, *Heterosyncracies*, 74-102; Traub, "Renaissance of Lesbianism." One of the ways erotic relations among women were resolved in early-modern texts is that one of the women becomes a man. See Amer, "Cross-Dressing"; Traub, "Renaissance of Lesbianism," 250-252. For a collection of some of the wide array of terms used by European writers in the seventeenth and eighteenth centuries to refer to what might be described as homoerotic relations among women, see Lanser, *Sexuality*, 16.
60. See DiGangi, *Sexual Types*, 77-79; Lochrie, *Heterosyncracies*, 104-136; Wagner, "Racing Gender"; Wahl, *Invisible Relations*, 27-34, 182-183.
61. As scholars have indicated, the elongated clitoris associated with the tribade at times was thought of as in-born and at times was attributed to prior practices of stimulation; in either case, it could mark a person as other-than-woman, as physically masculine or masculinized in ways marked by the term hermaphrodite. See Lochrie, *Heterosyncracies*, 82-88; Wahl, *Invisible Relations*, 23-27.
62. DeVun, *The Shape of Sex*, 202.
63. DeVun, *The Shape of Sex*, 66, 40-101.
64. On uses of the term in the eighteenth and nineteenth centuries in Great Britain and the United States, see Boag, *Re-Dressing*, 183, 187; Manion, *Female Husbands*, 110-111, 127-132; Reis, *Bodies in Doubt*.
65. Lochrie, *Heterosyncracies*, xiv.
66. Lochrie, *Heterosyncracies*, xxii.
67. Lanser, *Sexuality*, 16.
68. Sanchez, "Use Me," 493-494.
69. Traub, *Thinking Sex*, 113, 152. Similarly, David Halperin suggests, "We need to find ways of asking how different historical cultures fashioned different sorts of links between sexual acts, on the one hand, and sexual tastes, styles, dispositions, characters, gender presentations, and forms of subjectivity, on the other" (*How to Do*, 43-44).
70. Cleves, "Beyond the Binaries," 467; LaFleur et al., "Introduction," 5.
71. Lochrie, *Heterosyncracies*, xxii.
72. Dinshaw, *Getting Medieval*, 6.
73. DeVun, *The Shape of Sex*, 35.
74. Laqueur, *Making Sex*, 4.
75. Laqueur, *Making Sex*, 96, 134. See also Hitchcock, *English Sexualities*. For discussion of similar ideas about bodies and the work of bodily humors in Islamicate contexts, see Ze'evi, *Producing Desire*. For discussion of the ways the two-body model appeared earlier, at least in medical discourses, see DeVun, *The Shape of Sex*.
76. Hitchcock, *English Sexualities*, 111, 26.
77. Hitchcock, *English Sexualities*, 81.
78. Traub, *Thinking Sex*, 152.
79. LaFleur, *The Natural History*, 36, 67-101.
80. Tompkins, *Racial Indigestion*, 3, 69.

81. Coviello, *Tomorrow's Parties*, 19–20.
82. See Amer, "Cross-Dressing"; Boone, *Homoerotics*; El-Rouayheb, *Before Homosexuality*.
83. See El-Rouayheb, *Before Homosexuality*; Epps, "Comparison"; Massad, *Desiring Arabs*; Ze'evi, *Producing Desire*.
84. Nussbaum, *Torrid Zones*, 135. See also Moore, *Dangerous Intimacies*, 49–54; Nussbaum, *Torrid Zones*, 35–45, 76–89, 135–166; Pearsall, *Polygamy*.
85. See Coviello, *Tomorrow's Parties*, 168–189; Marcus, *Between Women*, 193–256.
86. Moore, *Dangerous Intimacies*, 12.
87. See Lanser, *Sexuality*; Marcus, *Between Women*; Traub, "Renaissance of Lesbianism"; Wahl, *Invisible Relations*.
88. Moore, *Dangerous Intimacies*, 82. See also Halberstam, *Female Masculinity*, 61–63.
89. Prior to the development of the category of homosexuality, affection and eroticism among white men also was in many ways less stigmatized. See Moon, *Disseminating Whitman*. On other kinds of nineteenth-century desire we might read as queer, see Coviello, *Tomorrow's Parties*. On the relation between nineteenth-century queernesses and processes of settler colonialism, see Rifkin, *Settler Common Sense*.
90. Manion, *Female Husbands*, 39.
91. Manion, *Female Husbands*, 50, 111.
92. On such laws, see Sears, *Arresting Dress*.
93. Boag, *Re-Dressing*, 2, 32, 67.
94. Boag, *Re-Dressing*, 6.
95. On the ways assumptions about trans presence in cities and among queer/trans communities obscures evidence of trans men in small towns and rural areas, see Skidmore, *True Sex*. Rather than being singled out for individual acts of gender-"crossing," though, people of color tended to be cast as collectively deviant and dangerous. As Clare Sears observes with respect to San Francisco, "city newspapers represented Chinese gender as a foreign and pathological formation, with men and women failing to embody the masculinity and femininity that editors deemed 'normal'" – enabling the kinds of crackdowns, deportations, and creation of segregated vice districts discussed earlier (*Arresting Dress*, 95).
96. Traub, *Thinking Sex*, 84; Lanser, *Sexuality*, 2, 16, 30.
97. The issue here, though, is not the same as the presumption of an unchanging, transhistorical lesbianism. For this kind of analysis, which seeks to restore what is presumed to be lesbians' invisibility using what is presented as a common-sensical understanding of the category, see Castle, *Apparitional*. For a critique of Castle's sense of history as redemptive in this way, see Jagose, *Inconsequence*.
98. Manion, *Female Husbands*, 11. For an earlier and slightly differently configured version of *trans-ing*, see Sears, *Arresting Dress*, 9.
99. Halberstam, *Female Masculinity*, 21, 46, 56–57.
100. Manion, *Female Husbands*, 139. Notable historical figures that can be associated with "female masculinity" who understood themselves as women who erotically

desired other women, such as Ann Lister in the early nineteenth century and Radclyffe Hall in the early twentieth century, quite specifically distanced themselves from persons assigned female at birth who sought to live as men. See Doan, *Fashioning Sapphism*, 89–90; Halberstam, *Female Masculinity*, 66, 93–96.
101. See Manion, *Female Husbands*, 127–132; Reis, *Bodies in Doubt*.
102. LaFleur et al., "Introduction," 11; LaFleur, "Epilogue," 374.
103. Lanser, *Sexuality*, 3, 39.
104. Dinshaw, *Getting Medieval*, 103–104; 111–112.
105. Bychowski, "Transgender Turn," 96, 104.
106. Hitchcock, *English Sexualities*, 58, 68, 70.
107. Hitchcock, *English Sexualities*, 68–69. For Heaney's description of mollies in these terms, see Heaney, *The New Woman*, 7, 155.
108. Hitchcock, *English Sexualities*, 67; Upchurch, *Before Wilde*, 85–95, 163–166.
109. Hale, "Consuming the Living," 319, 320.
110. Larson, "Laid Open," 351, 361.
111. DeVun and Tortorici, "Trans," 519.
112. Some of sexology's most important figures were Karl Ulrichs, Richard von Krafft-Ebing, Havelock Ellis, Richard Carpenter, and Magnus Hirschfeld.
113. Halberstam, *Female Masculinity*, 83.
114. Heaney, *The New Woman*, 3, 23; Katz, *The Invention*, 52.
115. See de Lauretis, *The Practice of Love*; Jagose, *Inconsequence*; Katz, *The Invention*.
116. Kahan, *The Book of Minor Perverts*, 15, 39.
117. Storr, "Transformations," 14, 17.
118. Until the 1930s, *heterosexual* itself was a term used to indicate excessive forms of desire that were seen as disruptive to social life (meaning matrimonial-reproductive relations). See Katz, *The Invention*; Stokes, *Color of Sex*.
119. On the uneven dissemination of, or popular investment in, sexological frameworks in small towns and rural areas, see Howard, *Men Like That*; Johnson, *Just Queer Folks*; Skidmore, *True Sex*.
120. Heaney, *The New Woman*, 4, 9. On the proliferation of categories of sexual and gender identity in the late nineteenth and early twentieth centuries that did not fit the terms of sexology, see also Chauncey, *Gay New York*.
121. Doan, *Fashioning Sapphism*, 133–137.
122. Kahan, *The Book of Minor Perverts*, 2.
123. Doan, *Fashioning Sapphism*, 126–163; Waters, "Havelock Ellis."
124. Doan, *Fashioning Sapphism*, 139. See also Heaney, *The New Woman*; Waters, "Havelock Ellis."
125. Fisher, "Sexual Politics," 59. See also Bristow, "Symond's History."
126. Duggan, *Sapphic Slashers*, 13–18.
127. Cohen, *Talk on the Wilde Side*, 4. On the changing character of criminal charges against men for homoerotic relations with other men in Great Britain during the nineteenth century, see also Upchurch, *Before Wilde*.
128. Cohen, *Talk on the Wilde Side*, 166.

129. Hurley, *Circulating Queerness*, 141, 193.
130. Although, sexological discourses also widely circulated internationally outside Europe and the United States. See Fiol-Matta, *Queer Mother*; Marhoefer, *Racism*; Sang, *Emerging Lesbian*.
131. Somerville, *Queering the Color Line*, 31, 33–37. See also Seitler, "Queer Physiognomies."
132. Carter, *Heart of Whiteness*, 6, 13, 98.
133. Ordover, *American Eugenics*, 78–80. On the role of animal husbandry in the development of eugenics discourse in the United States, see Johnson, *Just Queer Folks*.
134. Somerville, *Queering the Color Line*, 15, 31. We further might consider how such eugenic ideologies live on into the late twentieth century, for example helping shape responses to HIV/AIDS (as discussed in Chapter 2).
135. Kunzel, *Criminal Intimacy*, 6, 48.
136. On these dynamics, see also Awkward-Rich, *Terrible We*; Clare, *Brilliant*; Pascoe, *What Comes Naturally*; Shah, *Stranger Intimacy*.
137. Roscoe, *Changing Ones*, 170, 182. On such comparative dynamics, and the role of colonial discourse/reportage in them, see also Marhoefer, *Racism*.
138. Nealon, *Foundlings*, 2.
139. Gill-Peterson, *Histories*, 138.
140. Meyerowitz, *How Sex Changed*, 44.
141. Meyerowitz, *How Sex Changed*, 17–49. On the history of surgical intervention for intersex people, see Gill-Peterson, *Histories*; Reis, *Bodies in Doubt*.
142. Heaney, *The New Woman*, 46–47.
143. Gill-Peterson, *Histories*, 16, 18.
144. Heaney, *The New Woman*, 27, 153–173.
145. Amin, "Gland," 603. Amin addresses how one of the most famous early figures for transsexuality, Lili Elbe, sought surgical intervention not solely as a mode of affirming her womanhood but also as part of an affirmation of the physical potential of Euro-whiteness, indicating "a disturbing genealogy of transgender that is implicated in eugenics" ("Gland," 593).
146. See Reiss, *Bodies in Doubt*; Skidmore, *True Sex*.
147. Gill-Peterson, *Histories*, 79, 100.
148. Gill-Peterson, *Histories*, 98.
149. Meyerowitz, *How Sex Changed*, 114–125.
150. Gill-Peterson, *Histories*, 80–81, 135–140; Meyerowitz, *How Sex Changed*, 66–73, 169–179.
151. Ellison, "Black Femme"; Gill-Peterson, *Histories*; Snorton, *Black on Both Sides*.
152. Halberstam, *Female Masculinity*, 173.
153. DeVun and Tortorici, "Trans," 521. Julian Carter suggests that within ordinary trans experience "developmental sequences, backward turns, and futural impulses coexist and intertwine," such that "transition wraps the body in the folds of social time": "Sex change does involve purposive movement toward an

embodied future, even as that future is summoned into being in and through a body that does not yet exist, and while the body that does exist in the present is the medium for the future body's becoming-form" ("Embracing Transition," 131, 141, 142).
154. Bychowski et al., "Trans*historicities," 674–675. See also Lau, "Between the Times." On identity documents as illustrating the ways the sexed body is conceptualized as the property of the state, see Salamon, Assuming.
155. Halberstam, In a Queer Time, 4; McCallum and Tuhkanen, "Becoming Unbecoming," 8, 9.
156. Muñoz, Cruising Utopia, 22, 195.
157. Freeman, Time Binds, 3. Freeman builds on Dana Luciano's notion of chronobiopolitics. See Luciano, Arranging Grief.
158. Dinshaw, How Soon Is Now, 4, 33.
159. See McClintock, Imperial Leather; Pérez, A Taste; Rohy, Anachronism; Ross, "Beyond the Closet."
160. Freccero, Queer/Early/Modern, 70.
161. Valerie Traub, though, has raised questions about the ways notions of queer temporality may overemphasize the critic's own identifications and desires as the prism through which to view the past while also associating linear time with heteronormativity: "Neither straight identity nor heterosexual desire is the same as linear time. Not every diachronic or chronological treatment of temporality need be normativitizing, nor is every linear arc sexually 'straight'" (Thinking Sex, 73).
162. Freeman, Time Binds, xiii, 65, 95.
163. Bychowski and Kim, "Visions," 10.
164. Halberstam, Trans*.
165. Goldberg and Menon, "Queering History," 1609.
166. Rohy, Anachronism, 129; Freccero, Queer/Early/Modern, 39. On the relationship between discourses of sexuality and conceptions of sequence, see Jagose, Inconsequence.
167. Cornum, "Space NDN's."
168. Whitehead, "Introduction," 10.
169. See Morgensen, Spaces between Us; Rifkin, When Did Indians; Towle and Morgan, "Romancing."
170. Lothian, Old Futures, 9, 23. This approach responds to Lee Edelman's argument in No Future that the figure of the Child represents an endemic *reproductive futurism* that presents the current heteronormative social order as necessary for survival and futurity. For an engagement with Edelman that mobilizes his work toward a critique of racialization and empire, see Schotten, Queer Terror.
171. Keeling, Queer Times, 22, 103, 174.
172. Lau, "Between the Times," 10, 15.
173. Muñoz, Cruising Utopia, 1, 49, 195.

Chapter 4

1. Ferguson, *Aberrations in Black*, 4.
2. Ferguson addresses this dynamic in terms of how African Americans' "fitness for citizenship [has been] measured in terms of how much their sexual, familial, and gender relations deviated from the bourgeois nuclear family model," itself understood as intrinsically white, and reciprocally, the Black middle class has insisted on "compliance with heteropatriarchal cultural standards as a way of proving their distance" from what were/are deemed "pathological subjects" as part of "claiming access to the state and civil society" (*Aberrations in Black*, 20, 75).
3. Ferguson, *Aberrations in Black*, 87.
4. Hong and Ferguson, "Introduction," 11.
5. Reddy, *Freedom with Violence*, 39.
6. Chen, *Trans Exploits*, 6.
7. Hong and Ferguson, "Introduction," 2.
8. Ellison et al., "We Got Issues," 162, 165.
9. Barker, "Introduction," 7.
10. On Indigenous-state relations in the United States and Canada, see Barker, *Native Acts*; Coulthard, *Red Skin*; Rifkin, *Manifesting*; Simpson, *Mohawk Interruptus*; Wilkins and Stark, *American Indian Politics*.
11. Denetdale, "Return," 72, 73.
12. Simpson, *As We Have Always Done*, 123.
13. Laing, *Urban Indigenous*, 28; Hunt, "Embodying," 116.
14. Miranda, "Extermination."
15. Simpson, *As We Have Always Done*, 52, 104. See also Allen, *The Sacred Hoop*; Povinelli, *Empire of Love*; Rifkin, *When Did Indians*.
16. TallBear, "Making Love," 151–152.
17. Pierce, "In Good Relations," 96–97.
18. Denetdale, "Return," 73.
19. Denetdale, "Return," 71, 87.
20. Denetdale, "Return," 91, 92.
21. Kauanui, *Paradoxes*, 74, 178.
22. Kauanui, *Paradoxes*, 119–156.
23. Kauanui, *Paradoxes*, 159.
24. Miranda, "Extermination," 268.
25. Miranda, "Extermination," 270.
26. Pyle, "Naming and Claiming," 575.
27. Pyle, "Naming and Claiming," 582. See also Besnier and Alexeyeff, "Gender on the Edge"; Lang, *Men as Women*; Maracle, "A Journey"; Pierce, "In Good Relations"; Roscoe, *Changing Ones*; Wesley, "Twin-Spirited Woman."
28. Justice, "Notes," 209, 219.

29. Osorio, *Remembering*, 13, 63, 83, 111. I should note that Osorio also seeks to challenge the sense of easy translation that I'm enacting in providing quick glosses for the Hawaiian terms.
30. Tatonetti, *Written by the Body*, 5.
31. Tatonetti, *Queerness*, 68, 160; Tatonetti, *Written by the Body*, 187.
32. Driskill et al., "Introduction," 12; Laing, *Urban Indigenous*, 2; Pyle, "Naming and Claiming," 577. On the use of Two-Spirit, see also Jacobs et al., *Two-Spirit People*; Morgensen, *Spaces between Us*; Wesley, "Twin-Spirited Woman."
33. Driskill et al., "Introduction," 14; Pyle, "Naming and Claiming," 575.
34. Pyle, "Women and 2Spirits," 87–88.
35. Laing, *Urban Indigenous*, 5, 54, 92.
36. Pyle, "Women and 2Spirits," 90; Hunt, "Embodying," 108. In another piece, Pyle and Danne Jobin ask, "How do Two-Spirit individuals both adapt and resist some of the signifiers mapped onto trans bodies? How can we discuss access to hormones and surgery and the ways in which these have created new possibilities for transgender embodiment that perhaps break away from older categories of winkte, nádleehí, or māhū without reifying questions of authenticity? How important/useful is to try and maintain continuity with such categories?" ("Transgender," 3). For such historical dynamics, see also Carroll, "Remembering Polingaysi." On contemporary experiences, see also Jacobs et al., *Two-Spirit People*.
37. Pyle, "Women and 2spirits," 85, 92.
38. Belcourt, "Can the Other."
39. Belcourt, "Indigenous Studies," 182, 183–184.
40. Gould, "Disobedience," 32, 41.
41. Womack, *Art as Performance*, 369, 380–381; Womack, "Suspicioning," 133.
42. Byrd, "What's Normative," 108, 109, 112.
43. Ferguson, *Aberrations in Black*, 41.
44. Ferguson, *Aberrations in Black*, 75; Johnson and Henderson, "Introduction," 3.
45. Hammonds, "Black (W)holes," 133, 138–139.
46. Cohen, "Deviance," 30.
47. Green, "Troubling the Waters," 67, 79.
48. Johnson, "Quare," 126–127, 149.
49. Dillon, *Fugitive Life*, 15.
50. Abdur-Rahman, *Against the Closet*, 36–37.
51. See Abdur-Rahman, *Against the Closet*; Ferguson, *Aberrations in Black*; Franke, *Wedlocked*; Haley, *No Mercy Here*; Mumford, *Interzones*; Scott, *Extravagant Abjection*; Snorton, *Black on Both Sides*. Much of this work also has been discussed in previous chapters.
52. Dillon, *Fugitive Life*, 5, 18, 140. On the issue of queer Black mobility amid institutionalized forms of injury, see also Avilez, *Black Queer*.
53. Ellison, "Black Femme," 6, 11.
54. Ellison, "The Labor," 10, 14.

55. Richardson, *Queer Limit*, 12–13.
56. Richardson, *Queer Limit*.
57. Macharia, *Frottage*, 12; Walcott, *Queer Returns*, 184.
58. Macharia, *Frottage*, 12, 64, 129.
59. Best, *None Like Us*, 7–8, 64, 65, 2, 131.
60. Allen, "Black/Queer/Diaspora," 215.
61. Ellis, *Territories*, 2, 3, 4.
62. Walcott, *Queer Returns*, 185, 147, 158.
63. Spillers, "Mama's Baby," 206–207, 214, 217, 228–229.
64. For work that explores this idea of *flesh*, see Snorton, *Black on Both Sides*; Weheliye, *Habeus*. For discussion of turning toward abjection, in ways that resonate with Spillers's argument, see Cruz, *Color of Kink*; Scott, *Extravagant Abjection*.
65. Bruce, "The Body Beautiful," 169.
66. Ross, *Sissy Insurgencies*, 20, 208, 25.
67. Ross, *Sissy Insurgencies*, 169, 173, 264.
68. Bey, *Black Trans*, 4, 33, 39, 67.
69. Keeling, *The Witch's Flight*, 64, 85, 87, 137, 149.
70. Tinsley, *Ezili's Mirrors*, 33, 36, 40.
71. Tinsley, *Ezili's Mirrors*, 4, 24.
72. Bailey, *Burch Queens*, 4, 19, 33, 35, 80.
73. Reid-Pharr, *Black Gay Man*, 116, 133. In this vein, Dwight McBride notes, "the politics of black respectability ... can be seen as laying the foundation for the necessary disavowal of black queers in dominant representations of the African American community, African American history, and African American studies" (*Why I Hate*, 38).
74. Stallings, *Funk the Erotic*, xii, 10, 122. Stallings asserts, "My ancestors were superfreaks, and I have clearly become a conduit for their continued activities in the afterlife" (*Funk the Erotic*, 149).
75. McBride, *Why I Hate*, 100–101, 124. Similarly, Reid-Pharr observes, "It is surprising, then, that so little within queer theory has been addressed to the question of how we inhabit our various bodies, especially how we fuck or, rather, what we think when we fuck," and he suggests that "the tendency to insist upon the innocence of our sex, the transparency of desire at the moment of penetration, is itself part of the complex ideological process by which whiteness is rendered invisible, unremarkable except in the presence of a spectacularized blackness" (*Black Gay Man*, 86, 88–89).
76. Holland, *Erotic Life*, 46.
77. Holland, *Erotic Life*, 60.
78. Holland, *Erotic Life*; Reid-Pharr, *Black Gay Man*.
79. Declue, "Let's Play," 218, 227.
80. Musser, *Sensual Excess*, 3, 23.
81. Musser, *Sensual Excess*, 141, 172.

82. Adeyemi, *Feels Right*, 8–9, 16, 62, 97, 100, 104.
83. The "x" in Latinx replaces conventional gendered attributions in Spanish and Portuguese, in which a person would need to be characterized as Latino or Latina. Emerging over the last decade or so, this change signals an effort to challenge assumptions about gender. Although, as Francisco J. Galarte notes, "The possibility of the 'x' does not relieve us of our responsibilities to interrogate how nonbinary or gender-neutral positionalities still emerge out of the binary oppositions that structure Chicano/a and Latino/a sex-gender-sexuality paradigms" (*Brown Trans Figurations*, 130). Scholarly and popular discourses, though, also have started using Latine, since it is a non-gendered form that works more readily within Spanish and Portuguese forms of pronunciation.
84. See Anzaldúa, "To(o) Queer"; Hames-Garcia, "Jotería Studies"; La Fountain-Stokes, *Queer Ricans*; La Fountain-Stokes, *Translocas*; Pierce et al., "Introduction"; Rizki, "Latin/x"; Rodríguez, *Queer Latinidad*. Terms for personal identity in Spanish and Portuguese also serve as analytic frameworks for considering relations among gender, sexuality, class, race, and migration. See cárdenas, *Poetic Operations*; Pérez, "Jotería Epistemologies"; Rizki, "Latin/x."
85. Rizki, "Latin/x," 147.
86. Pierce et al., "Introduction," 322, 323.
87. Cantú, *Sexuality of Migration*, 76.
88. Mandujano, "Privatized Deportation," 178, 186. Many of the people arriving as migrants who are classified as Latinx or primarily as citizens of the countries they are leaving, though, are Indigenous, including many who may not speak Spanish. See Speed, *Incarcerated Stories*.
89. Alvarez et al., *Transmovimientos*, xx–xxi.
90. These include direct US support for undemocratic governments, the massive political and economic shifts due to US-led free trade agreements, debt and austerity conditions created by loans from the US-dominated International Monetary Fund (IMF) and World Bank, and US invasions and interventions largely justified through the wars on drugs and terror. See Beltrán, *Cruelty as Citizenship*; Luibhéid, "Treated neither with Respect nor Dignity"; Heidenreich, *Nepantla²*; Mandujano, "Privatized Deportation"; Speed, *Incarcerated Stories*.
91. Luibhéid, "Treated neither with Respect nor Dignity," 33. See also Cantú, *Sexuality of Migration*; Chávez, *Queer Migration*; Luibhéid, *Entry Denied*; Somerville, "Queer Loving."
92. Chávez, *Queer Migration*, 79–111.
93. Brady, *Extinct Lands*, 11.
94. Cantú, *Sexuality of Migration*, 42.
95. Negrón-Muntaner, "When I Was," 512.
96. See La Fountain-Stokes, *Queer Ricans*; León, "Exorbitant"; Rodríguez, *Sexual Futures*.
97. Negrón-Muntaner, "When I Was," 516, 520.

98. Negrón-Muntaner, "When I Was," 516, 514. See also La Fountain-Stokes, *Queer Ricans*.
99. La Fountain-Stokes, *Translocas*, 16–17.
100. Decena, *Tacit Subjects*, 3, 10, 64.
101. Rodríguez, *Sexual Futures*, 2, 4, 5, 10.
102. Pérez, *The Decolonial Imaginary*, 26, 124.
103. cárdenas, *Poetic Operations*, 133, 150.
104. Puerto Rican nationalism could also be considered a minority nationalism, but since Puerto Rico has a specific legal status as its own separate unit of governance, and it is geographically distinct from the continental United States and held as an unincorporated territory, its national(ist) discourses in many ways have more in common with those of an independent country than the forms taken by Chicanx nationalism.
105. Gaspar de Alba, *(Un)Framing*, 92.
106. Esquiel, *With Her Machete*, 3. This gendered narrative of betrayal resonates with and gains force from a longstanding account of Spanish conquest and racial mixture as arising out of a woman's betrayal. Malintzin, an early sixteenth-century Nahua woman, often has been portrayed as *La Malinche* (perhaps most famously by Octavio Paz), the supposed lover of the Spanish conqueror Hernán Cortés who sold out her people to him and who is taken to be the treacherous (symbolic) *mother* of the mestizo race – the mixture of European/white and Indigenous/Indian people. See also Alarcón, "Chicana's Feminist Literature"; Arrizón, *Queering Mestizaje*; Gaspar de Alba, *(Un)Framing*; Pérez, *The Decolonial Imaginary*; Yarbro-Bejarano, *Wounded Heart*.
107. Rodríguez, *Next of Kin*, 135, 145.
108. See Arrizón, *Queering Mestizaje*; Esquibel, *With Her Machete*; Gaspar de Alba, *(Un)Framing*; Heidenreich, *Nepantla^2*; Rodríguez, *Next of Kin*; Trujillo, "La Virgen."
109. Rivera-Severa, *Performing*, 29, 174–175, 194–196.
110. Rodríguez, *Queer Latinidad*, 10, 40.
111. Soto, *Reading*, 6, 121.
112. Muñoz, *The Sense of Brown*, 11, 46, 121, 136.
113. Galarte, *Brown Trans Figurations*, 18, 59.
114. Vargas, "Ruminations," 715–716; Alvarez, "Finding Sequins," 619–620.
115. Eng, *Racial Castration*, 24.
116. Takagi, "Maiden Voyage," 3.
117. Eng and Hom, "Introduction," 5–6.
118. See Eng, *Racial Castration*; Luibhéid, *Entry Denied*; Shah, *Stranger Intimacy*.
119. Eng, *Racial Castration*, 217.
120. Ponce, *Beyond the Nation*, 7.
121. See, *Decolonized*, xi.
122. See Ponce, *Beyond the Nation*; Rafael, *White Love*; Rodríguez, *Suspended Apocalypse*; See, *Decolonized*.

123. Ponce, *Beyond the Nation*, 56.
124. See, *Decolonized*, 116, 117.
125. Mendoza, *Metroimperial*, 25.
126. Mendoza, *Metroimperial*, 36–37.
127. Manalansan, *Global Divas*, 11–13.
128. Manalansan, *Global Divas*, 13. Manalansan also notes of his interviewees, "Many informants perceived the term *Asian* only in terms of geography and believed that significant differences existed between other Asians and themselves. They perceived *Asian* to mean East Asians – Japanese, Korean, and Chinese. A number of informants mentioned having more cultural affinity with Latinos" (*Global Divas*, 128).
129. See Eng, *Racial Castration*; Sueyoshi, *Discriminating Sex*.
130. Das Gupta, *Unruly Immigrants*; Shah, *Stranger Intimacy*.
131. Eng and Hom, "Introduction," 3.
132. Eng, *Racial Castration*, 199, 182.
133. Aguilar-San Juan, "Going Home," 25.
134. Hong Sohn, *Inscrutable*, 30–31, 67–68.
135. Fung, "Looking," 116, 118, 121. On the implications of such dominant tropes for gay Asian American self-perceptions, see Han, *Geisha*. On the transnational dynamics of the trope of the white man/Asian native boy dyad, see Lim, *Brown Boys*.
136. Eng, *Racial Castration*, 2, 21.
137. Nguyen, *A View*, 14, 17.
138. Nguyen, *A View*, 12, 80, 114.
139. Wu, *Sticky Rice*, 13, 142.
140. Manalansan et al., "Journeys," 1.
141. Wu, *Sticky Rice*, 160.
142. Huang, *Surface Relations*, 73, 83, 99, 153.
143. Puar, *Terrorist Assemblages*, 35, 119.
144. See Said, *Orientalism*.
145. Puar, *Terrorist Assemblages*, 4, 5, 169.
146. Kapadia, *Insurgent Aesthetics*, 29, 36.
147. Lee, "Toward a Queer Korean," 185, 186.
148. Nguyen, "Queer Dis/inheritance," 221.
149. Das Gupta, *Unruly Immigrants*, 57, 60.
150. Lee, "Toward a Queer Korean," 193.
151. Gopinath, *Impossible Desires*, 7, 9, 11.
152. Gopinath, *Unruly Visions*, 15.
153. We might note in this vein the tendency in the US context of talking about Asian diasporas in ways that ignore the significant presence of people and groups who would be considered *Asian* who have ties to the Caribbean, especially through histories of indenture and British imperial relations. See Das Gupta, *Unruly Immigrants*, 202; Gopinath, *Impossible Desires*, 169–181.

154. Lim, *Brown Boys*, 96, 97, 173.
155. Gopinath, *Unruly Visions*, 5, 60.
156. Gopinath, *Impossible Desires*, 103, 118.
157. Manalansan, *Global Divas*, ix, 43, 79–80.
158. Tompkins, "Intersections," 177.

Chapter 5

1. For a significant overview of scholarship on these issues prior to the early 1990s, see Weston, "Lesbian/Gay."
2. Gramling and Dutta, "Introduction," 339–340.
3. Arondeker and Patel, "Area Impossible," 152.
4. King, "There Are No Lesbians Here," 34.
5. See Chiang et al., "Trans-in-Asia."
6. Cruz-Malavé and Manalansan, "Introduction," 2.
7. Grewal and Kaplan, "Global Identities," 669, 670.
8. Povinelli and Chauncey, "Thinking Sexuality," 442.
9. Grewal and Kaplan, "Global Identities," 670–671.
10. Arondeker and Patel, "Area Impossible," 155; Chiang et al., "Trans-in-Asia," 299.
11. I should note that this chapter addresses a range of scholarship from the 1990s through the moment of writing (2024), and while I'm focused on the conceptual and methodological principles at play among the studies I discuss, I'm particularly mindful of the danger with regard to places outside the West of treating them as if they were suspended in time. For that reason, I want to include this reminder that the dynamics, terminologies, and policies discussed here may have changed in the time since any given work of scholarship was published, so the statements about given countries and regions should not be taken as necessarily indicating the current state of things there (also remembering that social dynamics and formations in a given place, at whatever scale, are always multiple).
12. Martin et al., "Introduction," 6.
13. Alexander, "Not Just," 6.
14. Alexander, "Not Just," 6, 7, 7–8. On its overturning, see Gosine, *Nature's Wild*. On economies of sexual labor (including sex tourism) within the Caribbean, see Kempadoo, *Sexing*.
15. Alexander, *Pedagogies*, 25, 26, 29. Alexander, though, also critiques Euro-American gay investments in tourism that promote "the conflation of the erotic and the exotic" and the "imperial production of sexual utopias" in ways that thwart, or at least significantly defer, the possibilities for something like global *gay* solidarity (*Pedagogies*, 69, 70).
16. Gosine, *Nature's Wild*, 6. On the British imposition of anti-sodomy and similar laws across the colonies, see Rao, *Out of Time*.

17. Gosine, *Nature's Wild*, 25.
18. Alexander, "Not Just," 21, 11.
19. Kempadoo, *Sexing*, 29, 34
20. Gosine, *Nature's Wild*, 7, 71.
21. Gosine, *Nature's Wild*, 75, 81. For discussion of a similar dynamic within African nations, see Currier and Migraine-George, "Queer Studies."
22. Hoad, *African Intimacies*, xxiii.
23. Hoad, *African Intimacies*, 56, 57.
24. Hoad, *African Intimacies*, 61, 67. The enshrinement of gay and lesbian rights in the South African constitution also positions the condemnation of queerness as part of processes for negotiating regional tensions, given the dominance of South Africa in terms of overall wealth and its tendency to be seen as more modern internationally. See Currier, *Out in Africa*; Munro, *South Africa*.
25. Massad, *Desiring Arabs*, 122, 112.
26. Massad, *Desiring Arabs*, 162–163.
27. Atshan, *Queer Palestine*, 3. On the history of the term, see Ritchie, "Pinkwashing"; Schulman, *Israel/Palestine*; Stelder, "Other Scenes."
28. Atshan, *Queer Palestine*, 111. On the importance of connecting critique of pinkwashing to critique of settler colonialism, in Israel and elsewhere, see Morgensen, "Queer Settler Colonialism."
29. Massad, *Desiring Arabs*, 39, 179, 185.
30. Ho, "Is Global Governance," 458, 463.
31. Hochberg, "Introduction," 507, 509.
32. In a similar vein, Nayroutz Abu Hatoum theorizes "the burden of queer Palestinians" (Stelder, "Other Scenes," 52).
33. Atshan, *Queer Palestine*, 10, 11, 189.
34. Atshan, *Queer Palestine*, 141. For discussion of the limits of pinkwashing as a frame for grasping the everyday confrontations of Palestinians with Israeli policies and popular images, see Ritchie, "Pinkwashing."
35. Dutta and Roy, "Decolonizing," 321, 323.
36. Dutta and Roy, "Decolonizing," 323.
37. Chatterjee, "Transgender," 312; Dutta and Roy, "Decolonizing," 329.
38. Jarrín, "Untranslatable," 358.
39. Jarrín, "Untranslatable," 366.
40. Addressing the role of sexologists in forms of official trans recognition in Mexico, Alba Pons Rabasa shows how the Mexican legalization of transgender health protocols coming out of the United States depathologizes gender nonnormativity but in ways that limit access to medical care due to "the individual financial cost of paying authorized sexology experts" to testify to a person's need for treatment ("From Representation," 396).
41. Benedicto, *Under Bright Lights*, 13, 14.
42. Martin et al., "Introduction," 7.
43. Benedicto, *Under Bright Lights*, 6, 3.

Notes to pages 181–189 241

44. Yue, "Trans-Singapore," 17–18, 21.
45. Wilson, *Intimate Economies*, 11, 103.
46. Wilson, *Intimate Economies*, 102–132.
47. Wilson, *Intimate Economies*, 132.
48. Wekker, *Politics*, 13, 193–194. On relations between sexuality and spirituality within Caribbean and Afrodiasporic networks, see also Alexander, *Pedagogies*; Gill, *Erotic Islands*; Tinsley, *Ezili's Mirrors*.
49. Wekker, *Politics*, 72, 77. For discussion of similar dynamics at play in *supi* relations among working-class women in Ghana, see Dankwa, *Knowing Women*.
50. Moussawi, *Disruptive Situations*, 5, 79, 106–107.
51. Moussawi, *Disruptive Situations*, 33, 59, 161.
52. Carrillo, *The Night Is Young*, 14, 16.
53. Carrillo, *The Night Is Young*, 35.
54. Carrillo, *The Night Is Young*, 80, 84.
55. Carrillo, *The Night Is Young*, 304.
56. Carrillo, *The Night Is Young*, 124–127.
57. Garrido, *Tortilleras*, 18, 37. On the national political scene and LGBT organizing in Mexico in this period, see de la Dehesa, *Queering*.
58. Garrido, *Tortilleras*, 12.
59. Garrido, *Tortilleras*, 50.
60. Sang, *Emerging Lesbian*, 9, 100.
61. Sang, *Emerging Lesbian*, 23, 102–103.
62. Sang, *Emerging Lesbian*, 123.
63. Boellstorff, "Perfect," 489.
64. Boellstorff, "Perfect," 484, 487.
65. Henry, "Queer Korea," 4, 5.
66. Henry, "Queer Korea," 3.
67. Mbasalaki, "Women," 38, 40, 45.
68. Tamale, "Researching," 20.
69. Ochoa, *Queen*, 3, 10, 210.
70. Ochoa, *Queen*, 158.
71. Ochoa, *Queen*, 177.
72. Reddy, *With Respect*, 2.
73. Reddy, *With Respect*, 32, 45–50, 102, 223.
74. See Reddy, *With Respect*; Saria, *Hijras*.
75. Saria, *Hijras*, 21, 61, 80–99.
76. Reddy, *With Respect*, 150; Saria, 16.
77. Saria, *Hijras*, 66; Reddy, *With Respect*, 100.
78. Saria, *Hijras*, 3. On colonial categorization and efforts to eliminate hijras, see Hinchy, *Governing Gender*.
79. Saria, *Hijras*, 4.
80. Kasmani, "Futuring Trans*," 97, 107.
81. Sinnott, *Toms and Dees*, 2.

82. Blackwood, *Falling*, 4, 126–127; Sinnott, *Toms and Dees*, 3, 45, 78.
83. Blackwood, *Falling*, 133.
84. Blackwood, *Falling*, 166; Sinnott, *Toms and Dees*, 30, 86, 111.
85. Boellstorff, *A Coincidence*, 78–113, 181–218.
86. On the history of such gender pluralism and its erosion in the seventeenth through nineteenth centuries, see Peletz, *Gender Pluralism*.
87. Sinnott, *Toms and Dees*, 38, 61.
88. Blackwood, *Falling*, 40.
89. Blackwood, *Falling*, 179–200; Sinnott, *Toms and Dees*, 151–166.
90. See Boellstorff, *A Coincidence*.
91. Liu, *Queer Marxism*, 14, 168. Liu sometimes speaks as if there were no significant work on Marxism already within queer and trans studies. For examples of Marxist analysis, see Ferguson, *Aberrations in Black*; Floyd, *Reification*; Gleeson and O'Rourke, *Transgender Marxism*; Hennessy, *Profit and Pleasure*.
92. Liu, *Queer Marxism*, 41, 43–44, 62, 143.
93. Howe, *Intimate Activism*, 57. Howe notes that, while the revived Sandinista government repealed the law enacted in 1992 that not only had criminalized consensual homoeroticism but even supposedly promoting it, the government then immediately outlawed abortion.
94. Howe, *Intimate Activism*, 24, 103. As Howe observes, though, this framing remains at odds with other modes of queer organizing that are more focused on combating national *homofobia* and specifically advocating for gay and lesbian rights. For a similar discursive strategy in Mexico, although for different political reasons, see de la Dehesa, *Queering*.
95. Roy, *Changing the Subject*, 37, 42–43.
96. Roy, *Changing the Subject*, 75.
97. Currier, *Out in Africa*, 20, 84.
98. De Mauro Rucovsky, "Travesti," 223, 230, 233, 235.
99. Rao, *Out of Time*, 175, 188, 216.
100. Diaz, "Biyuti," 408, 410.
101. Rao, *Out of Time*, 33, 45, 47. Similarly, Niko Besnier and Kalissa Alexeyeff observe with respect to the prominence of gender-nonconforming people in the Pacific Islands and the simultaneous hostility to them in many places, "How can rejection and acceptance rub shoulders in such a spectacularly contradictory fashion/These seemingly incommensurable positions cannot simply be explained away as the result of Christian dogmatism interloping upon a 'traditional' laissez-faire, since in many parts of the Pacific Christianity is so intricately intertwined with the socio-cultural order that it is *defined* as tradition" ("Gender on the Edge," 4).
102. Rao, *Out of Time*, 162.
103. Savci, *Queer*, 3, 10.
104. Savci, *Queer*, 107.
105. Hegarty, "Under the Lights," 357, 365.

106. Najmabadi, *Professing Selves*, 18–20.
107. Najmabadi, *Professing Selves*, 53, 70, 136–138.
108. Najmabadi, *Professing Selves*, 203–230.
109. Najmabadi, *Professing Selves*, 175, 244.
110. Rofel, *Desiring China*, 13, 148, 149–150.
111. Rofel, *Desiring China*, 3.
112. Amar, *Security*, 55, 56.
113. Amar, *Security*, 7, 15.
114. Amar, *Security*, 66, 74. On LGBT organizing in Brazil in this period, see de la Dehesa, *Queering*.
115. Amar, *Security*, 35.
116. Puri, *Sexual States*, 5, 13.
117. Puri, *Sexual States*, 52.
118. Puri, *Sexual States*, 150.
119. Fiol-Matta, *Queer Mother*, 214.
120. Fiol-Matta, *Queer Mother*, 6, 29, 66.
121. Wong, "Queer Vernacularism," 51.
122. Wong, "Queer Vernacularism," 53, 64.
123. Wong, "Queer Vernacularism," 59. Wong also argues that such minor-to-minor networks can circulate critiques of normalizing social forms, transmitting images that work in the interest of solidarity with and among gender-nonconforming people pushed to the economic margins – as in the film *Bugis Street* about the elimination of trans space in that area in Singapore (discussed in the first section) ("Queer Vernacularism," 61–64).
124. Martin, *Backward Glances*, 6, 15.
125. Martin, *Backward Glances*, 64.
126. Martin, *Backward Glances*, 132. As discussed in the previous section, *tomboy* has come to be used across East and Southeast Asia as a way of addressing persons designated female at birth who express a wide range of masculine gender identities, and this terminology seems likely to have originated in Taiwan through contact with US GIs during the 1960s (Martin, *Backward Glances*, 94–95).
127. Green-Simms, *Queer African Cinemas*, 38, 83.
128. On the popular and media association of queerness with money and corruption across West Africa, see Thomann and Currier, "Sex and Money."
129. Green-Simms, *Queer African Cinemas*, 4–5, 38, 53–55, 92.
130. Gopinath, *Unruly Visions*, 6, 10, 20.
131. Gopinath, *Unruly Visions*, 140, 174.
132. Bernard Shomali, *Between Banat*, 7–8, 12.
133. Bernard Shomali, *Between Banat*, 62, 88, 132.
134. Bernard Shomali, *Between Banat*, 140, 141, 145, 174.
135. Chiang, *Transtopia*, 10. On the ways nonwestern concepts from elsewhere are interpellated into Sinophone frameworks, see Tan, "Beijing."

136. Chiang, *Transtopia*, 98–130, 173–205. On the complex dynamics surrounding the concept of tongzhi, see also Martin, *Backward Glances*; Martin et al., "Introduction." Chiang specifically critiques Peter Liu's analysis, discussed earlier (*Transtopia*, 71–74.)
137. Hayes, *Queer Nations*, 8, 17, 136, 264.
138. Fiereck et al., "Queering-to-Come," 364.
139. See Mamdani, *Citizen and Subject*; Tamale, *Decolonization*, 83–117.
140. Fiereck et al., "Queering-to-Come," 366. See also Ayebazibwe, "Traditional African Systems."
141. Fiereck et al., "Queering-to-Come," 365. For a statement that emerges out of regional organizing in southern Africa, see "African LGBTI Declaration."
142. See Hamzić, "Temporal Nonconformity"; Hossain, "De-Indianizing Hijra."
143. Rizki, "Latin/x," 148, 149.
144. See Santana, "Mais Viva"; Valencia, "Necropolitics"; Wayar, "Latin American *Travesti*."
145. Sedgwick, *Touching Feeling*, 128, 147.

Bibliography

Abdur-Rahman, Aliyyah I. *Against the Closet: Black Political Longing and the Erotics of Race*. Durham: Duke University Press, 2012.

The ACT UP/NY Women and AIDS Book Group (eds.). *Women, AIDS & Activism*. Boston: South End Press, 1990.

Adeyemi, Kemi. *Feels Right: Black Queer Women and the Politics of Partying in Chicago*. Durham: Duke University Press, 2022.

Afal, Ahmed. "Beyond Hooking Up: Tales from Grindr in Pakistan," in *Pakistan Desires: Queer Futures Elsewhere*. Ed. Omar Kasmani. Durham: Duke University Press, 2023. 184–202.

"African LGBTI Declaration," in *African Sexualities: A Reader*. Ed. Sylvia Tamale. Dakar: Pambazuka Press, 2011. 182.

Aguilar-San Juan, Karin. "Going Home: Enacting Justice in Queer Asian American," in *Q & A: Queer in Asian America*. Ed. David L. Eng and Alice Y Hom. Philadelphia: Temple University Press. 1998. 25–40.

Ahmed, Sara. "An Affinity of Hammers." *TSQ* 3.1–2 (2016): 22–34.

The Cultural Politics of Emotion. New York: Routledge, 2004.

Living a Feminist Life. Durham: Duke University Press, 2017.

Queer Phenomenology: Orientations, Objects, Others. Durham: Duke University Press, 2006.

Ahuja, Neel. "Intimate Atmospheres: Queer Theory in a Time of Extinction." *GLQ* 21.2–3 (2015): 365–385.

Aizura, Aren. *Mobile Subjects: Transnational Imaginaries of Gender Reassignment*. Durham: Duke University Press, 2018.

Alarcón, Norma. "Chicana's Feminist Literature: A Re-vision through Malintzin/ or Malintzin Putting Flesh Back on the Object," in *This Bridge Called My Back: Writings by Radical Women of Color* (1981). Ed. Cherríe L. Moraga and Gloria E. Anzaldúa. Berkeley, CA: Third Woman Press, 2002. 202–211.

"The Theoretical Subject(s) of *This Bridge Called My Back* and Anglo-American Feminism," in *Making Face, Making Soul / Haciendo Caras: Creative and Critical Perspectives by Women of Color*. Ed. Gloria Anzaldúa. San Francisco: Aunt Lute Books, 1990. 356–369.

Alexander, M. Jacqui. "Not Just (Any) *Body* Can Be a Citizen: The Politics of Law, Sexuality, and Postcoloniality in Trinidad and Tobago and the Bahamas." *Feminist Review* 48.1 (1994): 5–23.

Pedagogies of Crossing: Meditations on Feminism, Sexual Politics, Memory, and the Sacred. Durham: Duke University Press, 2005.

Allen, Jafari S. "Black/Queer/Diaspora at the Current Conjuncture." *GLQ* 18.2–3 (2012): 211–248.

——— *There's a Disco Ball between Us: A Theory of Black Gay Life*. Durham: Duke University Press, 2022.

Allen, Paula Gunn. *The Sacred Hoop: Recovering the Feminine in American Indian Traditions*. Boston: Beacon Press, 1992.

Alvarez, Eddy Francisco, Jr. "Finding Sequins in the Rubble: Stitching Together an Archive of Trans Latina Los Angeles." *TSQ* 3.3–4 (2016): 618–627.

Alvarez, Eddy Francisco, Jr., Magda García, and Ellie D. Hernández. "Introduction: Trans Vida in Extraordinary Times," in *Transmovimientos: Latinx Queer Migrations, Bodies, and Spaces*. Ed. Ellie D. Hernández, Eddy Franciso Alvarez Jr., and Magda García. Lincoln: University of Nebraska Press, 2021. xv–xxiv.

Amar, Paul. *The Security Archipelago: Human-Security States, Sexuality Politics, and the End of Neoliberalism*. Durham: Duke University Press, 2013.

Amer, Sahar. "Cross-Dressing and Female Same-Sex Marriage in Medieval French and Arabic Literatures," in *Islamicate Sexualities: Translations across Temporal Geographies of Desire*. Ed. Kathryn Babayan and Afsaneh Najmabadi. Cambridge: Harvard University Press, 2008. 72–113.

Amin, Kadji. *Disturbing Attachments: Genet, Modern Pederasty, and Queer History*. Durham: Duke University Press, 2017.

——— "Gland, Eugenics, and Rejuvenation in *Man into Woman*: A Biopolitical Genealogy of Transsexuality." *TSQ* 5.4 (2018): 589–605.

Anzaldúa, Gloria. *Borderlands, La Frontera: The New Mestiza* (1987). San Francisco: Aunt Lute Books, 1999.

——— "To(o) Queer the Writer – Loca, Escritora y Chicana," in *The Gloria Anzaldúa Reader*. Ed. AnaLouise Keating. Durham: Duke University Press, 2009. 163–175.

——— "(Un)natural Bridges, (Un)safe Spaces," in *The Gloria Anzaldúa Reader*. Ed. AnaLouise Keating. Durham: Duke University Press, 2009. 243–248.

Arondeker, Anjali. *For the Record: On Sexuality and the Colonial Archive in India*. Durham: Duke University Press, 2009.

Arondeker, Anjali, and Geeta Patel. "Area Impossible: Notes toward an Introduction." *GLQ* 22.2 (2016): 151–171.

Arrizón, Alicia. *Queering Mestizaje: Transculturation and Performance*. Ann Arbor: University of Michigan Press, 2006.

Arvas, Abdulhamit. "Performing and Desiring Gender Variance in the Early Modern Ottoman Empire," in *Trans Historical: Gender Plurality before the Modern*. Ed. Greta LaFleur, Masha Raskolnikov, and Anna Klosowska. Ithaca, NY: Cornell University Press, 2021. 160–177.

Asetoyer, Charon. "First There Was Smallpox," in *Women, AIDS & Activism*. Ed. The ACT UP/NY Women & AIDS Book Group. Boston: South End Press, 1990. 91–94.

Atshan, Sa'ed. *Queer Palestine and the Empire of Critique*. Stanford, Stanford University Press, 2020.
Avilez, GerShun. *Black Queer Freedom: Spaces of Injury and Paths of Desire*. Urbana: University of Illinois Press, 2020.
Awkward-Rich, Cameron. *The Terrible We: Thinking with Trans Maladjustment*. Durham: Duke University Press, 2022.
Ayebazibwe, Jennifer Shinto. "Traditional African Systems of Land Ownership and Their Impact on Lesbian Women," in *Routledge Handbook of Queer African Studies*. Ed. S. N. Nyeck. New York: Routledge, 2019. 15–24.
Bailey, Marlon M. *Butch Queens Up in Pumps: Gender, Performance, and Ballroom Culture in Detroit*. Ann Arbor: University of Michigan Press, 2013.
Bailey, Marlon M., Darius Bost, Jennifer Brier, Angelique Harris, Johnnie Ray Kornegay III, Linda Villarosa, Dagmawi Woubshet, Marissa Miller, and Dana D. Hines. "Souls Forum: The Black AIDS Epidemic." *Souls* 21.2-3 (2019): 215–226.
Baril, Alexandre. "Transness as Debility: Rethinking Intersections between Trans and Disabled Embodiments." *Feminist Review* 111 (2015): 59–74.
Barker, Joanne. "Introduction: Critically Sovereign," in *Critically Sovereign: Indigenous Gender, Sexuality, and Feminist Studies*. Ed. Joanne Barker. Durham: Duke University Press, 2017. 1–44.
Native Acts: Law, Recognition, and Cultural Authenticity. Durham: Duke University Press, 2011.
Bauer, Robin. "Transgressive and Transformative Gendered Sexual Practices and White Privileges: The Case of the Dyke/Trans BDSM Communities." *WSQ* 36.3-4 (2008): 233–253.
Beam, Joseph. "Brother to Brother: Words from the Heart," in *In the Life: A Black Gay Anthology* (1986). Ed. Joseph Beam. Washington, DC: Redbone Press, 2008. 180–191.
"Introduction: Leaving the Shadows Behind," in *In the Life: A Black Gay Anthology* (1986). Ed. Joseph Beam. Washington, DC: Redbone Press, 2008. xix–xxiv.
Beauchamp, Tony. *Going Stealth: Transgender Politics and U.S. Surveillance Practices*. Durham: Duke University Press, 2019.
Belcourt, Billy-Ray. "Can the Other of Native Studies Speak?" decolonization.wordpress.com, February 1, 2016.
"Indigenous Studies beside Itself." *Somatechnics* 7.2 (2017): 182–184.
Bell, Cei. "The Radicalqueens Trans-formation," in *Smash the Church, Smash the State!: The Early Years of Gay Liberation*. Ed. Tommi Avicolli Mecca. San Francisco: City Lights Books, 2009. 116–134.
Beltrán, Cristina. *Cruelty as Citizenship: How Migrant Suffering Sustains White Democracy*. Minneapolis: University of Minnesota Press, 2020.
Benedicto, Bobby. *Under Bright Lights: Gay Manila and the Global Scene*. Minneapolis: University of Minnesota Press, 2014.

Berger, Michele Tracy. *Workable Sisterhood: The Political Journey of Stigmatized Women with HIV/AIDS.* Princeton, NJ: Princeton University Press, 2004.

Berkowitz, Richard, and Michael Callen. *How to Have Sex in an Epidemic* (1983), in *We Are Everywhere: A Historical Sourcebook of Gay and Lesbian Politics.* Ed. Mark Blasius and Shane Phelan. New York: Routledge, 1997. 571–574.

(with Richard Dworkin). "We Know Who We Are: Two Gay Men Declare War on Promiscuity" (1982), in *We Are Everywhere: A Historical Sourcebook of Gay and Lesbian Politics.* Ed. Mark Blasius and Shane Phelan. New York: Routledge, 1997. 563–571.

Berlant, Lauren, and Elizabeth Freeman. "Queer Nationality," in *Fear of a Queer Planet.* Ed. Michael Warner. Minneapolis: University of Minnesota Press, 1993. 193–229.

Berlant, Lauren, and Michael Warner. "Sex in Public." *Critical Inquiry* 24.2 (1998): 548–566.

Bernard Shomali, Mejdulene. *Between Banat: Queer Arab Critique and Transnational Arab Archives.* Durham: Duke University Press, 2023.

Bersani, Leo. "Is the Rectum a Grave?," in *AIDS: Cultural Analysis, Cultural Activism.* Ed. Douglas Crimp. Cambridge: MIT Press, 1988. 197–222.

Besnier, Niko, and Kalissa Alexeyeff. "Gender on the Edge: Identities, Politics, Transformations," in *Gender on the Edge: Transgender, Gay, and Other Pacific Islanders.* Ed. Niko Besnier and Kalissa Alexeyeff. Honolulu: University of Hawai'i Press, 2014. 1–32.

Best, Stephen. *None Like Us: Blackness, Belonging, Aesthetic Life.* Durham: Duke University Press, 2018.

Bettcher, Talia Mae. "Trapped in the Wrong Theory: Rethinking Trans Oppression and Resistance." *Signs* 39.2 (2014): 383–406.

Bey, Marquis. *Black Trans Feminism.* Durham: Duke University Press, 2022.

Bhanji, Nael. "Trans/scriptions: Homing Desires, (Trans)sexual Citizenship, and Racialized Bodies," in *The Transgender Studies Reader 2.* Ed. Susan Stryker and Aren Z. Aizura. New York: Routledge, 2013. 512–526.

binaohan, B. *Decolonizing Trans/gender 101.* Toronto: biyuti publishing, 2014.

Blackwell, Maylei. *¡Chicana Power!: Contested Histories of Feminism in the Chicano Movement.* Austin: University of Texas Press, 2011.

Blackwell, Maylei, Floridalma Boj Lopez, and Luis Urrieta, Jr. "Introduction: Critical Latinx Indigeneities." *Latino Studies* 15.2 (2017): 126–137.

Blackwood, Evelyn. *Falling into the Lesbi World: Desire and Difference in Indonesia.* Honolulu: University of Hawai'i Press, 2010.

Blasius, Mark, and Shane Phelan (eds.). *We Are Everywhere: A Historical Sourcebook of Gay and Lesbian Politics.* New York: Routledge, 1997.

Boag, Peter. *Re-Dressing America's Frontier Past.* Berkeley: University of California Press, 2011.

Boellstorff, Tom. *A Coincidence of Desires: Anthropology, Queer Studies, Indonesia.* Durham: Duke University Press, 2007.

"The Perfect Path: Gay Men, Marriage, Indonesia." *GLQ* 5.4 (1999): 473–510.

Boone, Joseph Allen. *The Homoerotics of Orientalism*. New York: Columbia University Press, 2014.
Bornstein, Kate. *Gender Outlaw: On Men, Women, and the Rest of Us*. New York: Vintage Books, 1995.
Bost, Darius. *Evidence of Being: The Black Gay Cultural Renaissance and the Politics of Violence*. Chicago: University of Chicago Press, 2019.
Brady, Mary Pat. *Extinct Lands, Temporal Geographies: Chicana Literature and the Urgency of Space*. Durham: Duke University Press, 2002.
Brant, Beth. *Writing as Witness: Essay and Talk*. Toronto: Women's Press, 1994.
Breines, Winifred. *The Trouble between Us: An Uneasy History of White and Black Women in the Feminist Movement*. New York: Oxford University Press, 2006.
Brier, Jennifer. *Infectious Ideas: U.S. Political Responses to the AIDS Crisis*. Chapel Hill: University of North Carolina Press, 2009.
Bristow, Joseph. "Symonds's History, Ellis's Heredity: *Sexual Inversion*," in *Sexology in Culture: Labelling Bodies and Desires*. Ed. Lucy Bland and Laura Doan. Chicago: University of Chicago Press, 1998. 79–99.
Bronstein, Carolyn. "Pornography, Trans Visibility, and the Demise of Tumblr." *TSQ* 7.2 (2020): 240–254.
Brown, Rita Mae. "Hanoi to Hoboken: A Round Trip Ticket" (1971), in *Out of the Closets: Voices of Gay Liberation, Twentieth-Anniversary Edition*. Ed. Karla Jay and Allen Young. New York: New York University Press, 1992. 195–201.
Brownworth, Victoria A. "Living Lesbian Nation," in *Smash the Church, Smash the State!: The Early Years of Gay Liberation*. Ed. Tommi Avicolli Mecca. San Francisco: City Lights Books, 2009. 99–107.
Bruce, La Marr Jurelle. "The Body Beautiful: Black Drag, American Cinema, and the Heteroperpetually Ever After," in *No Tea, No Shade: New Writings in Black Queer Studies*. Ed. E. Patrick Johnson. Durham: Duke University Press, 2016. 166–195.
Bunch, Charlotte. "Lesbians in Revolt" (1972), in *We Are Everywhere: A Historical Sourcebook of Gay and Lesbian Politics*. Ed. Mark Blasius and Shane Phelan. New York: Routledge, 1997. 420–423.
Butler, Judith. *Bodies That Matter: On the Discursive Limits of "Sex."* New York: Routledge, 1993.
Gender Trouble: Feminism and the Subversion of Identity (1990). New York: Routledge, 2006.
Undoing Gender. New York: Routledge, 2004.
Bychowski, M. W. "The Transgender Turn: Eleanor Rykener Speaks Back," in *Trans Historical: Gender Plurality before the Modern*. Ed. Greta LaFleur, Masha Raskolnikov, and Anna Klosowska. Ithaca, NY: Cornell University Press, 2021. 95–113.
Bychowski, M. W., Howard Chiang, Jack Halberstam, Jacob Lau, Kathleen P. Long, Marcia Ochoa, and C. Riley Snorton. "Trans*historicities: A Roundtable." *TSQ* 5.4 (2018): 658–685.

Bychowski, M. W., and Dorothy Kim. "Visions of Medieval Trans Feminism: An Introduction." *Medieval Feminist Forum* 55.1 (2019): 6–41.

Byrd, Jodi. "What's Normative Got to Do with It?: Toward Indigenous Queer Relationality." *Social Text* 38.4 (2020): 105–123.

Califia, Patrick. "Feminism and Sadomasochism" (1981), in *We Are Everywhere: A Historical Sourcebook of Gay and Lesbian Politics*. Ed. Mark Blasius and Shane Phelan. New York: Routledge, 1997. 522–528.

———. *Sex Changes: The Politics of Transgenderism*. San Francisco: Cleis Press, 1997.

Cantú, Lionel, Jr. *The Sexuality of Migration: Border Crossings and Mexican Immigrant Men*. Ed. Nancy A. Naples and Salvador Vidal-Ortiz. New York: New York University Press, 2009.

Carastathis, Anna. *Intersectionality: Origins, Contestations, Horizons*. Lincoln: University of Nebraska Press, 2016.

cárdenas, micha. *Poetic Operations: Trans of Color Art in Digital Media*. Durham: Duke University Press, 2022.

Carrillo, Héctor. *The Night Is Young: Sexuality in Mexico in the Time of AIDS*. Chicago: University of Chicago Press, 2002.

Carroll, Alicia. "Remembering Polingaysi: A Queer Recovering of *No Turning Back* as a Decolonial Text." *Studies in American Indian Literatures* 26.1 (2014): 54–80.

Carter, Julian. "Embracing Transition, or Dancing in the Folds of Time," in *The Transgender Studies Reader 2*. Ed. Susan Stryker and Aren Z. Aizura. New York: Routledge, 2013. 130–143.

Carter, Julian B. *The Heart of Whiteness: Normal Sexuality and Race in America, 1880–1940*. Durham: Duke University Press, 2007.

Cartwright, Ryan Lee. *Peculiar Places: A Queer Crip History of White Rural Nonconformity*. Chicago: University of Chicago Press, 2021.

Castle, Terry. *The Apparitional Lesbian: Female Homosexuality and Modern Culture*. New York: Columbia University Press, 1993.

Chatterjee, Shradda. "Transgender Shifts: Notes on Resignification of Gender and Sexuality in India." *TSQ* 5.3 (2018): 311–320.

Chauncey, George. *Gay New York: Gender, Urban Culture, and the Making of the Gay Male World, 1890–1940*. New York: Basic Books, 1994.

Chávez, Karma R. *The Borders of AIDS: Race, Quarantine, and Resistance*. Seattle: University of Washington Press, 2021.

———. *Queer Migration Politics: Activist Rhetoric and Coalitional Possibilities*. Urbana: University of Illinois Press, 2013.

Chen, Jian Neo. *Trans Exploits: Trans of Color Cultures and Technologies in Movement*. Durham: Duke University Press, 2019.

Chen, Mel Y. *Animacies: Biopolitics, Racial Mattering, and Queer Affect*. Durham: Duke University Press, 2012.

Cheng, Jih-Fei, Alexandra Juhasz, and Nishant Shahani (eds.). *AIDS and the Distribution of Crises*. Durham: Duke University Press, 2020.

Chess, Simone, Colby Gordon, and Will Fisher. "Introduction: Early Modern Trans Studies." *Journal for Early Modern Cultural Studies* 19.4 (2019): 1–25.

Chiang, Howard. *Transtopia in the Sinophone Pacific*. New York: Columbia University Press, 2021.
Chiang, Howard, Todd A. Henry, and Helen Hok-Sze Leung. "Trans-in-Asia, Asia-in-Trans: An Introduction." *TSQ* 5.3 (2018): 298–310.
Chicago Gay Liberation. "Working Paper for the Revolutionary People's Constitutional Convention" (1970), in *Out of the Closets: Voices of Gay Liberation, Twentieth-Anniversary Edition*. Ed. Karla Jay and Allen Young. New York: New York University Press, 1992. 346–352.
Clare, Eli. *Brilliant Imperfection: Grappling with Cure*. Durham: Duke University Press, 2017.
Exile and Pride: Disability, Queerness, and Liberation, new ed. Durham: Duke University Press, 2015.
Clarke, Cheryl. "The Failure to Transform: Homophobia in the Black Community," in *Home Girls: A Black Feminist Anthology* (1983). Ed. Barbara Smith. New Brunswick, NJ: Rutgers University Press, 2000. 190–201.
"Lesbianism: An Act of Resistance," in *This Bridge Called My Back: Writings by Radical Women of Color* (1981). Ed. Cherríe L. Moraga and Gloria E. Anzaldúa. Berkeley, CA: Third Woman Press, 2002. 141–151.
Cleves, Rachel Hope. "Beyond the Binaries in Early America: Special Issue Introduction." *Early American Studies* 12.3 (2014): 459–468.
Cohen, Cathy J. *The Boundaries of Blackness: AIDS and the Breakdown of Black Politics*. Chicago: University of Chicago Press, 1999.
"Deviance as Resistance: A New Research Agenda for the Study of Black Politics." *Du Bois Review* 1.1 (2004): 27–45.
"Punks, Bulldaggers, and Welfare Queens: The Radical Potential of Queer Politics?" *GLQ* 3.4 (1997): 437–465.
Cohen, Ed. *Talk on the Wilde Side: Toward a Genealogy of a Discourse on Male Sexualities*. Routledge: New York, 1993.
Cole, C. L., and L. C. Cate. "Compulsory Gender and Transgender Existence: Adrienne Rich's Queer Possibility." *WSQ* 36.3–4 (2008): 279–287.
Colebrook, Clare. "What Is It Like to Be a Human?" *TSQ* 2.2 (2015): 227–243.
Combahee River Collective. "The Combahee River Collective Statement" (1977), in *How We Get Free: Black Feminism and the Combahee River Collective*. Ed. Keeanga-Yamahtta Taylor. Chicago: Haymarket Books, 2017. 15–27.
Corbman, Rachel. "Tool Optimism: A History of the 1979 *Second Sex* Conference and the Afterlives of Audre Lorde," in *The Routledge Companion to Intersectionalities*. Ed. Jennifer Nash and Samantha Pinto. Routledge: New York, 2023. 57–67.
Cornum, Lou. "The Space NDN's Star Map." http://thenewinquiry.com/the-space-ndns-star-map. Accessed June 29, 2017.
Cornwell, Anita. "From a Soul Sister's Notebook" (1972), in *We Are Everywhere: A Historical Sourcebook of Gay and Lesbian Politics*. Ed. Mark Blasius and Shane Phelan. New York: Routledge, 1997. 364–366.

Coulthard, Glen Sean. *Red Skin, White Masks: Rejecting the Colonial Politics of Recognition*. Minneapolis: University of Minnesota Press, 2014.
Coviello, Peter. *Make Yourselves Gods: Mormons and the Unfinished Business of American Secularism*. Chicago: University of Chicago Press, 2019.
Tomorrow's Parties: Sex and the Untimely in Nineteenth-Century America. New York: New York University Press, 2013.
Crenshaw, Kimberlé. "Demarginalizing the Intersection of Race and Sex: A Black Feminist Critique of Antidiscrimination Doctrine, Feminist Theory and Antiracist Politics." *Chicago Law Forum* 1 (1989): 139–167.
"Mapping the Margins: Intersectionality, Identity Politics, and Violence against Women of Color." *Stanford Law Review* 43.6 (1991): 1241–1299.
Crimp, Douglas. *Melancholia and Moralism: Essays on AIDS and Queer Politics*. Cambridge: MIT Press, 2002.
Crimp, Douglas, and Adam Rolston. *AIDS DemoGraphics*. Seattle: Bay Press, 1990.
Cruz, Ariane. *The Color of Kink: Black Women, BDSM, and Pornography*. New York: New York University Press, 2016.
Cruz-Malavé, Arnaldo, and Martin F. Manalansan IV. "Introduction: Dissident Sexualities/ Alternative Globalisms," in *Queer Globalizations: Citizenship and the Afterlife of Colonialism*. Ed. Arnaldo Cruz-Malavé and Martin F. Manalansan IV. New York: New York University Press, 2002. 1–12.
Currah, Paisley. *Sex Is As Sex Does: Governing Transgender Identity*. New York: New York University Press, 2022.
Currier, Ashley. *Out in Africa: LGBT Organizing in Namibia and South Africa*. Minneapolis: University of Minnesota Press, 2012.
Currier, Ashley, and Thérèse Migraine-George. "Queer Studies/African Studies: An (Im)possible Transaction?" *GLQ* 22.2 (2016): 281–305.
Cvetkovich, Ann. *An Archive of Feelings: Trauma, Sexuality, and Lesbian Public Cultures*. Durham: Duke University Press, 2003.
Depression: A Public Feeling. Durham: Duke University Press, 2012.
Dankwa, Serena Owusua. *Knowing Women: Same-Sex Intimacies, Gender, and Identity in Postcolonial Ghana*. New York: Cambridge University Press, 2021.
Das Gupta, Monisha. *Unruly Immigrants: Rights, Activism, and Transnational South Asian Politics in the United States*. Durham: Duke University Press, 2006.
Dean, Tim. *Unlimited Intimacy: Reflections on the Subculture of Barebacking*. Chicago: University of Chicago Press, 2009.
Decena, Carlos Ulises. *Tacit Subjects: Belonging and Same-Sex Desire among Dominican Immigrant Men*. Durham: Duke University Press, 2011.
Declue, Jennifer. "Let's Play: Exploring Cinematic Black Lesbian Fantasy, Pleasure, and Pain," in *No Tea, No Shade: New Writings in Black Queer*

Studies. Ed. E. Patrick Johnson. Durham: Duke University Press, 2016. 216–238.

de la Dehesa, Rafael. *Queering the Public Sphere in Mexico and Brazil: Sexual Rights Movements in Emerging Democracies.* Durham: Duke University Press, 2010.

Delany, Samuel R. *Times Square Red, Times Square Blue.* New York: New York University Press, 1999.

de Lauretis, Teresa. *The Practice of Love: Lesbian Sexuality and Perverse Desire.* Bloomington: Indiana University Press, 1994.

"Queer Theory: Lesbian and Gay Sexualities – An Introduction." *differences* 3.2 (1991): iii–xviii.

De Mauro Rucovsky, Martín. "The *Travesti* Critique of the Gender Identity Law in Argentina." Trans. Ian Russell. *TSQ* 6.2 (2019): 223–238.

D'Emilio, John. *Sexual Politics, Sexual Communities: The Making of a Homosexual Minority in the United States, 1940–1970.* 2nd ed. Chicago: University of Chicago Press, 1998.

Denetdale, Jennifer. "'Return to 'The Uprising at Beautiful Mountain in 1913': Marriage and Sexuality in the Making of the Modern Navajo Nation," in *Critically Sovereign: Indigenous Gender, Sexuality, and Feminist Studies,* Ed. Joanne Barker. Durham: Duke University Press, 2017. 69–98.

De Souza, Igor H. "Elenx de Céspedes: Indeterminate Genders in the Spanish Inquisition," in *Trans Historical: Gender Plurality before the Modern.* Ed. Greta LaFleur, Masha Raskolnikov, and Anna Klosowska. Ithaca, NY: Cornell University Press, 2021. 42–67.

DeVun, Leah. *The Shape of Sex: Nonbinary Gender from Genesis to the Renaissance.* New York: Columbia University Press, 2021.

DeVun, Leah and Zeb Tortorici. "Trans, Time, and History." *TSQ* 5.4 (2018): 518–539.

Diaz, Robert. "*Biyuti* from Below: Contemporary Philippine Cinema and the Transing of *Kabaklaan*." *TSQ* 5.3 (2018): 404–424.

DiGangi, Mario. *Sexual Types: Embodiment, Agency, and Dramatic Character from Shakespeare to Shirley.* Philadelphia: University of Pennsylvania Press, 2011.

Dillon, Stephen. *Fugitive Life: The Queer Politics of the Prison State.* Durham: Duke University Press, 2018.

Dinshaw, Carolyn. *Getting Medieval: Sexualities and Communities, Pre- and Postmodern.* Durham: Duke University Press, 1999.

How Soon Is Now?: Medieval Texts, Amateur Readers, and the Queerness of Time. Durham: Duke University Press, 2012.

"Dispatches on the Globalization of AIDS," in *AIDS and the Distribution of Crises.* Ed. Jih-Fei Cheng, Alexandra Juhasz, and Nishant Shahani. Durham: Duke University Press, 2020. 29–59.

Doan, Laura. *Fashioning Sapphism: The Origins of a Modern English Lesbian Culture.* New York: Columbia University Press, 2001.

Driskill, Qwo-Li, Chris Finley, Brian Joseph Gilley, and Scott Lauria Morgensen. "Introduction," in *Queer Indigenous Studies: Critical Interventions in Theory, Politics, and Literature*. Ed. Qwo-Li Driskill, et al. Tucson: University of Arizona Press, 2011. 1–30.

Duberman, Martin. *Stonewall: The Definitive Story of the LGBTQ Rights Uprising that Changed America* (1993). New York: Plume, 2019.

Duggan, Lisa. "Censorship in the Name of Feminism" (1984), in *Sex Wars: Sexual Dissent and Political Culture*, 10th Anniversary Edition. Ed. Lisa Duggan and Nan D. Hunter. New York: Routledge, 2006. 29–39.

"The New Homonormativity: The Sexual Politics of Neoliberalism," in *Materializing Democracy: Toward a Revitalized Cultural Politics*. Ed. Russ Castronovo and Dana D. Nelson. Durham: Duke University Press, 2002. 175–194.

Sapphic Slashers: Sex, Violence, and American Modernity. Durham: Duke University Press, 2000.

Duggan, Lisa, Nan D. Hunter, and Carole S. Vance. "False Promises: Feminist Antipornography Legislation" (1985), in *Sex Wars: Sexual Dissent and Political Culture*, 10th Anniversary Edition. Ed. Lisa Duggan and Nan D. Hunter. New York: Routledge, 2006. 43–64.

Dutta, Aniruddha, and Raina Roy. "Decolonizing Transgender in India: Some Reflections." *TSQ* 1.3 (2014): 320–337.

Edelman, Lee. *No Future: Queer Theory and the Death Drive*. Durham: Duke University Press, 2004.

El-Rouayheb, Khaled. *Before Homosexuality in the Arab-Islamic World, 1500–1800*. Chicago: University of Chicago Press, 2005.

Ellis, Nadia. *Territories of the Soul: Queered Belonging in the Black Diaspora*. Durham: Duke University Press, 2015.

Ellison, Treva. "Black Femme Praxis and the Promise of Black Gender." *The Black Scholar* 49.1 (2019): 6–16.

"The Labor of Werqing It: The Performance and Protest Strategies of Sir Lady Java," in *Trap Door: Trans Cultural Production and the Politics of Visibility*. Ed. Tourmaline, Eric A. Stanley, and Johanna Burton. Cambridge: MIT Press, 2017. 1–22.

Ellison, Treva, K. Marshall Green, Matt Richardson, and C. Riley Snorton. "We Got Issues: Toward a Black/Trans* Studies." *TSQ* 4.2 (2017): 162–169.

El-Tayeb, Fatima. *European Others: Queering Ethnicity in Postnational Europe*. Minneapolis: University of Minnesota Press, 2011.

Eng, Chris A. "'Give It Up, Kwang': Disavowing Asian Labor and Queer/Trans of Color Critique in *Hedwig and the Angry Inch*." *Theatre Journal* 70.2 (2018): 173–193.

Eng, David L. *The Feeling of Kinship: Queer Liberalism and the Racialization of Intimacy*. Durham: Duke University Press, 2010.

Racial Castration: Managing Masculinity in Asian America. Durham: Duke University Press, 2001.

Eng, David L., Jack Halberstam, and José Esteban Muñoz. "What's Queer about Queer Studies Now?" *Social Text* 23.3-4 (2005): 1-17.

Eng, David L., and Alice Y. Hom. "Introduction," in *Q & A: Queer in Asian America*. Ed. David L. Eng and Alice Y Hom. Philadelphia: Temple University Press. 1998. 1-21.

Eng, David L., and Jasbir K. Puar. "Introduction: Left of Queer." *Social Text* 145 (2020): 1-24.

Enke, Finn. "Collective Memory and the Transfeminist 1970s: Toward a Less Plausible History." *TSQ* 5.1 (2018): 9-29.

"The Education of Little Cis: Cisgender and the Discipline of Opposing Bodies," in *The Transgender Studies Reader 2*. Ed. Susan Stryker and Aren Z. Aizura. New York: Routledge, 2013. 234-247.

Enke, A. Finn. "Introduction: Transfeminist Perspectives," in *Transfeminist Perspectives in and beyond Transgender and Gender Studies*. Ed. A. Finn Enke. Philadelphia: Temple University Press, 2012. 1-15.

Epps, Brad. "Comparison, Competition, and Cross-Dressing: Cross-Cultural Analysis in a Contested World," in *Islamicate Sexualities: Translations across Temporal Geographies of Desire*. Ed. Kathryn Babayan and Afsaneh Najmabadi. Cambridge: Harvard University Press, 2008. 114-160.

Esquiel, Catrióna Rueda. *With Her Machete in Her Hand: Reading Chicana Lesbians*. Austin: University of Texas Press, 2006.

Farmer, Paul. *AIDS and Accusation: Haiti and the Geography of Blame*, Rev. ed. Berkeley: University of California Press, 2006.

Fawaz, Ramzi. *Queer Forms*. New York: New York University Press, 2022.

Faye, Shon. *The Transgender Issue: An Argument for Justice*. London: Penguin Books, 2021.

Feinberg, Leslie. *Stone Butch Blues* (1993). Los Angeles, CA: Alyson Books, 2003.

Transgender Warriors: Making History from Joan of Arc to Dennis Rodman. Boston: Beacon Press, 1996.

Trans Liberation: Beyond Pink or Blue. Boston: Beacon Press, 1998.

Ferguson, Roderick A. *Aberrations in Black: Toward a Queer of Color Critique*. Minneapolis: University of Minnesota Press, 2004.

One-Dimensional Queer. Medford, MA: Polity Press, 2019.

Fiereck, Kirk, Neville Hoad, and Danai S. Mupotsa. "A Queering-to-Come." *GLQ* 26.3 (2020): 363-376.

Fink, Marty. *Forget Burial: HIV Kinship, Disability, and Queer/Trans Narratives of Care*. New Brunswick, NJ: Rutgers University Press, 2022.

Fiol-Matta, Licia. *A Queer Mother for the Nation: The State and Gabriela Mistral*. Minneapolis: University of Minnesota Press, 2002.

Fisher, Will. "The Sexual Politics of Victorian Historiographical Writing about the 'Renaissance.'" *GLQ* 14.1 (2008): 41-67.

Floyd, Kevin. *The Reification of Desire: Toward a Queer Marxism*. Minneapolis: University of Minnesota Press, 2005.

Foucault, Michel. *The History of Sexuality*, vol. I (1976). Trans. Robert Hurley (1978). New York: Vintage Books, 1990.
Franke, Katherine. *Wedlocked: The Perils of Marriage Equality*. New York: New York University Press, 2015.
Freccero, Carla. *Queer/Early/Modern*. Durham: Duke University Press, 2006.
Freeman, Elizabeth. *Time Binds: Queer Temporalities, Queer Histories*. Durham: Duke University Press, 2010.
Fung, Richard. "Looking for My Penis: The Eroticized Asian in Gay Video Porn," in *Q & A: Queer in Asian America*. Ed. David L. Eng and Alice Y. Hom. Philadelphia: Temple University Press, 1998. 115–134.
Fuss, Diana. *Identification Papers: Readings on Psychoanalysis, Sexuality, and Culture*. New York: Routledge, 1995.
 "Inside/Out," in *Inside/Out: Lesbian Theories, Gay Theories*. Ed. Diana Fuss. New York: Routledge, 1991. 1–10.
Galarte. Francisco J. *Brown Trans Figurations: Rethinking Race, Gender, and Sexuality in Chicanx/Latinx Studies*. Austin: University of Texas Press, 2021.
Gamble, Joseph. "Towards a Trans Philology." *Journal for Early Modern Cultural Studies* 19.4 (2019): 26–44.
Gan, Jessi. "'Still at the Back of the Bus': Sylvia Rivera's Struggle," in *The Transgender Studies Reader 2*. Ed. Susan Stryker and Aren Z. Aizura. New York: Routledge, 2013. 291–301.
Garber, Linda. *Identity Poetics: Race, Class, and the Lesbian-Feminist Roots of Queer Theory*. New York: Columbia University Press, 2001.
Garrido, Anahi Russo. *Tortilleras Negotiating Intimacy: Love, Friendship, and Sex in Queer Mexico City*. New Brunswick, NJ: Rutgers University Press, 2020.
Garrido, Germán. "The World in Question: A Cosmopolitical Approach to Gay/Homosexual Liberation Movements in/and the 'Third World' (from Argentina to the United States)." *GLQ* 27.3 (2021): 379–406.
Gaspar de Alba, Alicia. *(Un)Framing the "Bad Woman": Sor Juana, Malinche, Coyolxauhqui, and Other Rebels with a Cause*. Austin: University of Texas Press, 2014.
"Gay Revolutionary Party Manifesto," in *Out of the Closets: Voices of Gay Liberation, Twentieth-Anniversary Edition*. Ed. Karla Jay and Allen Young. New York: New York University Press, 1992. 342–345.
Geary, Adam M. *Antiblack Racism and the AIDS Epidemic: State Intimacies*. New York: Palgrave Macmillan, 2014.
 "Paradigmatic." *TSQ* 7.4 (2020): 573–584.
Getachew, Adom. *Worldmaking after Empire: The Rise and Fall of Self-Determination*. Princeton, NJ: Princeton University Press, 2020.
Getsy, David J. "Capacity." *TSQ* 1.1 (2014): 47–49.
Ghosh, Bishnupriya. "The Costs of Living: Reflections on Global Health Crises," in *AIDS and the Distribution of Crises*. Ed. Jih-Fei Cheng, Alexandra Juhasz, and Nishant Shahani. Durham: Duke University Press, 2020. 60–75.

Gill, Lyndon K. *Erotic Islands: Art and Activism in the Queer Caribbean.* Durham: Duke University Press, 2018.
Gill-Peterson, Jules. *Histories of the Transgender Child.* Minneapolis: University of Minnesota Press, 2018.
— "Trans of Color Liberation: An Unauthorized History of the Future," in *The Routledge Companion to Intersectionalities.* Ed. Jennifer Nash and Samantha Pinto. New York: Routledge, 2023. 325–334.
Gilman, Sander L. "AIDS and Syphilis: The Iconography of Disease," in *AIDS: Cultural Analysis, Cultural Activism.* Ed. Douglas Crimp. Cambridge: MIT Press, 1988. 87–108.
Gleeson, Jules Joanne. "How Do Gender Transitions Happen?," in *Transgender Marxism.* Ed. Jules Joanne Gleeson and Elle O'Rourke. London: Pluto Press, 2021. 70–84.
Gleeson, Jules Joanne, and Elle O'Rourke (eds.). *Transgender Marxism.* London: Pluto Press, 2021.
Goldberg, Jonathan. *Sodometries: Renaissance Texts, Modern Sexualities.* Stanford, CA: Stanford University Press, 1992.
Goldberg, Jonathan, and Madhavi Menon. "Queering History." *PMLA* 120.5 (2005): 1608–1617.
González, Deena J. "Speaking Secrets: Living Chicana Theory," in *Living Chicana Theory.* Ed. Carla Trujillo. Berkeley, CA: Third Woman Press, 1998. 46–77.
Gopinath, Gayatri. *Impossible Desires: Queer Diasporas and South Asian Public Cultures.* Durham: Duke University Press, 2005.
— *Unruly Visions: The Aesthetic Practices of Queer Diaspora.* Durham: Duke University Press, 2018.
Gosine, Andil. *Nature's Wild: Love, Sex, and Law in the Caribbean.* Durham: Duke University Press, 2021.
Gossett, Che. "Silhouettes of Defiance: Memorializing Historical Sites of Queer and Transgender Resistance in an Age of Neoliberal Inclusivity," in *The Transgender Studies Reader 2.* Ed. Susan Stryker and Aren Z. Aizura. New York: Routledge, 2013. 580–590.
— "We Will Not Rest in Peace: AIDS Activism, Black Radicalism, Queer and/or Trans Resistance," in *Queer Necropolitics.* Ed. Jin Haritaworn. New York: Routledge, 2015. 31–50.
Gossett, Che, and Eva Hayward. "Monica Jones: An Interview." *TSQ* 7.4 (2020): 611–614.
— "Trans in a Time of HIV/AIDS." *TSQ* 7.4 (2020): 527–553.
Gould, Deborah B. *Moving Politics: Emotion and ACT UP's Fight against AIDS.* Chicago: University of Chicago Press, 2009.
Gould, Janice. "Disobedience (in Language) in Texts by Lesbian Native Americans." *ARIEL: A Review of International English Literature* 25.1 (1994): 32–44.

Grahn, Judy. *A Simple Revolution: The Making of an Activist Poet.* San Francisco: Aunt Lute Books, 2013.
Gramling, David, and Aniruddha Dutta. "Introduction." *TSQ* 3.3–4 (2016): 333–356.
Gray, Mary L. *Out in the Country: Youth, Media, and Queer Visibility in Rural America.* New York: New York University Press, 2009.
Green, K. Marshall. "Troubling the Waters: Mobilizing a Trans* Analytic," in *No Tea, No Shade: New Writings in Black Queer Studies.* Ed. E. Patrick Johnson. Durham: Duke University Press, 2016. 65–82.
Green-Simms, Lindsey B. *Queer African Cinemas.* Durham: Duke University Press, 2022.
Grewal, Inderpal, and Caren Kaplan. "Global Identities: Theorizing Transnational Studies of Sexuality." *GLQ* 7.4 (2001): 663–679.
Grover, Jan Zita. "AIDS: Keywords," in *AIDS: Cultural Analysis, Cultural Activism.* Ed. Douglas Crimp. Cambridge: MIT Press, 1988. 17–30.
Guidotti-Hernández, Nicole M. *Unspeakable Violence: Remapping U.S. and Mexican National Imaginaries.* Durham: Duke University Press, 2011.
Halberstam, Jack. *Female Masculinity.* Durham: Duke University Press, 1998.
   In a Queer Time and Place: Transgender Bodies, Subcultural Lives. New York: New York University Press, 2005.
   Trans: A Quick and Quirky Account of Gender Variability.* Oakland: University of California Press, 2018.
Hale, C. Jacob. "Consuming the Living, Dis(re)membering the Dead in the Butch/FTM Borderlands." *GLQ* 1.2 (1998): 311–348.
Haley, Sarah. *No Mercy Here: Gender, Punishment, and the Making of Jim Crow Modernity.* Chapel Hill: University of North Carolina Press, 2016.
Hall, Kim F. *Things of Darkness: Economies of Race and Gender in Early Modern England.* Ithaca, NY: Cornell University Press, 1995.
Hall, Lisa Kahaleole. "Bitches in Solitude: Identity Politics and Lesbian Community," in *Sisters, Sexperts, Queers: Beyond the Lesbian Nation.* Ed. Arlene Stein. New York: Penguin Books, 1993. 218–229.
   "Difference," in *Keywords for Gender and Sexuality Studies.* Ed. Kyla Wazana Tompkins, Aren Z. Aizura, Aimee Bahng, Karma R. Chávez, Mishuana Goeman, and Amber Jamilla Musser. New York: New York University Press, 2021. 71–73.
Halperin, David M. *How to Do the History of Homosexuality.* Chicago: University of Chicago Press, 2002.
Hames-García, Michael. "Jotería Studies, or the Political Is Personal." *Aztlán: A Journal of Chicano Studies* 39.1 (2014): 135–141.
Hammonds, Evelyn. "Black (W)holes and the Geometry of Black Female Sexuality." *differences* 6.2–3 (1994): 126–145.
Hammonds, Evelynn. "Race, Sex, AIDS: The Construction of 'Other.'" *Radical America* 20.6 (1988): 28–36.

Hamzić, Vanja. "Temporal Nonconformity: Being There Together as *Khwajasara* in a Time of One's Own," in *Pakistan Desires: Queer Futures Elsewhere*. Ed. Omar Kasmani. Durham: Duke University Press, 2023. 126–145.
Han, C. Winter. *Geisha of a Different Kind: Race and Sexuality in Gaysian America*. New York: New York University Press, 2018.
Hancock, Ange-Marie. *Intersectionality: An Intellectual History*. New York: Oxford University Press, 2016.
Haney López, Ian F. *White by Law: The Legal Construction of Race*. New York: New York University Press, 1996.
Hanhardt, Christina B. *Safe Space: Gay Neighborhood History and the Politics of Violence*. Durham: Duke University Press, 2013.
Haritaworn, Jin. *Queer Lovers and Hateful Others: Regenerating Violent Times and Places*. London: Pluto Press, 2015.
Harper, Philip Brian. *Private Affairs: Critical Ventures in the Culture of Social Relations*. New York: New York University Press, 1999.
Harper, Philip Brian, Anne McClintock, José Esteban Muñoz, and Trish Rosen. "Queer Transexions of Race, Nation, and Gender: An Introduction." *Social Text* 52/53 (1997): 1–4.
Hart, Lynda. *Between the Body and the Flesh: Performing Sadomasochism*. New York: Columbia University Press, 1998.
Hartman, Saidiya. *Wayward Lives, Beautiful Experiments: Intimate Histories of Social Upheaval*. New York: W. W. Norton and Co., 2019.
Hayes, Jarrod. *Queer Nations: Marginal Sexualities in the Maghreb*. Chicago: University of Chicago Press, 2000.
Hayward, Eva. "Lessons from a Starfish," in *The Transgender Studies Reader 2*. Ed. Susan Stryker and Aren Z. Aizura. New York: Routledge, 2013. 178–188.
Heaney, Emma. *The New Woman: Literary Modernism, Queer Theory, and the Trans Feminine Allegory*. Evanston, IL: Northwestern University Press, 2017.
"Women-Identified Women: Trans Women in 1970s Lesbian Feminist Organizing" *TSQ* 3.1–2 (2016): 137–145.
Hegarty, Benjamin. "Under the Lights, Onto the Stage: Becoming *Waria* through National Glamour in New Order Indonesia." *TSQ* 5.3 (2018): 355–377.
Heidenreich, Linda. *Nepantla^2: Transgender Mestiz@ Histories in Times of Global Shift*. Lincoln: University of Nebraska Press, 2020.
Hemmings, Clare. *Why Stories Matter: The Political Grammar of Feminist Theory*. Durham: Duke University Press, 2011.
Hemphill, Essex. "Introduction," in *Brother To brother: New Writings by Black Gay Men*. Ed. Essex Hemphill (conceived by Joseph Beam). Boston: Alyson Publications, 1991. xv–xxxi.
Heng, Geraldine. *The Invention of Race in the European Middle Ages*. New York: Cambridge University Press, 2018.
Hennessy, Rosemary. *Profit and Pleasure: Sexual Identities in Late Capitalism*. New York: Routledge, 2000.

Henry, Todd A. "Queer Korea: Toward a Field of Engagement," in *Queer Korea*. Ed. Todd A. Henry. Durham: Duke University Press, 2020. 1–52.

Herring, Scott. *Another Country: Queer Anti-Urbanism*. New York: New York University Press, 2010.

Hesford, Victoria. *Feeling Women's Liberation*. Durham: Duke University Press, 2013.

Higashida, Cheryl. *Black Internationalist Feminism: Women Writers of the Black Left, 1945–1995*. Urbana: University of Illinois Press, 2011.

Hill-Meyer, Tobi. "Where the Trans Women Aren't: The Slow Inclusion of Trans Women in Feminist and Queer Porn," in *The Feminist Porn Book: The Politics of Producing Pleasure*. Ed. Tristan Taormino, Celine Parreñas Shimizu, Constance Penley, and Mireille Miller-Young. New York: The Feminist Press, 2013. 155–163.

Hinchy, Jessica. *Governing Gender and Sexuality in Colonial India: The Hijra, c. 1850–1900*. New York: Cambridge University Press, 2019.

Hird, Myra J. "Animal Trans," in *The Transgender Studies Reader 2*. Ed. Susan Stryker and Aren Z. Aizura. New York: Routledge, 2013. 156–167.

Hitchcock, Tim. *English Sexualities, 1700–1800*. London: Macmillan Press, 1997.

Ho, Josephine. "Is Global Governance Bad for East Asian Queers?" *GLQ* 14.4 (2008): 457–479.

Hoad, Neville. *African Intimacies: Race, Homosexuality, and Globalization*. Minneapolis: University of Minnesota Press, 2007.

Hobson, Emily K. *Lavender and Red: Liberation and Solidarity in the Gay and Lesbian Left*. Oakland: University of California Press, 2016.

Hochberg, Gill Z. "Introduction: Israelis, Palestinians, Queers: Points of Departure." *GLQ* 16.4 (2010): 493–516.

Holland, Sharon. *The Erotic Life of Racism*. Durham: Duke University Press, 2012.

Hollibaugh, Amber L. *My Dangerous Desires: A Queer Girl Dreaming Her Way Home*. Durham: Duke University Press, 2000.

Hollibaugh, Amber, and Cherríe Moraga. "What We're Rollin' Around in Bed With," in *My Dangerous Desires: A Queer Girl Dreaming Her Way Home*. Amber L. Hollibaugh. Durham: Duke University Press, 2000. 62–84.

Hom, Alice Y. "Unifying Differences: Lesbian of Color Community Building in Los Angeles and New York, 1970s–1980s." Diss. Claremont Graduate University, 2011.

Hong, Grace Kyungwon. *Death beyond Disavowal: The Impossible Politics of Difference*. Minneapolis: University of Minnesota Press, 2015.

Hong, Grace Kyungwon, and Roderick A. Ferguson. "Introduction," in *Strange Affinities: The Gender and Sexual Politics of Comparative Racialization*. Ed. Grace Kyungwon Hong and Roderick A. Ferguson. Durham: Duke University Press, 2011. 1–24.

Hong Sohn, Stephen. *Inscrutable Belongings: Queer Asian North American Fiction*. Stanford, CA: Stanford University Press, 2018.

Hoppe, Trevor. *Punishing Disease: HIV and the Criminalization of Sickness.* Oakland: University of California Press, 2018.

Horswell, Michael J. *Decolonizing the Sodomite: Queer Tropes of Sexuality in Colonial Andean Culture.* Austin: University of Texas Press, 2005.

Hossain, Adnan. "De-Indianizing Hijra: Intraregional Effacements and Inequalities in South Asian Queer Space." *TSQ* 5.3 (2018): 321–331.

Howard, John. *Men Like That: A Southern Queer History.* Chicago: University of Chicago Press, 1999.

Howe, Cymene. *Intimate Activism: The Struggle for Sexual Rights in Postrevolutionary Nicaragua.* Durham: Duke University Press, 2013.

Huang, Vivian L. *Surface Relations: Queer Forms of Asian American Inscrutability.* Durham: Duke University Press, 2022.

"Wither Asian American Lesbian Feminist Thought?" *Diacritics* 48.3 (2020): 40–58.

Hunt, Sarah. "Embodying Self-Determination: Beyond the Gender Binary," in *Determinants of Indigenous Peoples' Health: Beyond the Social.* Ed. Margo Greenwood, Sarah de Leeuw, and Nicole Marie Lindsay. Toronto: Canadian Scholars, 2018. 104–119.

Hunter, Nan D. "Contextualizing the Sexuality Debates: A Chronology 1966–2005," in *Sex Wars: Sexual Dissent and Political Culture*, 10th Anniversary Edition. Ed. Lisa Duggan and Nan D. Hunter. New York: Routledge, 2006. 15–28.

Hurley, Natasha. *Circulating Queerness: Before the Gay and Lesbian Novel.* Minneapolis: University of Minnesota, 2018.

Jacobs, Sue-Ellen, Wesley Thomas, and Sabine Lang. *Two-Spirit People: Native American Gender Identity, Sexuality, and Spirituality.* Urbana: University of Illinois Press, 1997.

Jagose, Annamarie. *Inconsequence: Lesbian Representation and the Logic of Sexual Sequence.* Ithaca, NY: Cornell University Press, 2002.

Queer Theory: An Introduction. New York: New York University Press, 1996.

Jarman, Michelle. "Dismembering the Lynch Mob: Intersecting Narratives of Disability, Race, and Sexual Menace," in *Sex and Disability.* Ed. Robert McRuer and Anna Mollow. Durham: Duke University Press, 2012. 89–107.

Jarrín, Alvaro. "Untranslatable Subjects: Travesti Access to Public Health Care in Brazil." *TSQ* 3.3–4 (2016): 357–375.

Jay, Karla. "Introduction" (1972), in *Out of the Closets: Voices of Gay Liberation*, Twentieth-Anniversary Edition. Ed. Karla Jay and Allen Young. New York: New York University Press, 1992. lxi–lxvii.

Johnson, Austin H. "Transnormativity: A New Concept and Its Validation through Documentary Film about Transgender Men." *Sociological Inquiry* 20.10 (2016): 1–27.

Johnson, Colin R. *Just Queer Folks: Gender and Sexuality in Rural America.* Philadelphia: Temple University Press, 2013.

Johnson, E. Patrick. "'Quare' Studies, or (Almost) Everything I Know about Queer Studies I Learned from My Grandmother," in *Black Queer Studies: A Critical Anthology*. Ed. E. Patrick Johnson and Mae G. Henderson. Durham: Duke University Press, 2005. 125–157.

Johnson, E. Patrick, and Mae G. Henderson. "Introduction: Queering Black Studies/ 'Quaring' Queer Studies," in *Black Queer Studies: A Critical Anthology*. Ed. E. Patrick Johnson and Mae G. Henderson. Durham: Duke University Press, 2005. 1–17.

Jolivette, Andrew J. *Indian Blood: HIV and Colonial Trauma in San Francisco's Two-Spirit Community*. Seattle: University of Washington Press, 2016.

Jordan-Zachary, Julia S. "Safe, Soulful Sex: HIV/AIDS Talk," in *AIDS and the Distribution of Crises*. Ed. Jih-Fei Cheng, Alexandra Juhasz, and Nishant Shahani. Durham: Duke University Press, 2020. 93–130.

Justice, Daniel Heath. "Notes toward a Theory of Anomaly." *GLQ* 16.1–2 (2010): 207–242.

Kafer, Alison. *Feminist, Queer, Crip*. Bloomington: Indiana University Press, 2013.

Kahan, Benjamin. *The Book of Minor Perverts: Sexology, Etiology, and the Emergences of Sexuality*. Chicago: University of Chicago Press, 2019.

Kapadia, Ronak K. *Insurgent Aesthetics: Security and the Queer Life of the Forever War*. Durham: Duke University Press, 2019.

Kasmani, Omar. "Futuring Trans* in Pakistan: Timely Reflections." *TSQ* 8.1 (2021): 96–112.

Katz, Jonathan Ned (ed.). *Gay American History: Lesbians and Gay Men in the U.S.A*. New York: Thomas Y. Crowell, 1976.

The Invention of Heterosexuality. New York: Penguin Books, 1996.

Kauanui, J. Kēhaulani. *Paradoxes of Hawaiian Sovereignty: Land, Sex, and the Colonial Politics of State Nationalism*. Durham: Duke University Press, 2018.

Keating, AnaLouise. "Introduction: Reading Gloria Anzaldúa, Reading Ourselves...: Complex Intimacies, Intricate Connections," in *The Gloria Anzaldúa Reader*. Ed. AnaLouise Keating. Durham: Duke University Press, 2009. 1–18.

Keegan, Cáel M. "Getting Disciplined: What's Trans* about Queer Studies Now?" *Journal of Homosexuality* 67.3 (2020): 384–397.

Lana and Lily Wachowski. Urbana: University of Illinois Press, 2018.

Keeling, Kara. *Queer Times, Black Futures*. New York: New York University Press, 2019.

The Witch's Flight: The Cinematic, the Black Femme, and the Image of Common Sense. Durham: Duke University Press, 2007.

Kempadoo, Kamala. *Sexing the Caribbean: Gender, Race, and Sexual Labor*. New York: Routledge, 2004.

Kennedy, Elizabeth Lapovsky and Madeline D. Davis. *Boots of Leather, Slippers of Gold: The History of a Lesbian Community*. New York: Penguin, 1994.

Kim, Dorothy. "Before Intersectionality," in *The Routledge Companion to Intersectionalities*. Ed. Jennifer Nash and Samantha Pinto. Routledge: New York, 2023. 313–324.

King, Katie. "'There Are No Lesbians Here': Lesbianisms, Feminisms, and Global Gay Formations," in *Queer Globalizations: Citizenship and the Afterlife of Colonialism*. Ed. Arnaldo Cruz-Malavé and Martin F. Manalansan IV. New York: New York University Press, 2002. 33–45.

Kissack, Terence. "Freaking Fag Revolutionaries: New York's Gay Liberation Front 1969-1971." *Radical History Review* 62 (1995): 104–134.

Koyama, Emi. "The Transfeminist Manifesto." www.eminism.org (2001).

"Whose Feminism Is It Anyway?: The Unspoken Racism of the Trans Inclusion Debate," in *The Transgender Studies Reader*. Ed. Susan Stryker and Stephen Whittle. New York: Taylor & Francis Group, 2006. 698–705.

Kramer, Larry. "1,112 and Counting" (1983), in *We Are Everywhere: A Historical Sourcebook of Gay and Lesbian Politics*. Ed. Mark Blasius and Shane Phelan. New York: Routledge, 1997. 578–586.

Krell, Elías Cosenza. "Is Transmisogyny Killing Trans Women of Color?: Black Trans Feminisms and the Exigencies of White Femininity." *TSQ* 4.2 (2017): 226–242.

Kunzel, Regina. *Criminal Intimacy: Prison and the Uneven History of Modern American Sexuality*. Chicago: University of Chicago Press, 2008.

LaFleur, Greta. "Epilogue: Against Consensus," in *Trans Historical: Gender Plurality before the Modern*. Ed. Greta LaFleur, Masha Raskolnikov, and Anna Klosowska. Ithaca, NY: Cornell University Press, 2021. 366–377.

The Natural History of Sexuality in Early America. Baltimore: Johns Hopkins University Press, 2018.

"Sex and 'Unsex': Histories of Gender Trouble in Eighteenth-Century North America." *Early American Studies* 12.3 (2014): 469–499.

LaFleur, Greta, Masha Raskolnikov, and Anna Klosowska. "Introduction: The Benefits of Being Trans Historical," in *Trans Historical: Gender Plurality before the Modern*. Ed. Greta LaFleur, Masha Raskolnikov, and Anna Klosowska. Ithaca, NY: Cornell University Press, 2021. 1–26.

La Fountain-Stokes, Lawrence. *Queer Ricans: Cultures and Sexualities in the Diaspora*. Minneapolis: University of Minnesota, 2009.

Translocas: The Politics of Puerto Rican Drag and Trans Performance. Ann Arbor: University of Michigan Press, 2021.

Laing, Marie. *Urban Indigenous Youth Reframing Two-Spirit*. New York: Routledge, 2021.

Lang, Sabine. *Men as Women, Women as Men: Changing Gender in Native American Cultures*. Austin: University of Texas Press, 1998.

Lanser, Susan S. *The Sexuality of History: Modernity and the Sapphic, 1565–1830*. Chicago: University of Chicago, 2014.

Laporte, Rita. "The Butch/Femme Question" (1971), in *We Are Everywhere: A Historical Sourcebook of Gay and Lesbian Politics*. Ed. Mark Blasius and Shane Phelan. New York: Routledge, 1997. 355-364.

Laqueur, Thomas. *Making Sex: Body and Gender from the Greeks to Freud*. Cambridge: Harvard University Press, 1990.

Larson, Scott. "Laid Open: Examining Genders in Early America," in *Trans Historical: Gender Plurality before the Modern*. Ed. Greta LaFleur, Masha Raskolnikov, and Anna Klosowska. Ithaca, NY: Cornell University Press, 2021. 350-365.

Latrónico, Néstor. "My Memories as a Gay Militant in NYC," in *Smash the Church, Smash the State!: The Early Years of Gay Liberation*. Ed. Tommi Avicolli Mecca. San Francisco: City Lights Books, 2009. 48-54.

Lau, Jacob Roberts. "Between the Times: Trans-Temporality and Historical Representations." Diss. UCLA, 2016.

Lavery, Grace. "Egg Theory's Early Style." *TSQ* 7.3 (2020): 383-398.

Lee, JeeYeun. "Toward a Queer Korean American Diasporic History," in *Q & A: Queer in Asian America*. Ed. David L. Eng and Alice Y. Hom. Philadelphia: Temple University Press, 1998. 185-209.

León, Christian. "Exorbitant Dust: Manuel Ramos Otero's Queer and Colonial Matters." *GLQ* 27.3 (2021): 357-377.

Leonard, Zoe. "Lesbians in the AIDS Crisis," in *Women, AIDS & Activism*. Ed. The ACT UP/NY Women & AIDS Book Group. Boston: South End Press, 1990. 113-118.

Leonard, Zoe, and Polly Thistlethwaite. "Prostitution and HIV Infection," in *Women, AIDS & Activism*. Ed. The ACT UP/NY Women & AIDS Book Group. Boston: South End Press, 1990. 177-186.

Leung, Helen Hok-Sze. "Always in Translation: Trans Cinema across Languages." *TSQ* 3.3-4 (2016): 433-447.

Lewis, Abram J. "Trans History in a Moment of Danger: Organizing within and beyond 'Visibility' in the 1970s," in *Trap Door: Trans Cultural Production and the Politics of Visibility*. Ed. Tourmaline, Eric A. Stanley, and Johanna Burton. Cambridge: The MIT Press, 2017. 57-66.

Lim, Eng-Beng. *Brown Boys and Rice Queens: Spellbinding Performance in the Asias*. New York: New York University Press, 2014.

Liu, Petrus. *Queer Marxism in Two Chinas*. Durham: Duke University Press, 2015.

Lochrie, Karma. *Heterosyncracies: Female Sexuality When Normal Wasn't*. Minneapolis: University of Minnesota Press, 2005.

Lorde, Audre. "Sadomasochism: Not about Condemnation," in *A Burst of Light and Other Essays* (1988). Garden City, NJ: Ixia Press, 2017. 1-9.

Sister Outsider: Essays and Speeches. Freedom, CA: Crossing Press, 1984.

Lothian, Alexis. *Old Futures: Speculative Fiction and Queer Possibility*. New York: New York University Press, 2018.

Love, Heather. *Feeling Backward: Loss and the Politics of Queer History*. Cambridge: Harvard University Press, 2007.

  Underdogs: Social Deviance and Queer Theory. Chicago: University of Chicago Press, 2021.

Luciano, Dana. *Arranging Grief: Sacred Time and the Body in Nineteenth-Century America*. New York: New York University Press, 2007.

Luciano, Dana, and Mel Y. Chen. "Has the Queer Ever Been Human?" *GLQ* 21.2–3 (2015): 183–207.

Lugones, María. "Heterosexualism and the Colonial/Modern Gender System." *Hypatia* 27.1 (2007): 186–209.

  Pilgrimages/Peregrinajes: Theorizing Coalition against Multiple Oppressions. New York: Rowman & Littlefield, 2003.

Luibhéid, Eithne. *Entry Denied: Controlling Sexuality at the Border*. Minneapolis: University of Minnesota Press, 2002.

  "'Treated neither with Respect nor with Dignity': Contextualizing Queer and Trans Migrant 'Illegalization,' Detention, and Deportation," in *Queer and Trans Migrations: Dynamics of Illegalization, Detention, and Deportation*. Ed. Eithne Luibhéid and Karma R. Chávez. Urbana: University of Illinois Press, 2020. 19–40.

Macharia, Keguro. *Frottage: Frictions of Intimacy across Black Diaspora*. New York: New York University Press, 2019.

Malatino, Hil. *Side Affects: On Being Trans and Feeling Bad*. Minneapolis: University of Minnesota Press, 2022.

Mamdani, Mahmood. *Citizen and Subject: Contemporary Africa and the Legacy of Late Colonialism*. Princeton, NJ: Princeton University Press, 1996.

Manalansan, Martin F., IV. *Global Divas: Filipino Gay Men in the Diaspora*. Durham: Duke University Press, 2003.

  "Race, Violence, and Neoliberal Spatial Politics in the Global City." *Social Text* 84–85.3–4 (2005): 141–155.

Manalansan, Martin F. IV, Alice Y. Hom, and Kale Bantigue Fajardo. "Journeys, Itineraries, Horizons: An Introduction," in *Q & A: Voices from Queer Asian North America*. Ed. Martin F. Manalansan IV, Alice Y. Hom, and Kale Bantigue Fajardo. Philadelphia: Temple University Press, 2021. 1–25.

Mandujano, Verónica. "The Privatized Deportation Center Complex y la trans mujer," in *Transmovimientos: Latinx Queer Migrations, Bodies, and Spaces*. Ed. Ellie D. Hernández, Eddy Franciso Alvarez Jr., and Magda García. Lincoln: University of Nebraska Press, 2021. 177–204.

Manion, Jen. *Female Husbands: A Trans History*. New York: Cambridge University Press, 2020.

Maracle, Aiyyana. "A Journey in Gender." *torquere: Journal of the Canadian Lesbian and Gay Studies Association* 2 (2000): 36–57.

Marcus, Sharon. *Between Women: Friendship, Desire, and Marriage in Victorian England*. Princeton, NJ: Princeton University Press, 2007.

Marhoefer, Laurie. *Racism and the Making of Gay Rights: A Sexologist, His Student, and the Empire of Queer Love*. Toronto: University of Toronto Press, 2022.

Martin, Biddy. *Femininity Played Straight: The Significance of Being Lesbian*. New York: Routledge, 1996.
Martin, Fran. *Backward Glances: Contemporary Chinese Cultures and the Female Homoerotic Imaginary*. Durham: Duke University Press, 2010.
Martin, Fran, Peter A. Jackson, Mark McLelland, and Audrey Yue. "Introduction," in *AsiaPacifiQueer: Rethinking Genders and Sexualities*. Ed. Fran Martin, Peter A. Jackson, Mark McLelland, and Audrey Yue. Urbana: University of Illinois Press, 2008. 1–27.
Massad, Joseph A. *Desiring Arabs*. Chicago: University of Chicago Press, 2007.
Masten, Jeffrey. *Queer Philologies: Sex, Language, and Affect in Shakespeare's Time*. Philadelphia: University of Pennsylvania Press, 2016.
Mbasalaki, Phoebe Kisubi. "Women Who Love Women: Negotiation of African Traditions and Kinship," in *Routledge Handbook of Queer African Studies*. Ed. S. N. Nyeck. New York: Routledge, 2019. 37–48.
McBride, Dwight A. *Why I Hate Abercrombie and Fitch: Essay Son Race and Sexuality*. New York: New York University Press, 2005.
McCallum, E. L., and Mikko Tuhkanen. "Becoming Unbecoming: Untimely Meditations," in *Queer Times, Queer Becomings*. Ed. E. L. McCallum and Mikko Tuhkanen. Albany: State University of New York Press, 2011. 1–25.
McClintock, Anne. *Imperial Leather: Race, Gender and Sexuality in the Colonial Contest*. New York: Routledge, 1995.
McKinney, Cait. "Crisis Infrastructures: AIDS Activism Meets Internet Regulation," in *AIDS and the Distribution of Crises*. Ed. Jih-Fei Cheng, Alexandra Juhasz, and Nishant Shahani. Durham: Duke University Press, 2020. 162–182.
Information Activism: A Queer History of Lesbian Media Technologies. Durham: Duke University Press, 2020.
Mendoza, Victor Román. *Metroimperial Intimacies: Fantasy, Racial-Sexual Governance, and the Philippines in U.S. Imperialism, 1899–1913*. Durham: Duke University Press, 2015.
Metzger, Sean, and Gina Masequesmay. "Introduction: Embodying Asian/American Sexualities," in *Embodying Asian/American Sexualities*. Ed. Gina Masequesmay and Sean Metzger. New York: Rowman & Littlefield Publishers, Inc., 2009. 1–22.
Meyerowitz, Joanne. *How Sex Changed: A History of Transsexuality in the United States*. Cambridge: Harvard University Press, 2002.
Mia, Valentina. "The Failures of SESTA/FOSTA: A Sex Worker Manifesto." *TSQ* 7.2 (2020): 237–239.
Miller-Young, Mireille. "Interventions: The Deviant and Defiant Art of Black Women Porn Directors," in *The Feminist Porn Book: The Politics of Producing Pleasure*. Ed. Tristan Taormino, Celine Parreñas Shimizu, Constance Penley, and Mireille Miller-Young. New York City: The Feminist Press, 2013. 105–120.

Miranda, Deborah A. "Extermination of the *Joyas: Gendercide in Spanish California.*" *GLQ* 16.1–2 (2010): 253–284.
Mirandé, Alfredo. *Behind the Mask: Gender Hybridity in a Zapotec Community.* Tucson: University of Arizona Press, 2017.
Mogul, Joey L., Andrea J. Ritchie, and Kay Whitlock (eds.). *Queer (In)Justice: The Criminalization of LGBT People in the United States.* Boston: Beacon Press, 2011.
Mollow, Anna, and Robert McRuer. "Introduction," in *Sex and Disability.* Ed. Robert McRuer and Anna Mollow. Durham: Duke University Press, 2012. 1–36.
Moon, Michael. *Disseminating Whitman: Revision and Corporeality in Leaves of Grass.* Cambridge: Harvard University Press, 1991.
Moore, Lisa L. *Dangerous Intimacies: Toward a Sapphic History of the British Novel.* Durham: Duke University Press, 1997.
Moraga, Cherríe. "La Güera," in *Loving the War Years: Lo Que Nunca Paso Por Sus Labios* (1983). Boston: South End Press, 2000. 42–50.
——— "A Long Line of Vendidas," in *Loving the War Years: Lo Que Nunca Paso Por Sus Labios* (1983). Boston: South End Press, 2000.
Moraga, Cherríe L., and Gloria E. Anzaldúa (eds.). *This Bridge Called My Back: Writings by Radical Women of Color* (1981). Berkeley, CA: Third Woman Press, 2002.
Morgan, Jennifer L. *Reckoning with Slavery: Gender, Kinship, and Capitalism in the Early Black Atlantic.* Durham: Duke University Press, 2021.
Morgan, Robin. "Lesbianism and Feminism: Synonyms or Contradictions?" (1973), in *We Are Everywhere: A Historical Sourcebook of Gay and Lesbian Politics.* Ed. Mark Blasius and Shane Phelan. New York: Routledge, 1997. 424–435.
Morgan, Tracy. "Butch-Femme and the Politics of Identity," in *Sisters, Sexperts, Queers: Beyond the Lesbian Nation.* Ed. Arlene Stein. New York: Penguin Books, 1993. 35–46.
Morgensen, Scott L. "Queer Settler Colonialism in Canada and Israel: Articulating Two-Spirit and Palestinian Queer Critiques." *Settler Colonial Studies* 2.2 (2012): 167–190.
——— *Spaces between Us: Queer Settler Colonialism and Indigenous Decolonization.* Minneapolis: University of Minnesota Press, 2011.
Moussawi, Ghassan. *Disruptive Situations: Fractal Orientalism and Queer Strategies in Beirut.* Philadelphia: Temple University Press, 2020.
Mumford, Kevin J. *Interzones: Black/White Sex Districts in Chicago and New York in the Early Twentieth Century.* New York: Columbia University Press, 1997.
Muñoz, José Esteban. *Cruising Utopia: The Then and There of Queer Futurity.* New York: New York University Press, 2009.
——— *Disidentifications: Queers of Color and the Performance of Politics.* Minneapolis: University of Minnesota, 1999.

The Sense of Brown. Ed. Joshua Chambers-Letson and Tavia Nyong'o. Durham: Duke University Press, 2020.

Munro, Brenna M. *South Africa and the Dream of Love to Come: Queer Sexuality and the Struggle for Freedom.* Minneapolis: University of Minnesota Press, 2012.

Musser, Amber Jamilla. *Sensual Excess: Queer Femininity and Brown Jouissance.* New York: New York University Press, 2018.

Najmabadi, Afsaneh. *Professing Selves: Transsexuality and Same-Sex Desire in Contemporary Iran.* Durham: Duke University Press, 2014.

Namaste, Viviane K. *Invisible Lives: The Erasure of Transsexual and Transgendered People.* Chicago: University of Chicago Press, 2000.

Nash, Jennifer. *Black Feminism Reimagined: After Intersectionality.* Durham: Duke University Press, 2018.

Nash, Jennifer, and Samantha Pinto (eds.). *The Routledge Companion to Intersectionalities.* Routledge: New York, 2023.

Ndaiye, Noémie. *Scripts of Blackness: Early Modern Performance Culture and the Making of Race.* Philadelphia: University of Pennsylvania Press, 2022.

Nealon, Christopher. *Foundlings: Lesbian and Gay Historical Emotion before Stonewall.* Durham: Duke University Press, 2001.

Negrón-Muntaner, Frances. "When I Was a Puerto Rican Lesbian: Meditations on *Brincando el Charco: Portrait of a Puerto Rican.*" *GLQ* 5.4 (1999): 511–526.

Nestle, Joan. *A Restricted Country.* Ithaca, NY: Firebrand Books, 1987.

Newton, Esther. *Mother Camp: Female Impersonators in America* (1972). Chicago: University of Chicago Press, 1979.

Nguyen, Ly Thuy. "Queer Dis/inheritance and Refugee Futures." *WSQ: Women's Studies Quarterly* 48.1-2 (2020): 218–235.

Nguyen, Tan Hoang. *A View from the Bottom: Asian American Masculinity and Sexual Representation.* Durham: Duke University Press, 2014.

Noble, Bobby. "Knowing Dick: Penetration and the Pleasures of Feminist Porn's Trans Man," in *The Feminist Porn Book: The Politics of Producing Pleasure.* Ed. Tristan Taormino, Celine Parreñas Shimizu, Constance Penley, and Mireille Miller-Young. New York City: The Feminist Press, 2013. 303–319.

"Trans. Panic.: Some Thoughts toward a Theory of Feminist Fundamentalism," in *Transfeminist Perspectives in and beyond Transgender and Gender Studies.* Ed. Finn Enke. Philadelphia: Temple University Press, 2012. 45–59.

Nunokawa, Jeff. "'All the Sad Young Men': AIDS and the Work of Mourning," in *Inside/Out: Lesbian Theories, Gay Theories.* Ed. Diana Fuss. New York: Routledge, 1991. 311–323.

Nurka, Camille. "Animal Techne: Transing Posthumanism." *TSQ* 2.2 (2015): 209–226.

Nussbaum, Felicity A. *Torrid Zones: Maternity, Sexuality, and Empire in Eighteenth-Century English Narratives*. Baltimore: Johns Hopkins University Press, 1995.
Nyong'o, Tavia. *The Amalgamation Waltz: Race, Performance, and the Ruses of Memory*. Minneapolis: University of Minnesota Press, 2009.
O'Brien, Michelle. "Tracing This Body: Transsexuality, Pharmaceuticals, and Capitalism," in *The Transgender Studies Reader 2*. Ed. Susan Stryker and Aren Z. Aizura. New York: Routledge, 2013. 56–65.
——— "Trans Work: Employment Trajectories, Labor Discipline and Gender Freedom," in *Transgender Marxism*. Ed. Jules Joanne Gleeson and Elle O'Rourke. London: Pluto Press, 2021. 47–61.
Ochoa, Marcia. *Queen for a Day: Transformistas, Beauty Queens, and the Performance of Femininity in Venezuela*. Durham: Duke University Press, 2014.
O'Daniel, Alyson. *Holding On: African American Women Surviving HIV/AIDS*. Lincoln: University of Nebraska Press, 2016.
Ordover, Nancy. *American Eugenics: Race, Queer Anatomy, and the Science of Nationalism*. Minneapolis: University of Minnesota Press, 2003.
Osorio, Jamaica Heolimeleikalani. *Remembering Our Intimacies: Mo'olelo, Aloha, 'Aina, and Ea*. Minneapolis: University of Minnesota Press, 2021.
Parker, Pat. "Revolution: It's Not Neat or Pretty or Quick," in *This Bridge Called My Back: Writings by Radical Women of Color* (1981). Ed. Cherríe L. Moraga and Gloria E. Anzaldúa. Berkeley, CA: Third Woman Press, 2002. 267–272.
——— "The 1987 March on Washington: The Morning Rally," in *The Complete Works of Pat Parker*. Ed. Julie R. Enszer. Dover, FL: Sinister Wisdom, Inc., 2018. 272–277.
Pascoe, Peggy. *What Comes Naturally: Miscegenation Law and the Making of Race in America*. New York: Oxford University Press, 2009.
Patton, Cindy. *Globalizing AIDS*. Minneapolis: University of Minnesota Press, 2002.
——— *Inventing AIDS*. New York: Routledge, 1990.
Pearsall, Sarah M. S. *Polygamy: An Early American History*. New Haven, CT: Yale University Press, 2019.
Peletz, Michael G. *Gender Pluralism: Southeast Asia since Early Modern Times*. New York: Routledge, 2009.
Penley, Constance, Celine Parreñas Shimizu, Mireille Miller-Young, and Tristan Taormino. "Introduction: The Politics of Producing Pleasure," in *The Feminist Porn Book: The Politics of Producing Pleasure*. Ed. Tristan Taormino, Celine Parreñas Shimizu, Constance Penley, and Mireille Miller-Young. New York City: The Feminist Press, 2013. 9–22.
People with AIDS/ARC. "The Denver Principles" (1983), in *We Are Everywhere: A Historical Sourcebook of Gay and Lesbian Politics*. Ed. Mark Blasius and Shane Phelan. New York: Routledge, 1997. 593–595.

Pérez, Daniel Enrique. "Jotería Epistemologies: Mapping a Research Agenda, Unearthing a Lost Heritage, and Building 'Queer Aztlán.'" *Aztlán: A Journal of Chicano Studies* 39.1 (2014): 143–154.

Pérez, Emma. *The Decolonial Imaginary: Writing Chicanas into History*. Bloomington: Indiana University Press, 1999.

Pérez, Hiram. *A Taste for Brown Bodies: Gay Modernity and Cosmopolitan Desire*. New York: New York University Press, 2015.

Pezzutto, Sophie, and Lynn Comella. "Trans Pornography: Mapping an Emerging Field." *TSQ* 7.2 (2020): 152–171.

Pierce, Joseph M. "In Good Relations: Native Adoption, Kinstillations, and the Grounding of Memory," in *Queer Kinship: Race, Sex, Belonging, Form*. Ed. Teagan Bradway and Elizabeth Freeman. Durham: Duke University Press, 2022. 95–118.

Pierce, Joseph M., María Amelia Viteri, Diego Falconí Trávez, Salvador Vidal-Ortiz, and Lourdes Martínez-Echazábal. "Introduction: *Cuir*/Queer Américas: Translation, Decoloniality, and the Incommensurable." *GLQ* 27.3 (2021): 321–327.

Pitts, Andrea. "Sylvia Rivera and the Fight against Carceral Medicine," in *Trans Philosophy*. Ed. Perry Zurn, Andrea J. Pitts, Talia Mae Bettch, and P. J. DiPietro. Minneapolis: University of Minnesota Press, 2024. 171–192.

Ponce, Martin Joseph. *Beyond the Nation: Diasporic Filipino Literature and Queer Reading*. New York: New York University Press, 2012.

Ports, Suki Terada (with Marion Bankzhaf). "Many Cultures, Many Approaches," in *Women, AIDS & Activism*. Ed. The ACT UP/NY Women & AIDS Book Group. Boston: South End Press, 1990. 107–111.

Povinelli, Elizabeth A. *The Empire of Love*. Durham: Duke University Press, 2006.

Povinelli, Elizabeth A., and George Chauncey. "Thinking Sexuality Transnationally: An Introduction." *GLQ* 5.4 (1999): 439–450.

Preciado, Paul B. *Can the Monster Speak?* Trans. Frank Wynne. London: Fitzcarraldo Editions, 2021.

Price Minter, Shannon. "Do Transsexuals Dream of Gay Rights?: Getting Real about Transgender Inclusion," in *Transgender Rights*. Ed. Paisley Currah, Richard M. Juang, and Shannon Price Minter. Minneapolis: University of Minnesota Press, 2006. 141–170.

Prosser, Jay. *Second Skins: The Body Narratives of Transsexuality*. New York: Columbia University Press, 1998.

Puar, Jasbir K. *The Right to Maim: Debility, Capacity, Disability*. Durham: Duke University Press, 2017.

Terrorist Assemblages: Homonationalism in Queer Times. Durham: Duke University Press, 2007.

Puri, Jyoti. *Sexual States: Governance and the Struggle over the Antisodomy Law in India*. Durham: Duke University Press, 2016.

Pyle, Kai. "Naming and Claiming: Recovering Ojibwe and Plains Cree Two-Spirit Language." *TSQ: Transgender Studies Quarterly* 5.4 (2018): 574–588.

"'Women and 2spirits': On the Marginalization of Transgender Indigenous People in Activist Rhetoric." *American Indian Culture and Research Journal* 43.3 (2019): 85–94.

Pyle, Kai Minosh, and Danne Jobin. "Transgender, Two-Spirit and Nonbinary Indigenous Literatures: Introduction." *Transmotion* 7.1 (2021): 1–9.

"Queers Read This; I Hate Straights" (1990), in *We Are Everywhere: A Historical Sourcebook of Gay and Lesbian Politics*. Ed. Mark Blasius and Shane Phelan. New York: Routledge, 1997. 773–780.

Rabasa, Alba Pons. "From Representation to Corposubjectivation: The Configuration of Transgender in Mexico City." *TSQ* 3.3–4 (2016): 388–411.

Radicalesbians. "Leaving the Gay Men Behind" (1970) in *Out of the Closets: Voices of Gay Liberation, Twentieth-Anniversary Edition*. Ed. Karla Jay and Allen Young. New York: New York University Press, 1992. 290–293.

"The Woman-Identified Woman" (1970), in *Out of the Closets: Voices of Gay Liberation, Twentieth-Anniversary Edition*. Ed. Karla Jay and Allen Young. New York: New York University Press, 1992. 172–177.

Rafael, Vincent L. *White Love and Other Events in Filipino History*. Durham: Duke University Press, 2000.

Rao, Rahul. *Out of Time: The Queer Politics of Postcoloniality*. New York: Oxford University Press, 2020.

"Rapping with a Street Transvestite Revolutionary: An Interview with Marcia [sic.] Johnson" (1972), in *Out of the Closets: Voices of Gay Liberation, Twentieth-Anniversary Edition*. Ed. New York: New York University Press, 1992. 112–120.

Rawson, K. J., and Cristan Williams. "*Transgender**: The Rhetorical Landscape of a Term." *Present Tense: A Journal of Rhetoric in Society* 3.2 (2014) (online).

Reddy, Chandan. *Freedom with Violence: Race, Sexuality, and the US State*. Durham: Duke University Press, 2011.

Reddy, Gayatri. *With Respect to Sex: Negotiating Hijra Identity in South India*. Chicago: University of Chicago Press, 2005.

Reid-Pharr, Robert F. *Black Gay Man*. New York: New York University Press, 2001.

Reis, Elizabeth. *Bodies in Doubt: An American History of Intersex*. Baltimore: Johns Hopkins University Press, 2021.

Rich, Adrienne. "Compulsory Heterosexuality and Lesbian Existence" (1980), in *Adrienne Rich's Poetry and Prose*. Ed. Barbara Charlesworth Gelpi and Albert Gelpi. New York: W. W. Norton & Company, 1993. 203–224.

"When We Dead Awaken: Writing as Re-Vision" (1971), in *Adrienne Rich's Poetry and Prose*. Ed. Barbara Charlesworth Gelpi and Albert Gelpi. New York: W. W. Norton & Company, 1993. 166–177.

Richardson, Matt. *The Queer Limit of Black Memory: Black Lesbian Literature and Irresolution*. Columbus: The Ohio State University Press, 2013.

Richie, Beth. *Arrested Justice: Black Women, Violence, and America's Prison Nation*. New York: New York University Press, 2012.
Rifkin, Mark. *Beyond Settler Time: Temporal Sovereignty and Indigenous Self-Determination*. Durham: Duke University Press, 2017.
— *Manifesting America: The Imperial Construction of U.S. National Space*. New York: Oxford University Press, 2009.
— *Settler Common Sense: Queerness and Everyday Colonialism in the American Renaissance*. Minneapolis: University of Minnesota Press, 2014.
— *When Did Indians Become Straight?: Kinship, the History of Sexuality, and Native Sovereignty*. New York: Oxford University Press, 2011.
Ritchie, Andrea J. *Invisible No More: Police Violence against Black Women and Women of Color*. Boston: Beacon Press, 2017.
Ritchie, Jason. "Pinkwashing, Homonationalism, and Israle-Palestine: The Conceits of Queer Theory and the Politics of the Ordinary." *Antipode* 47.3 (2015): 616–634.
Rivera-Servera, Rámon H. *Performing Queer Latinidad: Dance, Sexuality, Politics*. Ann Arbor: University of Michigan Press, 2012.
Rizki, Cole. "Latin/x American Trans Studies: Toward a *Travesti*-Trans Analytic." *TSQ* 6.2 (2019): 145–155.
Roane, J. T. "Black Harm Reduction Politics in the Early Philadelphia Epidemic." *Souls: A Critical Journal of Black Politics, Culture, and Society* 21.2–3 (2019): 144–152.
Roberts, James C. "Pre-Now," in *Smash the Church, Smash the State!: The Early Years of Gay Liberation*. Ed. Tommi Avicolli Mecca. San Francisco: City Lights Books, 2009. 43–47.
Rodríguez, Dylan. *Suspended Apocalypse: White Supremacy, Genocide, and the Filipino Condition*. Minneapolis: University of Minnesota Press, 2009.
Rodríguez, Juana María. *Queer Latinidad: Identity Practices, Discursive Spaces*. New York: New York University Press, 2003.
— *Sexual Futures, Queer Gestures, and Other Latina Longings*. New York: New York University Press, 2014.
Rodríguez, Richard T. *Next of Kin: The Family in Chicano/a Cultural Politics*. Durham: Duke University Press, 2009.
Rofel, Lisa. *Desiring China: Experiments in Neoliberalism, Sexuality, and Public Culture*. Durham: Duke University Press, 2007.
Rohy, Valerie. *Anachronism and Its Others: Sexuality, Race, Temporality*. Albany: State University of New York Press, 2009.
Román, David. *Acts of Intervention: Performance, Gay Culture, and AIDS*. Bloomington: Indiana University Press, 1998.
Roque Ramírez, Horacio. "'That's *My* Place!': Negotiating Racial, Sexual, and Gender Politics in San Francisco's Gay Latino Alliance, 1975–1983." *Journal of the History of Sexuality* 12.4 (2004): 224–258.

Roscoe, Will. *Changing Ones: Third and Fourth Genders in Native North America.* New York: St. Martin's Griffin, 1998.
Ross, Marlon B. "Beyond the Closet as Raceless Paradigm," in *Black Queer Studies: A Critical Anthology.* Ed. E. Patrick Johnson and Mae G. Henderson. Durham: Duke University Press, 2005. 161–189.
——— *Sissy Insurgencies: A Racial Anatomy of Unfit Manliness.* Durham: Duke University Press, 2022.
Rouhi, Leyla. "A Handsome Boy among Those Barbarous Turks: Cervantes's Muslims and the Art and Science of Desire," in *Islamicate Sexualities: Translations across Temporal Geographies of Desire.* Ed. Kathryn Babayan and Afsaneh Najmabadi. Cambridge: Harvard University Press, 2008. 41–71.
Roy, Srila. *Changing the Subject: Feminist and Queer Politics in Neoliberal India.* Durham: Duke University Press, 2022.
Royles, Dan. *To Make the Wounded Whole: The African American Struggle against HIV/AIDS.* Chapel Hill: University of North Carolina Press, 2020.
Rubin, Gayle. "Blood under the Bridge: Reflections on 'Thinking Sex'" (2010), in *Deviations: A Gayle Rubin Reader.* Durham: Duke University Press, 2011. 194–223.
——— "The Leather Menace: Comments on Politics and S/M" (1982), in *Deviations: A Gayle Rubin Reader.* Durham: Duke University Press, 2011. 109–136.
——— "Of Catamites and Kings: Reflections on Butch, Gender, and Boundaries" (1992), in *Deviations: A Gayle Rubin Reader.* Durham: Duke University Press, 2011. 241–253.
——— "Thinking Sex: Notes for a Radical Theory of the Politics of Sexuality" (1984), in *Deviations: A Gayle Rubin Reader.* Durham: Duke University Press, 2011. 137–181.
Rubin, Henry. *Self-Made Men: Identity and Embodiment among Transsexual Men.* Nashville, TN: Vanderbilt University Press, 2003.
Rubright, Marjorie. "Transgender Capacity in Thomas Dekker and Thomas Middleton's *The Roaring Girl* (1611)." *Journal for Early Modern Cultural Studies* 19.4 (2019): 45–74.
Said, Edward. *Orientalism.* New York: Vintage Books, 1979.
Salamon, Gayle. *Assuming a Body: Transgender and Rhetorics of Materiality.* New York: Columbia University Press, 2010.
Saldaña-Portillo, María Josefina. *The Revolutionary Imagination in the Americas and the Age of Development.* Durham: Duke University Press, 1993.
Samer, Rox. *Lesbian Potentiality and Feminist Media in the 1970s.* Durham: Duke University Press, 2022.
Samuels, Ellen. *Fantasies of Identification: Disability, Gender, Race.* New York: New York University Press, 2014.
Sanchez, Melissa E. *Shakespeare and Queer Theory.* New York: Bloomsbury, 2020.
——— "'Use Me but as Your Spaniel': Feminism, Queer Theory, and Early Modern Sexualities." *PMLA* 127.3 (2012): 493–511.

Sandoval, Chela. "Feminism and Racism: A Report on the 1981 National Women's Studies Association Conference," in *Making Face, Making Soul/Haciendo Caras: Creative and Critical Perspectives by Feminists of Color.* Ed. Gloria Anzaldúa. San Francisco: Aunt Lute Books, 1990. 55–71.
 "U.S. Third World Feminism: The Theory and Method of Oppositional Consciousness in the Postmodern World." *Genders* 10 (Spring 1991): 1–24.
Sang, Tze-lan D. *The Emerging Lesbian: Female Same-Sex Desire in Modern China.* Chicago: University of Chicago Press, 2003.
Santana, Dora Silva. "Mais Viva!: Reassembling Transness, Blackness, and Feminism." *TSQ* 6.2 (2019): 210–222.
Saria, Vaibhav. *Hijras, Lovers, Brothers: Surviving Sex and Poverty in Rural India.* New York: Fordham University Press, 2021.
Savci, Evren. *Queer in Translation: Sexual Politics under Neoliberal Islam.* Durham: Duke University Press, 2021.
Schalk, Sami. *Bodyminds Reimagined: (Dis)ability, Race, and Gender in Black Women's Speculative Fiction.* Durham: Duke University Press, 2018.
Schotten, C. Heike. *Queer Terror: Life, Death, and Desire in the Settler Colony.* New York: Columbia University Press, 2018.
Schulman, Sarah. *Israel/Palestine and the Queer International.* Durham: Duke University Press, 2012.
 Let the Record Show: A Political History of ACT UP New York, 1987–1993. New York: Picador, 2021.
Scott, Darieck. *Extravagant Abjection: Blackness, Power, and Sexuality in the African American Literary Imagination.* New York: New York University, 2010.
Sears, Clare. *Arresting Dress: Cross-Dressing, Law, and Fascination in Nineteenth-Century San Francisco.* Durham: Duke University Press, 2015.
Sedgwick, Eve Kosofsky. *Epistemology of the Closet.* Berkeley: University of California Press, 1990.
 Tendencies. Durham: Duke University Press, 1993.
 Touching Feeling: Affect, Pedagogy, Performativity. Durham: Duke University Press, 2003.
See, Sarita Echavez. *The Decolonized Eye: Filipino American Art and Performance.* Minneapolis: University of Minnesota Press, 2009.
Seitler, Dana. "Queer Physiognomies; Or, How Many Ways Can We Do the History of Sexuality?" *Criticism* 46.1 (2004): 71–102.
Serano, Julia. *Whipping Girl: A Transsexual Woman on Sexism and the Scapegoating of Femininity* (2007). 2nd ed. Berkeley, CA: Seal Press, 2016.
Shah, Nayan. *Stranger Intimacy: Contesting Race, Sexuality, and the Law in the North American West.* Berkeley: University of California Press, 2011.
Shahani, Nishant. "How to Survive the Whitewashing of AIDS: Global Pasts, Transnational Futures." *QED* 3.1 (2016): 1–33.

Shelley, Martha. "Gay Is Good" (1970), in *Out of the Closets: Voices of Gay Liberation, Twentieth-Anniversary Edition*. Ed. Karla Jay and Allen Young. New York: New York University Press, 1992. 31–34.
Shugar, Dana R. *Separatism and Women's Community*. Lincoln: University of Nebraska Press, 1995.
Shumsky, Ellen. "The Radicalesbian Story: An Evolution of Consciousness" (1970, 1972), in *Smash the Church, Smash the State!: The Early Years of Gay Liberation*. Ed. Tommi Avicolli Mecca. San Francisco: City Lights Books, 2009. 190–196.
Siebers, Tobin. "A Sexual Culture for Disabled People," in *Sex and Disability*. Ed. Robert McRuer and Anna Mollow. Durham: Duke University Press, 2012. 37–53.
Sigal, Pete. "Gendered Power, the Hybrid Self, and Homosexual Desire in Late Colonial Yucatan," in *Infamous Desire: Male Homosexuality in Colonial Latin America*. Ed. Pete Sigal. Chicago: University of Chicago Press, 2003. 102–133.
  (ed.). *Infamous Desire: Male Homosexuality in Colonial Latin America*. Chicago: University of Chicago Press, 2003.
Simpson, Audra. *Mohawk Interruptus: Political Life across the Borders of Settler States*. Durham: Duke University Press, 2014.
Simpson, Leanne Betasamosake. *As We Have Always Done: Indigenous Freedom through Radical Resistance*. Minneapolis: University of Minnesota Press, 2017.
Sinnott, Megan J. *Toms and Dees: Transgender Identity and Same-Sex Relationships in Thailand*. Honolulu: University of Hawai'i Press, 2004.
Skidmore, Emily. *True Sex: The Lives of Trans Men at the Turn of the Twentieth Century*. New York: New York University Press, 2017.
Smith, Barbara. "Introduction," in *Home Girls: A Black Feminist Anthology* (1983). Ed. Barbara Smith. New Brunswick, NJ: Rutgers University Press, 2000. xxi–lviii.
Smyth, Cherry. *Lesbians Talk Queer Notions*. London: Scarlet Press, 1992.
Snediker, Michael D. *Contingent Figure: Chronic Pain and Queer Embodiment*. Minneapolis: University of Minnesota Press, 2021.
Snorton, C. Riley. *Black on Both Sides: A Racial History of Trans Identity*. Minneapolis: University of Minnesota Press, 2017.
  Nobody Is Supposed to Know: Black Sexuality on the Down Low. Minneapolis: University of Minnesota Press, 2014.
Snorton, C. Riley, and Jin Haritaworn. "Trans Necropolitics: A Transnational Reflection on Violence, Death, and the Trans of Color Afterlife," in *The Transgender Studies Reader 2*. Ed. Susan Stryker and Aren Z. Aizura. New York: Routledge, 2013. 66–76.
Somerville, Siobhan B. "Introduction," in *The Cambridge Companion to Queer Studies*. Ed. Siobhan B. Somerville. New York: Cambridge University Press, 2020. 1–14.

Queering the Color Line: Race and the Invention of Homosexuality in American Culture. Durham: Duke University Press, 2000.

"Queer Loving." *GLQ* 11.3 (2005): 335–370.

Soto, Sandra K. *Reading Chican@ Like a Queer: The De-mastery of Desire.* Austin: University of Texas Press, 2010.

Spade, Dean. *Normal Life: Administrative Violence, Critical Trans Politics, and the Limits of Law.* Rev. ed. Durham: Duke University Press, 2015.

Speed, Shannon. *Incarcerated Stories: Indigenous Women Migrants and Violence in the Settler-Capitalist State.* Chapel Hill: University of North Carolina Press, 2019.

Spillers, Hortense J. "Mama's Baby, Papa's Maybe: An American Grammar Book" (1987), in *Black, White, and in Color: Essays on American Literature and Culture.* Ed. Hortense J. Spillers. Chicago: University of Chicago Press, 2003. 203–229.

Springer, Kimberly. *Living for the Revolution: Black Feminist Organizations, 1968–1980.* Durham: Duke University Press, 2005.

Stallings, L. H. *Funk the Erotic: Transaesthetics and Black Sexual Cultures.* Urbana: University of Illinois Press, 2015.

Stanley, Eric. "The Affective Commons: Gay Shame, Queer Hate, and Other Collective Feelings." *GLQ* 24.4 (2018): 489–508.

Stanley, Eric A., and Nat Smith (eds.). *Captive Genders: Trans Embodiment and the Prison Industrial Complex.* Baltimore: AK Press, 2015.

"Statement of the Male Homosexual Workshop" (1970), in *We Are Everywhere: A Historical Sourcebook of Gay and Lesbian Politics.* Ed. Mark Blasius and Shane Phelan. New York: Routledge, 1997. 402–403.

Stavig, Ward. "Political 'Abominations' and Private Reservation: The Nefarious Sin, Homosexuality, and Cultural Values in Colonial Peru," in *Infamous Desire: Male Homosexuality in Colonial Latin America.* Ed. Pete Sigal. Chicago: University of Chicago Press, 2003. 134–151.

Stein, Arlene. *Sex and Sensibility: Stories of a Lesbian Generation.* Berkeley: University of California Press, 1997.

Steinbock, Eliza. *Shimmering Images: Trans Cinema, Embodiment, and the Aesthetics of Change.* Durham: Duke University Press, 2019.

Stelder, Mikki. "Other Scenes of Speaking: Listening to Palestinian Anticolonial-Queer Critique." *Journal of Palestinian Studies* 47.3 (2018): 45–61.

Stokes, Mason. *The Color of Sex: Whiteness, Heterosexuality, and the Fictions of White Supremacy.* Durham: Duke University Press, 2001.

Stoler, Ann Laura. *Race and the Education of Desire: Foucault's History of Sexuality and the Colonial Order of Things.* Durham: Duke University Press, 1995.

Stoller, Nancy E. *Lessons from the Damned: Queers, Whores, and Junkies Respond to AIDS.* New York: Routledge, 1998.

Stone, Sandy. "The *Empire* Strikes Back: A Posttranssexual Manifesto." *Camera Obscura* 10.2 (1992): 150–176.

Storr, Mel. "Transformations: Subjects, Categories, and Cures in Krafft-Ebbing's Sexology," in *Sexology in Culture: Labelling Bodies and Desires*. Ed. Lucy Bland and Laura Doan. Chicago: University of Chicago Press, 1998. 11–26.

Strub, Whitney. "Trans Porn Genealogy beyond the Queer Canon: Kim Christy, Joey Silvera, and the Hetero-Industrial Production of Transsexuality." *TSQ* 7.2 (2020): 174–191.

Stryker, Susan. "(De)Subjugated Knowledges: An Introduction to Transgender Studies," in *The Transgender Studies Reader*. Ed. Susan Stryker and Stephen Whittle. New York: Taylor & Francis, 2006. 1–17.

"My Words to Victor Frankenstein above the Village of Chamounix: Performing Transgender Rage." *GLQ* 1.3 (1994): 237–254.

Transgender History: The Roots of Today's Revolution. Rev. ed. New York: Seal Press, 2017.

Stryker, Susan, and Aren Z. Aizura. "Introduction: Transgender Studies 2.0," in *The Transgender Studies Reader 2*. Ed. Susan Stryker and Aren Z. Aizura. New York: Routledge, 2013. 1–12.

Stryker, Susan, and Paisley Currah. "Introduction." *TSQ* 1.1–2 (2014): 1–18.

Stryker, Susan, Paisley Currah, and Lisa Jean Moore. "Introduction: Trans-, Trans, or Transgender?" *WSQ* 36.3–4 (2008): 11–22.

Sueyoshi, Amy. *Discriminating Sex: White Leisure and the Making of the American "Oriental."* Champaign: University of Illinois Press, 2018.

Sullivan, Nikki. *A Critical Introduction to Queer Theory*. New York: New York University Press, 2003.

Takagi, Dana Y. "Maiden Voyage: Excursion into Sexuality and Identity Politics in Asian America." *Amerasia Journal* 20.1 (1994): 1–17.

TallBear, Kim. "Making Love and Relations beyond Settler Sex and Family," in *Making Kin Not Population*. Ed. Adele E. Clarke and Donna Haraway. Chicago: Prickly Paradigm Press, 2018. 145–166.

Tallie, T. J. *Queering Colonial Natal: Indigeneity and the Violence of Belonging in Southern Africa*. Minneapolis: University of Minnesota Press, 2019.

Tamale, Sylvia. *Decolonization and Afro-Feminism*. Quebec: Daraja Press, 2020.

"Researching and Theorising Sexualities in Africa," in *African Sexualities: A Reader*. Ed. Sylvia Tamale. Dakar: Pambazuka Press, 2011. 11–36.

Tan, Jin. "Beijing Meets Hawai'i: Reflections on *Ku'er*, Indigeneity, and Queer Theory." *GLQ* 23.1 (2017): 137–150.

Tatonetti, Lisa. *The Queerness of Native American Literature*. Minneapolis: University of Minnesota Press, 2014.

Written by the Body: Gender Expansiveness and Indigenous Non-Cis Masculinities. Minneapolis: University of Minnesota Press, 2021.

Taylor, Keeanga-Yamahtta (ed.). *How We Get Free: Black Feminism and the Combahee River Collective*. Chicago: Haymarket Books, 2017.

Taylor, Liza. *Feminism in Coalition: Thinking with US Women of Color Feminism*. Durham: Duke University Press, 2022.

Taylor, Verta, and Leila J. Rupp. "Women's Culture and Lesbian Feminist Activism: A Reconsideration of Cultural Feminism." *Signs* 19.1 (1993): 32–61.

Third World Gay Revolution. "The Oppressed Shall Not Become the Oppressor," in *We Are Everywhere: A Historical Sourcebook of Gay and Lesbian Politics*. Ed. Mark Blasius and Shane Phelan. New York: Routledge, 1997. 400–401.

"What We Want, What We Believe" (1971), in *Out of the Closets: Voices of Gay Liberation, Twentieth-Anniversary Edition*. Ed. Karla Jay and Allen Young. New York: New York University Press, 1992. 363–367.

Thomann, Matthew, and Ashley Currier. "Sex and Money in West Africa: The 'Money' Problem in West African Sexual Diversity Politics," in *Routledge Handbook of Queer African Studies*. Ed. S. N. Nyeck. New York: Routledge, 2019. 200–212.

Thomas, Greg. *The Sexual Demon of Colonial Power: Pan-African Embodiment and Erotic Schemes of Empire*. Bloomington: Indiana University Press, 2007.

Thompson, Becky. "Multiracial Feminism: Recasting the Chronology of Second Wave Feminism." *Feminist Studies* 28.2 (2002): 337–360.

Tinsley, Omise`eke Natasha. *Ezili's Mirrors: Imagining Black Queer Genders*. Durham: Duke University Press, 2018.

Tompkins, Kyla Wazana. "Intersections of Race, Gender, and Sexuality: Queer of Color Critique," in *The Cambridge Companion to American Gay and Lesbian Literature*. Ed. Scott Herring. New York: Cambridge University Press, 2015. 173–189.

Racial Indigestion: Eating Bodies in the Nineteenth Century. New York: New York University Press, 2012.

Tompkins, Kyla Wazana, Aren Z. Aizura, Aimee Bahng, Karma R. Chávez, Mishuana Goeman, and Amber Jamilla Musser (eds.). *Keywords for Gender and Sexuality Studies*. New York: New York University Press, 2021.

Tongson, Karen. *Relocations: Queer Suburban Imaginaries*. New York: New York University Press, 2011.

Tortorici, Zeb. *Sins against Nature: Sex and Archives in Colonial New Spain*. Durham: Duke University Press, 2018.

Towle, Evan B., and Lynn M. Morgan. "Romancing the Transgender Native: Rethinking the Use of the 'Third Gender' Concept." *GLQ* 8.4 (2002): 469–497.

Traub, Valerie. "The Renaissance of Lesbianism in Early Modern England." *GLQ* 7.2 (2001): 245–263.

Thinking Sex with the Early Moderns. Philadelphia: University of Pennsylvania Press, 2016.

Treichler, Paula A. *How to Have Theory in an Epidemic: Cultural Chronicles of AIDS*. Durham: Duke University Press, 1999.

Trujillo, Carla. "La Virgen de Guadalupe and Her Reconstruction in Chicana Lesbian Desire," in *Living Chicana Theory*. Ed. Carla Trujillo. Berkeley, CA: Third Woman Press, 1998. 214–231.

Upchurch, Charles. *Before Wilde: Sex between Men in Britain's Age of Reform*. Berkeley: University of California Press, 2009.

Valencia, Sayak. "Necropolitics, Postmortem/Transmortem Politics, and Transfeminisms in the Sexual Economies of Death." Trans. Olga Arnaiz Zhuavleva. *TSQ* 6.2 (2019): 180–193.

Valentine, David. *Imagining Transgender: An Ethnography of a Category*. Durham: Duke University Press, 2007.

Valentine, Gill. "Making Space: Lesbian Separatist Communities in the United States," in *Contested Countryside Cultures: Otherness, Marginality, and Rurality*. Ed. Paul Cloke and Jo Little. New York: Routledge, 1997. 109–122.

Valk, Anne M. "Living a Feminist Lifestyle: The Intersection of Theory and Action in a Lesbian Feminist Collective." *Feminist Studies* 28.2 (2002): 303–332.

Vargas, Deborah R. "Ruminations on *Lo Sucio* as a Latino Queer Analytic." *American Quarterly* 66.3 (2014): 715–726.

Vernon, Irene S. *Native Americans and HIV/AIDS*. Lincoln: University of Nebraska Press, 2001.

Wagner, Sydness. "Racing Gender to the Edge of the World: Decoding the Transmasculine Amazon Cannibal in Early Modern Travel Writing." *Journal for Early Modern Cultural Studies* 19.4 (2019): 137–155.

Wahl, Elizabeth Susan. *Invisible Relations: Representations of Female Intimacy in the Age of Enlightenment*. Stanford, CA: Stanford University Press, 1999.

Walcott, Rinaldo. *Queer Returns: Essays on Multiculturalism, Diaspora, and Black Studies*. Ontario: Insomniac Press, 2016.

Warner, Michael. "Introduction," in *Fear of a Queer Planet: Queer Politics and Social Theory*. Ed. Michael Warner. Minneapolis: University of Minnesota Press, 1993. vii–xxxi.

"New English Sodom." *American Literature* 64.1 (1992): 19–47.

The Trouble with Normal: Sex, Politics, and the Ethics of Queer Life. New York: The Free Press, 1999.

Wat, Eric C. *Love Your Asian Body: AIDS Activism in Los Angeles*. Seattle: University of Washington Press, 2021.

Waters, Chris. "Havelock Ellis, Sigmund Freud and the State: Discourses of Homosexual Identity in Interwar Britain," in *Sexology in Culture: Labelling Bodies and Desires*. Ed. Lucy Bland and Laura Doan. Chicago: University of Chicago Press, 1998. 165–179.

Watney, Simon. *Practices of Freedom: Selected Writings on HIV/AIDS*. Durham: Duke University Press, 1994.

Wayar, Marlene. "Latin American *Travesti*/Trans Theory" (trans. Rocio Picon-Rivière), in *Trans Philosophy*. Ed. Perry Zurn, Andrea J. Pitts, Talia Mae Bettch, and P. J. DiPietro. Minneapolis: University of Minnesota Press, 2024. 254–278.

Weheliye, Alexander G. *Habeas Viscus: Racializing Assemblages, Biopolitics, and Black Feminist Theories of the Human.* Durham: Duke University Press, 2014.

Weiss, Margot. *Techniques of Pleasure: BDSM and the Circuits of Sexuality.* Durham: Duke University Press, 2011.

Wekker, Gloria. *The Politics of Passion: Women's Sexual Culture in the Afro-Surinamese Diaspora.* New York: Columbia University Press, 2006.

Wesley, Saylesh. "Twin-Spirited Woman: Sts'iyóye semstíyexw slhá:li." *TSQ* 1.3 (2014): 338–351.

West, Isaac. *Transforming Citizenships: Transgender Articulations of the Law.* New York: New York University Press, 2014.

Weston, Kath. "Lesbian/Gay Studies in the House of Anthropology." *Annual Review of Anthropology* 22 (1993): 339–367.

——— *Long Slow Burn: Sexuality and Social Science.* New York: Routledge, 1998.

Whitehead, Joshua. "Introduction," in *Love after the End: An Anthology of Two-Spirit and Indigiqueer Speculative Fiction.* Ed. Joshua Whitehead. Vancouver: Arsenal Pulp Press, 2020.

Wiegman, Robyn, and Elizabeth A. Wilson. "Introduction: Antinormativity's Queer Conventions." *differences* 26.1 (2015): 1–25.

Wilchins, Riki Anne. *Read My Lips: Sexual Subversion and the End of Gender.* Milford, CT: Firebrand Books, 1997.

Wilkerson, Abby L. "Normate Sex and Its Discontents," in *Sex and Disability.* Ed. Robert McRuer and Anna Mollow. Durham: Duke University Press, 2012. 183–207.

Wilkins, David E., and Heidi Kiiwetinepinesiik Stark. *American Indian Politics and the American Political System.* New York: Rowman & Littlefield Publishers, 2017.

Willey, Angela. *Undoing Monogamy: The Politics of Science and the Possibilities of Biology.* Durham: Duke University Press, 2016.

Williams, Cristan. "Radical Inclusion: Recounting the Trans Inclusive History of Radical Feminism." *TSQ* 3.1–2 (2016): 254–258.

Wilson, Ara. *The Intimate Economies of Bangkok: Tomboys, Tycoons, and Avon Ladies in the Global City.* Berkeley: University of California Press, 2004.

Wittman, Carl. "A Gay Manifesto" (1969), in *Out of the Closets: Voices of Gay Liberation, Twentieth-Anniversary Edition.* Ed. Karla Jay and Allen Young. New York: New York University Press, 1992. 330–342.

Womack, Craig. "Suspicioning: Imaging a Debate between Those Who Get Confused, and Those Who Don't, When They Read Critical Responses to the Poems of Joy Harjo, or What's an Old-Timey Gay Boy Like Me to Do?" *GLQ* 16.1–2 (2010): 133–155.

Womack, Craig S. *Art as Performance, Story as Criticism: Reflections on Native Literary Aesthetics.* Norman: University of Oklahoma Press, 2009.

——— *Red on Red: Native American Literary Separatism.* Minneapolis: University of Minnesota Press, 1999.

Wong, Alvin K. "Queer Vernacularism: Minor Transnationalism across Hong Kong and Singapore." *Cultural Dynamics* 12.1–2 (2020): 49–67.
Wong, Edlie L. *Racial Reconstruction: Black Inclusion, Chinese Exclusion, and the Fictions of Citizenship.* New York: New York University Press, 2015.
Woo, Merle. "Letter to Ma," in *This Bridge Called My Back: Writings by Radical Women of Color* (1981). Ed. Cherríe L. Moraga and Gloria E. Anzaldúa. Berkeley, CA: Third Woman Press, 2002. 154–163.
    "Stonewall Was a Riot – Now We Need a Revolution," in *Smash the Church, Smash the State!: The Early Years of Gay Liberation.* Ed. Tommi Avicolli Mecca. San Francisco: City Lights Books, 2009. 282–294.
Woubshet, Dagmawai. *The Calendar of Loss: Race, Sexuality and Mourning in the Early Era of AIDS.* Baltimore: Johns Hopkins University Press, 2015.
Wu, Cynthia. *Sticky Rice: A Politics of Intraracial Desire.* Philadelphia: Temple University Press, 2018.
Yarbro-Bejarano, Yvonne. *The Wounded Heart: Writing on Cherríe Moraga.* Austin: University of Texas Press, 2001.
Yergeau, Melanie. *Authoring Autism: On Rhetoric and Neurological Queerness.* Durham: Duke University Press, 2018.
Yingling, Thomas. "AIDS in America: Postmodern Governance, Identity, and Experience," in *Inside/Out: Lesbian Theories, Gay Theories.* Ed. Diana Fuss. New York: Routledge, 1991. 291–310.
Young, Allen. "Out of the Closets, into the Streets" (1971), in *Out of the Closets: Voices of Gay Liberation, Twentieth-Anniversary Edition.* Ed. Karla Jay and Allen Young. New York: New York University Press, 1992. 6–31.
Young, Cynthia A. *Soul Power: Culture, Radicalism, and the Making of a U.S. Third World Left.* Durham: Duke University Press, 2006.
Yue, Audrey. "Trans-Singapore: Some Notes toward Queer Asia as Method." *Inter-Asia Cultural Studies* 18.1 (2017): 10–24.
Zazanis, Noah. "Social Reproduction and Social Cognition: Theorizing (Trans)gender Identity Development in Community Context," in *Transgender Marxism.* Ed. Jules Joanne Gleeson and Elle O'Rourke. London: Pluto Press, 2021. 33–46.
Ze'evi. Dror. *Producing Desire: Changing Sexual Discourse in the Ottoman Middle East, 1500–1900.* Berkeley: University of California Press, 2006.

Index

Abdur-Rahman, Aliyyah I., 146
Abelove, Henry, 115
Aberrations in Black (Ferguson), 136
ablebodiedness, 47
ablenormativity, 47
ACT UP – the AIDS Coalition to Unleash Power, 85
Adeyemi, Kemi, 153
affective commons, queer identity and, 46
Africa
  Black diaspora and, 147
  customary law and queer culture in, 202
  film depictions of queerness in, 200
  queer and trans policies in, 176
Afri-queer fugitivity, 200
agency, Butler's discussion of, 23
Aguilar-San Juan, Karin, 165
Ahmed, Sara, 28, 41, 71, 218
Ahuja, Neel, 52
AIDS (Acquired Immunodeficiency Syndrome) epidemic
  criminalization processes in response to, 88
  history of, 81
  impact of loss from, 89
  queer paradigm concerning, 83
  racialized response to, 86
  terminology of, 222
Alexander, M. Jacqui, 174
Allen, Jafari S., 91, 148
Allen, Paula Gunn, 77, 139
Alvarez, Jr., Eddy Francisco, 161

amalgamation, racism and, 105
Amar, Paul, 197
American Psychiatric Association (APA), transgender activism and, 95
Americans with Disabilities Act (ADA), trans healthcare omitted from, 50
Amin, Kadji, 128, 231
analytics, in queer and trans studies, 108
androgyne, terminology of, 112
animacy hierarchy, 51
anti-Asian sentiment and policy, 161
antinormativity, in queer and trans studies, 13
Anzaldúa, Gloria, 75, 79, 158
Applied Behavioral Analysis (ABA), 49
'aqi (Chumash gender identity), 141
Arab and Muslim populations
  queer and trans culture in, 177
  transnational formation of, 201
Araujo, Gwen Amber Rose, 161
Arondeker, Anjali, 103, 172
Asian American studies, 161, 238
Asians
  colonial racialization of, 107
  global capitalism's impact on, 180
  queer vernacularism in, 198
AsiaPacifiQueer, 180
Asiatic Barred Zone, 162
Atshan, Sa'ed, 177, 179
autism, neuroqueerness and, 48
autoeroticism, 38

Awkward-Rich, Cameron, 50
ayakwao/ayekkwe, 141
Aztlán, Chicanx idea of, 159

Bailey, Marlon M., 151
bakla (Philippines), 33, 169, 193
Ballroom culture, 151
Baril, Alexandre, 50
Barker, Joanne, 138
  Barnard Conference, *see also* "The Scholar and the Feminist IX: Towards a Politics of Sexuality"
bathroom bills, emergence of, 210
BDSM
  Black women's participation in, 69
  class and race and, 217
  lesbian feminism and, 62, 67
Beam, Joseph, 91
Beauvoir, Simone de, 22
Belcourt, Billy-Ray, 143
Benedicto, Bobby, 180
Benjamin, Harry, 8
Berkowitz, Richard, 90
Berlant, Lauren, 11
Best, Stephen, 147
Bey, Marquis, 149
Bhanji, Nael, 31
binaohan, b., 33
binary, trans studies critique of, 29
biopolitics/biopower, sexuality and, 100
Black church, sex and gender roles and, 149
Black feminism, intersectionality and, 220
Black femmes, 150
Black identity
  citizenship and, 233
  criminalization of, 106
  deviancy linked to, 106, 145
  slavery's erasure of, 104, 134
  temporality and, 133
  transsexuality and, 130
Black kink, 152
Black nationalism, anti-queer discourse in, 151

Black Panthers' Revolutionary People's Constitutional Convention, 60
Black queer culture
  AIDS epidemic and, 86, 90
  Black disavowal of, 235
  homophobia and, 77
  queer theory and, 45
Black sissiness, 149
Black Studies
  Black realness in, 151
  queer and trans scholarship in, 148
  sexuality and gender in, 145
Black women, *see also* women of color feminism: evolution of
  BDSM and, 69
  Black Studies and role of, 145
  incarceration of, 106
  Indigenous queer and trans studies in relation to, 144
  lesbian feminism and, 66
  in queer studies, 80
  South African queer and trans culture and, 186
  in Suriname, sexuality and identity of, 182
Blackwell, Maylei, 80
Blackwood, Evelyn, 189
Boag, Peter, 118
Bodies That Matter (Butler), 22
body, *see also* embodiment
  in Black Studies, 148
  in disability studies, 47
  gender and, 22
  trans experience and, 27, 128
Boellstorff, Tom, 185
Bollywood film industry, 169
Bornstein, Kate, 1, 92, 95
Bost, Darius, 90
"Boston marriages", 117
bottomhood, in Asian American studies, 165
Boys Don't Cry (film), 95
Brady, Mary Pat, 156
Brant, Beth, 76, 139

Brazil, queer and trans culture and politics in, 180, 187, 192, 197
Brown, Rita Mae, 216
brownness, Latinx concept of, 160
Brownworth, Victoria, 65
Bunch, Charlotte, 64
Burns, Randy, 62
butch/femme identities, 66, 217
Butler, Judith, 1
    foundations of queer and trans studies and, 19
    on gender and sexuality, 20, 50, 52
    on humanness, 47
    influences in work of, 208
    trans experience and power for, 27
Bychowski, M. W., 120
Byrd, Jodi, 144

Califia, Patrick, 96
Callen, Michael, 90
Cambodian Americans, 164
Cameron, Barbara, 62
Camp Trans, 95
Cantú, Lionel, 155
capitalist expansion and intervention
    Asian countries and impact of, 180
    queer and trans studies and, 171, 173, 196
    queer diaspora and, 201
cárdenas, micha, 158
Caribbean culture
    Asian influence in, 238
    Black Studies and, 150
    Latinx studies and, 154
    postcolonial queer and trans politics in, 174
Carillo, Héctor, 184
Carter, Julian, 126
Cartwright, Ryan Lee, 48
Cauldwell, David O., 127
Chauncey, George, 173
Chen, Jian Neo, 33, 137
Chen, Mel, 51
Chiang, Howard, 202
Chicana feminism, 80

Chicanx queer and trans studies, 159
China, queer and trans culture in, 185, 190, 195
Chinese Americans, history of, 162
Chinese Exclusion Act (1882), 162
Christopher Street Liberation Day Parade (1973), 60
chrononormativity, 131
cis time, 130, 134
cisnormativity
    defined, 2
    in queer and trans studies, 12
cissexual privilege, 29
citizenship
    in Asian American studies, 161
    Chinese cultural citizenship articulation, 195
    in Latinx studies, 160
    racialization of, 107, 233
    undocuqueer movement and, 156
Clare, Eli, 44, 47
Clarke, Cheryl, 77
class dynamics
    AIDS epidemic and, 83
    Black Studies and, 147
    Filipino gay culture and, 180
    Foucault on sexuality and, 100
    Gay Liberation Movement and, 58
    hijra community and, 188
    imperialism and, 102
    in histories of sexuality and gender identity, 100
    Latinx studies and, 160
    lesbian feminism and, 67, 216
    Muslim cultures and, 178
    normativity in framework of, 111
    queer and trans status and, 121
    sexology and, 124
    transgender activism and, 93
    women of color feminism and, 72
Cleves, Rachel Hope, 109, 114
closet thinking
    minoritization and, 40
    whiteness and, 42

coalition-building, women of color feminism and, 77
Cohen, Cathy, 2, 86, 145
Cohen, Ed, 125
colonialism, *see also* imperialism
   AIDS epidemic and re-emergence of, 82, 87
   in Black Studies, 147
   criminalization of sexuality and, 197
   gender and sexual deviancy and, 102
   in Native American and Indigenous studies, 137
   in queer and trans studies, 174, 204
   race and empire and, 101
   Southeast Asian gender concepts and influence of, 190
   women and, 237
colonialnormativity, 164
Combahee River Collective, 73, 219
Comella, Lynn, 70
coming out, history of, 57
Compton's Cafeteria Riot (1966), 56
compulsory heterosexuality, 65
Compulsory Medical Plan (Argentina), 192
Cooper Do-Nuts protest (1959), 56
Cornum, Lou, 132
Cornwell, Anita, 66
Cortés, Hernán, 103
Coviello, Peter, 116
criminalization of sexual activity and gender identity
   AIDS epidemic and, 88
   Black identity and, 106
   decriminalization policies as pushback against, 197
   homoeroticism linked to, 126
   third-world queer and trans cultures and, 215
Crimp, Douglas, 89
Cruz, Ariane, 69
Cumming, Jane, 117
customary law, African queer culture and, 203
Cvetkovich, Ann, 45

Daughters of Bilitis, 56
de Lauretis, Theresa, 1, 6
De Mauro Rucovsky, Martin, 192
Decena, Carlos Ulises, 157
Declue, Jennifer, 152
decolonial imaginary, in Latinx queer and trans studies, 158
decolonizing trans/gender 101 (binaohan), 33
degeneration, colonial concepts of, 125
Denetdale, Jennifer, 138, 140
deviancy
   Asian immigrants linked to, 164
   Blackness linked to, 106, 145
   imperialism and, 102
   sociological studies of, 213
diaspora
   in Asian American studies, 168
   in Black Studies, 147
   gender identity and, in Latinx queer and trans studies, 31, 157
   queer diaspora, 200
difference, women of color feminism and role of, 75
DiGangi, Mario, 110
Dillon, Stephen, 146
Dinshaw, Carolyn, 108, 120, 131
disability studies
   gender and sexuality in, 48
   medical model in, 47
   queer and trans scholarship and, 47
Dixon, Melvin, 91
down-low concept, AIDS epidemic and, 86
drag
   Butler's discussion of, 24
   in ballroom culture, 149
Duberman, Martin, 56
Duggan, Lisa, 12, 124
Dutta, Aniruddha, 171, 179

Edelman, Lee, 232
Elbe, Lili, 231
Elliott, Beth, 71, 218
Ellis, Havelock, 124

Ellis, Nadia, 148
Ellison, Treva, 146
embodiment
  in disability studies, 49
  historical understandings of, 111, 114
  Indigenous concepts of, 141
  in trans studies, 27
empire of critique, 179
Employment Nondiscrimination Act, 95
Eng, David, 162, 164
Enke, Finn, 70
environment, sexuality and influence of, 115
Epistemology of the Closet (Sedgwick), 1, 34
eroticism
  in Black Studies, 152
  historical understandings of, 111, 115–116
  inversion and, 122
erotohistoriography, 132
Esquiel, Catrióna Rueda, 159
eugenics
  deviancy in theories of, 126
  sexuality and, 48
Ezili (Caribbean spirit figure), 150

family
  AIDS epidemic and discourse of, 82
  in Asian American studies, 163
  in Black Studies, 148, 152
  Chicanx la familia concept of, 159
  imperialism and image of, 102
  Native and Indigenous studies and framework of, 139
  Sedgwick on identity and, 38
Fawaz, Ramzi, 54
Feinberg, Leslie, 1, 94, 96
female husband, 117
female masculinity, 119, 229
femininity
  in Asian American studies, 166
  in Black Studies, 150
  Venezuelan concepts of, 187

"femininism", feminism, 67, *see also* women of color feminism, *see also* lesbian feminism
  Black women and, 66
  intersectionality in, 220
  legacy of, 97
  media images and normalization of, 199
  sexism and, 63
  whiteness and, 66
feminotopia literary genre, 116
Ferguson, Roderick, 55, 136, 145
Fielding, Henry, 117
Fiereck, Kirk, 203
Filipinos, history in US of, 163
Fiol-Matta, Licia, 198
Fisher, Will, 124
flesh, in Black Studies, 148
Foote, Stephanie, 123
Foucault, Michel, 10, 35, 39, 99
Frazier, Demita, 73
Freccero, Carla, 131
Freeman, Elizabeth, 131
Fung, Richard, 165
funk, Black sexuality and gender and, 151

Galarte, Francisco J. H., 161
Galen, 114
Gaspar de Alba, Alicia, 159
Gay Activists Alliance (GAA), 60, 214
Gay American Indians (GAI), 62
Gay International, 177
gay liberation
  legacy of, 97
  origins of, 55
  pushback against, 60
  racism and, 61
Gay Liberation Front (GLF)
  evolution of, 56, 214
  lesbian feminism and, 63
Gay Shame organization, 46
gay terminology, evolution of, 58
Gay Women's Liberation, 63

Geary, Adam, 83
gender
  AIDS epidemic and, 83
  in Asian American studies, 162
  in Black Studies, 145
  disability and, 48
  evolution linked to, 126, 129
  gay liberation separation from, 60
  historical understanding of, 116
  in nature, 114
  international dynamics in identity and expression of, 179
  inversion and, 122
  Islamic countries' policies concerning, 194
  nonwestern gender identity concepts and, 186
  philology of, 109
  queer and trans of color studies and, 137
  queer theory and, 4
  sexuality and, 20
  slavery's impact on, 104
  Southeast Asian concepts of, 189
  trans studies and, 7, 28
gender-affirming care, *see also* medical
Gender Identity Law (Argentina), 192
Gender Trouble (Butler), 20, 24
Gill-Peterson, Jules, 129
GLF Women, 215
glocalqueering, 169
Goldberg, Jonathan, 103, 111
Gopinath, Gayatri, 168, 201
Gosine, Andil, 175
Gossett, Che, 55
Gould, Janice, 144
Grahn, Judy, 65
Gramling, David, 171
Green, Marshall, 145
Green-Simms, Lindsey B., 200
GRID (gay-related immune deficiency), 81
Grover, Jan Zita, 81

HAART (highly active antiretroviral therapies), 87
Halberstam, Jack, 44, 119, 122, 130
Hale, C. Jacob, 121
Haley, Sarah, 106
Hall, Lisa Kahaleole, 77
Hall, Radclyffe, 67, 124
Hammonds, Evelyn, 87, 145
Haritaworn, Jin, 32, 43
Harrington, J. P., 141
Hart, Lynda, 69
Hartman, Saidiya, 107
Hawai'i, 140, 142
Hayes, Jarrod, 202
Hayward, Eva, 52
Heaney, Emma, 121, 123, 128
Hemmings, Clare, 54
Hemphill, Essex, 91
Henry, Todd A., 185
Herring, Scott, 44
heteronormativity
  AIDS epidemic and, 81
  evolution linked to, 51
  Native and Indigenous Studies in framework of, 139
heterosexuality
  Butler's discussion of, 21
  compulsory heterosexuality, 65
  normative historical framing of, 113
  terminology of, 230
  women's liberation and, 63
hijra (India), 32, 187, 203
historiography
  eroticism and embodiment and, 113–114, 134
  of gender and sexuality terminology, 109
Hitchcock, Tim, 115, 120
HIV (human immunodeficiency virus)
  gender differences in infection from, 83
  origins of, 81
Ho, Josephine, 178
Hoad, Neville, 176, 203

Holland, Sharon, 80, 152
Hollibaugh, Amber, 68
Hom, Alice, 73, 162
homoeroticism
  historical figures linked to, 124
  press coverage of, 124
  terminology of, 119, 229
homonationalism, 13
homonormativity, 12
homosexuality
  Butler's definition of, 22
  Sedgwick on models of, 36
  terminology of, 122
Hong, Grace Kyungwon, 75, 136
Howe, Cymene, 191
Howe, James, 118
Huang, Vivian L., 166
human rights, queer and trans policies and, 178
humanness
  nonhumans and evolutionary theory and, 51
  queer scholarship and, 47
human-security governance ideology, queer and trans policies and politics and, 197
Hurley, Natasha, 125

identity
  Indigenous concepts of, 141
  in queer and trans studies, 2, 6, 10
  women of color feminism and, 73, 97
immigration
  Asian American studies and, 161
  gender and sexuality and, 108, 161
  gender identity and, 31
  Latinx queer and trans studies and, 155
  of Filipinos, 164
  whiteness policies and, 226
Immigration Act of 1924, 162
imperialism, *see also* colonialism
  in Philippines, 163
  Latinx queer and trans studies and, 156

queer and trans studies and, 16, 173, 204
India
  caste system and trans identity in, 192
  hijra culture in, 31, 187
Indian Women's Movement, 191
Indigenous sexual and gender diversity
  AIDS epidemic and, 87
  in Chicanx scholarship, 159
  colonialist framing of, 103, 141
  gay liberation and, 62
  inversion discourse and, 127
  Native lesbian writing and, 144
  queer and trans of color scholarship and, 137
  temporality in research on, 132
  Two-Spirit framework for, 142
  Western frameworks for, 121
  white appropriation of, 43
  women of color feminism and, 76
Indonesia, queer and trans culture in, 185, 189, 194
international aid, queer and trans policies and, 178
intersectionality, Black feminism and, 220
intersex
  Indigenous cultures and, 141
  terminology of, 111, 119
interzones, nonwhiteness and criminality and, 107
inversion, 122
Iran, gender and identity policies in, 195
Irigaray, Luce, 216
Islamophobia
  deviancy linked to, 103, 167
  queer and trans politics and, 194
  sodomy linked in, 111, 116
Israel, queer and trans politics in, 177

Jagose, Annamarie, 9
Japanese Americans, 161
Jay, Karla, 58

Johnson, Patrick, 145
Jolivette, Andrew, 87
Jorgensen, Christine, 129
Julien, Isaac, 91
Justice, Daniel Heath, 141

Kahan, Benjamin, 123
Kapadia, Ronak K., 167
Kauanui, J. Kēhaulani, 140
Keeling, Kara, 150
Kempadoo, Kamala, 175
King, Katie, 172
kinlessness, Spillers's concept of, 148
kinship structures, in Native and Indigenous studies, 139, 141
Korea, queer and trans culture in, 185
Korean Americans, 161, 164, 168
Koyama, Emi, 2
Krafft-Ebing, Richard von, 123–124
Kramer, Larry, 90

La Fountain-Stokes, Lawrence, 157
Ladies of Llangollen, 117
LaFleur, Greta, 109, 115
Laing, Marie, 139, 143
Lanser, Susan, 113
Lansing, Susan, 119–120
Laporte, Rita, 66, 217
Laqueur, Thomas, 114
Laramee, Myra, 142
Larson, Scott, 121
late-carbon capitalism, 52
Latin America, regional queer and trans networks in, 203
Latina feminism, 158
latinidad, 160
Latinx queer and trans studies, 154, 236
Latrónico, Néstor, 61
Lau, Jacob, 130, 133
Lebanon, queer community in, 183
Lee, JeeYeun, 168
lesbian continuum, 65
lesbian feminism
   Black studies and, 146
   evolution of, 62, 215–216
   legacy of, 97
   media images and normalization of, 199
Lesbian Herstory Archives, 66, 72
lesbian potentiality, 62
lesbian terminology, 63
   historiography and, 118, 228
LGBT history, Blackness and, 146
Librado, Kitsepawit Fernando, 141
Lim, Eng-Beng, 169
Liu, Peter, 190
local, role in queer and trans studies of, 172
Lochrie, Karma, 113
Lorde, Audre, 75, 146
Lothian, Alexis, 133
Love, Heather, 46
Luciano, Dana, 51
Lugones, María, 79
Luibhéid, Eithne, 108

Macharia, Keguro, 147
Maghreb, sexuality and gender in, 202
Malatino, Hil, 46
Malintzin, 237
Manalansan, Martin F., 164, 169
Mandujano, Verónica, 155
Manion, Jen, 118–119
March on Washington for Lesbian, Gay, and Bisexual Equal Rights (1993), 95
Marcos, Ferdinand, 164
Marlowe, Christopher, 124
marriage
   in Asian American studies, 163
   colonial and imperial management of, 104
   for Indigenous peoples, 140
   racial boundaries in laws on, 107
Martin, Fran, 199
Marxism, queer and trans studies and, 190, 242
masculinity
   in Asian American studies, 165

masculinity (cont.)
  in Black Studies, 149
  in queer and trans studies, 119
Massad, Joseph, 177
Masten, Jeffrey, 109
masturbation, 38
Mattachine Society, 56
Mbasalaki, Phoebe Kisubi, 186
McBride, Dwight, 152
McClintock, Anne, 102, 131
McRuer, Robert, 48
media images, normativity promotion through, 199
medical research, *see also* gender-affirming care
medical systems and research
  inversion and, 122
  on homosexuality, 124
  queer and trans politics and, 179, 192
  slave experiments in, 105
melancholy historicism, Black Studies and, 147
Mendoza, Victor Román, 164
mestiza consciousness, 79
metaphysics of substance, 22
metronormativity, 44
Mexican–American War (1846–1848), 156
Mexico
  in Chicanx queer and trans studies, 159
  queer and trans culture in, 184, 240
Michelangelo, 124
Michigan Womyn's Music Festival, 3, 71, 95
minoritization
  disidentification and, 41
  of sexual identity, 36, 40
Minter, Shannon Price, 60
Miranda, Deborah, 139, 141
miscegenation, 105
Mistral, Gabriela, 198
Mitchell, Alice, 124
mo'olelo (Hawaiian story/chant), 142

model minority, in Asian American studies, 164
mollies and molly houses, defined, 120
Mollow, Anna, 48
Money, John, 129
Moraga, Cherríe, 74, 136
Morbidity and Mortality Weekly Report, 80
Morgan, Lynn Marie, 32
Morgan, Robin, 71
Moussawi, Gloria, 183
Mumford, Kevin, 107
Muñoz, José Esteban, 41, 133, 148, 160
Mupotsa, Danai, 203
Muslim populations
  deviancy linked to, 103, 167
  Islamic theology, gender and sexuality and, 116
  queer and trans culture in, 177
  sodomy linked to, 111, 116
  transnational Arabness and, 201
Muslims, *see also* Islamophobia

Namibia, LGBT issues in, 192
Nash, Jennifer, 220
National Black Feminist Organization, 219
nationalism, queer and trans politics and, 198
Native American studies, *see* Indigenous sexual and gender diversity
nativism, in third-world queer and trans studies, 182
nature, gender and sexuality and, 114
Navajo Nation, US government transformation of, 140
Nealon, Christopher, 127
Negrón-Muntaner, Frances, 157
neoliberal Islam, 194
neoliberalism, 196
Nestle, Joan, 66, 217
neuroqueerness, 48
Nguyen, Lu Thuy, 168
Nguyen, Tan Hoang, 166

Nicaragua, gender and sexuality activism in, 191, 242
nongovernmental organizations (NGOs), queer and trans politics and, 191
nonhumans, 51
non-urban space, 44
normativity
　in disability studies, 49
　Foucault on sexuality and, 100
　human health and well-being linked to, 126
　media promotion of queer and trans identity and, 199
　queer and trans people of color and, 136
　queer and trans politics and, 198
　in queer and trans studies, 11, 120
　racial and imperial dynamics of, 126, 134
　in sex research, 122
　social norms, 30
Nyong'o, Tavia, 105

O'Brien, Michelle, 31
O'Leary, Jean, 60
Ochoa, Marcia, 187
Ogborn, Anne, 95
oppositional consciousness, 78
Orientalism, 167
Osorio, Jamaica Heolimeleikalani, 142

Pacific Islands, gender nonconformity in, 242
Page Act (1875), 162
pain, queer theory and, 49
Pakistan, queer and trans culture in, 188, 203
Palestinians, 178
Paris Is Burning (film), 25
Parker, Pat, 66, 78
Patel, Geeta, 172
patriarchy
　Butler's critique of, 32
　colonialism and, 77
　feminists of color and, 66
　gender stereotypes and, 93
　hegemonic structure of, 20
　Indigenous family structure and, 139
　Indigenous resistance to, 143
　Latinx studies and, 154
　lesbian feminism and, 62
　normativity and, 112
Patton, Cindy, 81
Pérez, Emma, 158
Pérez, Hiram, 43
performativity
　Butler on body and, 23
　transgender and, 28
personal responsibility rhetoric, AIDS epidemic and, 88
Pezzuto, Sophie, 69
Philippines
　queer and trans culture in, 180, 193
　US occupation of, 163
philology of gender and sexuality, 109
pinkwashing, 177
polygamy
　colonial-imperial view of, 104
　in Native and Indigenous culture, 140
Ponce, Martin Joseph, 163
pornography
　Black lesbians and, 152
　lesbian feminism and, 67, 69, 217
pornotrope, Spillers's concept of, 148
postcolonialisn, queer and trans studies and, 174
Povinelli, Elizabeth, 173
power, 97
PrEP – preexposure prophylaxis, AIDS epidemic and, 87
primitiveness, eugenics and fear of, 126
prison sex, deviancy linked to, 126
property rights, racialization of, 107
Prosser, Jay, 28
Psychopathia Sexualis (Krafft-Ebing), 124

Puar, Jasbir, 50
public health, queer and trans politics and, 179
Puerto Ricans, Latinx queer and trans studies and, 156, 237
Pyle, Kai, 141, 143

queer
  as scholarly subject, 6
  Butler's discussion of, 25
  defined, 3
queer diaspora, 200
queer paradigm, AIDS epidemic and, 83
queer people of color
  scholarship on, 136
queer theory
  AIDS epidemic and, 89
  Asian American studies, 161
  Black Studies and, 145
  Black.female.queer in, 80
  de Lauretis on, 5
  disability studies and, 49
  evolution of, 1
  global dynamics in, 171
  history and, 14, 16, 134
  imperial and capitalist expansion/intervention and, 173
  Latinx studies in, 154
  origins of, 19
  power in, 9
  race, diaspora, and empire and, 14
  Sedgwick's contributions to, 37
  temporalities and, 130, 232
  terminology and norms in, 108, 118
  trans studies in relation to, 205
queer vernacularism, global cosmopolitanism and, 198, 243

race and racism, *see also* Black Studies, *see also* trans people of color, *see also* women of color feminism
  AIDS epidemic and, 83
  in Asian American studies, 162
  Asian identity and, 107
  Black Studies and, 145
  colonialism and, 101
  cross-racial relationships, deviancy linked to, 126
  disidentification and minoritization and, 41
  gay liberation and, 61
  gender and sexuality and, 105, 227
  in Latinx studies, 160
  lesbian feminism and, 66, 69
  queer and trans studies and, 16, 25, 152
  trans vulnerability and, 32
  women's romantic friendships and, 117
Radicalesbians, 63
Rao, Rahul, 192–193
Raymond, Janice, 93
Reagon, Bernice Johnson, 77
realness, Butler's discussion of, 26
Reddy, Chandan, 136
Reddy, Gayatri, 187
regional queer and trans networks, queer diaspora and, 202
Reid-Pharr, Robert, 151
representation, queer and trans studies and, 6
repressive hypothesis, Foucault on sexuality and, 39, 99
reproductive futurism, 232
respectability politics, Black Studies and, 145, 151
Rich, Adrienne, 65
Richardson, Matt, 147
Riggs, Marlon, 91
risk groups
  AIDS epidemic, 81
  four H's — homosexuals, heroin addicts (intravenous drug users), Haitians, and hemophiliacs classification, AIDS epidemic and, 81
Ritchie, Andrea, 33
Rivera, Sylvia, 60

Rivera-Servera, Rámon H., 160
Rizki, Cole, 154
Rodríguez, Juana María, 158
Rohy, Valerie, 132
Roscoe, Will, 127
Ross, Marlon B., 42, 149
Roy, Raina, 179
Rubin, Gayle, 67
Rubin, Henry, 28
Rubright, Marjorie, 110, 120
Ryan White CARE Act, 88
Rykener, Eleanor, 120

sadomasochism, 69
sahq (Arabic female same-sex activity), 201
Saint, Assotto, 91
Salamon, Gayle, 30
Samer, Rox, 62, 72
Sandoval, Chela, 78
Sang, Tze-lan D., 185
sapphic terminology, 227
Saria, Vaibhav, 188
Savci, Evren, 194
Scott, Darieck, 45
secondary marginalization, AIDS epidemic and, 86
Sedgwick, Eve Kosofsky
  on closet thinking, 40
  on humanness, 47
  queer and trans studies origins and, 19, 34
  queer representation and, 37
  queer theory and influence of, 1, 15
  reparative orientation theory of, 206
  social norms assembly and disassembly and, 42, 52
separatism, lesbian feminism and, 65
Serano, Julia, 28
sex traficking, feminist activism concerning, 218
sex wars, lesbian feminism and, 67, 69
sex work, AIDS epidemic and, 84, 222

sexism
  gay liberation and, 59
  lesbian feminism and, 63
sexological discourse, 122
sexuality
  in Asian American studies, 162
  disability and, 48
  gender and, 20
  history of, 99, 113
  in Latinx Studies, 160
  in nature, 114
  omission in Black Studies of, 145
  philology of, 109
  practices and marginalized identities and, 222
  queer and trans for color and, 137
  queer theory and, 4
  racialization of, 106
  trans studies and, 7
Shah, Nayan, 107
Shelley, Martha, 57
Shepard, Matthew, 44
Shomali, Bernard, 201
Siebers, Tobin, 48
Simpson, Leanne Betasamosake, 139
Sims, James Marion, 105
Singapore, queer and trans culture in, 181
Sinnott, Megan, 189
Sir Lady Jay, 146
slavery, 104
slavery, impact on gender and sexuality of, 134, 145
Smith, Barbara, 73, 78
Smith, Beverly, 73
Snediker, Michael, 49
Snorton, C. Riley, 32, 86, 105
social and intellectual movements, queer and trans studies and, 15
social norms
  queering and transing of, 120
sodomy
  colonial references to, 103
  Indigenous cultures linked to, 141
  legal status of, 221

sodomy (cont.)
　mollies and molly houses and, 121
　terminology of, 110
Somerville, Siobhan, 12, 126
Soto, Sandra K., 160
South Africa, queer and trans culture in, 186, 192, 240
Southern Comfort conference, 95
sovereignty, for Native and Indigenous peoples, 138, 143
Spade, Dean, 33
Spanish–American War (1898), 156
Spillers, Hortense J., 148
Stallings, L. H., 151
Stanley, Eric, 46
Stein, Arlene, 64
Stein, Gertrude, 67
"sticky rice" pairings, 166
Stoler, Ann Laura, 101
Stone, Sandy, 71, 92
Stonewall 25, 95
Stonewall Riot (1969), 55
Storr, Mel, 123
straight time, 130, 134
Street Transvestites Action Revolutionaries (STAR), 59
Stryker, Susan, 60, 93, 119
Suharto, authoritarian regime of, 185, 194
Sullivan, Nikki, 9, 12
Summit of South American–Arab Countries (2005), 197
Suriname, Black women's sexuality and identity in, 182
suspicioning, 144
Symonds, John Addington, 124
systems and research
　in Brazil, 180
　evolution of, 92, 128
　role of law in, 192
　in Singapore, 181
　transgender activism and, 95

Taiwan, queer and trans culture in, 190
Takagi, Dana, 162
TallBear, Kim, 139
Tallie, T. J., 104, 226
Tamale, Sylvia, 186
Tatonetti, Lisa, 142
Taylor, Liza, 77
Teena, Brandon, 44, 95, 224
TERFs (trans-exclusionary radical feminists), 62
terrorist, in queer and trans studies, 167
Thailand, queer and trans culture in, 181, 189
The History of Sexuality, Vol. 1 (Foucault), 99
The Lesbian Tide, 71
"The Scholar and the Feminist IX: Towards a Politics of Sexuality" (Barnard Conference), 67
The Transsexual Empire (Raymond), 93
"Thinking Sex" (Rubin), 68
third gender ideology, 31, 180
Third International Gathering of American Indian and First Nations Gays and Lesbians, 142
third wave feminism, 72
Third World Gay Revolution movement, 61
third-world queer studies
　imperialist and capitalist expansion and, 180
　specificity beyond authenticity and nativism, 181
　terminology in, 218
Thomas, Greg, 42
Tinsley, Omise'eke Natasha, 150
tom (tomboi) in Southeast Asian cultures, 189, 243
Tompkins, Kyla Wazana, 115
Tongson Karen, 45
tongzhi (Chinese queer terminology), 191, 202
Towle, Evan B., 32
transfemininity, 121, 123

Trans Historical collection, 114
trans people of color
  scholarship on, 136
  vulnerabiity of, 32
trans studies
  AIDS epidemic and, 89
  Asian American studies, 161
  assertions of newness about, 109
  Black Studies and, 145
  Blackness and slavery and, 105
  core self perceptions in, 209
  disability studies and, 49
  early transgender writing and activism, 91
  embodiment in, 27, 231
  evolution of, 1
  gay liberation and, 59
  gender and sexuality in, 7
  global dynamics in, 171
  history and, 14, 134
  imperialist and capitalist expansion/intervention and, 173
  Indigenous studies and, 138
  Latinx studies, 154
  lesbian feminism and, 66, 70
  origins of, 19
  queer theory in relation to, 205
  race, diaspora, and empire and, 14
  temporalities in, 131
  terminology and norms in, 108, 118
  universality in, 32
  women of color in, 25
trans*temporal kinship, 141
Transgender Nation, 95
Transgender Studies Reader, 7
transgender, definitions of, 7, 91, 119
transloca performance, 157
transnormativity, defined, 13
Transsexual Menace, 95
transsexuality
  emergence of category, 127
  terminology of, 8, 94
transtopia, queer diaspora as, 202
transvestites, defined, 8
Traub, Valerie, 109, 113, 115, 118

travestis (Brazil), 180, 187, 192, 197
Treaty of Guadalupe Hidalgo, 156
Treichler, Paula, 82
tribadism, 111, 119, 228
Trinidad and Tobago, queer and trans policies in, 175
Tubman, Harriet, 73
Turkey, queer and trans studies in, 194
Two-Spirit terminology, 142, 234

Uganda, anti-homosexual legislation in, 193
Ulrichs, Karl, 122
undocuqueer movement, 156
universalization of sexual identity, 36

Venezuela, gender identity in, 187
vernacular sexology, 123
Vietnamese Americans, 161, 164, 168

Walcott, Ronaldo, 148
Ward, Freda, 124
Warner, Michael, 11, 111
Watney, Simon, 82
Wekker, Gloria, 182
West Coast Lesbian Conference (1973), 71
West, Isaac, 30
whiteness
  civilization advancement linked to, 125
  gay liberation movement and dominance of, 61
  homosexuality and heterosexuality and, 42
  lesbian feminism and, 66
"Whose Feminism Is It Anyway?" (Koyama), 2
Wiegman, Robin, 13
Wilchins, Riki Anne, 29, 95, 225
Wilde, Oscar, 124
Wilkerson, Abby, 49
Wilson, Ara, 181
Wilson, Elizabeth, 13

winkte (Lakota), 32
Wittig, Monique, 216
Wittman, Carl, 56
Womack, Craig, 144
women, 63
   categorization politics and, 3, 20, 32
   lesbian feminism identification of, 64
   tribadism in, 112
Women Against Pornography, 68
women of color feminism, *see also* Black women
   definitions of, 219
   evolution of, 72
   legacy of, 97
women's liberation movement, 63
"womyn-born womyn", 71
Wong, Alvin K., 198
Woo, Merle, 55, 75
Woubshet, Dagmawi, 89
"wrong body" narrative, trans studies and, 94
Wu, Cynthia, 166

Yergeau, Melanie, 49
Young, Allen, 57

Cambridge Introductions to...

Authors

Margaret Atwood Heidi Macpherson
Jane Austen (second edition) Janet Todd
Mikhail Bakhtin Ken Hirschkop
Samuel Beckett Ronan McDonald
Walter Benjamin David Ferris
Lord Byron Richard Lansdown
Chaucer Alastair Minnis
Chekhov James N. Loehlin
J. M. Coetzee Dominic Head
Samuel Taylor Coleridge John Worthen
Joseph Conrad John Peters
Jacques Derrida Leslie Hill
Charles Dickens Jon Mee
Emily Dickinson Wendy Martin
George Eliot Nancy Henry
T. S. Eliot John Xiros Cooper
William Faulkner Theresa M. Towner
F. Scott Fitzgerald Kirk Curnutt
Michel Foucault Lisa Downing
Robert Frost Robert Faggen
Gabriel Garcia Marquez Gerald Martin
Nathaniel Hawthorne Leland S. Person
Zora Neale Hurston Lovalerie King
James Joyce Eric Bulson
Kafka Carolin Duttlinger
Thomas Mann Todd Kontje
Christopher Marlowe Tom Rutter
Herman Melville Kevin J. Hayes
Milton Stephen B. Dobranski
George Orwell John Rodden and John Rossi
Sylvia Plath Jo Gill
Edgar Allan Poe Benjamin F. Fisher
Ezra Pound Ira Nadel
Marcel Proust Adam Watt
Jean Rhys Elaine Savory
Edward Said Conor McCarthy
Shakespeare Emma Smith
Shakespeare's Comedies Penny Gay
Shakespeare's History Plays Warren Chernaik
Shakespeare's Poetry Michael Schoenfeldt
Shakespeare's Tragedies Janette Dillon
Tom Stoppard William W. Demastes
Harriet Beecher Stowe Sarah Robbins
Mark Twain Peter Messent
Edith Wharton Pamela Knights
Walt Whitman M. Jimmie Killingsworth
Virginia Woolf Jane Goldman
William Wordsworth Emma Mason
W. B. Yeats David Holdeman

Topics

American Literary Realism Phillip Barrish
American Poetry Since 1945 Andrew Epstein
The American Short Story Martin Scofield
Anglo-Saxon Literature Hugh Magennis
British Poetry, 1945–2010 Eric Falci
British Fiction, 1900–1950
Contemporary American Fiction Stacey Olster

Comedy Eric Weitz
Creative Writing David Morley
Early English Theatre Janette Dillon
Early Modern Drama, 1576–1642 Julie Sanders
The Eighteenth-Century Novel April London
Eighteenth-Century Poetry John Sitter
English Theatre, 1660–1900 Peter Thomson
French Literature Brian Nelson
Francophone Literature Patrick Corcoran
German Poetry Judith Ryan
Literary Posthumanism Joseph Tabbi
Literature and the Environment Timothy Clark
Modern British Theatre Simon Shepherd
Modern Irish Poetry Justin Quinn
Modernism Pericles Lewis
Modernist Poetry Peter Howarth
Narrative (second edition) H. Porter Abbott
Narrative (third edition) H. Porter Abbott
The Nineteenth-Century American Novel Gregg Crane
The Novel Marina MacKay
Old Norse Sagas Margaret Clunies Ross
Performance Theory Simon Shepherd
Postcolonial Literatures C. L. Innes
Postmodern Fiction Bran Nicol
Romantic Poetry Michael Ferber
Russian Literature Caryl Emerson
Satire Jonathan Greenberg
Scenography Joslin McKinney and Philip Butterworth
The Short Story in English Adrian Hunter
Theatre Directing Christopher Innes and Maria Shevtsova
Theatre Historiography Thomas Postlewait
Theatre and Literature of the Absurd Michael Y. Bennett
Theatre Studies Christopher B. Balme
Tragedy Jennifer Wallace
Victorian Poetry Linda K. Hughes

For EU product safety concerns, contact us at Calle de José Abascal, 56–1º,
28003 Madrid, Spain or eugpsr@cambridge.org.

www.ingramcontent.com/pod-product-compliance
Lightning Source LLC
LaVergne TN
LVHW020341260326
834688LV00045B/1475